CHAPTER 28

MY NAME IS...

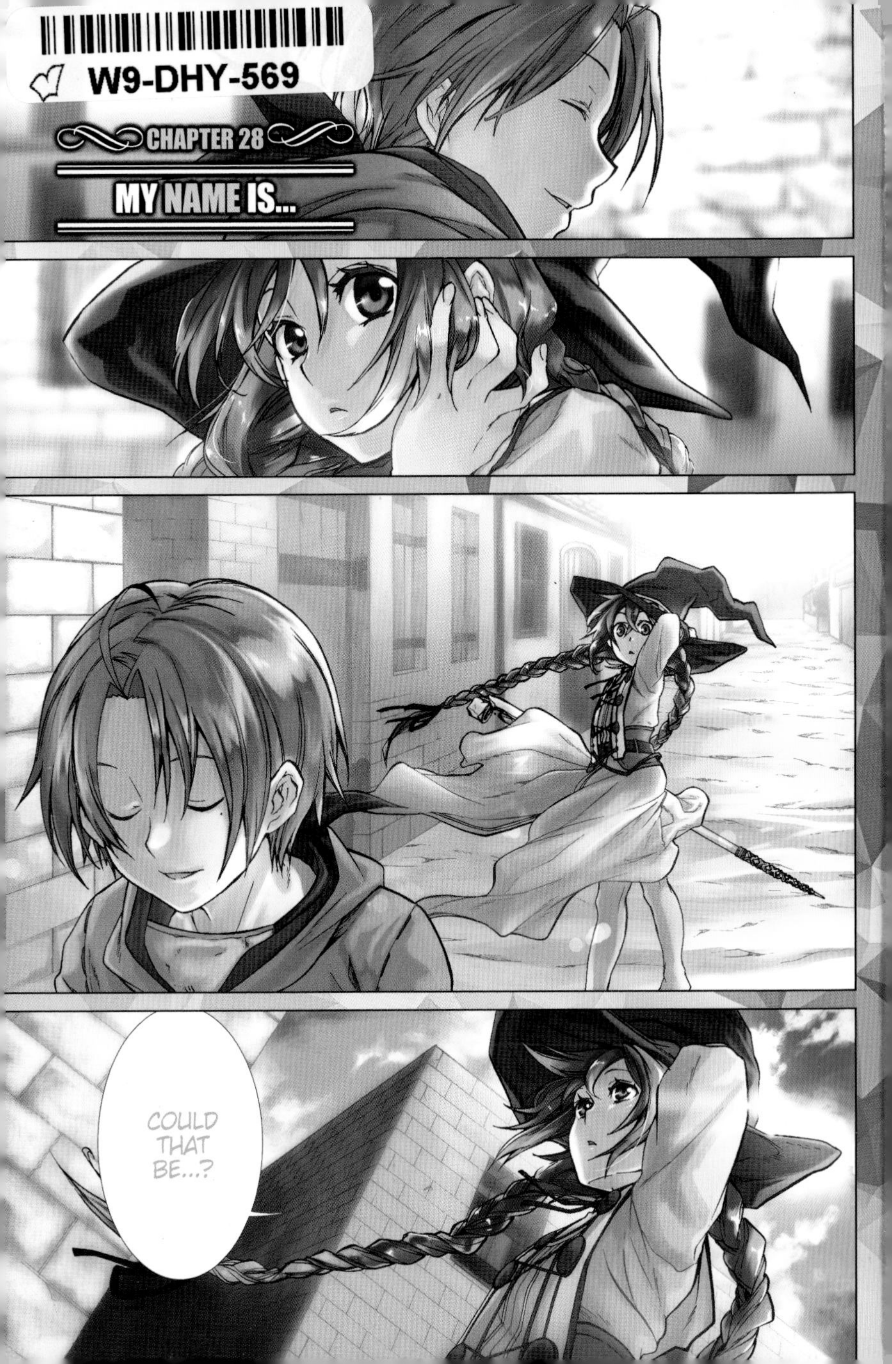
COULD THAT BE...?

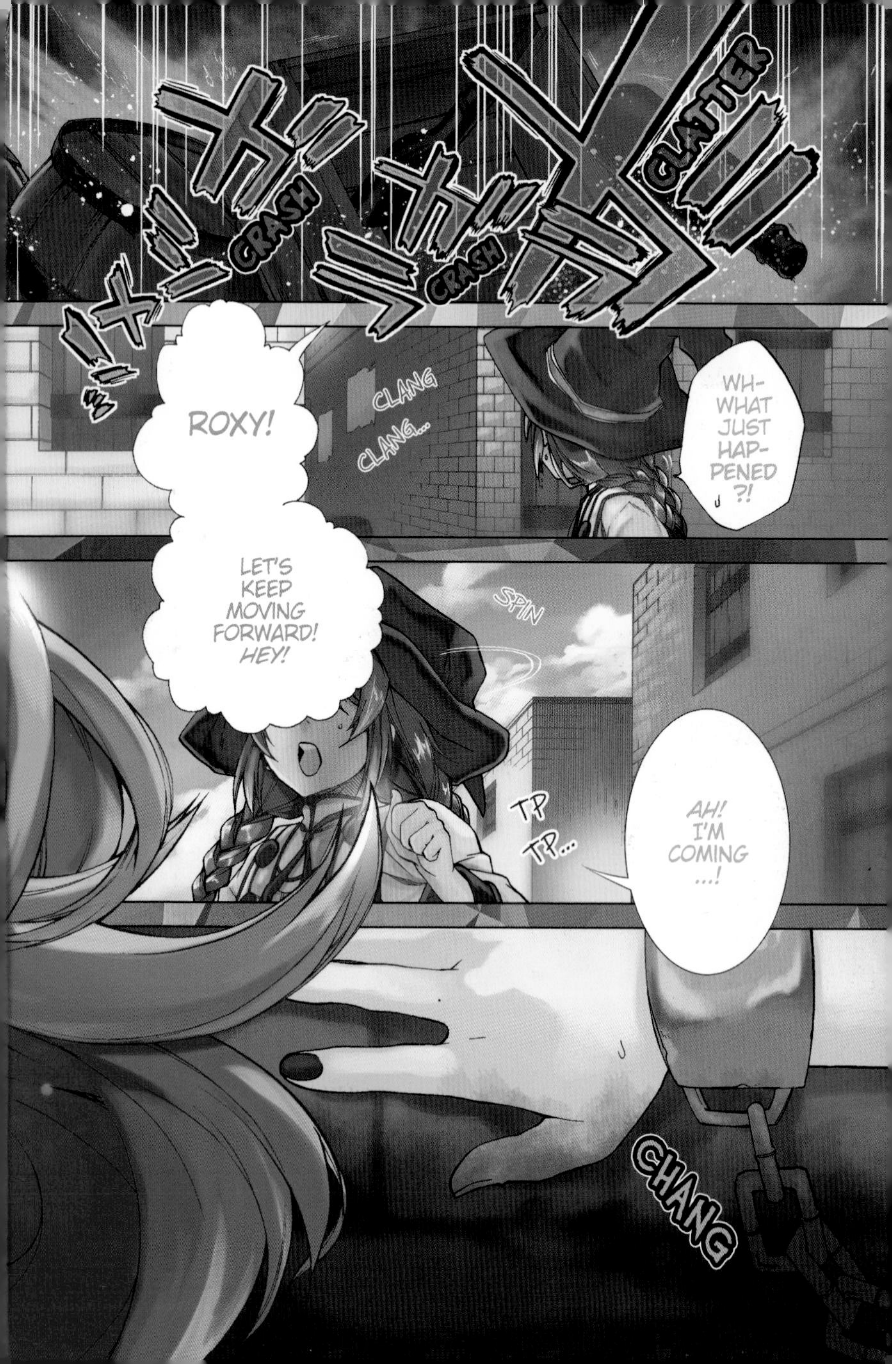
CLATTER
CRASH
CRASH
WH-WHAT JUST HAP-PENED?!
CLANG CLANG...
ROXY!
SPIN
LET'S KEEP MOVING FORWARD! HEY!
AH! I'M COMING...!
TP TP...
CHANG

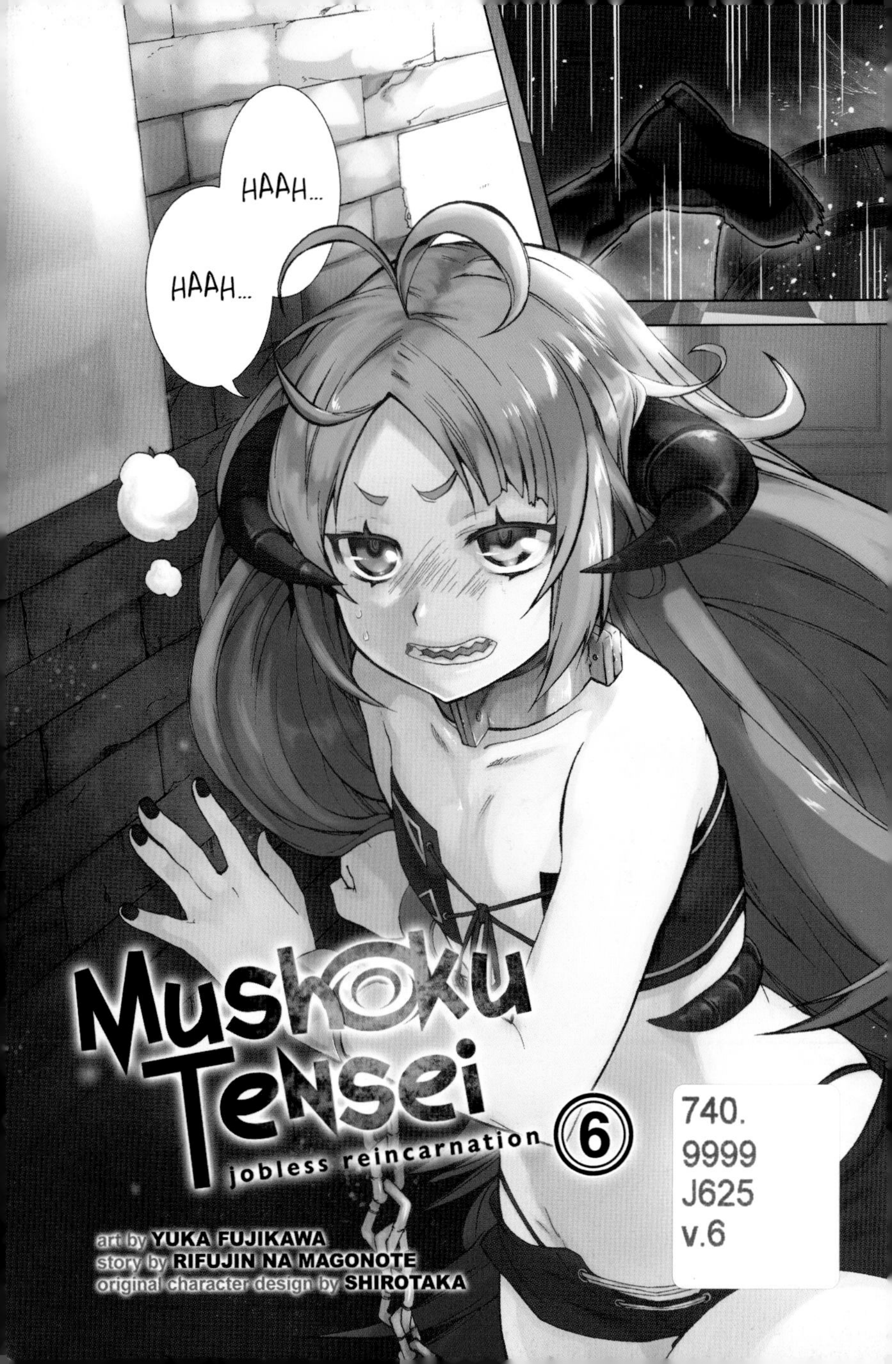
HAAH...
HAAH...

Mushoku Tensei
jobless reincarnation 6

art by YUKA FUJIKAWA
story by RIFUJIN NA MAGONOTE
original character design by SHIROTAKA

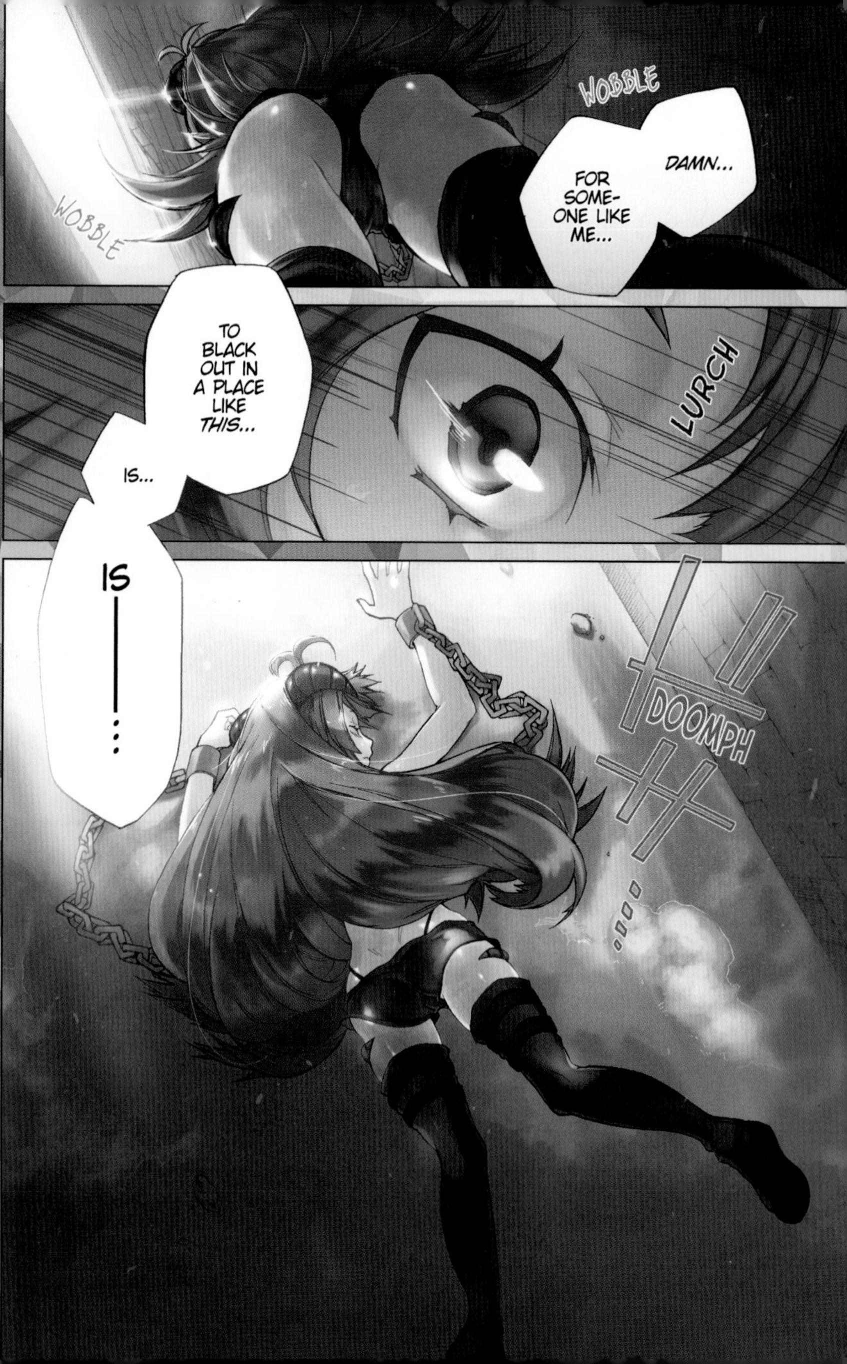
WOBBLE
DAMN...
FOR SOME-ONE LIKE ME...
WOBBLE
LURCH
TO BLACK OUT IN A PLACE LIKE *THIS*...
IS...
DOOMPH
IS——...

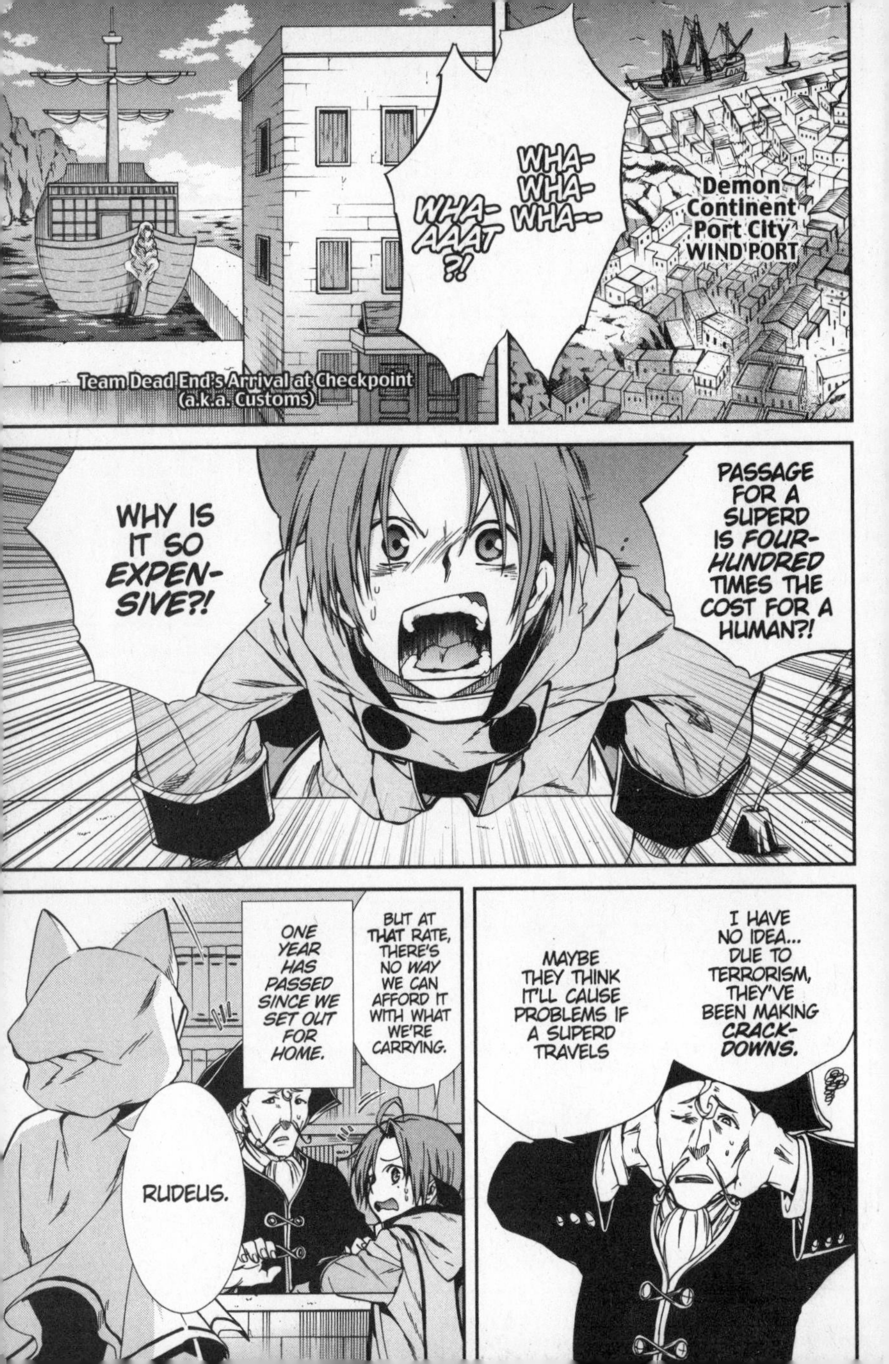
Demon Continent Port City WIND PORT
WHA-WHA-WHA-- WHA-AAAT?!
Team Dead End's Arrival at Checkpoint (a.k.a. Customs)
PASSAGE FOR A SUPERD IS FOUR-HUNDRED TIMES THE COST FOR A HUMAN?!
WHY IS IT SO EXPEN-SIVE?!
I HAVE NO IDEA... DUE TO TERRORISM, THEY'VE BEEN MAKING CRACK-DOWNS.
MAYBE THEY THINK IT'LL CAUSE PROBLEMS IF A SUPERD TRAVELS
BUT AT THAT RATE, THERE'S NO WAY WE CAN AFFORD IT WITH WHAT WE'RE CARRYING.
ONE YEAR HAS PASSED SINCE WE SET OUT FOR HOME.
RUDEUS.

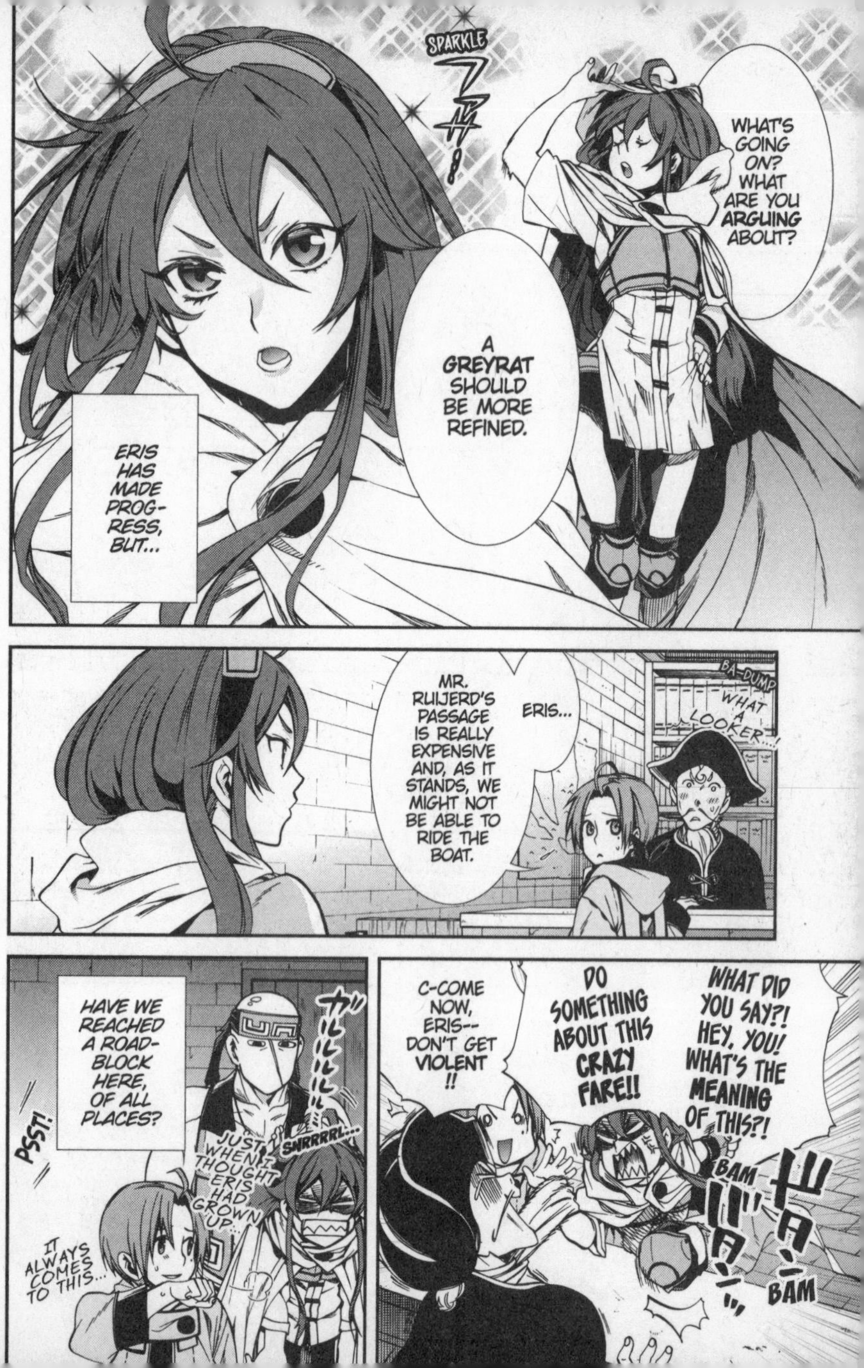
SPARKLE
WHAT'S GOING ON? WHAT ARE YOU ARGUING ABOUT?
A GREYRAT SHOULD BE MORE REFINED.
ERIS HAS MADE PROG-RESS, BUT...
BA-DUMP
WHAT A LOOKER...!
ERIS...
MR. RUIJERD'S PASSAGE IS REALLY EXPENSIVE AND, AS IT STANDS, WE MIGHT NOT BE ABLE TO RIDE THE BOAT.
WHAT DID YOU SAY?! HEY, YOU! WHAT'S THE MEANING OF THIS?!
DO SOMETHING ABOUT THIS CRAZY FARE!!
C-COME NOW, ERIS-- DON'T GET VIOLENT !!
BAM
BAM
HAVE WE REACHED A ROAD-BLOCK HERE, OF ALL PLACES?
SNRRRRL...
JUST WHEN I THOUGHT ERIS HAD GROWN UP...
PSST!
IT ALWAYS COMES TO THIS...

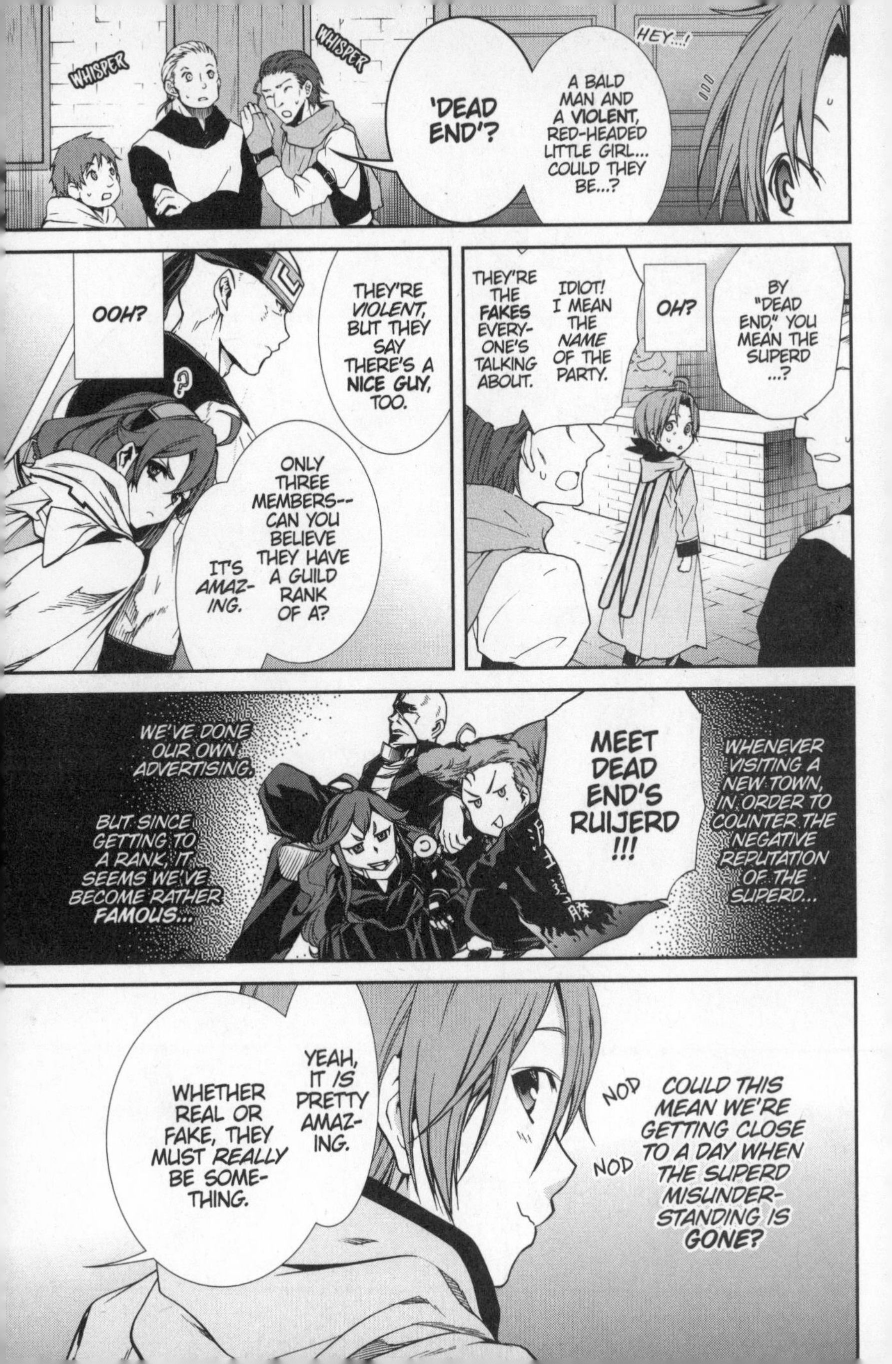
HEY...!
A BALD MAN AND A VIOLENT, RED-HEADED LITTLE GIRL... COULD THEY BE...?
'DEAD END'?
WHISPER
WHISPER
BY "DEAD END," YOU MEAN THE SUPERD ...?
OH?
IDIOT! I MEAN THE NAME OF THE PARTY.
THEY'RE THE FAKES EVERYONE'S TALKING ABOUT.
THEY'RE VIOLENT, BUT THEY SAY THERE'S A NICE GUY, TOO.
OOH?
ONLY THREE MEMBERS--CAN YOU BELIEVE THEY HAVE A GUILD RANK OF A?
IT'S AMAZING.
WHENEVER VISITING A NEW TOWN, IN ORDER TO COUNTER THE NEGATIVE REPUTATION OF THE SUPERD...
MEET DEAD END'S RUIJERD !!!
WE'VE DONE OUR OWN ADVERTISING.
BUT SINCE GETTING TO A RANK, IT SEEMS WE'VE BECOME RATHER FAMOUS...
COULD THIS MEAN WE'RE GETTING CLOSE TO A DAY WHEN THE SUPERD MISUNDERSTANDING IS GONE?
NOD
NOD
YEAH, IT IS PRETTY AMAZING.
WHETHER REAL OR FAKE, THEY MUST REALLY BE SOMETHING.

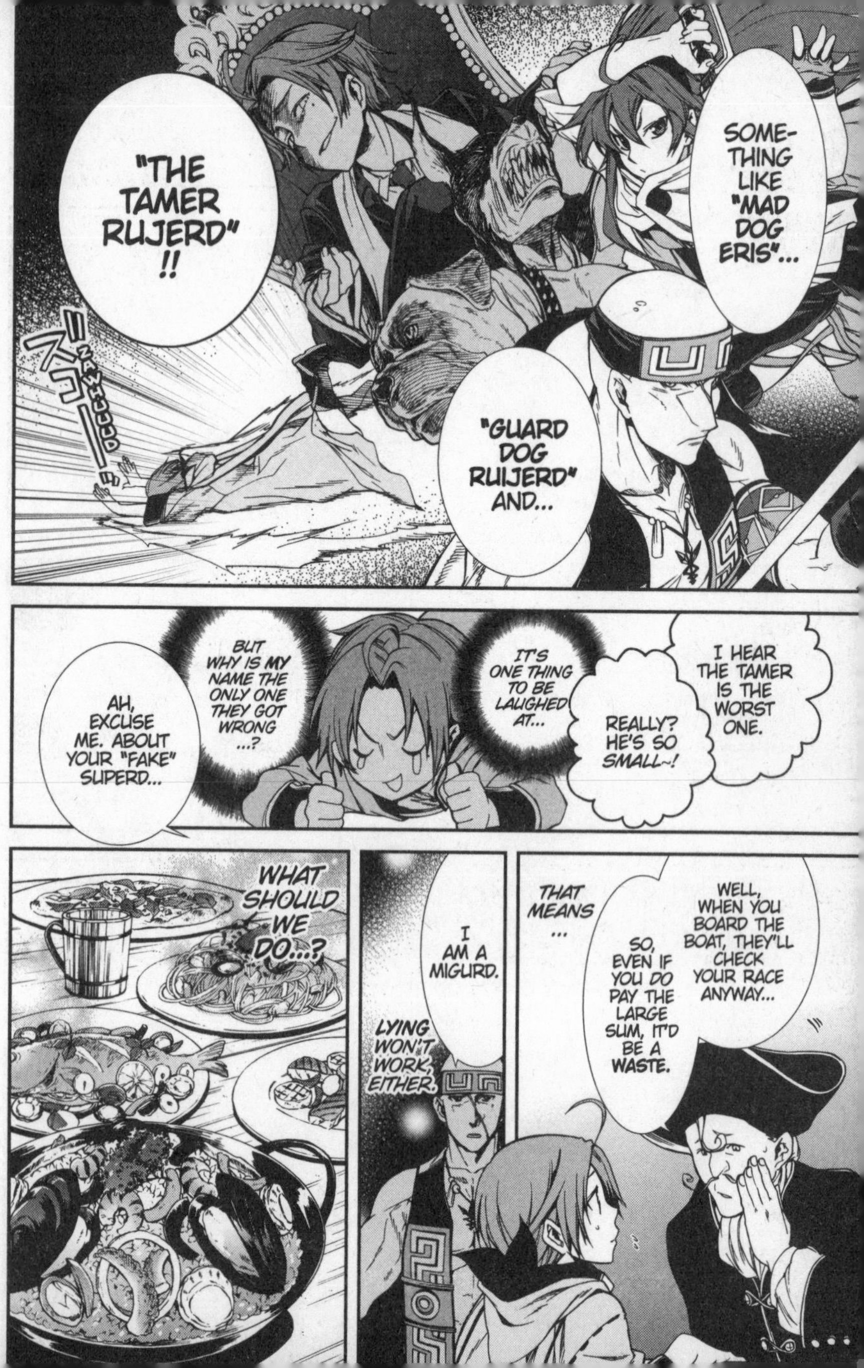
SOMETHING LIKE "MAD DOG ERIS"...
"GUARD DOG RUIJERD" AND...
"THE TAMER RUJERD" !!
ZAWHUUD
I HEAR THE TAMER IS THE WORST ONE.
REALLY? HE'S SO SMALL~!
IT'S ONE THING TO BE LAUGHED AT...
BUT WHY IS MY NAME THE ONLY ONE THEY GOT WRONG ...?
AH, EXCUSE ME. ABOUT YOUR "FAKE" SUPERD...
WELL, WHEN YOU BOARD THE BOAT, THEY'LL CHECK YOUR RACE ANYWAY...
SO, EVEN IF YOU *DO* PAY THE LARGE SUM, IT'D BE A WASTE.
THAT MEANS ...
I AM A MIGURD.
LYING WON'T WORK, EITHER.
WHAT SHOULD WE DO...?

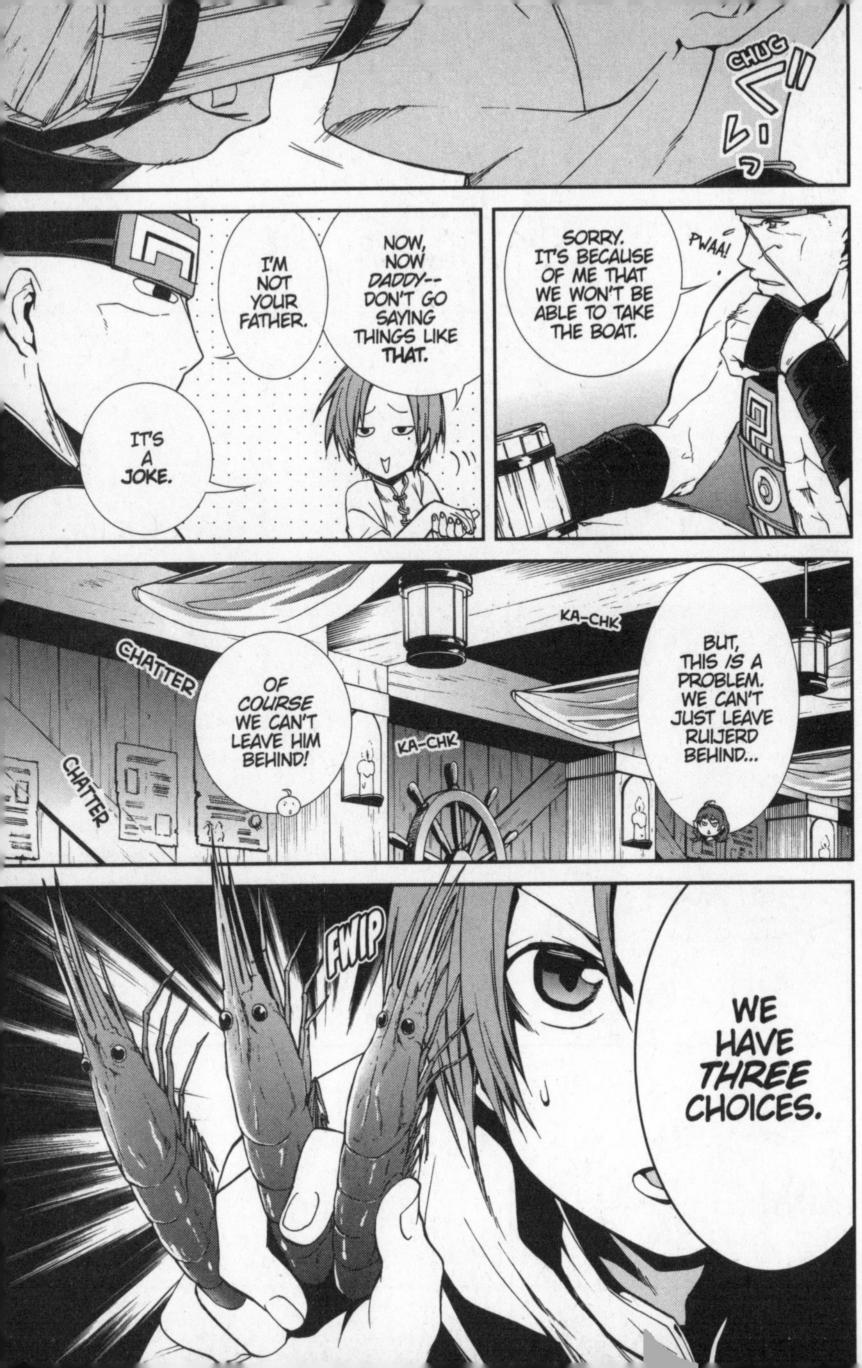
CHUG
PWAA!
SORRY. IT'S BECAUSE OF ME THAT WE WON'T BE ABLE TO TAKE THE BOAT.
NOW, NOW *DADDY*-- DON'T GO SAYING THINGS LIKE **THAT.**
I'M NOT YOUR FATHER.
IT'S A JOKE.
KA-CHK
BUT, THIS *IS* A PROBLEM. WE CAN'T JUST LEAVE RUIJERD BEHIND...
KA-CHK
OF COURSE WE CAN'T LEAVE HIM BEHIND!
CHATTER
CHATTER
WE HAVE *THREE* CHOICES.
FWIP

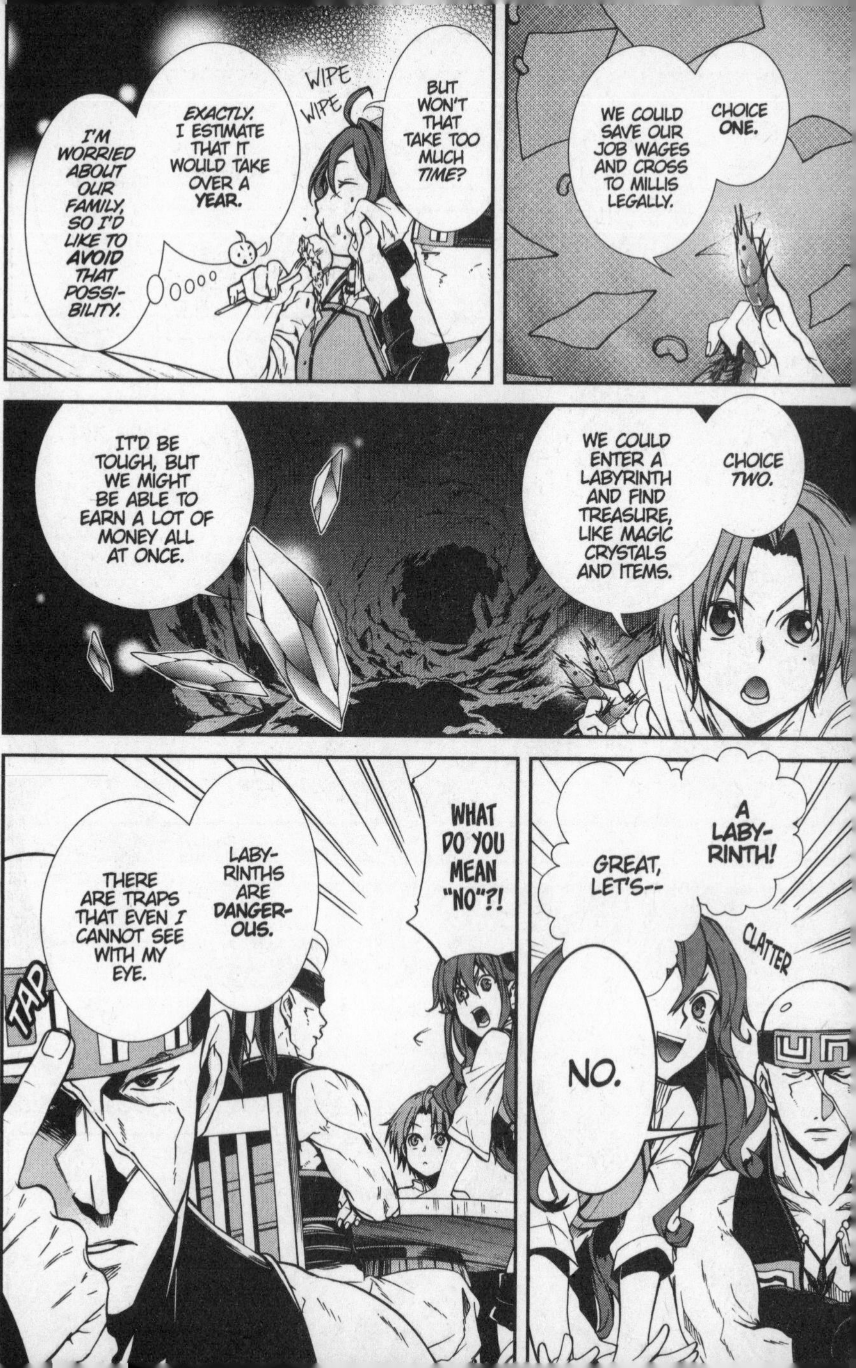

CHOICE ONE.
WE COULD SAVE OUR JOB WAGES AND CROSS TO MILLIS LEGALLY.
BUT WON'T THAT TAKE TOO MUCH TIME?
WIPE WIPE
EXACTLY. I ESTIMATE THAT IT WOULD TAKE OVER A YEAR.
I'M WORRIED ABOUT OUR FAMILY, SO I'D LIKE TO AVOID THAT POSSIBILITY.
CHOICE TWO.
WE COULD ENTER A LABYRINTH AND FIND TREASURE, LIKE MAGIC CRYSTALS AND ITEMS.
IT'D BE TOUGH, BUT WE MIGHT BE ABLE TO EARN A LOT OF MONEY ALL AT ONCE.
A LABYRINTH!
GREAT, LET'S--
CLATTER
NO.
WHAT DO YOU MEAN "NO"?!
LABYRINTHS ARE DANGEROUS.
THERE ARE TRAPS THAT EVEN I CANNOT SEE WITH MY EYE.
TAP

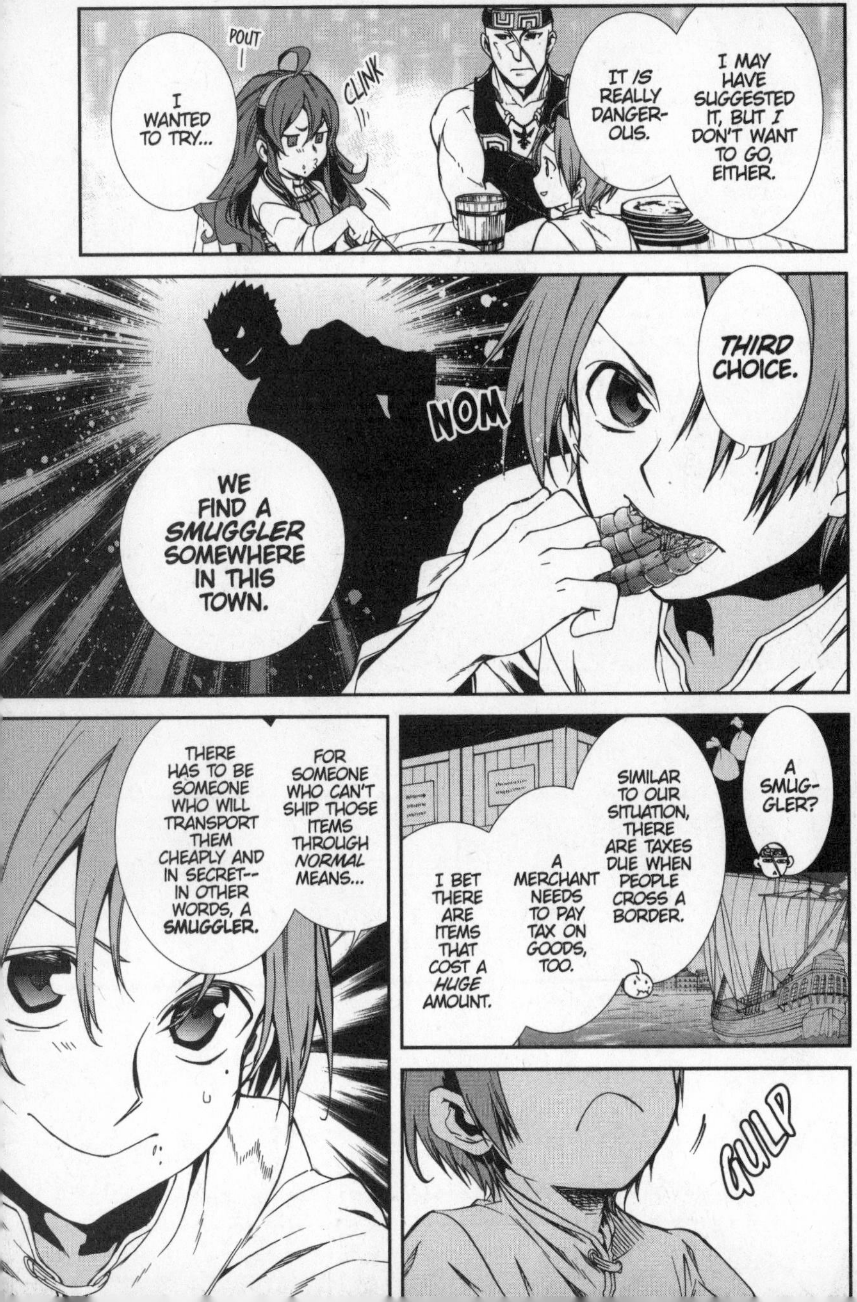
I MAY HAVE SUGGESTED IT, BUT I DON'T WANT TO GO, EITHER.
IT IS REALLY DANGEROUS.
CLINK
POUT
I WANTED TO TRY...
THIRD CHOICE.
NOM
WE FIND A SMUGGLER SOMEWHERE IN THIS TOWN.
A SMUGGLER?
SIMILAR TO OUR SITUATION, THERE ARE TAXES DUE WHEN PEOPLE CROSS A BORDER.
A MERCHANT NEEDS TO PAY TAX ON GOODS, TOO.
I BET THERE ARE ITEMS THAT COST A HUGE AMOUNT.
GULP
FOR SOMEONE WHO CAN'T SHIP THOSE ITEMS THROUGH NORMAL MEANS...
THERE HAS TO BE SOMEONE WHO WILL TRANSPORT THEM CHEAPLY AND IN SECRET-- IN OTHER WORDS, A SMUGGLER.

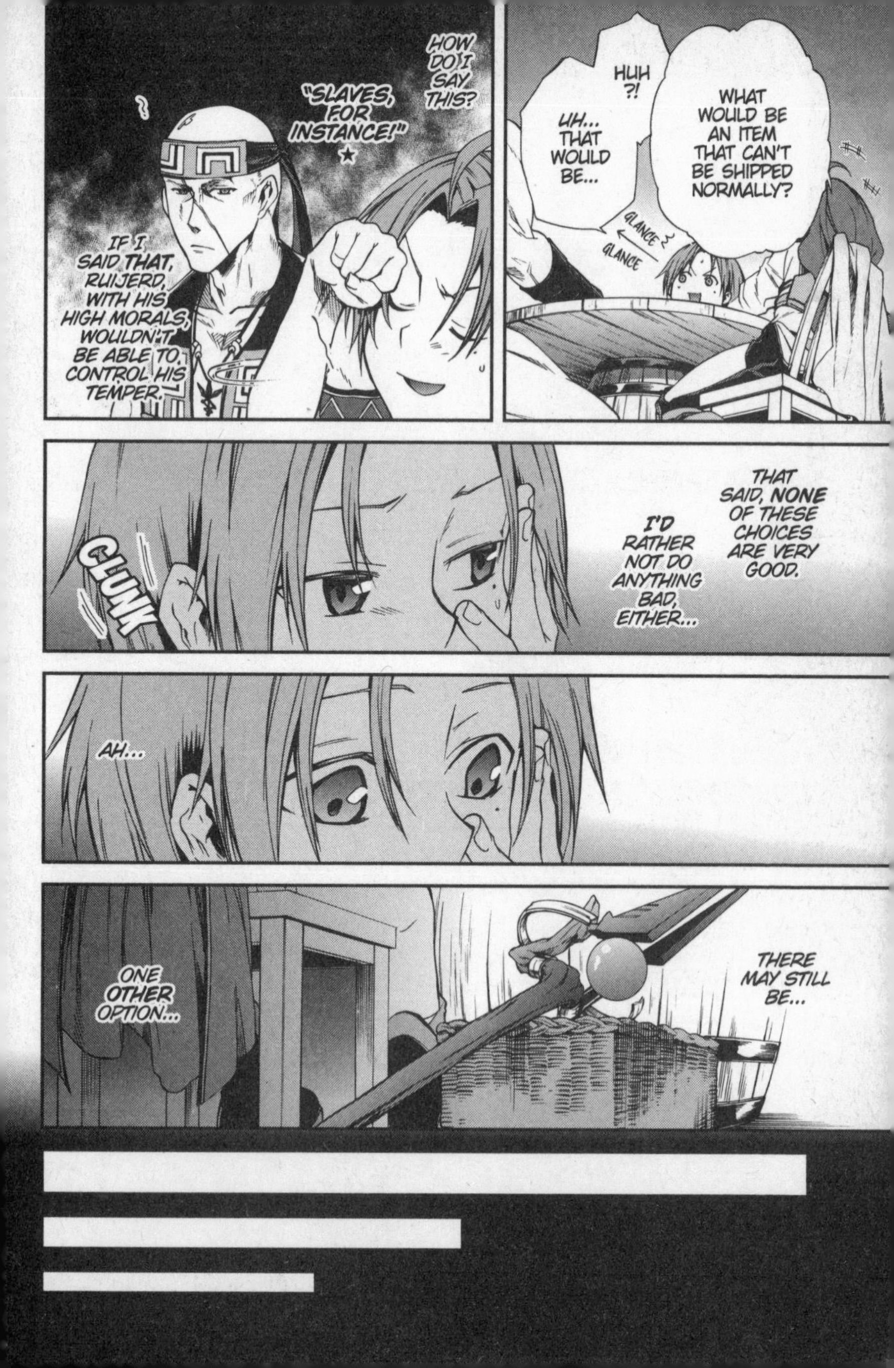
WHAT WOULD BE AN ITEM THAT CAN'T BE SHIPPED NORMALLY?
HUH ?!
UH... THAT WOULD BE...
GLANCE
GLANCE
HOW DO I SAY THIS?
"SLAVES, FOR INSTANCE!" ★
?
IF I SAID THAT, RUIJERD, WITH HIS HIGH MORALS, WOULDN'T BE ABLE TO CONTROL HIS TEMPER.
THAT SAID, NONE OF THESE CHOICES ARE VERY GOOD.
I'D RATHER NOT DO ANYTHING BAD, EITHER...
CLUNK
AH...
THERE MAY STILL BE...
ONE OTHER OPTION...

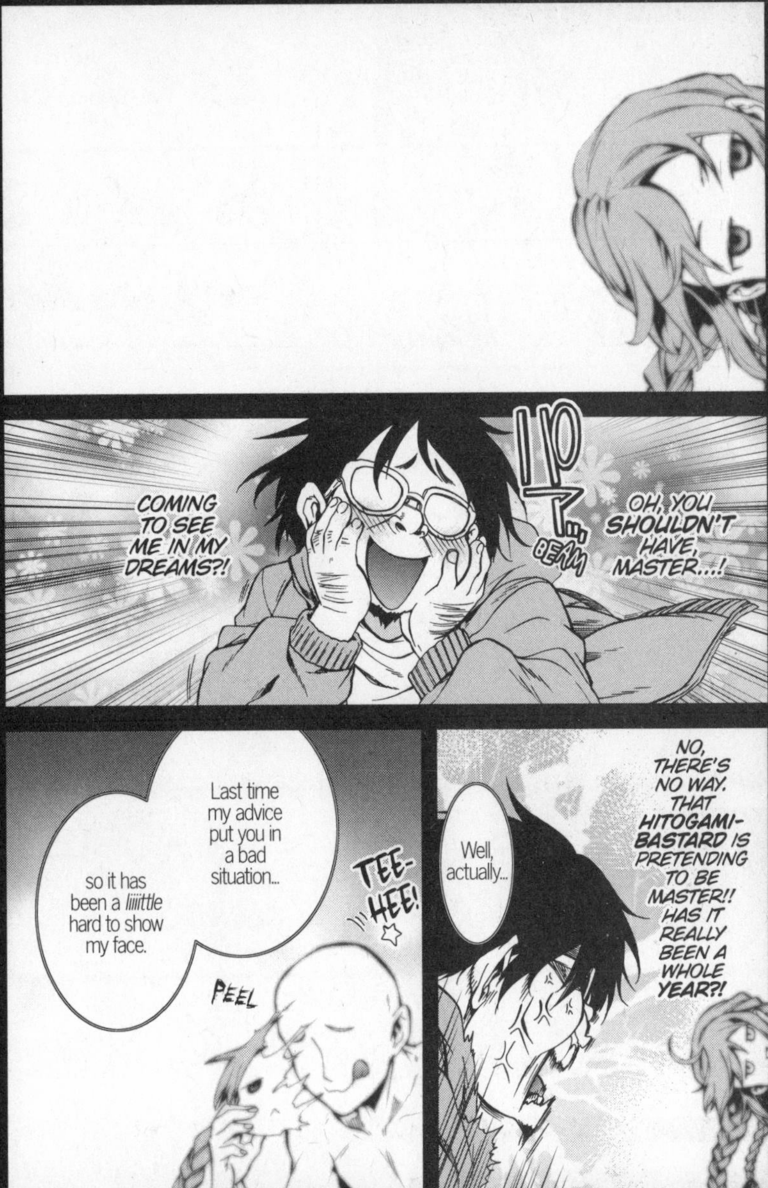
OH, YOU SHOULDN'T HAVE, MASTER...!
BEAM
COMING TO SEE ME IN MY DREAMS?!
NO, THERE'S NO WAY. THAT HITOGAMI-BASTARD IS PRETENDING TO BE MASTER!! HAS IT REALLY BEEN A WHOLE YEAR?!
Well, actually...
TEE-HEE!
Last time my advice put you in a bad situation...
so it has been a *liiiittle* hard to show my face.
PEEL

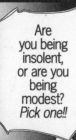

HUH?! DON'T GET IT MIXED UP.
YOU MAY'VE GIVEN ME ADVICE BEFORE, BUT I MADE THE MISTAKE ON MY OWN.
POINT
BUT, SINCE YOU'RE HERE!... PLEASE TELL ME WHAT THE RIGHT THING TO DO WAS!!
DUUUN
Are you being insolent, or are you being modest? Pick one!!
Hmm... Even if you ask for the 'right' thing...
If you had just positioned the pea hunters as guards, then you and Ruijerd should have gotten along just fine.
EH? THAT WAS ALL I NEEDED TO DO?
SHOCK
That's right~!
But I enjoyed watching things play out in a way I did not predict.
I DIDN'T ENJOY IT ONE BIT.
Well, that's true. You cried, after all.
Waah waah~! ♪
YOU BASTARD...!
Hee hee... I'm sorry, I'm sorry.
Fine-- I will make it up to you by giving you a piece of advice.

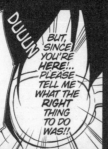

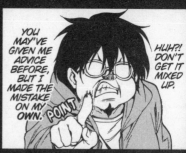

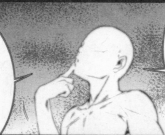

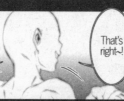

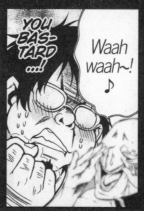

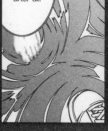

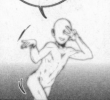

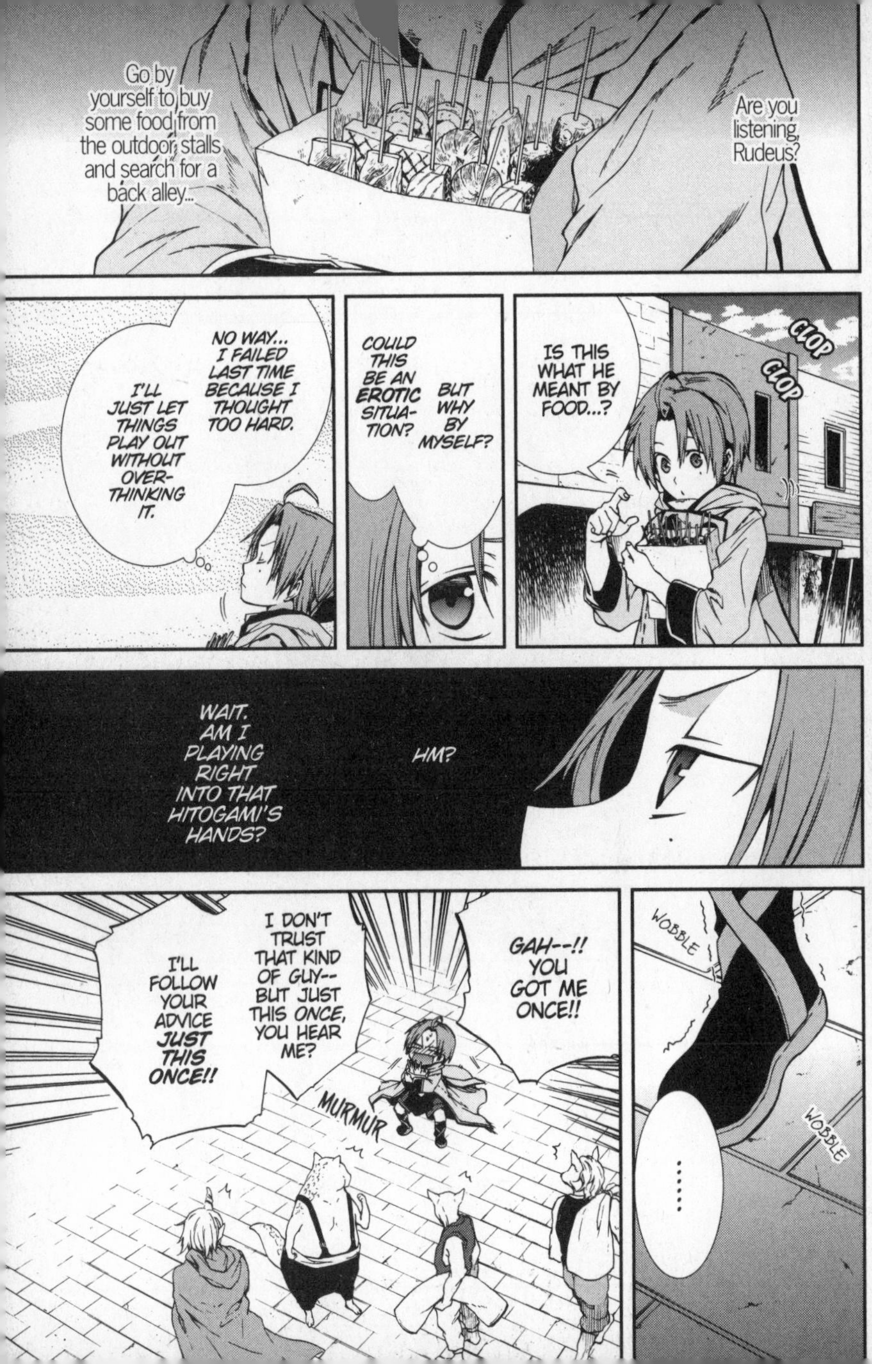
Are you listening, Rudeus?
Go by yourself to buy some food from the outdoor stalls and search for a back alley...
CLOP
CLOP
IS THIS WHAT HE MEANT BY FOOD...?
COULD THIS BE AN EROTIC SITUATION?
BUT WHY BY MYSELF?
NO WAY... I FAILED LAST TIME BECAUSE I THOUGHT TOO HARD.
I'LL JUST LET THINGS PLAY OUT WITHOUT OVER-THINKING IT.
HM?
WAIT. AM I PLAYING RIGHT INTO THAT HITOGAMI'S HANDS?
WOBBLE
WOBBLE
......
GAH--!! YOU GOT ME ONCE!!
I DON'T TRUST THAT KIND OF GUY-- BUT JUST THIS ONCE, YOU HEAR ME?
I'LL FOLLOW YOUR ADVICE JUST THIS ONCE!!
MURMUR

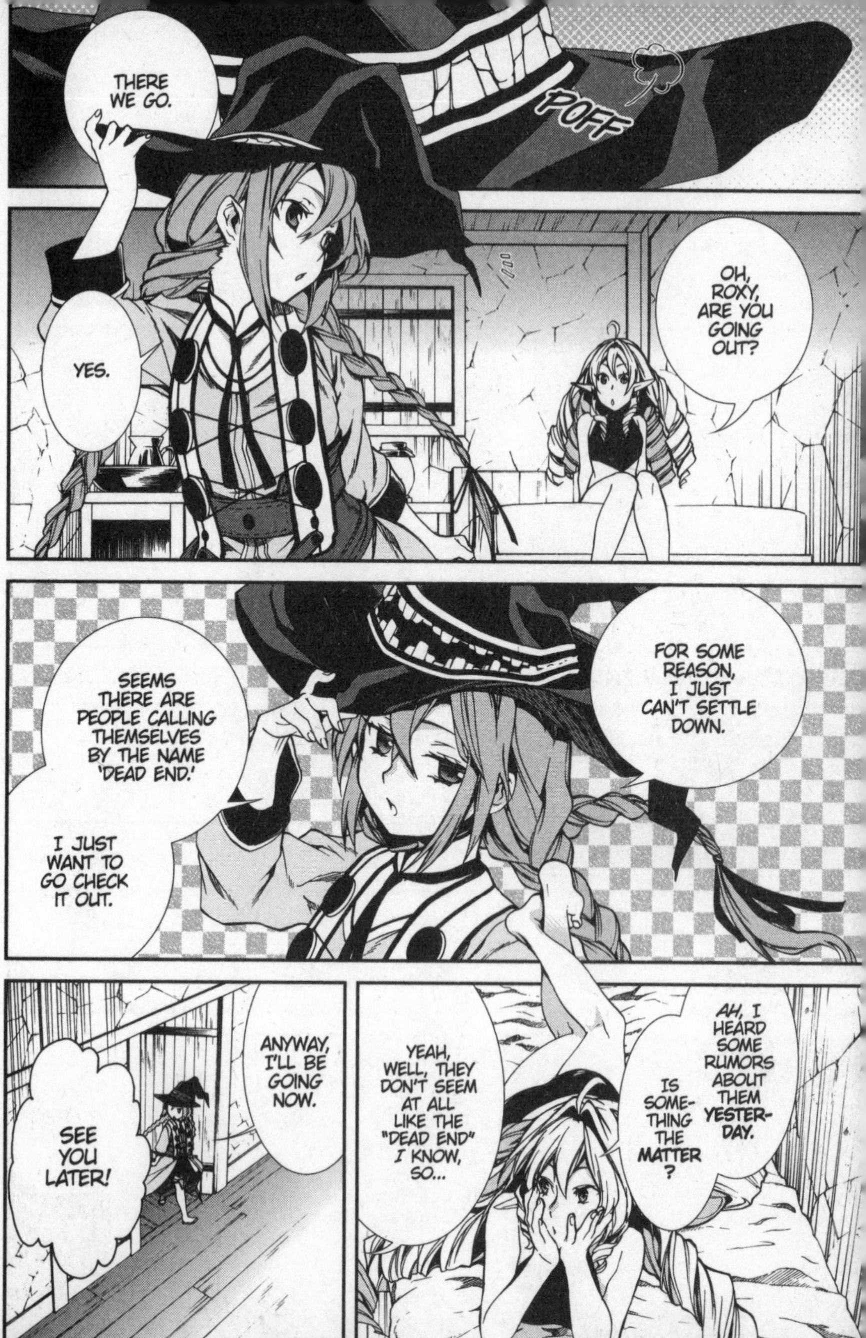
POFF
THERE WE GO.
OH, ROXY, ARE YOU GOING OUT?
YES.
FOR SOME REASON, I JUST CAN'T SETTLE DOWN.
SEEMS THERE ARE PEOPLE CALLING THEMSELVES BY THE NAME 'DEAD END.'
I JUST WANT TO GO CHECK IT OUT.
AH, I HEARD SOME RUMORS ABOUT THEM YESTER-DAY.
IS SOME-THING THE MATTER?
YEAH, WELL, THEY DON'T SEEM AT ALL LIKE THE "DEAD END" I KNOW, SO...
ANYWAY, I'LL BE GOING NOW.
SEE YOU LATER!

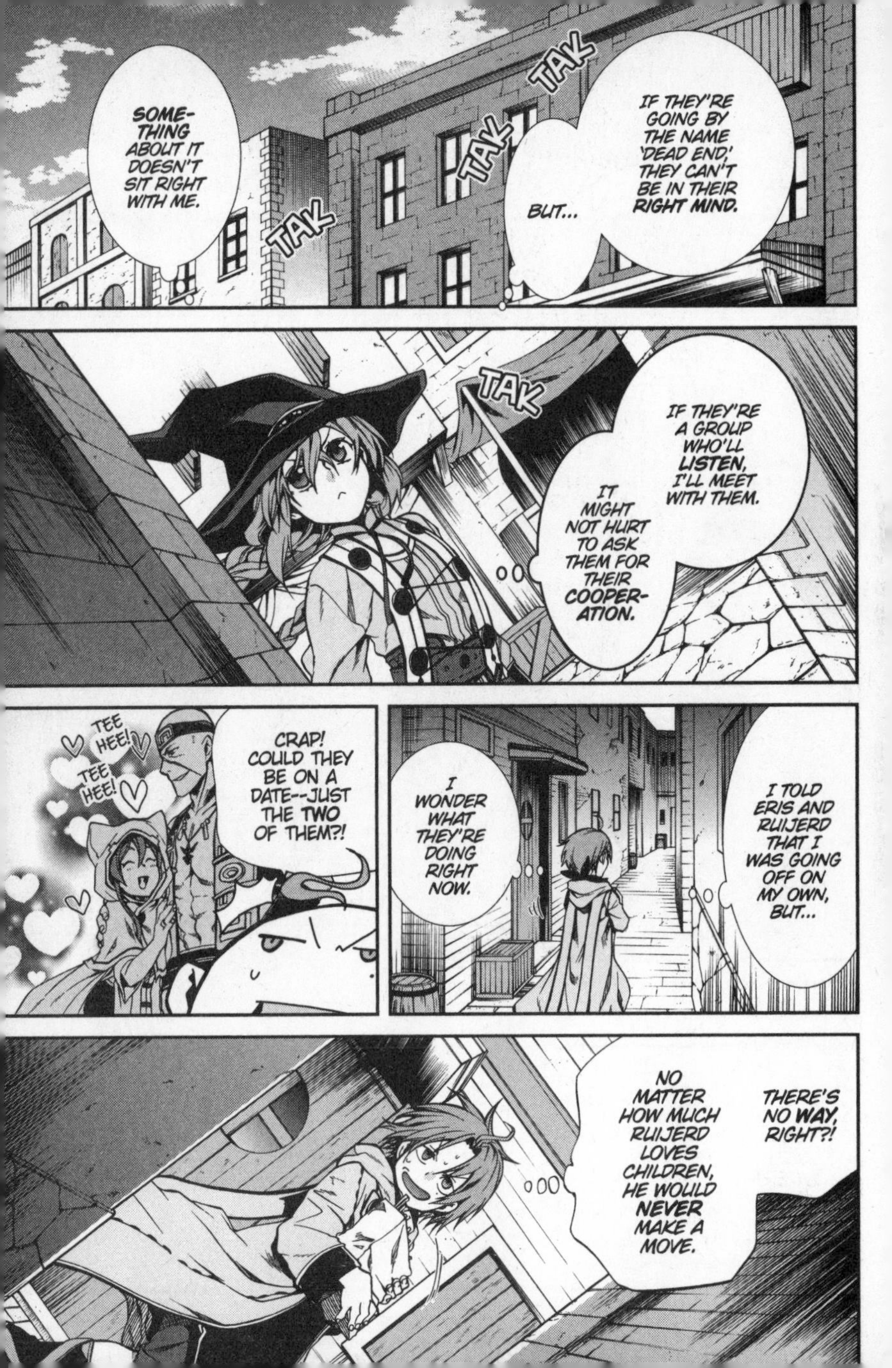
TAK
TAK
IF THEY'RE GOING BY THE NAME 'DEAD END,' THEY CAN'T BE IN THEIR RIGHT MIND.
BUT...
TAK
SOMETHING ABOUT IT DOESN'T SIT RIGHT WITH ME.
TAK
TAK
IF THEY'RE A GROUP WHO'LL LISTEN, I'LL MEET WITH THEM.
IT MIGHT NOT HURT TO ASK THEM FOR THEIR COOPERATION.
I TOLD ERIS AND RUIJERD THAT I WAS GOING OFF ON MY OWN, BUT...
I WONDER WHAT THEY'RE DOING RIGHT NOW.
CRAP! COULD THEY BE ON A DATE--JUST THE TWO OF THEM?!
TEE HEE!
TEE HEE!
THERE'S NO WAY, RIGHT?!
NO MATTER HOW MUCH RUIJERD LOVES CHILDREN, HE WOULD NEVER MAKE A MOVE.

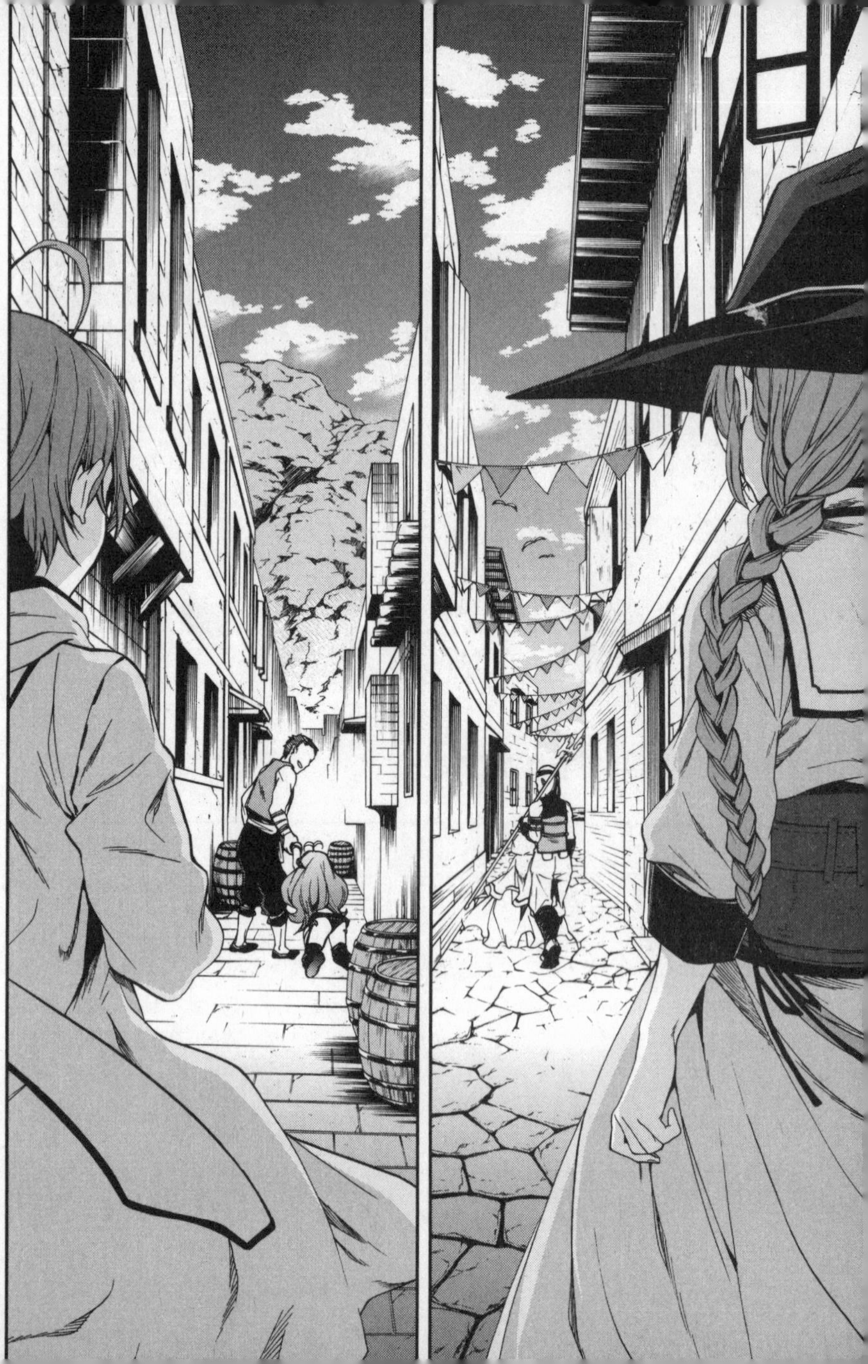

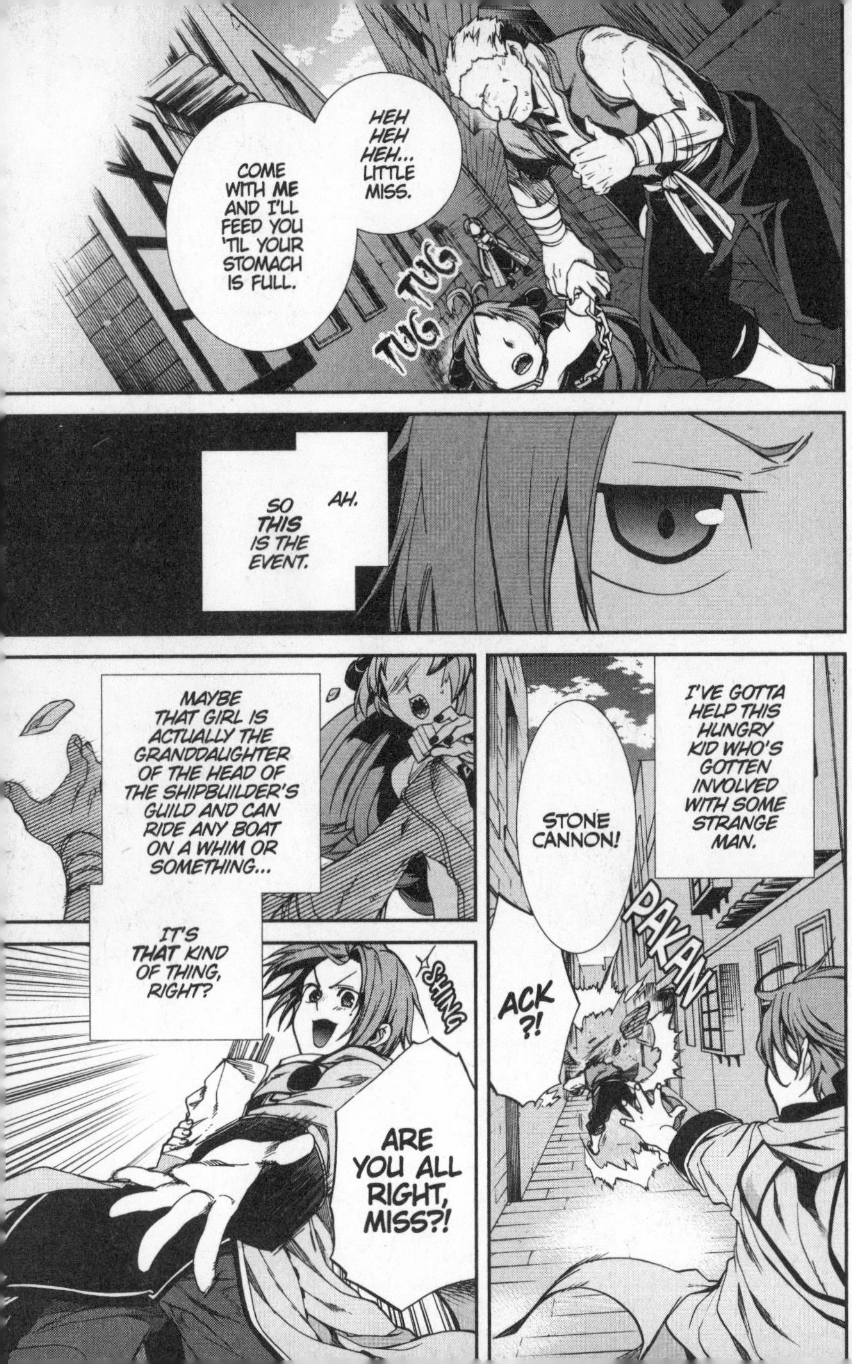
HEH HEH HEH... LITTLE MISS.
COME WITH ME AND I'LL FEED YOU 'TIL YOUR STOMACH IS FULL.
TUG TUG
AH.
SO THIS IS THE EVENT.
I'VE GOTTA HELP THIS HUNGRY KID WHO'S GOTTEN INVOLVED WITH SOME STRANGE MAN.
STONE CANNON!
PAKAN
ACK ?!
MAYBE THAT GIRL IS ACTUALLY THE GRANDDAUGHTER OF THE HEAD OF THE SHIPBUILDER'S GUILD AND CAN RIDE ANY BOAT ON A WHIM OR SOMETHING...
IT'S THAT KIND OF THING, RIGHT?
SHING
ARE YOU ALL RIGHT, MISS?!

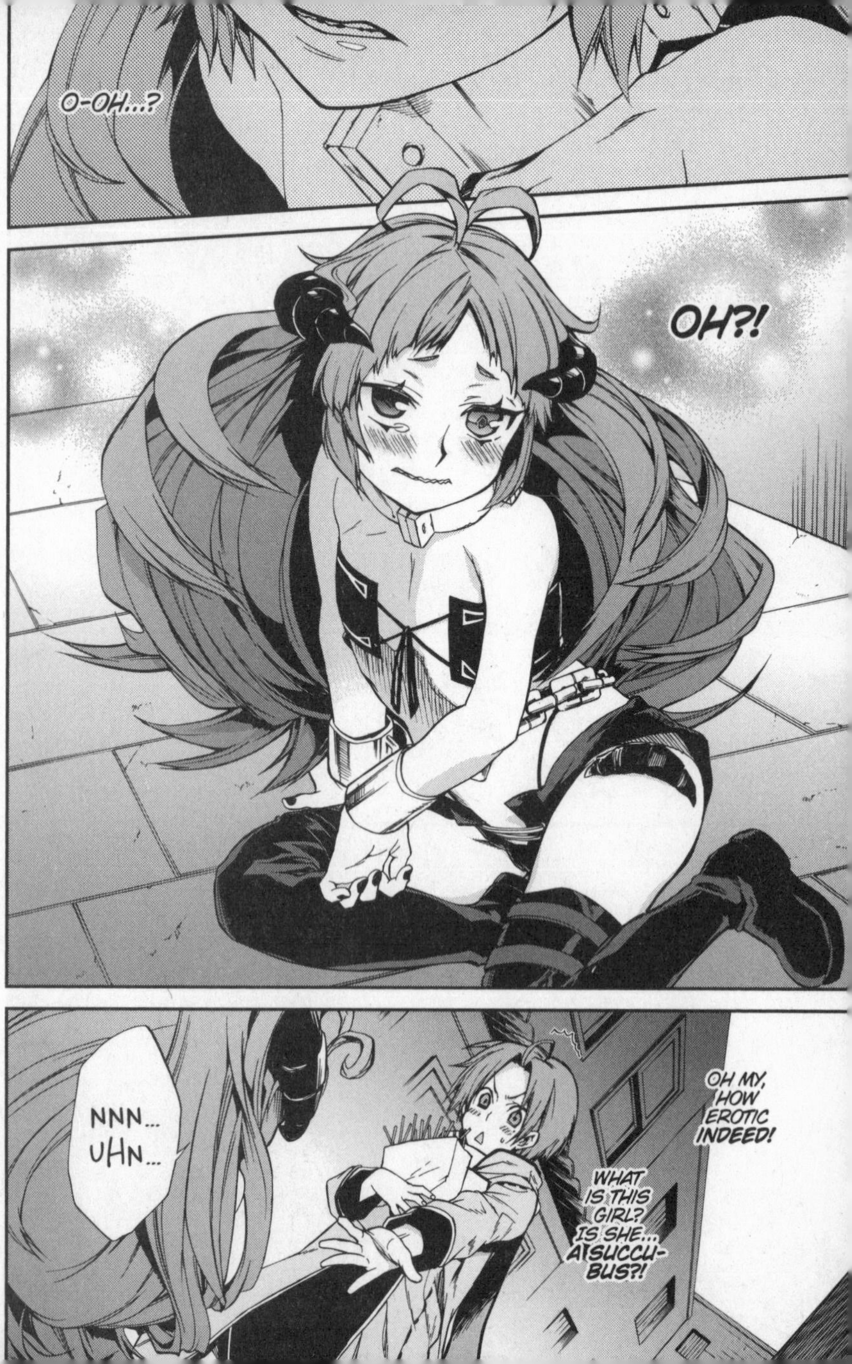
O-OH...?
OH?!
OH MY, HOW EROTIC INDEED!
WHAT IS THIS GIRL? IS SHE... A SUCCU-BUS?!
NNN... UHN...

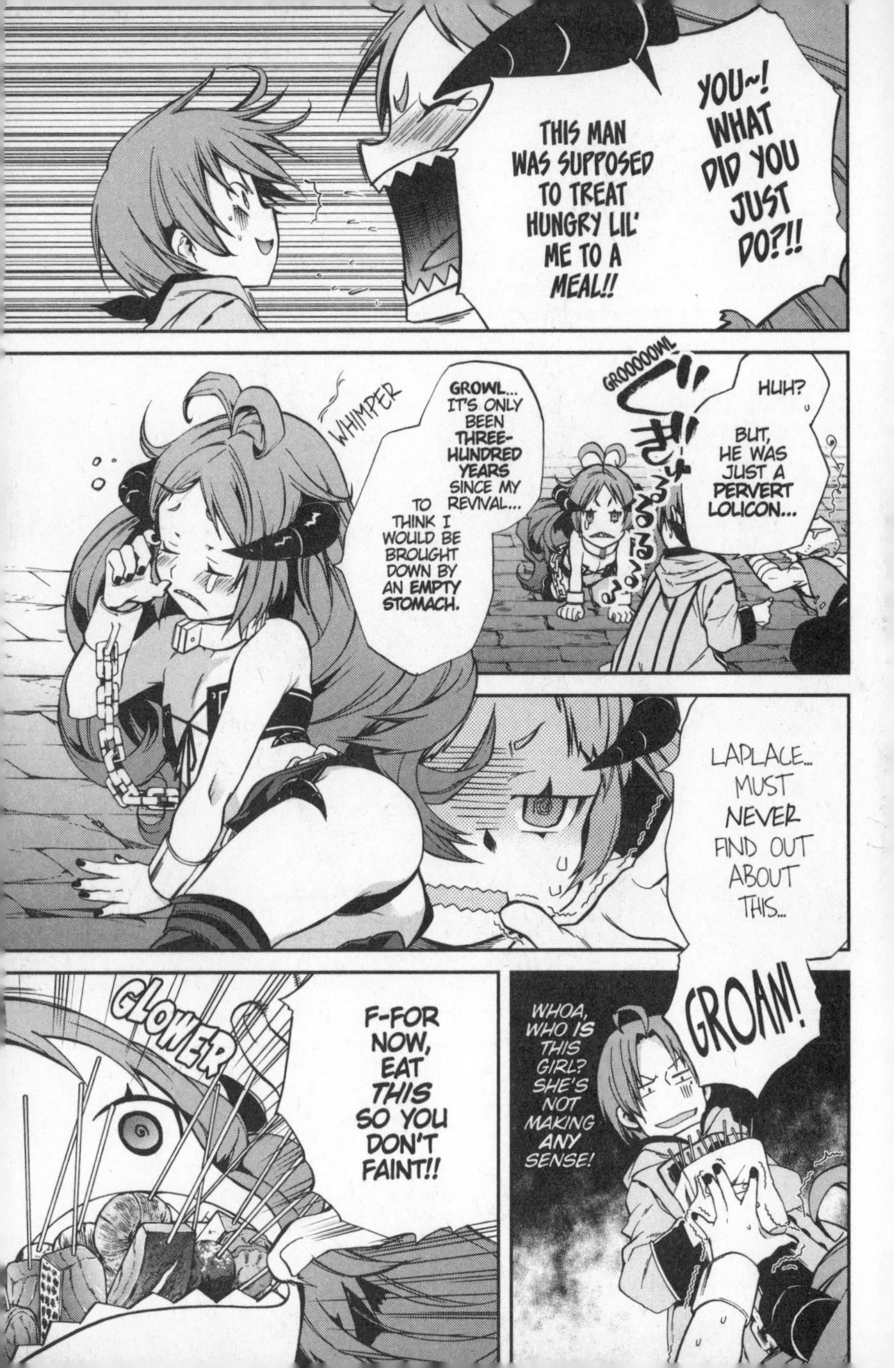
YOU~! WHAT DID YOU JUST DO?!!
THIS MAN WAS SUPPOSED TO TREAT HUNGRY LIL' ME TO A MEAL!!
HUH?
BUT, HE WAS JUST A PERVERT LOLICON...
GROOOOOWL
GROWL... IT'S ONLY BEEN THREE-HUNDRED YEARS SINCE MY REVIVAL...
TO THINK I WOULD BE BROUGHT DOWN BY AN EMPTY STOMACH.
WHIMPER
LAPLACE... MUST NEVER FIND OUT ABOUT THIS...
GROAN!
WHOA, WHO IS THIS GIRL? SHE'S NOT MAKING ANY SENSE!
GLOWER
F-FOR NOW, EAT THIS SO YOU DON'T FAINT!!

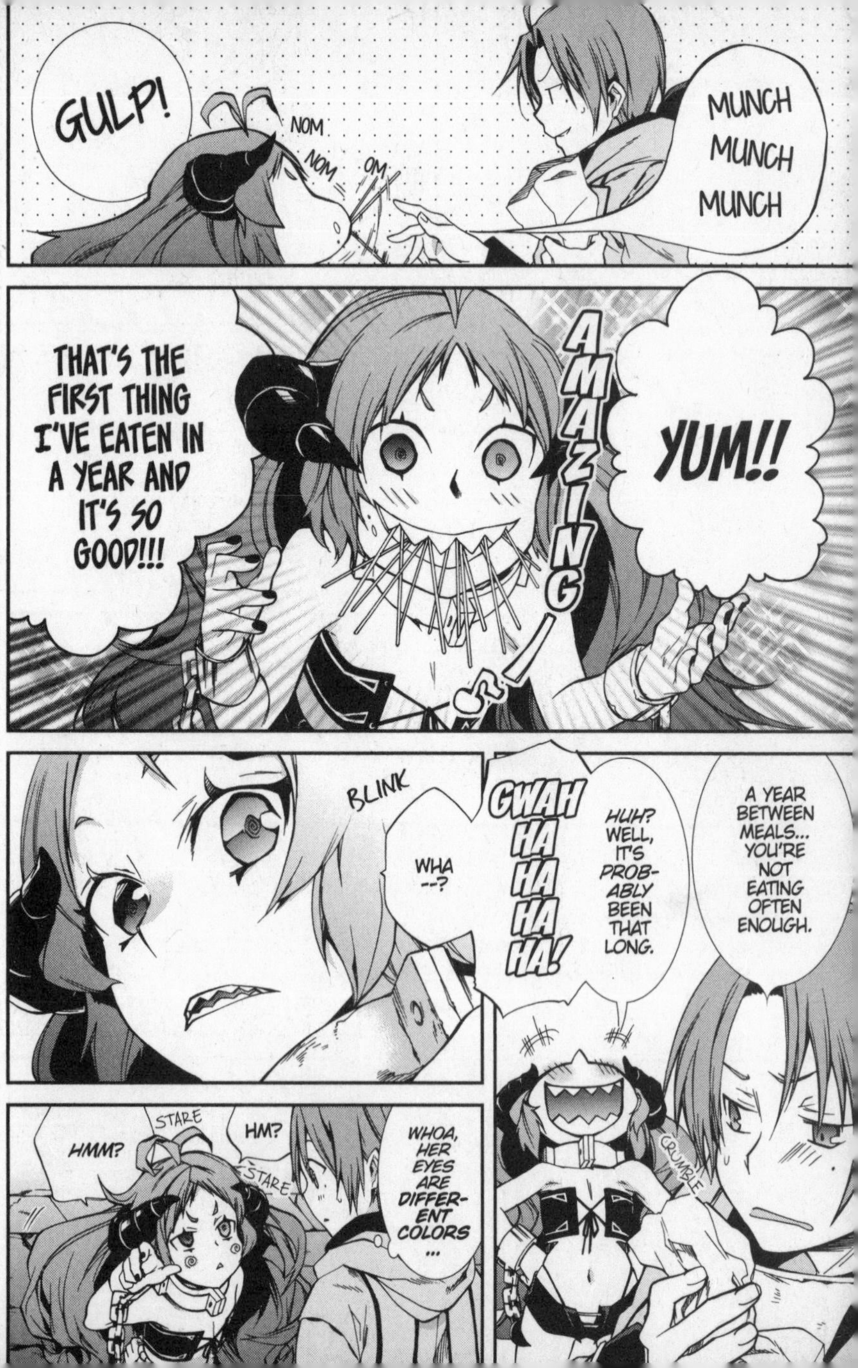
MUNCH
MUNCH
MUNCH
NOM
NOM
OM
GULP!
YUM!!
AMAZING
THAT'S THE FIRST THING I'VE EATEN IN A YEAR AND IT'S SO GOOD!!!
A YEAR BETWEEN MEALS... YOU'RE NOT EATING OFTEN ENOUGH.
HUH? WELL, IT'S PROB-ABLY BEEN THAT LONG.
GWAH HA HA HA HA HA!
CRUMBLE
WHA--?
BLINK
WHOA, HER EYES ARE DIFFER-ENT COLORS...
HM?
STARE
HMM?
STARE

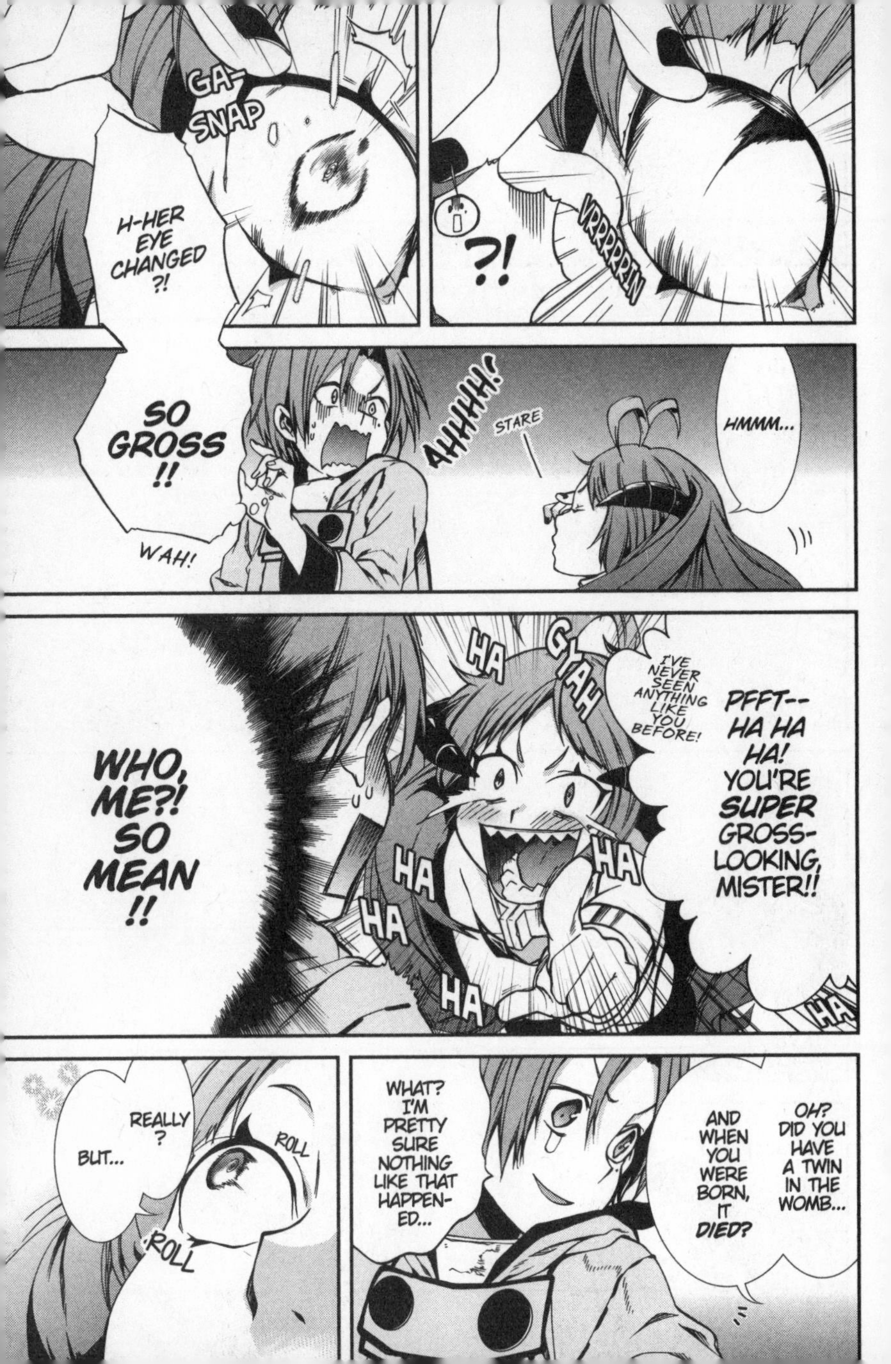
VRRRRRRIN
?!
GA-SNAP
H-HER EYE CHANGED ?!
HMMM...
STARE
AHHHH!
SO GROSS !!
WAH!
PFFT-- HA HA HA! YOU'RE SUPER GROSS-LOOKING, MISTER!!
I'VE NEVER SEEN ANYTHING LIKE YOU BEFORE!
GYAH
HA
HA
HA
HA
HA
HA
WHO, ME?! SO MEAN !!
OH? DID YOU HAVE A TWIN IN THE WOMB...
AND WHEN YOU WERE BORN, IT DIED?
WHAT? I'M PRETTY SURE NOTHING LIKE THAT HAPPENED...
ROLL
REALLY ?
BUT...
ROLL

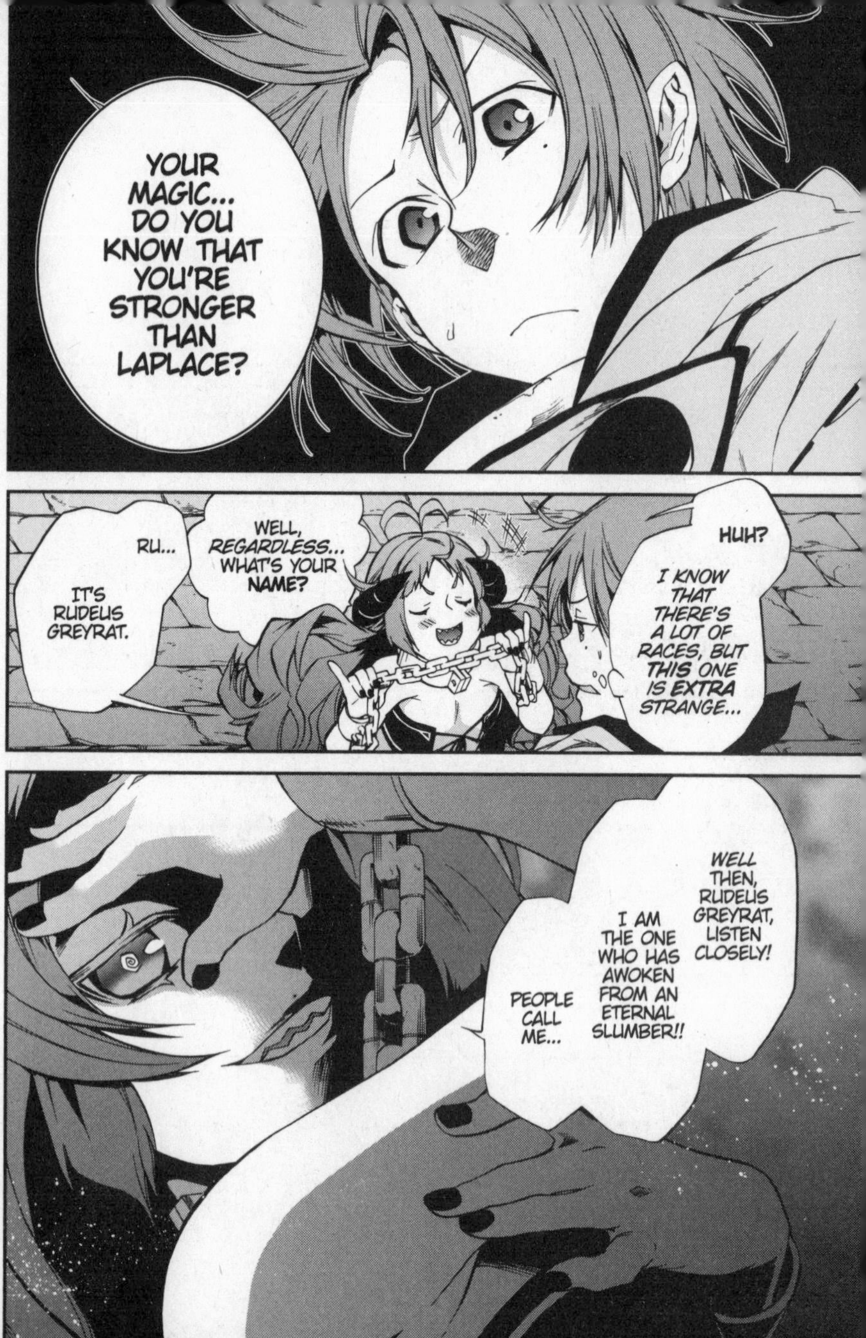
YOUR MAGIC... DO YOU KNOW THAT YOU'RE STRONGER THAN LAPLACE?
HUH?
I KNOW THAT THERE'S A LOT OF RACES, BUT THIS ONE IS EXTRA STRANGE...
WELL, REGARDLESS... WHAT'S YOUR NAME?
RU...
IT'S RUDEUS GREYRAT.
WELL THEN, RUDEUS GREYRAT, LISTEN CLOSELY!
I AM THE ONE WHO HAS AWOKEN FROM AN ETERNAL SLUMBER!!
PEOPLE CALL ME...

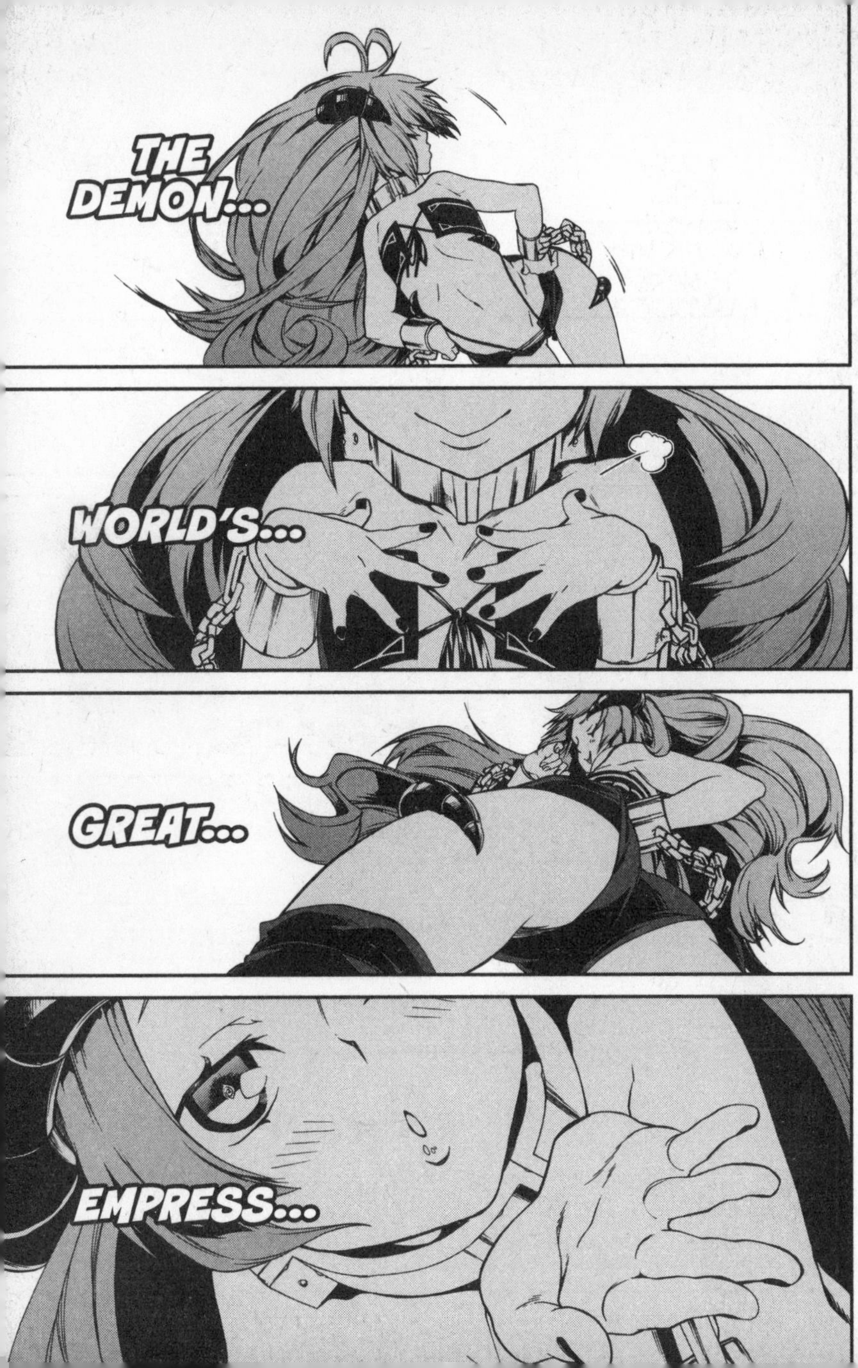
THE DEMON...
WORLD'S...
GREAT...
EMPRESS...

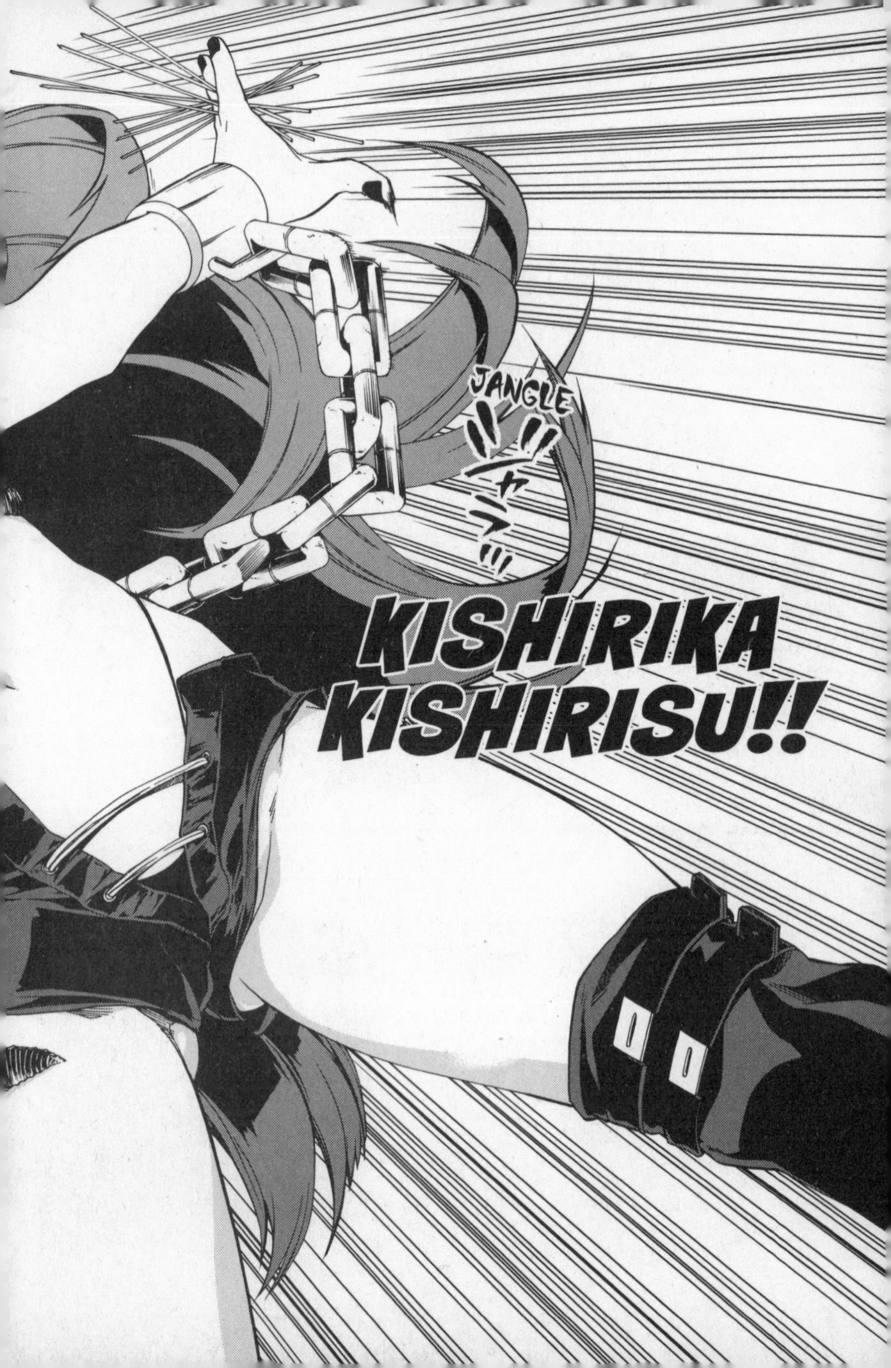
JANGLE
KISHIRIKA KISHIRISU!!

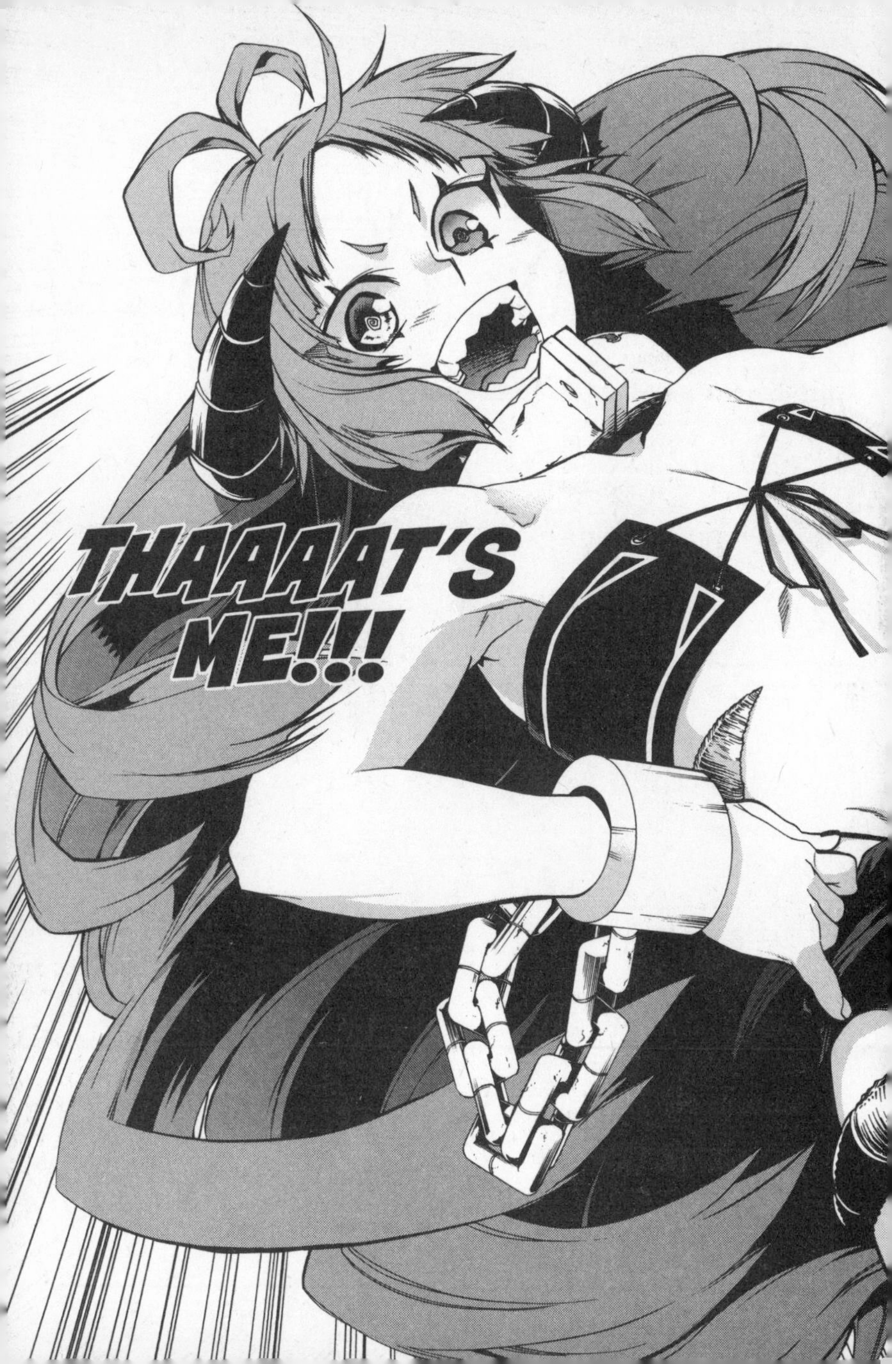
THAAAAT'S ME!!!

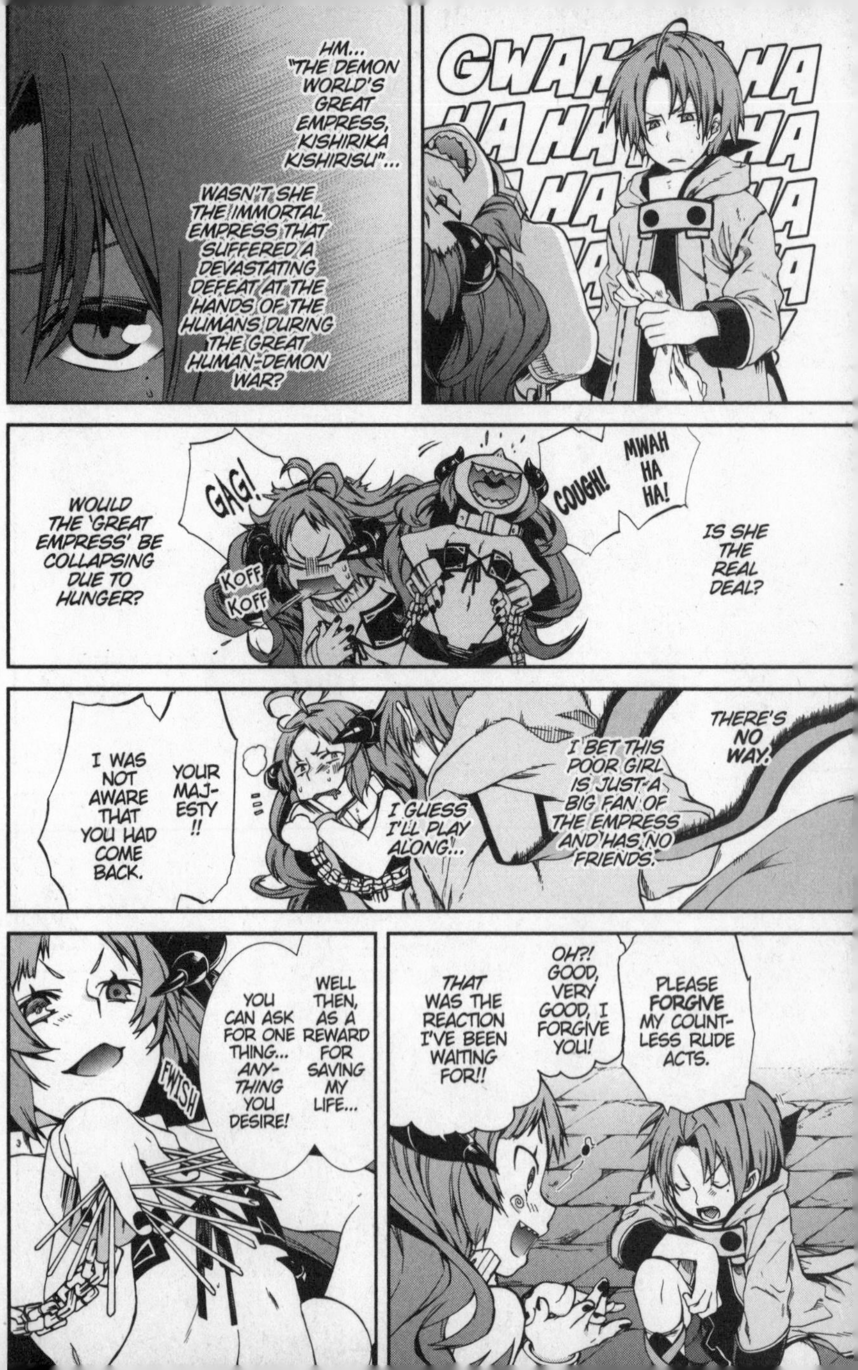
GWAH HA HA HA HA HA HA HA HA HA HA
HM... "THE DEMON WORLD'S GREAT EMPRESS, KISHIRIKA KISHIRISU"...
WASN'T SHE THE IMMORTAL EMPRESS THAT SUFFERED A DEVASTATING DEFEAT AT THE HANDS OF THE HUMANS DURING THE GREAT HUMAN-DEMON WAR?
IS SHE THE REAL DEAL?
MWAH HA HA!
COUGH!
GAG!
KOFF KOFF
WOULD THE 'GREAT EMPRESS' BE COLLAPSING DUE TO HUNGER?
THERE'S NO WAY.
I BET THIS POOR GIRL IS JUST A BIG FAN OF THE EMPRESS AND HAS NO FRIENDS.
I GUESS I'LL PLAY ALONG...
YOUR MAJESTY!!
I WAS NOT AWARE THAT YOU HAD COME BACK.
PLEASE FORGIVE MY COUNTLESS RUDE ACTS.
OH?! GOOD, VERY GOOD, I FORGIVE YOU!
THAT WAS THE REACTION I'VE BEEN WAITING FOR!!
WELL THEN, AS A REWARD FOR SAVING MY LIFE...
YOU CAN ASK FOR ONE THING... ANY-THING YOU DESIRE!
FWISH

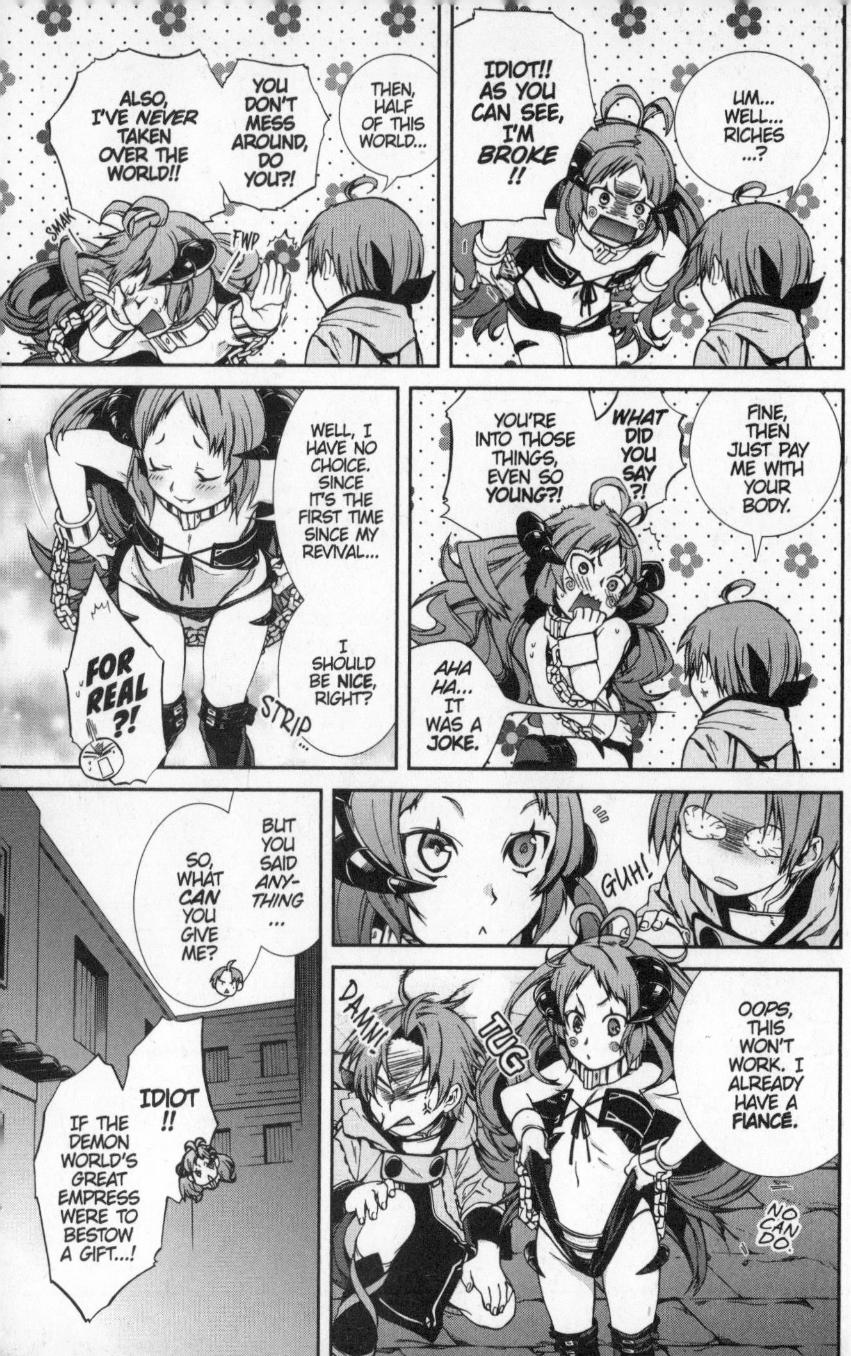
UM... WELL... RICHES ...?
IDIOT!! AS YOU CAN SEE, I'M *BROKE* !!
THEN, HALF OF THIS WORLD...
YOU DON'T MESS AROUND, DO YOU?!
ALSO, I'VE *NEVER* TAKEN OVER THE WORLD!!
SMAK
FWP
FINE, THEN JUST PAY ME WITH YOUR BODY.
WHAT DID YOU SAY ?!
YOU'RE INTO THOSE THINGS, EVEN SO YOUNG?!
AHA HA... IT WAS A JOKE.
WELL, I HAVE NO CHOICE. SINCE IT'S THE FIRST TIME SINCE MY REVIVAL...
I SHOULD BE NICE, RIGHT?
STRIP...
FOR REAL ?!
GUH!
OOPS, THIS WON'T WORK. I ALREADY HAVE A FIANCÉ.
TUG
DAMN!
NO CAN DO.
BUT YOU SAID ANYTHING...
SO, WHAT *CAN* YOU GIVE ME?
IDIOT !!
IF THE DEMON WORLD'S GREAT EMPRESS WERE TO BESTOW A GIFT...!

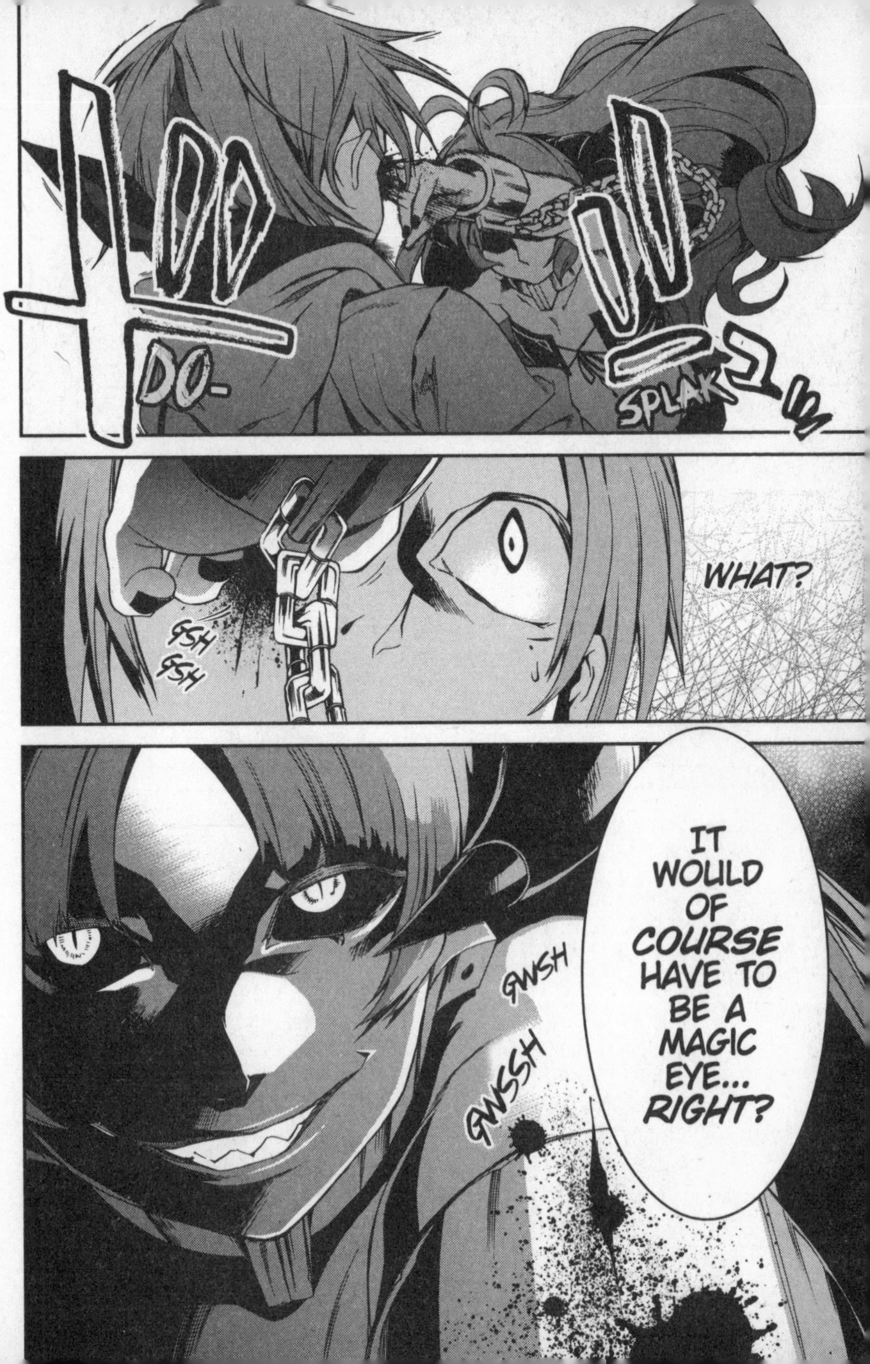
SPLAK
DO-
WHAT?
GSH
GSH
IT WOULD OF COURSE HAVE TO BE A MAGIC EYE... RIGHT?
GWSH
GWSSH

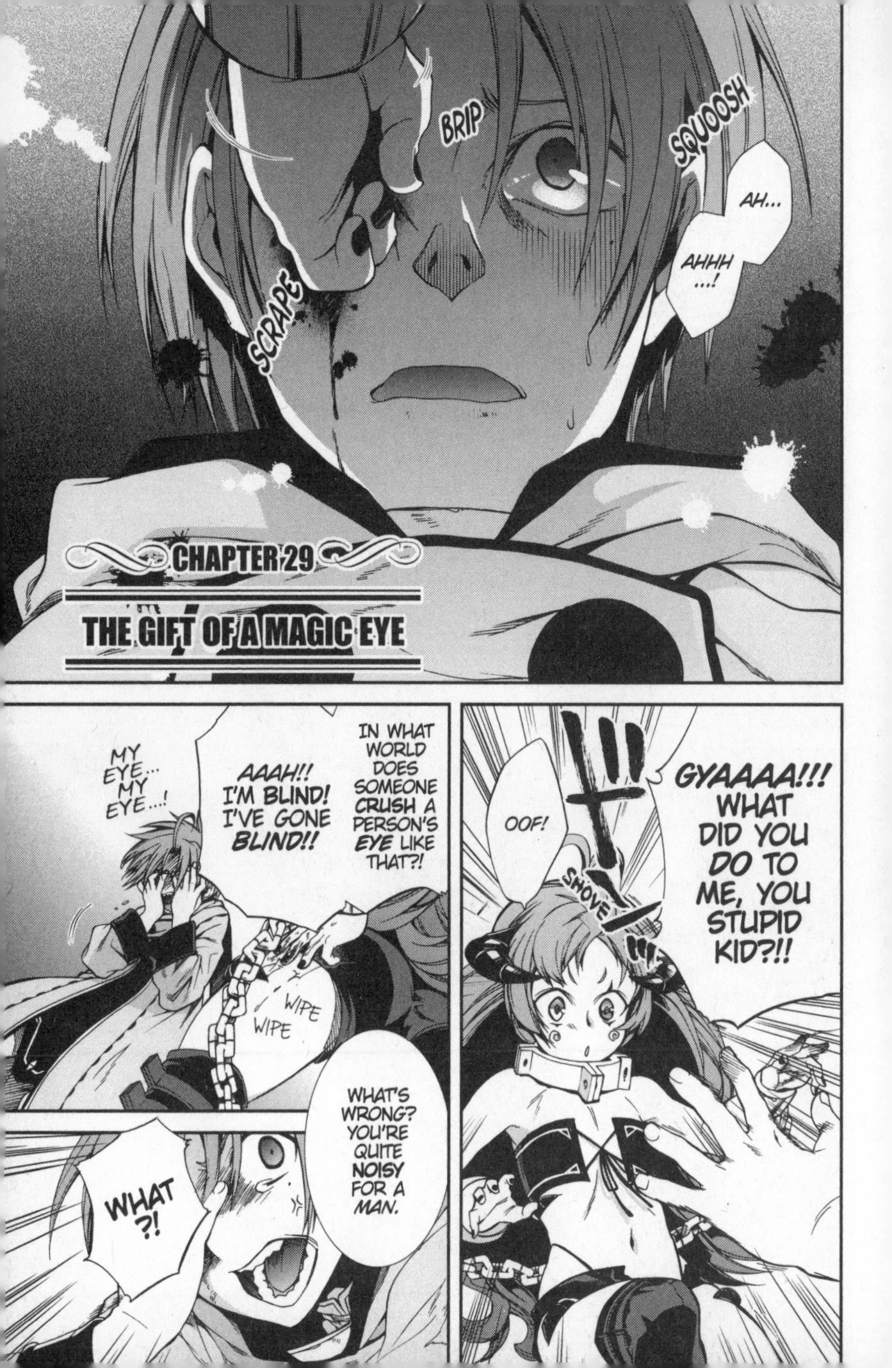
SQUOOSH
AH...
AHHH ...!
BRIP
SCRAPE
CHAPTER 29
THE GIFT OF A MAGIC EYE
GYAAAA!!! WHAT DID YOU DO TO ME, YOU STUPID KID?!!
OOF!
SHOVE
IN WHAT WORLD DOES SOMEONE CRUSH A PERSON'S EYE LIKE THAT?!
AAAH!! I'M BLIND! I'VE GONE BLIND!!
MY EYE... MY EYE...!
WIPE WIPE
WHAT'S WRONG? YOU'RE QUITE NOISY FOR A MAN.
WHAT ?!

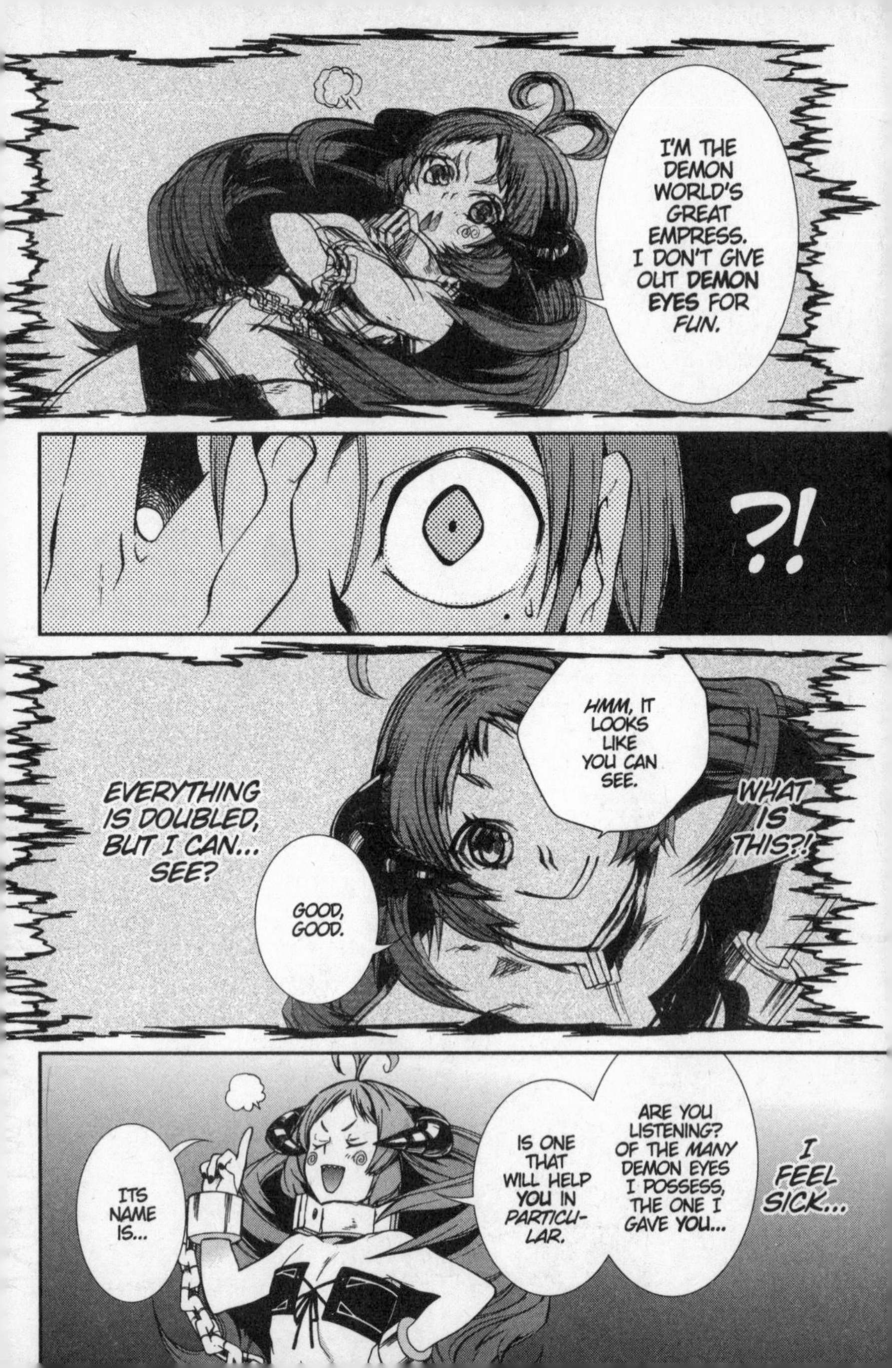
I'M THE DEMON WORLD'S GREAT EMPRESS. I DON'T GIVE OUT DEMON EYES FOR FUN.
?!
WHAT IS THIS?!
HMM, IT LOOKS LIKE YOU CAN SEE.
EVERYTHING IS DOUBLED, BUT I CAN... SEE?
GOOD, GOOD.
I FEEL SICK...
ARE YOU LISTENING? OF THE MANY DEMON EYES I POSSESS, THE ONE I GAVE YOU...
IS ONE THAT WILL HELP YOU IN PARTICULAR.
ITS NAME IS...

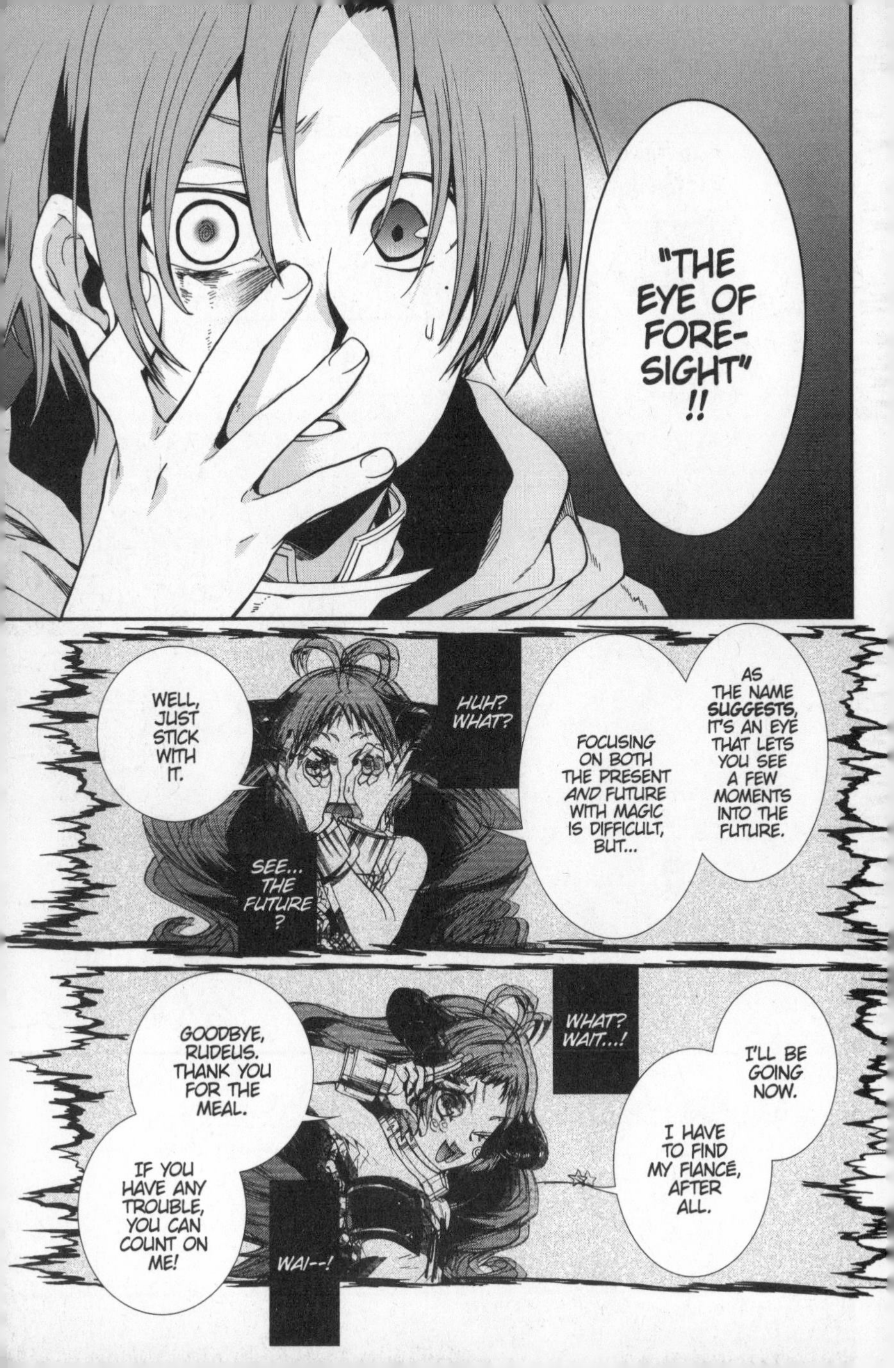
"THE EYE OF FORE-SIGHT"!!
AS THE NAME SUGGESTS, IT'S AN EYE THAT LETS YOU SEE A FEW MOMENTS INTO THE FUTURE.
FOCUSING ON BOTH THE PRESENT AND FUTURE WITH MAGIC IS DIFFICULT, BUT...
HUH? WHAT?
WELL, JUST STICK WITH IT.
SEE... THE FUTURE?
I'LL BE GOING NOW.
I HAVE TO FIND MY FIANCÉ, AFTER ALL.
WHAT? WAIT...!
GOODBYE, RUDEUS. THANK YOU FOR THE MEAL.
IF YOU HAVE ANY TROUBLE, YOU CAN COUNT ON ME!
WAI--!

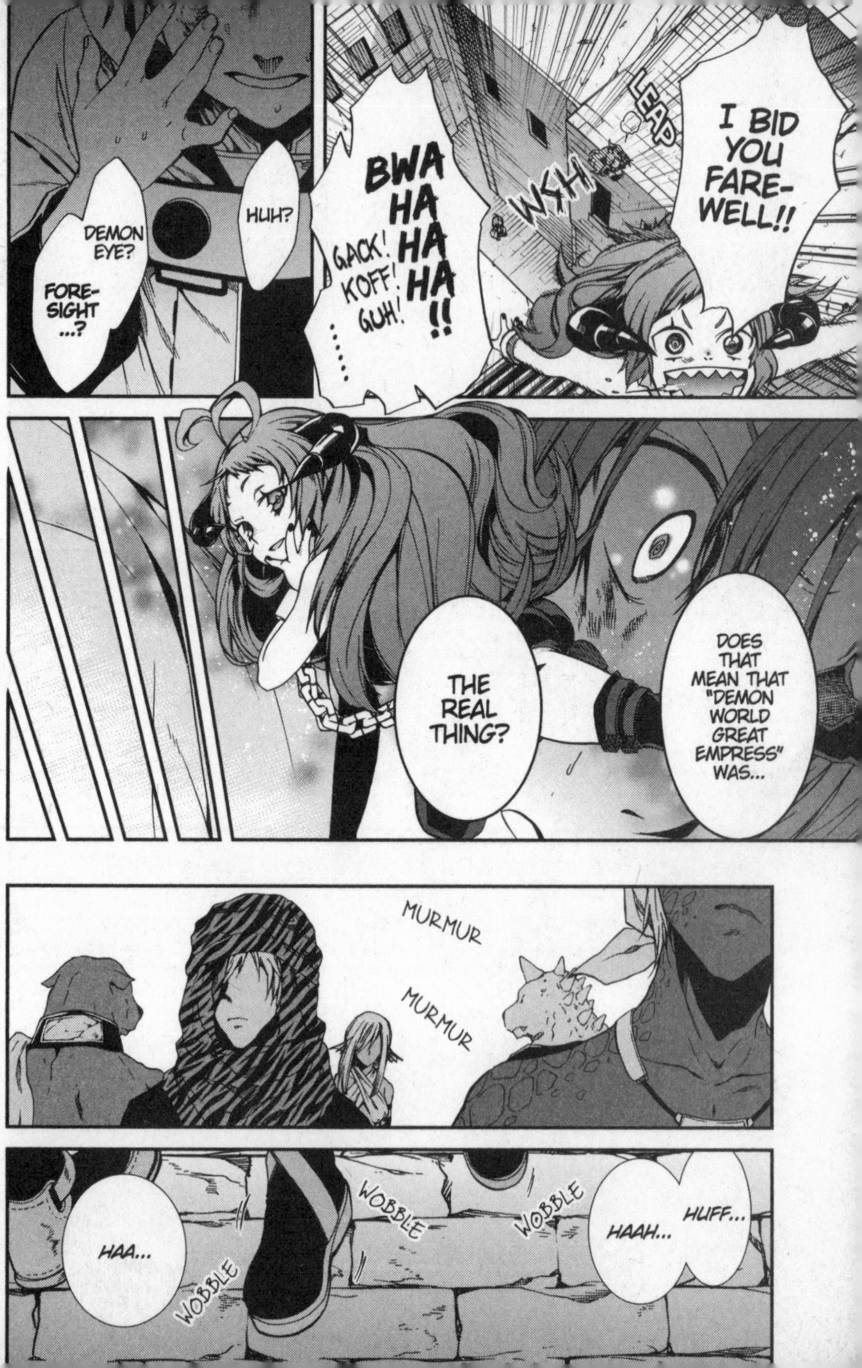
I BID YOU FARE-WELL!!
LEAP
WSH
BWA HA HA HA!!
GACK! KOFF! GUH!
......
HUH?
DEMON EYE?
FORE-SIGHT ...?
DOES THAT MEAN THAT "DEMON WORLD GREAT EMPRESS" WAS...
THE REAL THING?
MURMUR
MURMUR
HUFF...
HAAH...
WOBBLE
WOBBLE
HAA...
WOBBLE

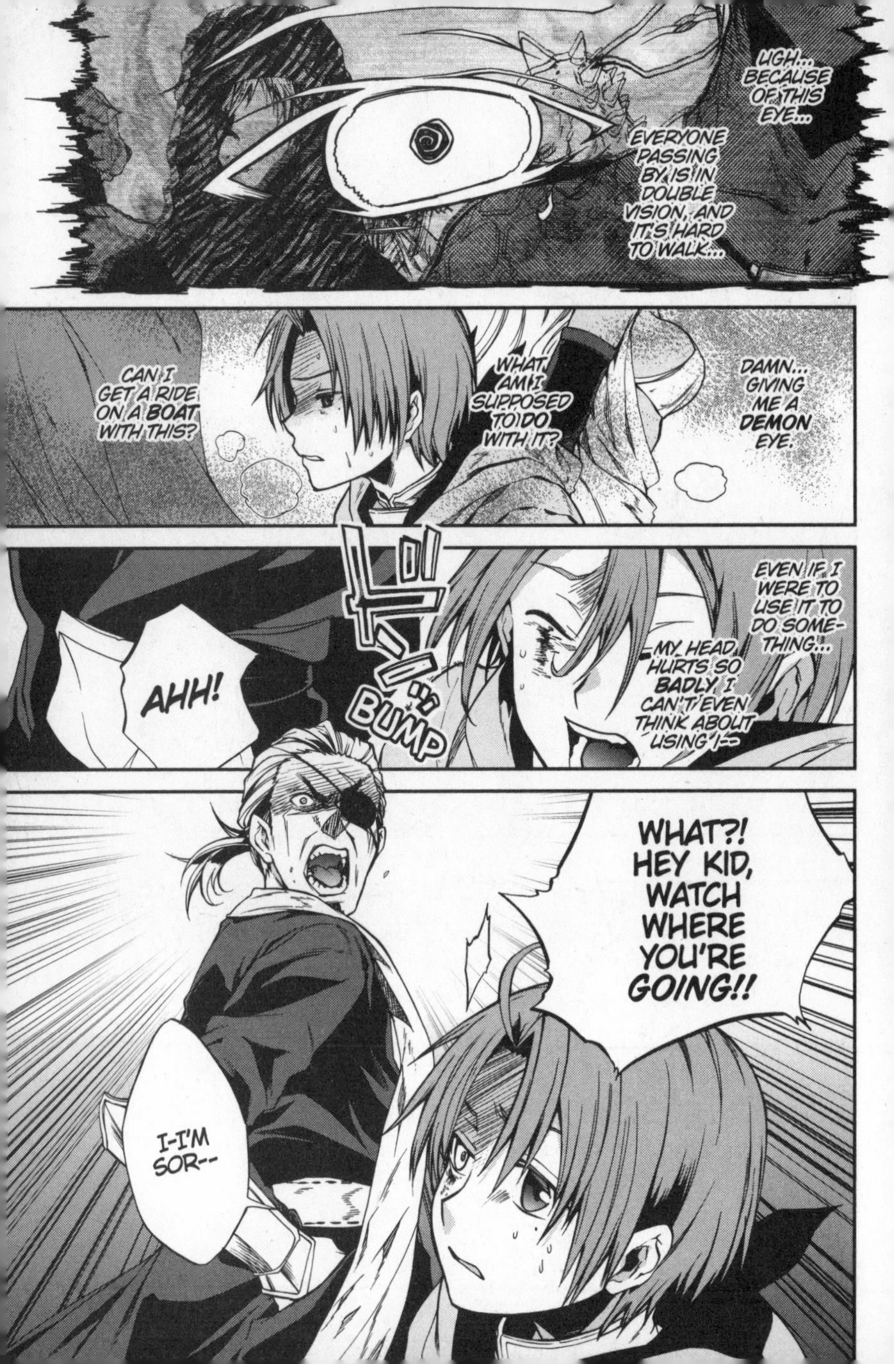
UGH... BECAUSE OF THIS EYE...
EVERYONE PASSING BY IS IN DOUBLE VISION, AND IT'S HARD TO WALK...
DAMN... GIVING ME A DEMON EYE.
WHAT AM I SUPPOSED TO DO WITH IT?
CAN I GET A RIDE ON A BOAT WITH THIS?
EVEN IF I WERE TO USE IT TO DO SOME-THING...
MY HEAD HURTS SO BADLY I CAN'T EVEN THINK ABOUT USING I--
BUMP
AHH!
WHAT?! HEY KID, WATCH WHERE YOU'RE GOING!!
I-I'M SOR--

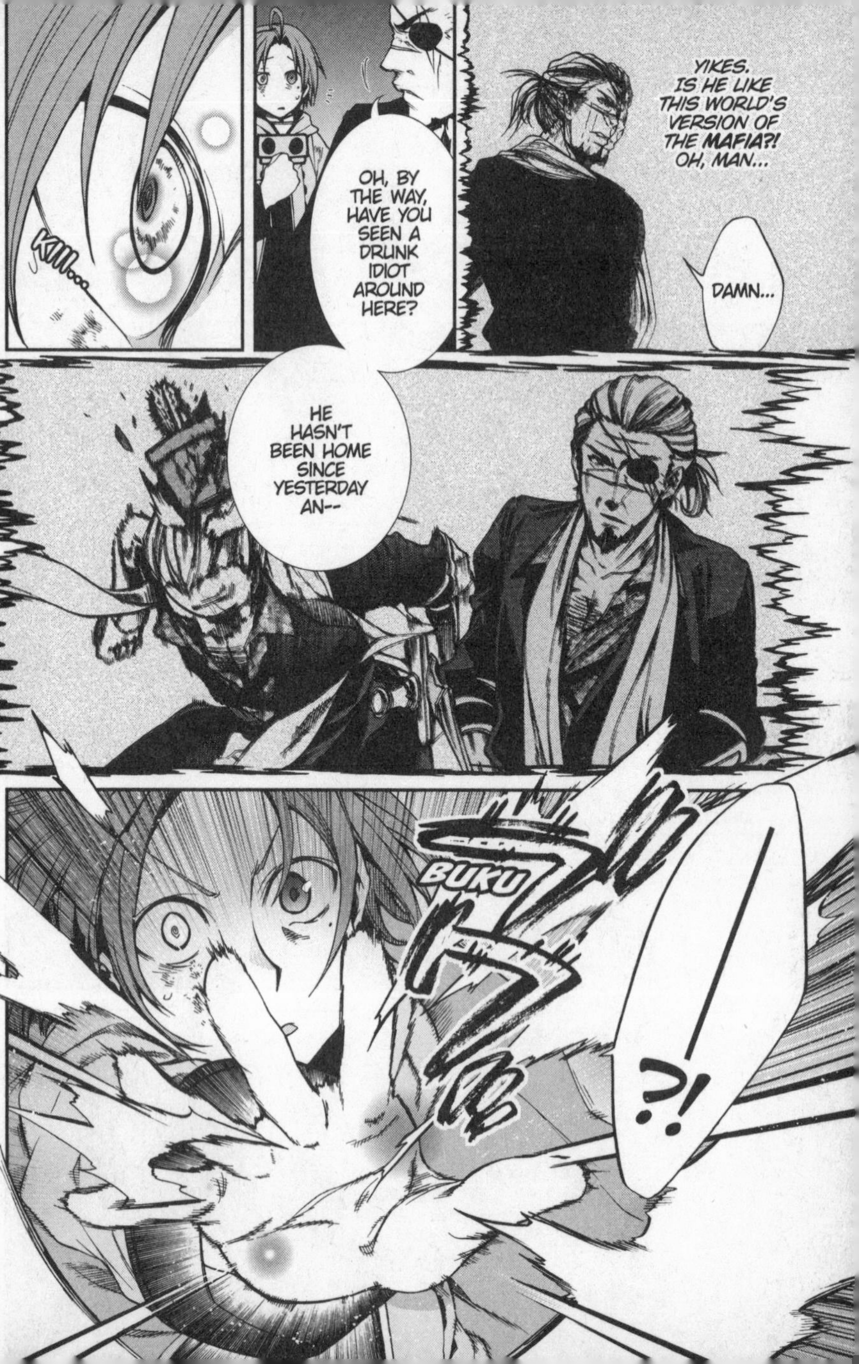
YIKES. IS HE LIKE THIS WORLD'S VERSION OF THE MAFIA?! OH, MAN...
DAMN...
OH, BY THE WAY, HAVE YOU SEEN A DRUNK IDIOT AROUND HERE?
KIII...
HE HASN'T BEEN HOME SINCE YESTERDAY AN--
BUKU
?!

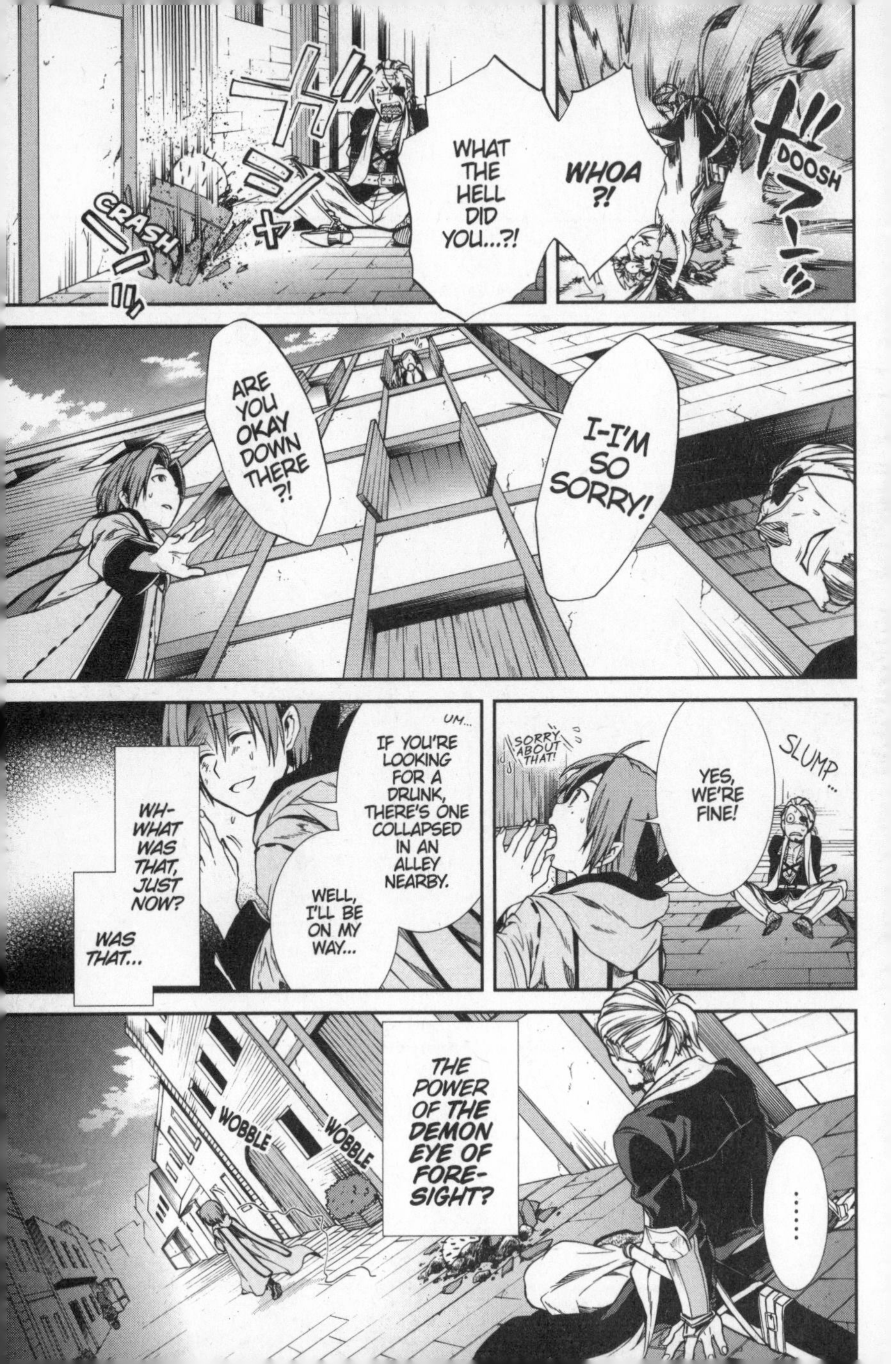
DOOSH
WHOA ?!
WHAT THE HELL DID YOU...?!
CRASH
I-I'M SO SORRY!
ARE YOU OKAY DOWN THERE ?!
SLUMP...
YES, WE'RE FINE!
SORRY ABOUT THAT!
UM...
IF YOU'RE LOOKING FOR A DRUNK, THERE'S ONE COLLAPSED IN AN ALLEY NEARBY.
WELL, I'LL BE ON MY WAY...
WH-WHAT WAS THAT, JUST NOW?
WAS THAT...
......
THE POWER OF THE DEMON EYE OF FORE-SIGHT?
WOBBLE
WOBBLE

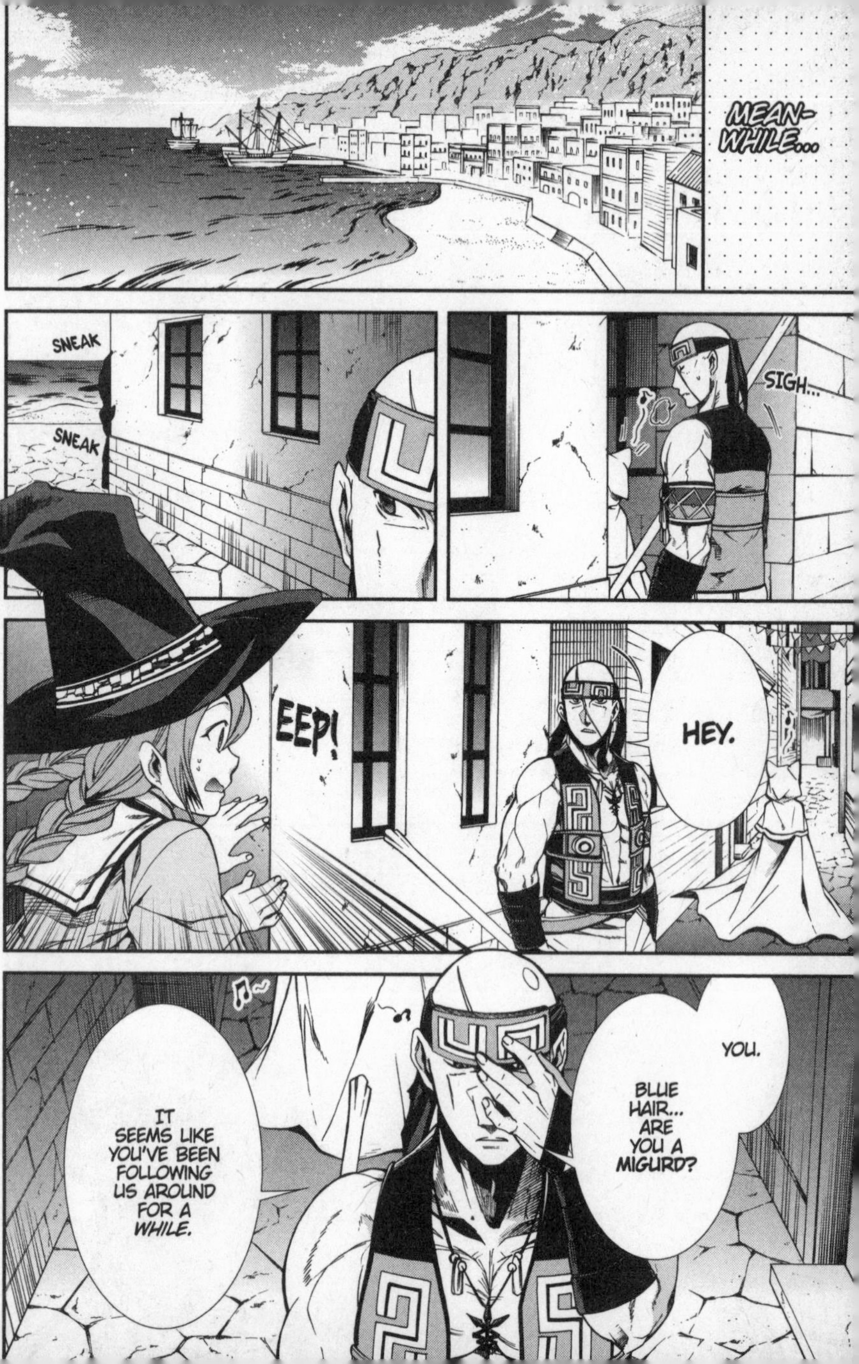
MEAN-WHILE...
SIGH...
SNEAK
SNEAK
HEY.
EEP!
YOU.
BLUE HAIR... ARE YOU A MIGURD?
IT SEEMS LIKE YOU'VE BEEN FOLLOWING US AROUND FOR A WHILE.

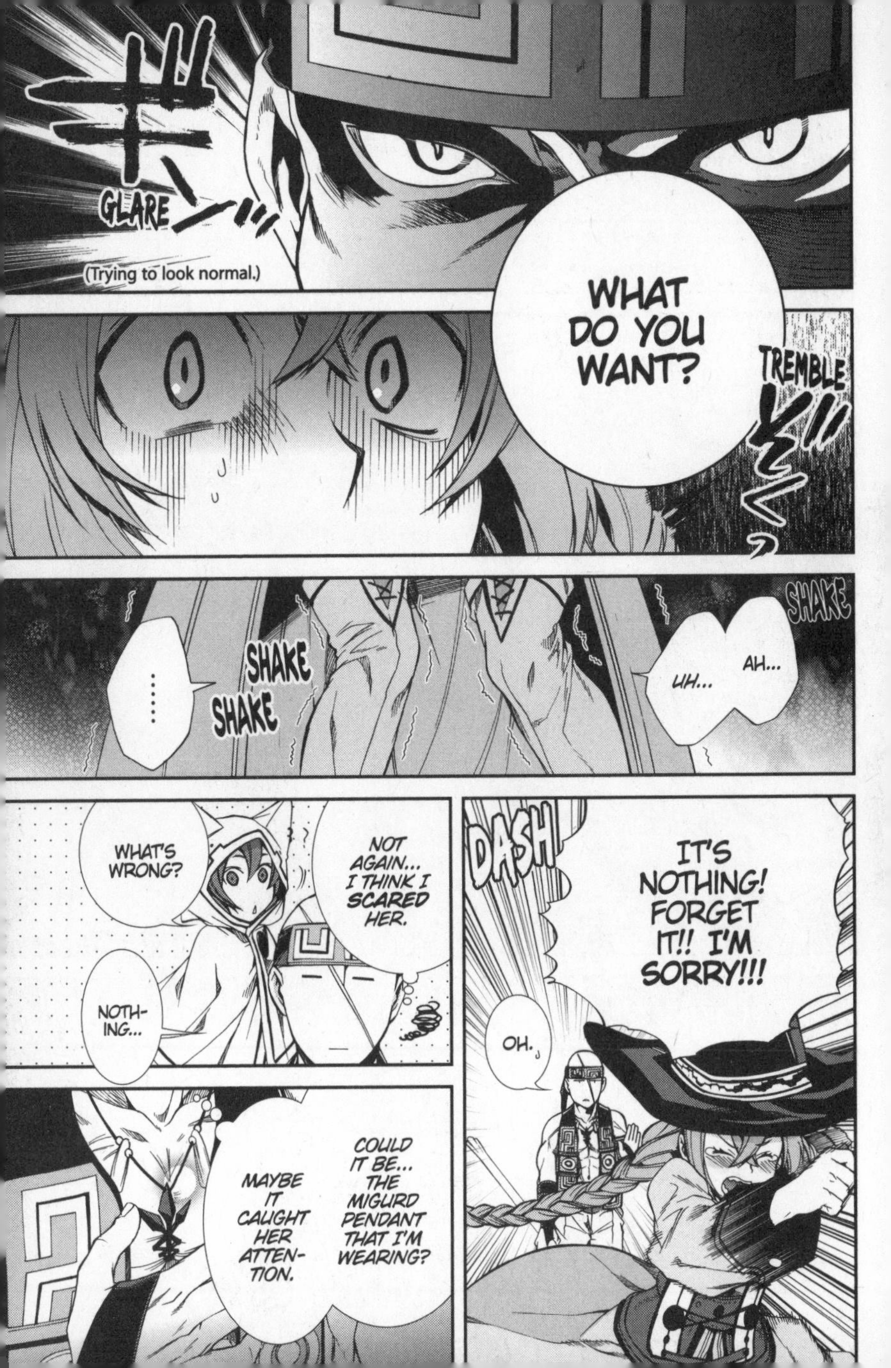
GLARE
(Trying to look normal.)
WHAT DO YOU WANT?
TREMBLE
SHAKE
AH... UH...
SHAKE SHAKE
......
DASH
IT'S NOTHING! FORGET IT!! I'M SORRY!!!
OH.
NOT AGAIN... I THINK I SCARED HER.
WHAT'S WRONG?
NOTH-ING...
COULD IT BE... THE MIGURD PENDANT THAT I'M WEARING?
MAYBE IT CAUGHT HER ATTEN-TION.

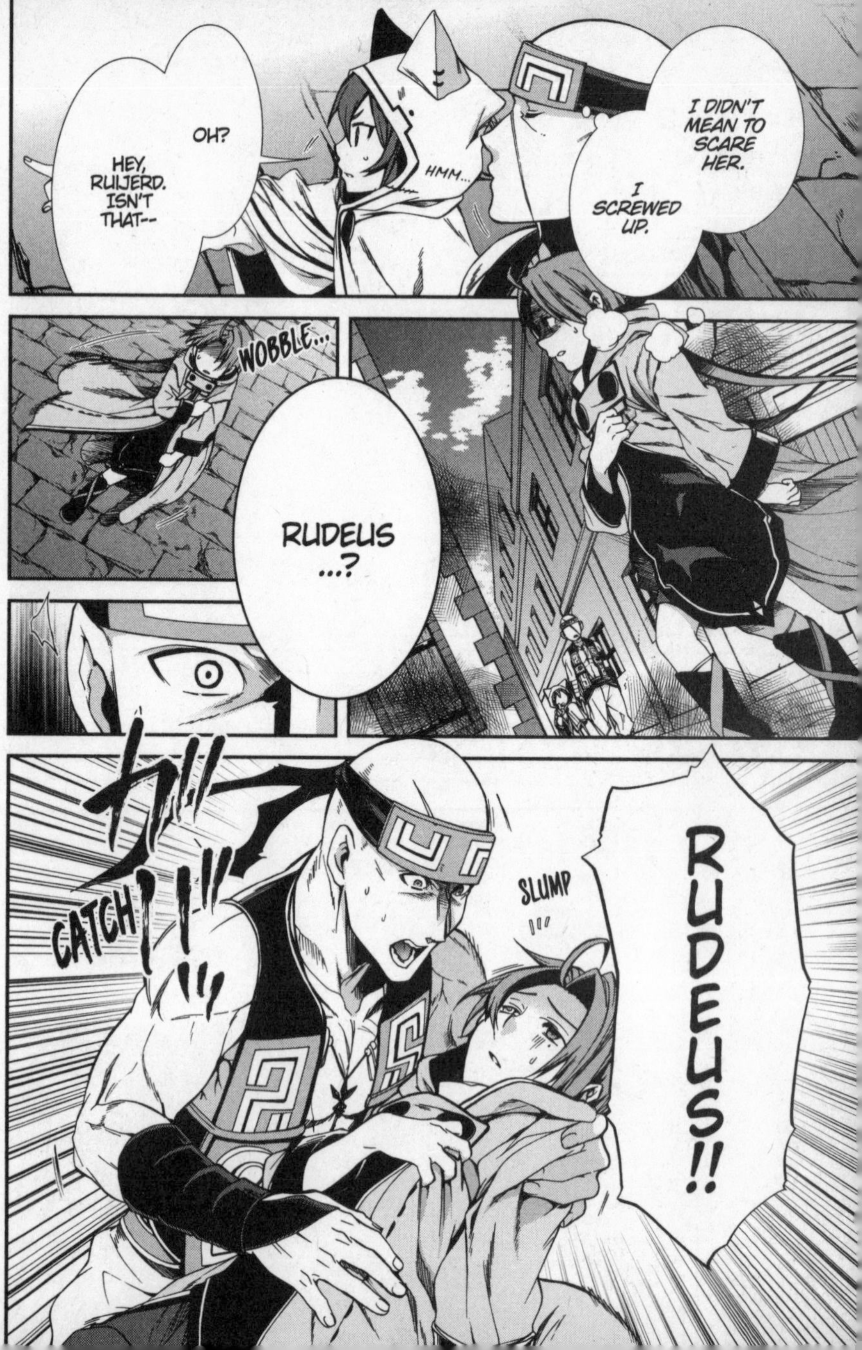
I DIDN'T MEAN TO SCARE HER.
I SCREWED UP.
HMM...
OH?
HEY, RUIJERD. ISN'T THAT--
RUDEUS ...?
WOBBLE...
RUDEUS!!
SLUMP
CATCH

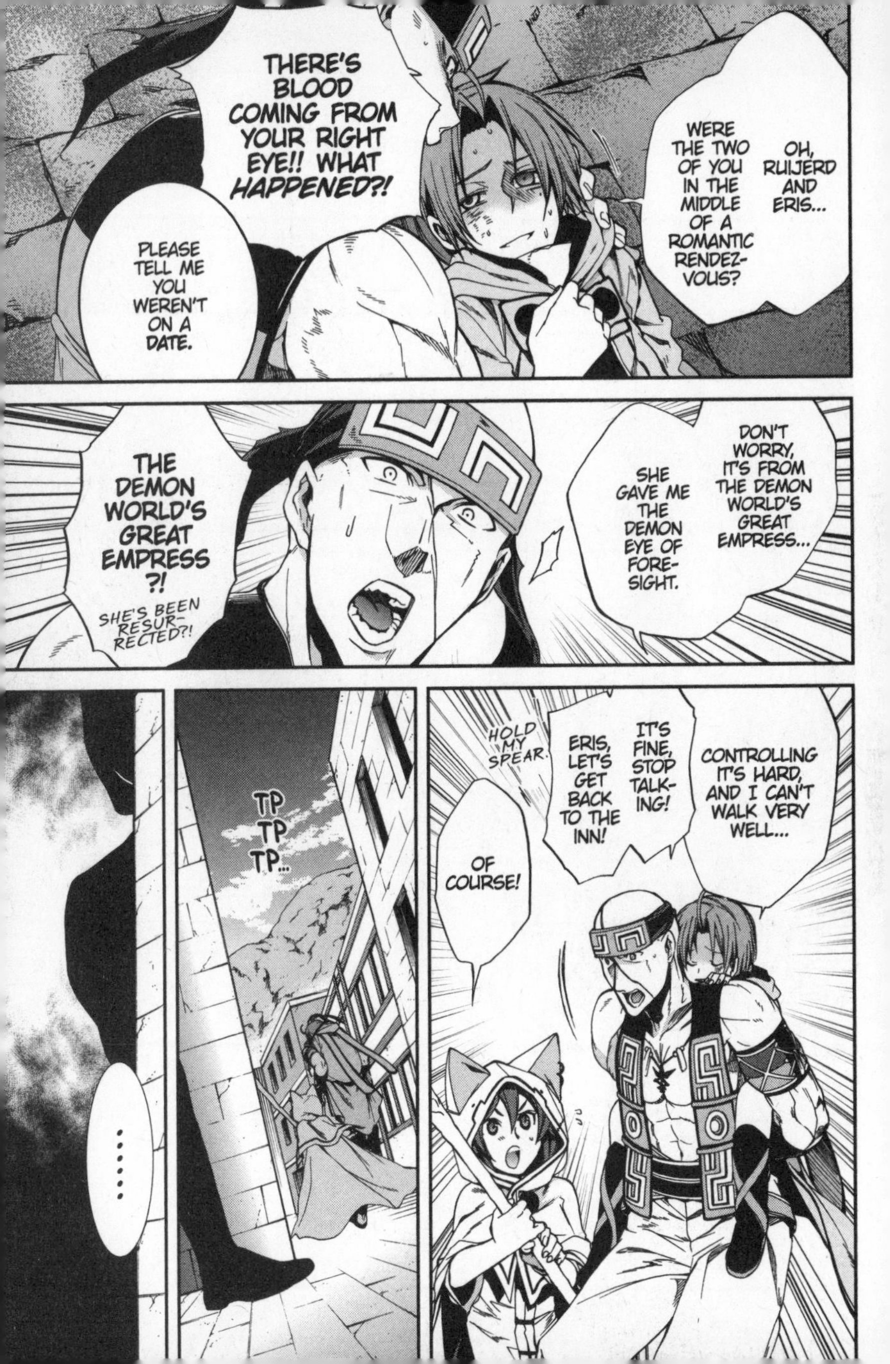
OH, RUIJERD AND ERIS...
WERE THE TWO OF YOU IN THE MIDDLE OF A ROMANTIC RENDEZ-VOUS?
THERE'S BLOOD COMING FROM YOUR RIGHT EYE!! WHAT HAPPENED?!
PLEASE TELL ME YOU WEREN'T ON A DATE.
DON'T WORRY, IT'S FROM THE DEMON WORLD'S GREAT EMPRESS...
SHE GAVE ME THE DEMON EYE OF FORE-SIGHT.
THE DEMON WORLD'S GREAT EMPRESS ?!
SHE'S BEEN RESUR-RECTED?!
CONTROLLING IT'S HARD, AND I CAN'T WALK VERY WELL...
IT'S FINE, STOP TALK-ING!
ERIS, LET'S GET BACK TO THE INN!
HOLD MY SPEAR.
OF COURSE!
TP TP TP...
......

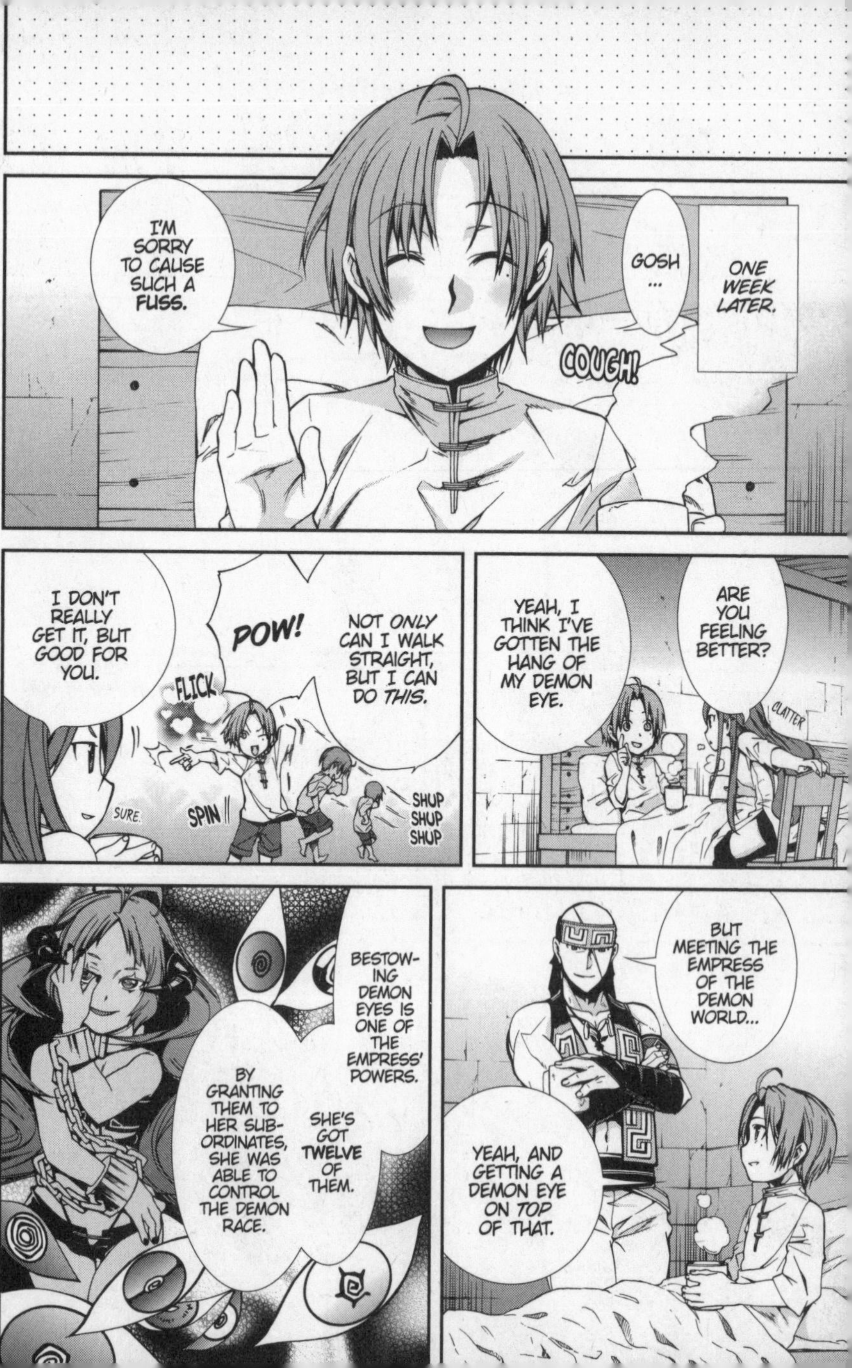

ONE WEEK LATER.
GOSH ...
COUGH!
I'M SORRY TO CAUSE SUCH A FUSS.
ARE YOU FEELING BETTER?
CLATTER
YEAH, I THINK I'VE GOTTEN THE HANG OF MY DEMON EYE.
NOT *ONLY* CAN I WALK STRAIGHT, BUT I CAN DO *THIS*.
POW!
FLICK
SHUP SHUP SHUP
SPIN
I DON'T REALLY GET IT, BUT GOOD FOR YOU.
SURE.
BUT MEETING THE EMPRESS OF THE DEMON WORLD...
YEAH, AND GETTING A DEMON EYE ON *TOP* OF THAT.
BESTOWING DEMON EYES IS ONE OF THE EMPRESS' POWERS.
BY GRANTING THEM TO HER SUBORDINATES, SHE WAS ABLE TO CONTROL THE DEMON RACE.
SHE'S GOT **TWELVE** OF THEM.

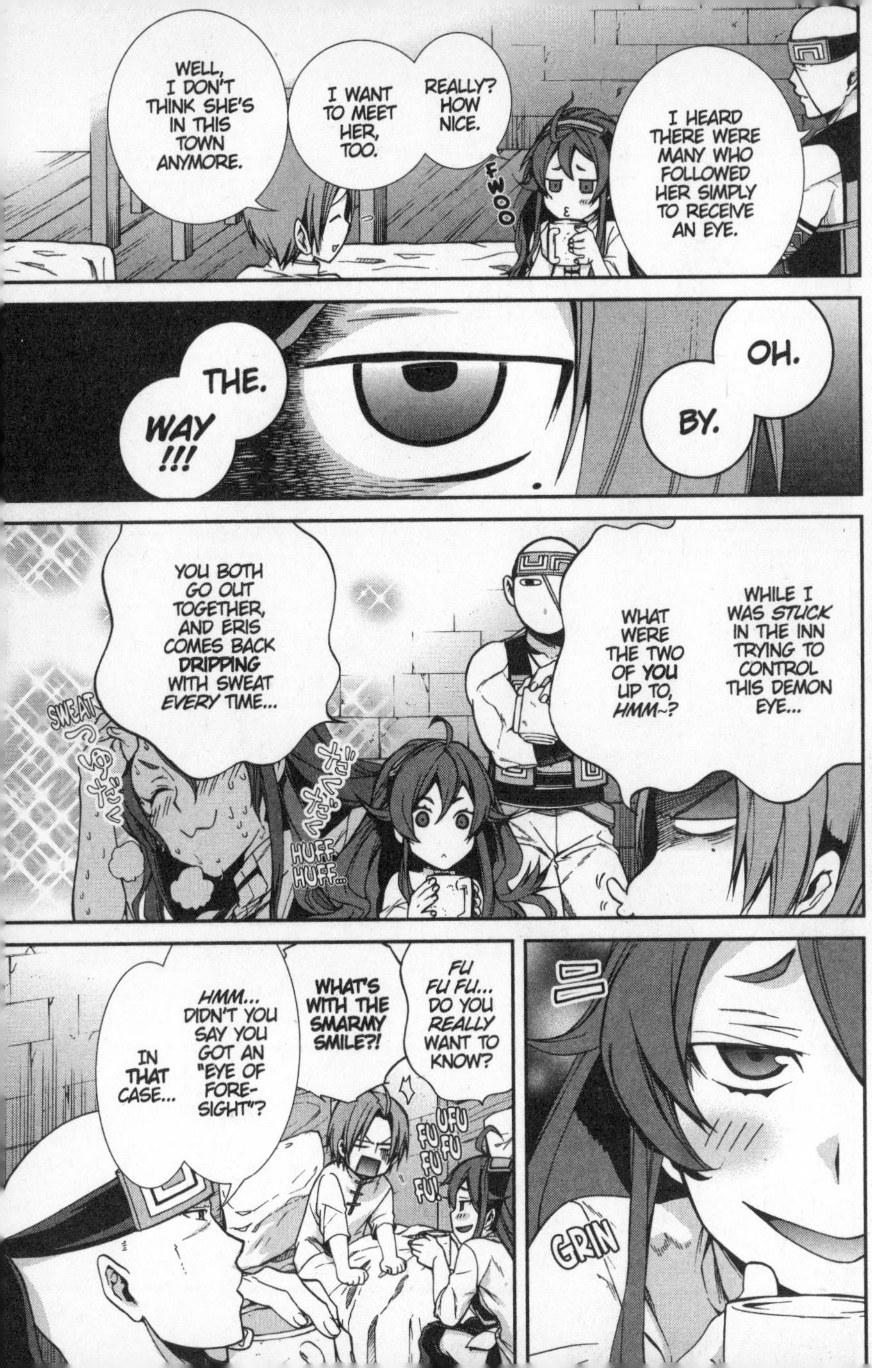
I HEARD THERE WERE MANY WHO FOLLOWED HER SIMPLY TO RECEIVE AN EYE.
FWOO
REALLY? HOW NICE.
I WANT TO MEET HER, TOO.
WELL, I DON'T THINK SHE'S IN THIS TOWN ANYMORE.
OH.
BY.
THE.
WAY!!!
WHILE I WAS STUCK IN THE INN TRYING TO CONTROL THIS DEMON EYE...
WHAT WERE THE TWO OF YOU UP TO, HMM~?
YOU BOTH GO OUT TOGETHER, AND ERIS COMES BACK DRIPPING WITH SWEAT EVERY TIME...
HUFF HUFF...
SWEAT
GRIN
FU FU FU... DO YOU REALLY WANT TO KNOW?
UFU FU FU FU FU!
WHAT'S WITH THE SMARMY SMILE?!
HMM... DIDN'T YOU SAY YOU GOT AN "EYE OF FORE-SIGHT"?
IN THAT CASE...

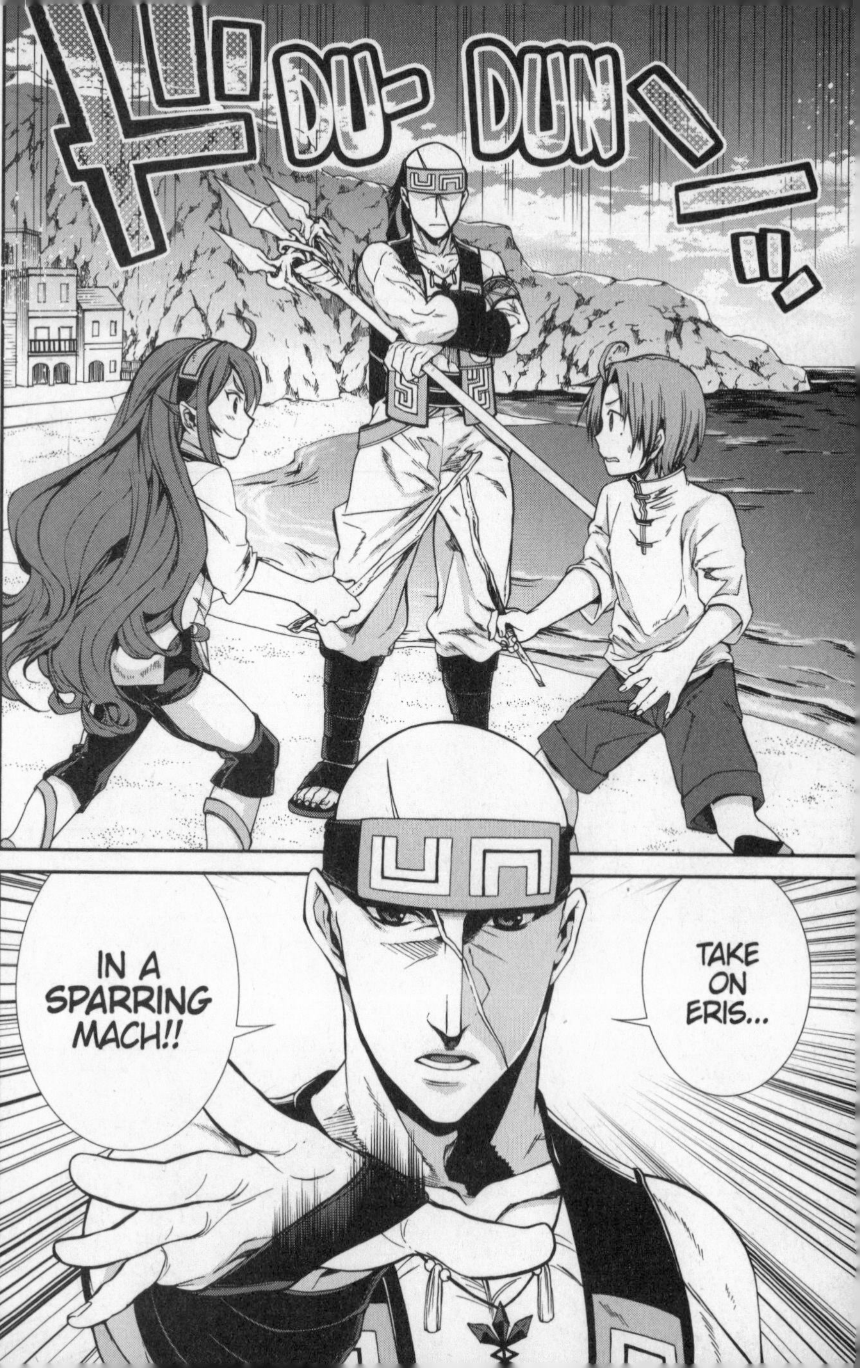
DU-DUN
TAKE ON ERIS...
IN A SPARRING MACH!!

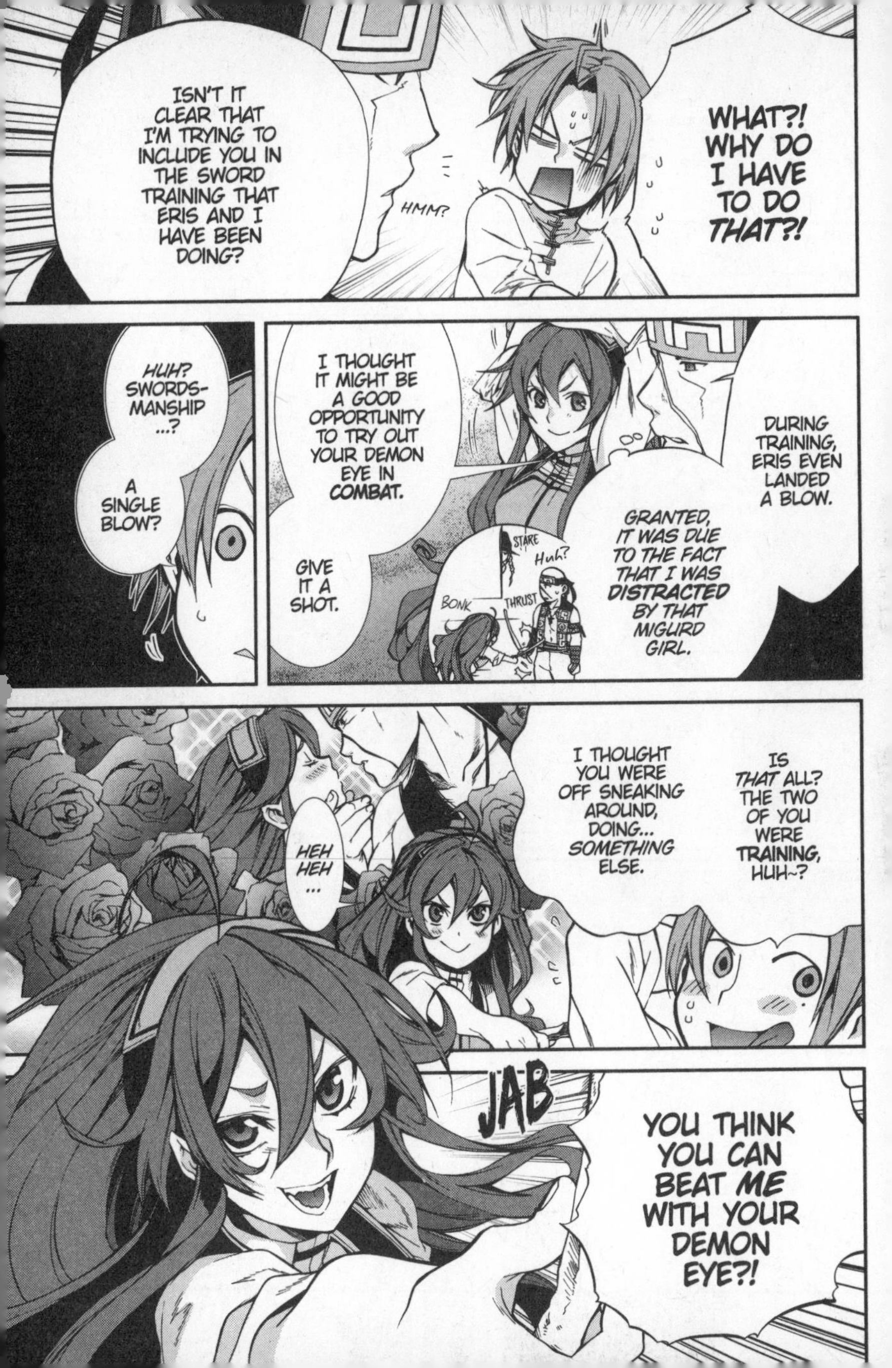
WHAT?! WHY DO I HAVE TO DO *THAT?!*
ISN'T IT CLEAR THAT I'M TRYING TO INCLUDE YOU IN THE SWORD TRAINING THAT ERIS AND I HAVE BEEN DOING?
HMM?
DURING TRAINING, ERIS EVEN LANDED A BLOW.
*GRANTED, IT WAS DUE TO THE FACT THAT I WAS **DISTRACTED** BY THAT MIGURD GIRL.*
STARE
Huh?
THRUST
BONK
I THOUGHT IT MIGHT BE A GOOD OPPORTUNITY TO TRY OUT YOUR DEMON EYE IN **COMBAT.**
GIVE IT A SHOT.
HUH? SWORDS-MANSHIP ...?
A SINGLE BLOW?
IS *THAT* ALL? THE TWO OF YOU WERE TRAINING, HUH~?
I THOUGHT YOU WERE OFF SNEAKING AROUND, DOING... SOMETHING ELSE.
HEH HEH ...
YOU THINK YOU CAN BEAT *ME* WITH YOUR DEMON EYE?!
JAB

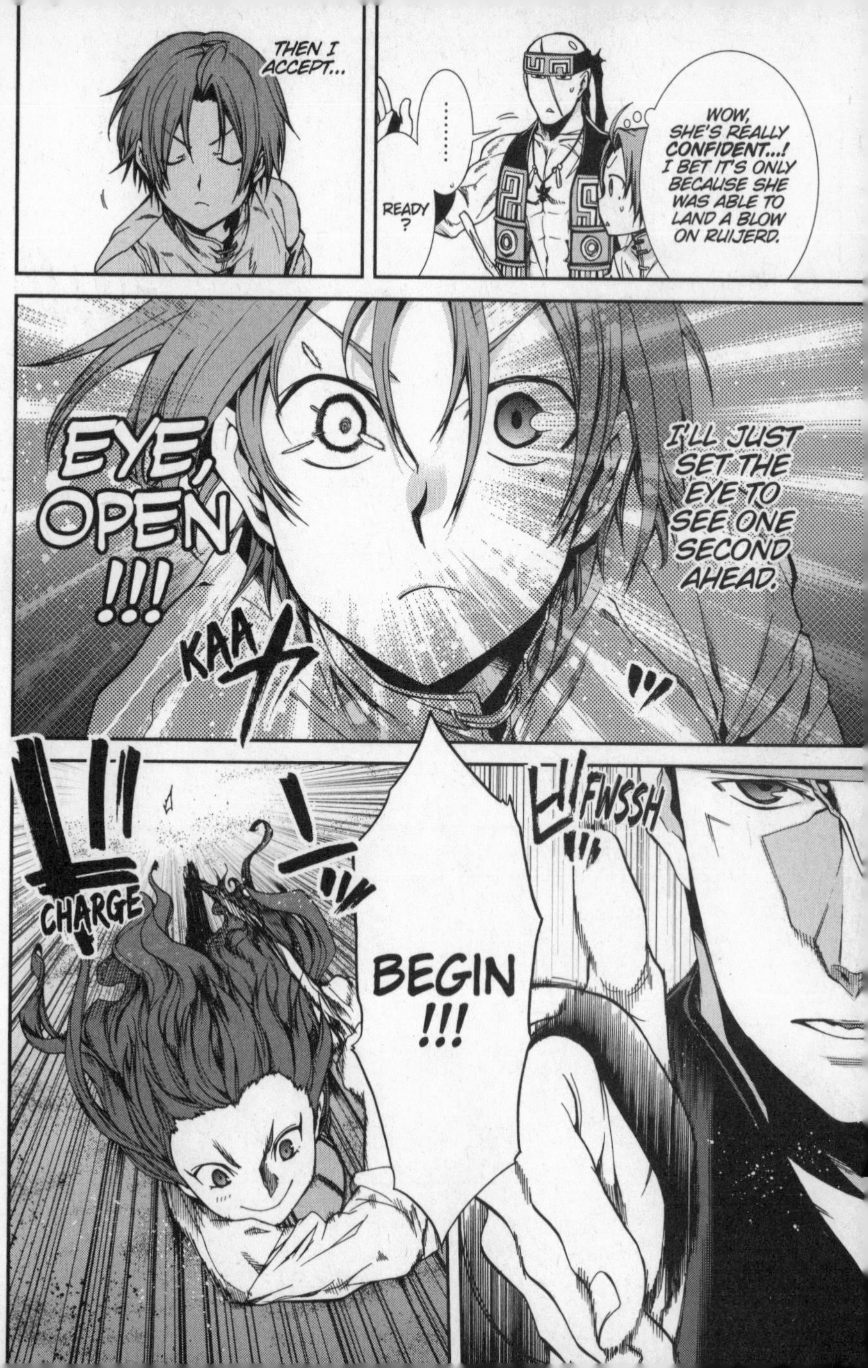
WOW, SHE'S REALLY CONFIDENT...! I BET IT'S ONLY BECAUSE SHE WAS ABLE TO LAND A BLOW ON RUIJERD.
......
READY?
THEN I ACCEPT...
I'LL JUST SET THE EYE TO SEE ONE SECOND AHEAD.
EYE, OPEN!!!
KAA
FWSSH
BEGIN!!!
CHARGE

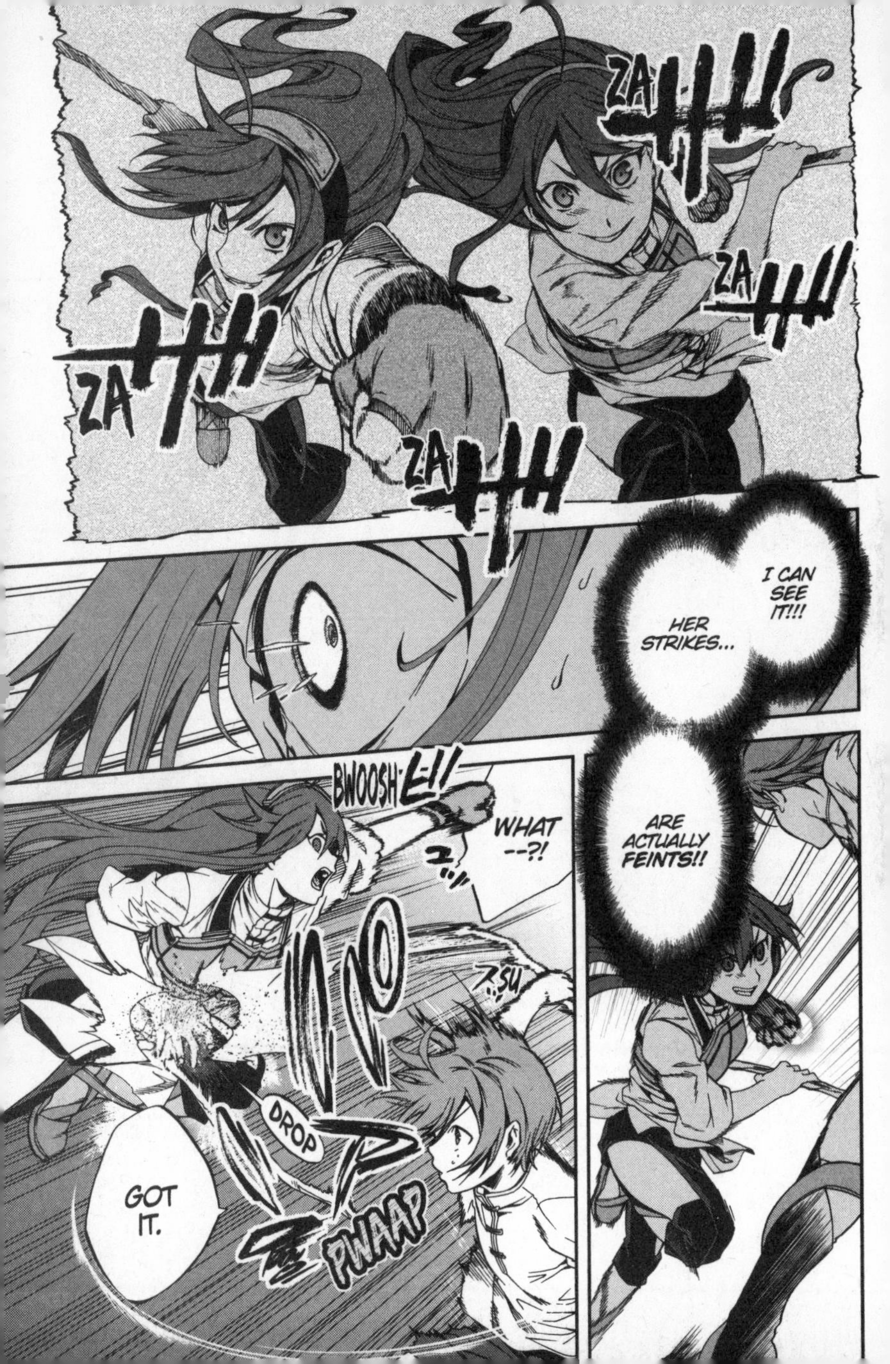
ZA!!!
ZA!!!
ZA!!!
ZA!!!
I CAN SEE IT!!!
HER STRIKES...
ARE ACTUALLY FEINTS!!
BWOOSH!!
WHAT --?!
SU
DROP
PWAAP
GOT IT.

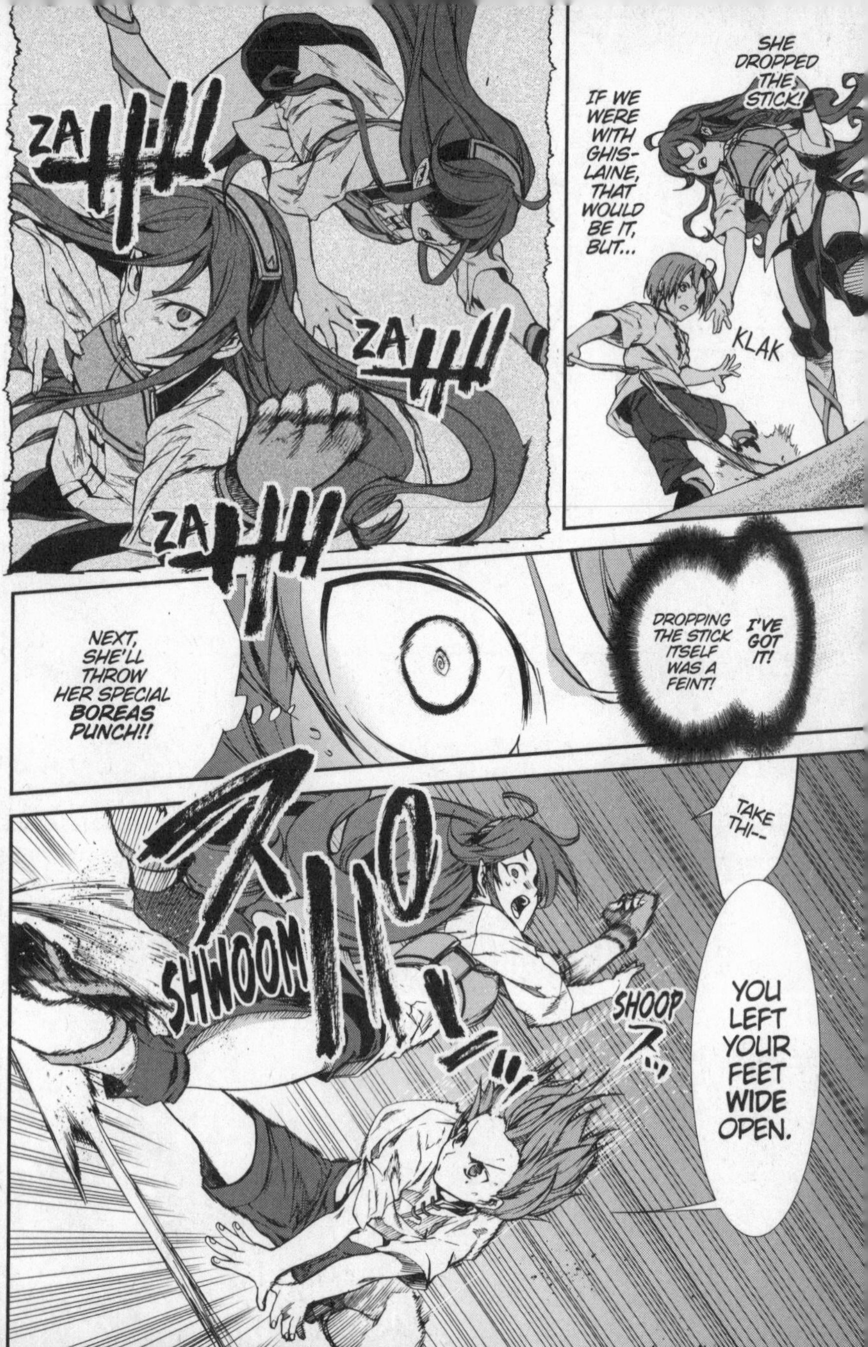
SHE DROPPED THE STICK!
IF WE WERE WITH GHISLAINE, THAT WOULD BE IT, BUT...
KLAK
ZA
ZA
ZA
I'VE GOT IT!
DROPPING THE STICK ITSELF WAS A FEINT!
NEXT, SHE'LL THROW HER SPECIAL BOREAS PUNCH!!
TAKE THI--
YOU LEFT YOUR FEET WIDE OPEN.
SHOOP
SHWOOM

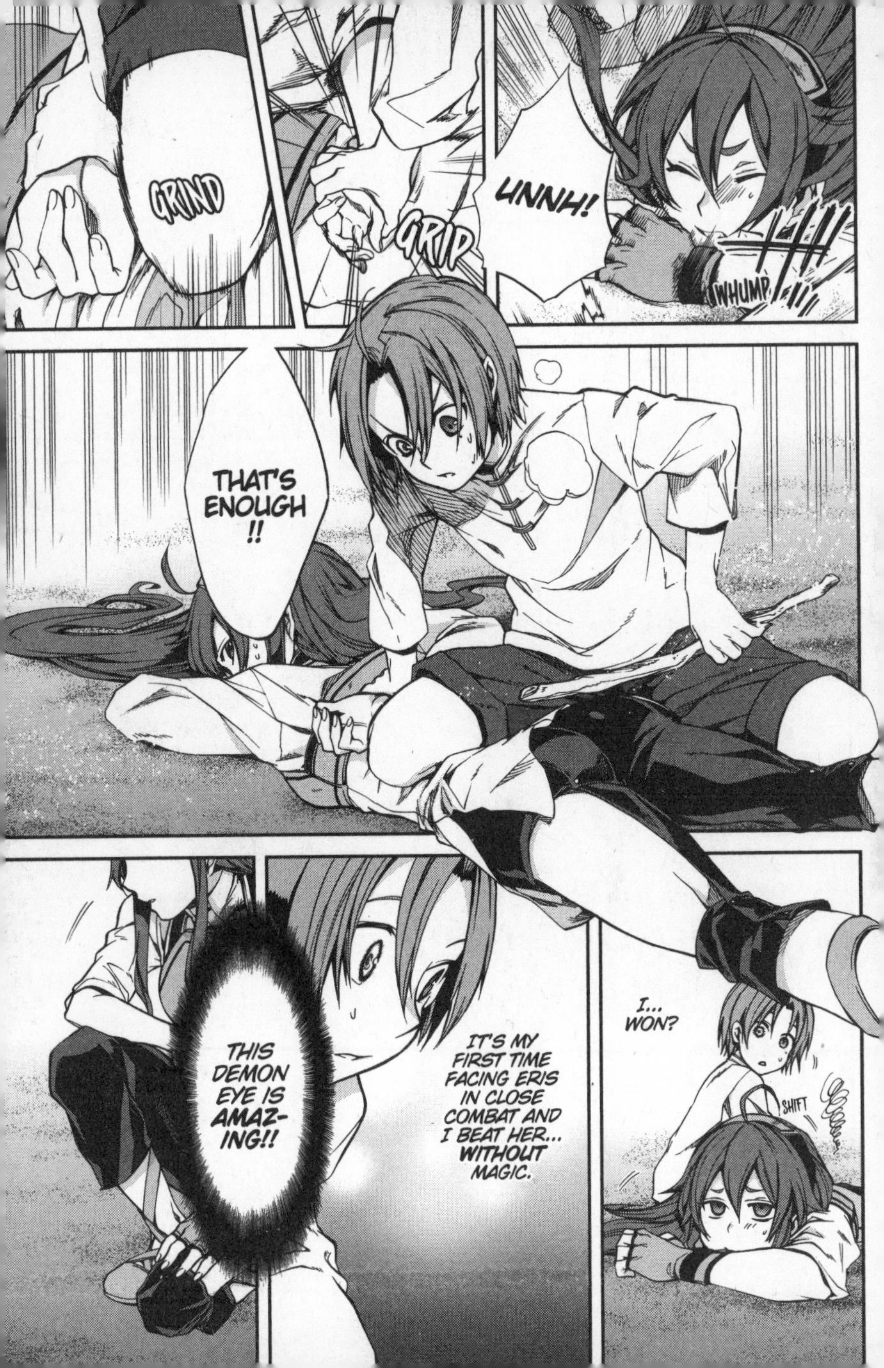
UNNH!
WHUMP
GRIP
GRIND
THAT'S ENOUGH!!
I... WON?
SHIFT
IT'S MY FIRST TIME FACING ERIS IN CLOSE COMBAT AND I BEAT HER... WITHOUT MAGIC.
THIS DEMON EYE IS AMAZ-ING!!

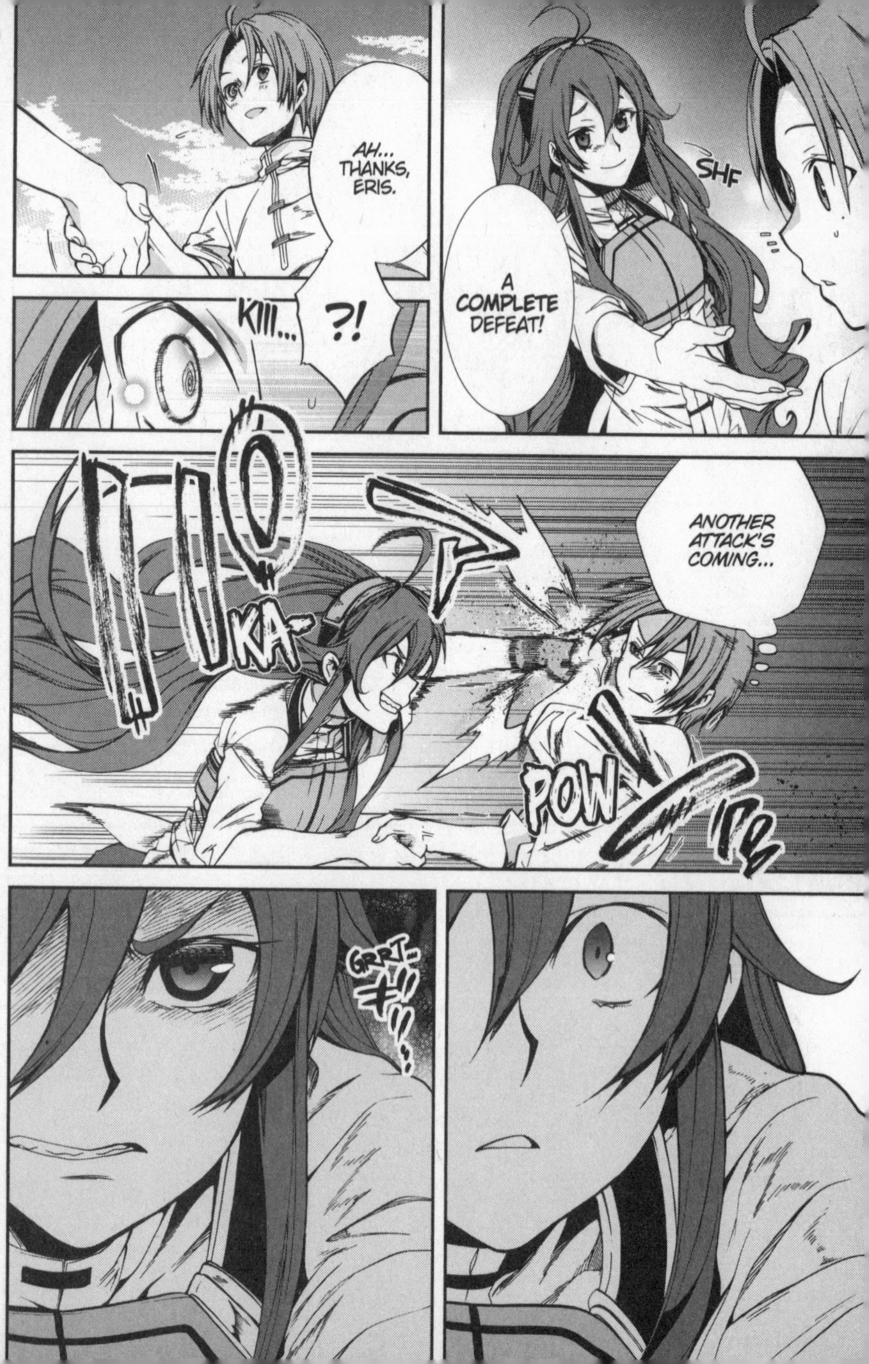
SHF
A COMPLETE DEFEAT!
AH... THANKS, ERIS.
KIII...
?!
ANOTHER ATTACK'S COMING...
KA-
POW
GRRT...!!

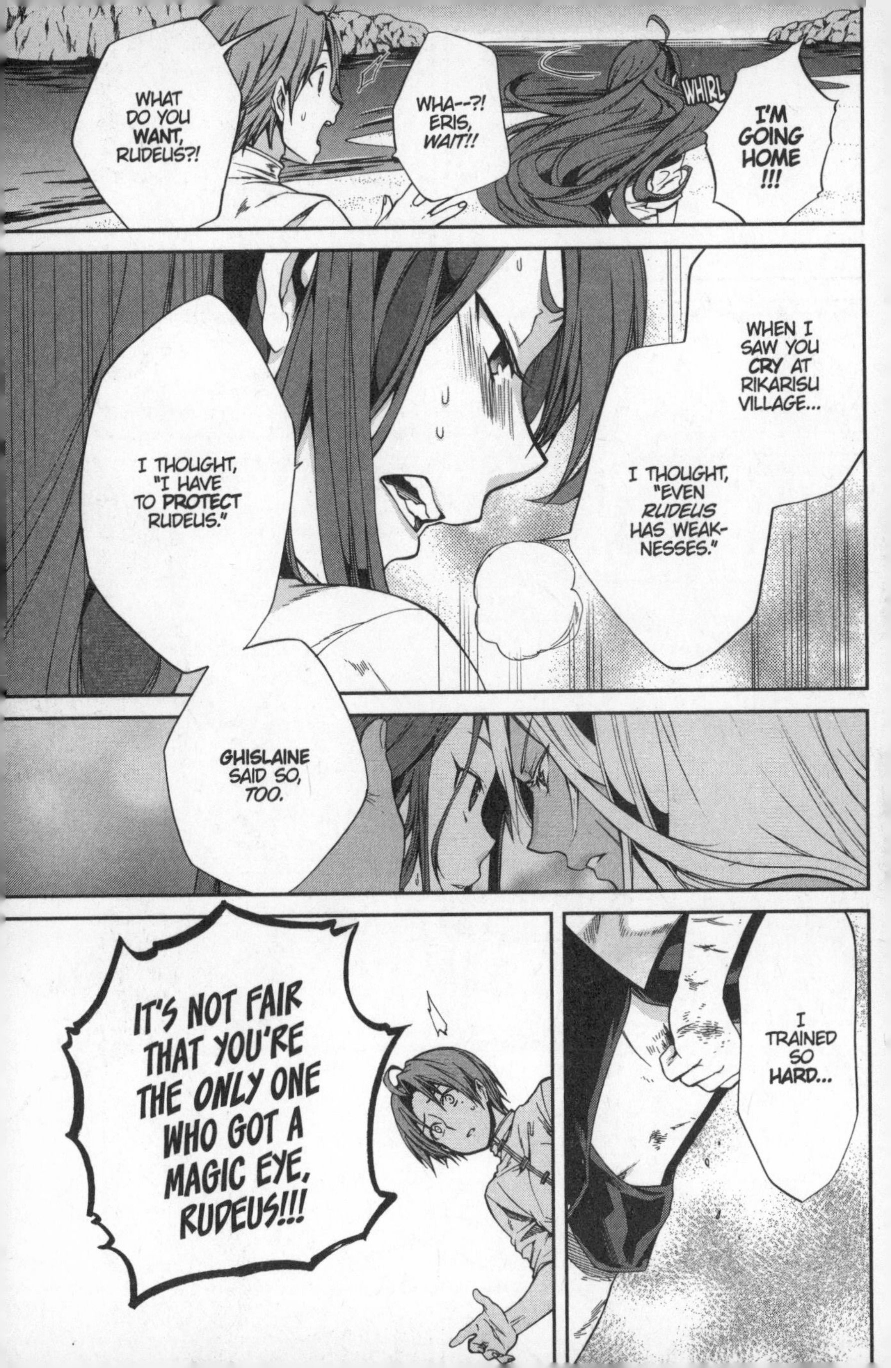
I'M GOING HOME!!!
WHIRL
WHA--?! ERIS, WAIT!!
WHAT DO YOU WANT, RUDEUS?!
WHEN I SAW YOU CRY AT RIKARISU VILLAGE...
I THOUGHT, "EVEN RUDEUS HAS WEAKNESSES."
I THOUGHT, "I HAVE TO PROTECT RUDEUS."
GHISLAINE SAID SO, TOO.
I TRAINED SO HARD...
IT'S NOT FAIR THAT YOU'RE THE ONLY ONE WHO GOT A MAGIC EYE, RUDEUS!!!

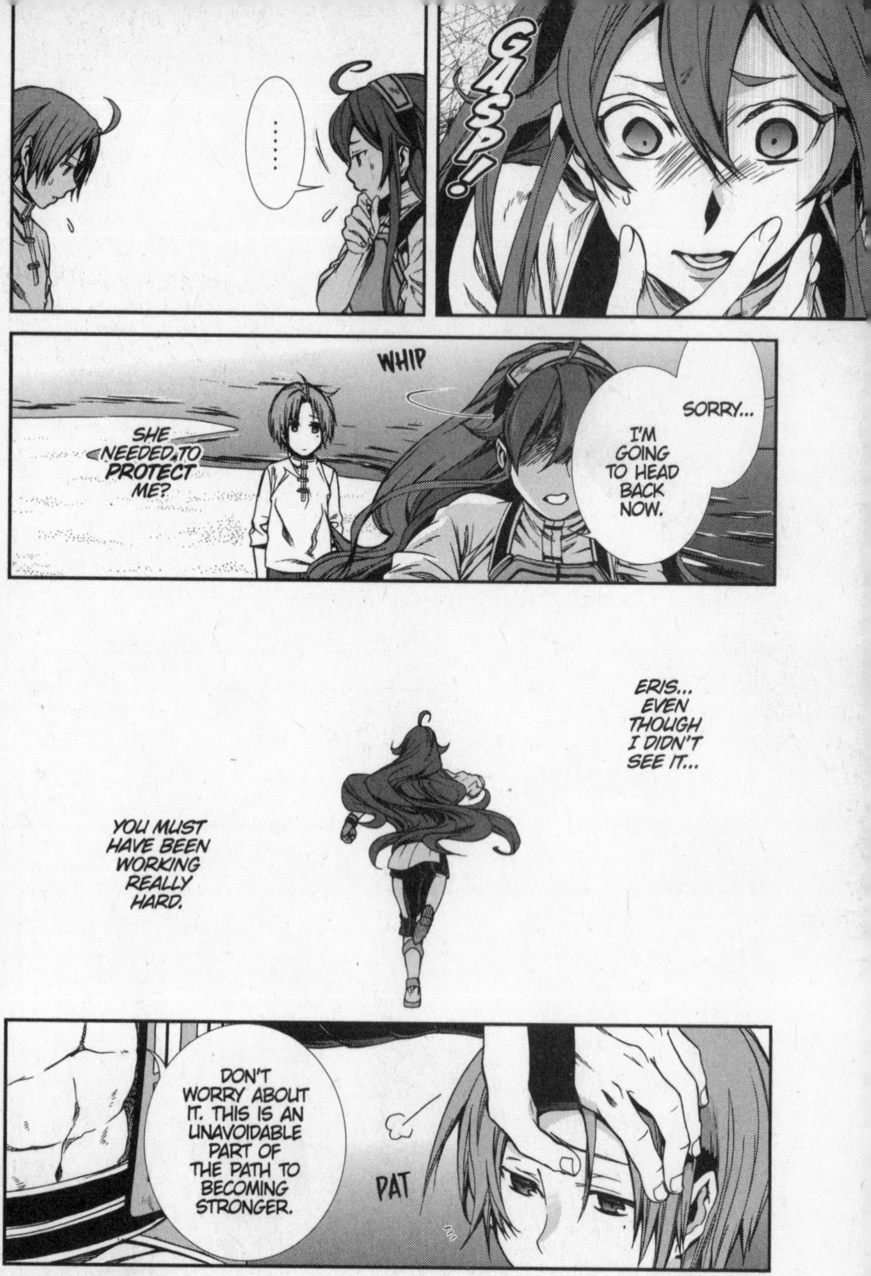
GASP!
……
SORRY... I'M GOING TO HEAD BACK NOW.
WHIP
SHE NEEDED TO PROTECT ME?
ERIS... EVEN THOUGH I DIDN'T SEE IT...
YOU MUST HAVE BEEN WORKING REALLY HARD.
DON'T WORRY ABOUT IT. THIS IS AN UNAVOIDABLE PART OF THE PATH TO BECOMING STRONGER.
PAT

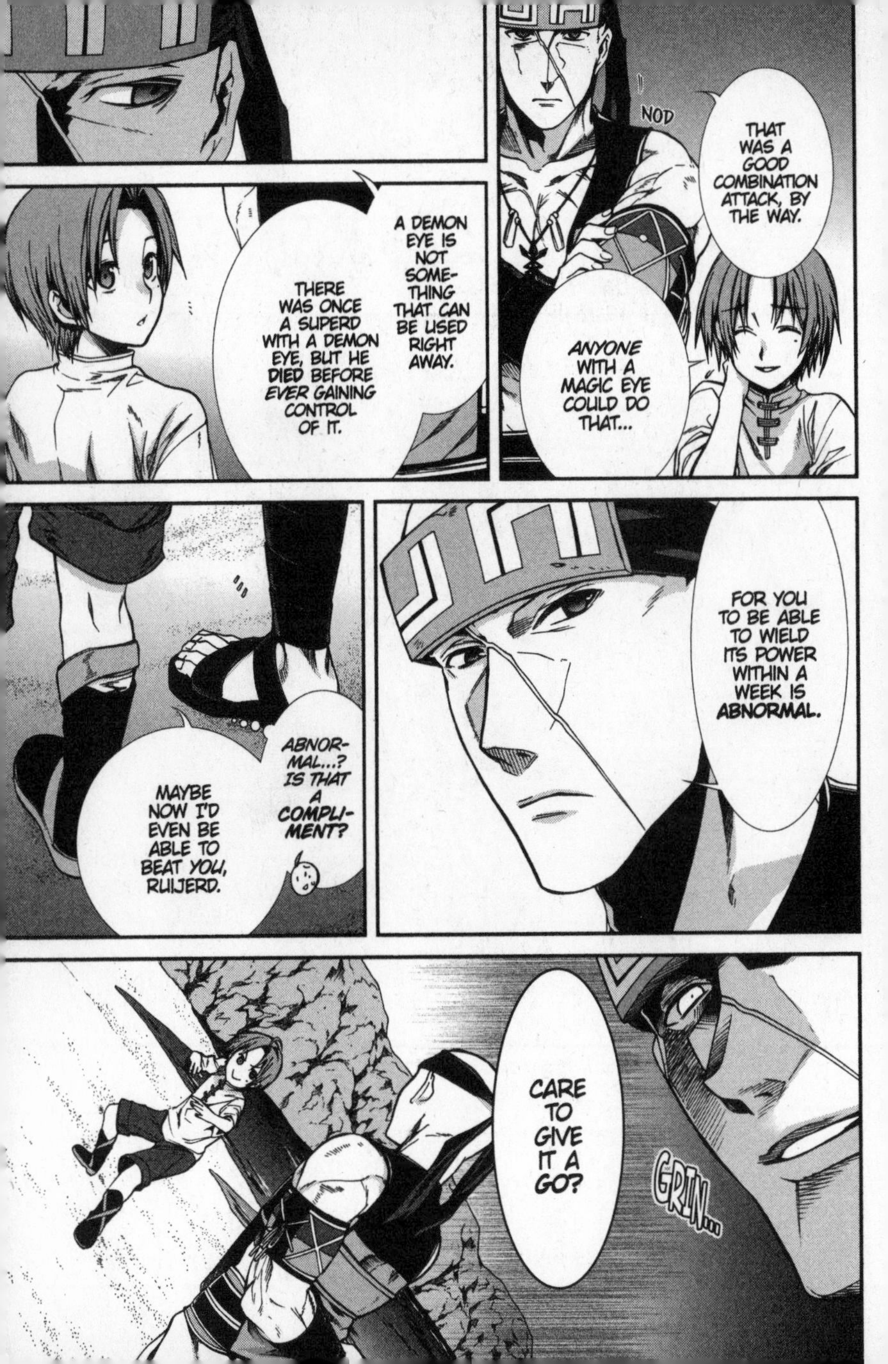
NOD
THAT WAS A GOOD COMBINATION ATTACK, BY THE WAY.
ANYONE WITH A MAGIC EYE COULD DO THAT...
A DEMON EYE IS NOT SOMETHING THAT CAN BE USED RIGHT AWAY.
THERE WAS ONCE A SUPERD WITH A DEMON EYE, BUT HE DIED BEFORE EVER GAINING CONTROL OF IT.
FOR YOU TO BE ABLE TO WIELD ITS POWER WITHIN A WEEK IS ABNORMAL.
ABNORMAL...? IS THAT A COMPLIMENT?
MAYBE NOW I'D EVEN BE ABLE TO BEAT YOU, RUIJERD.
GRIN...
CARE TO GIVE IT A GO?

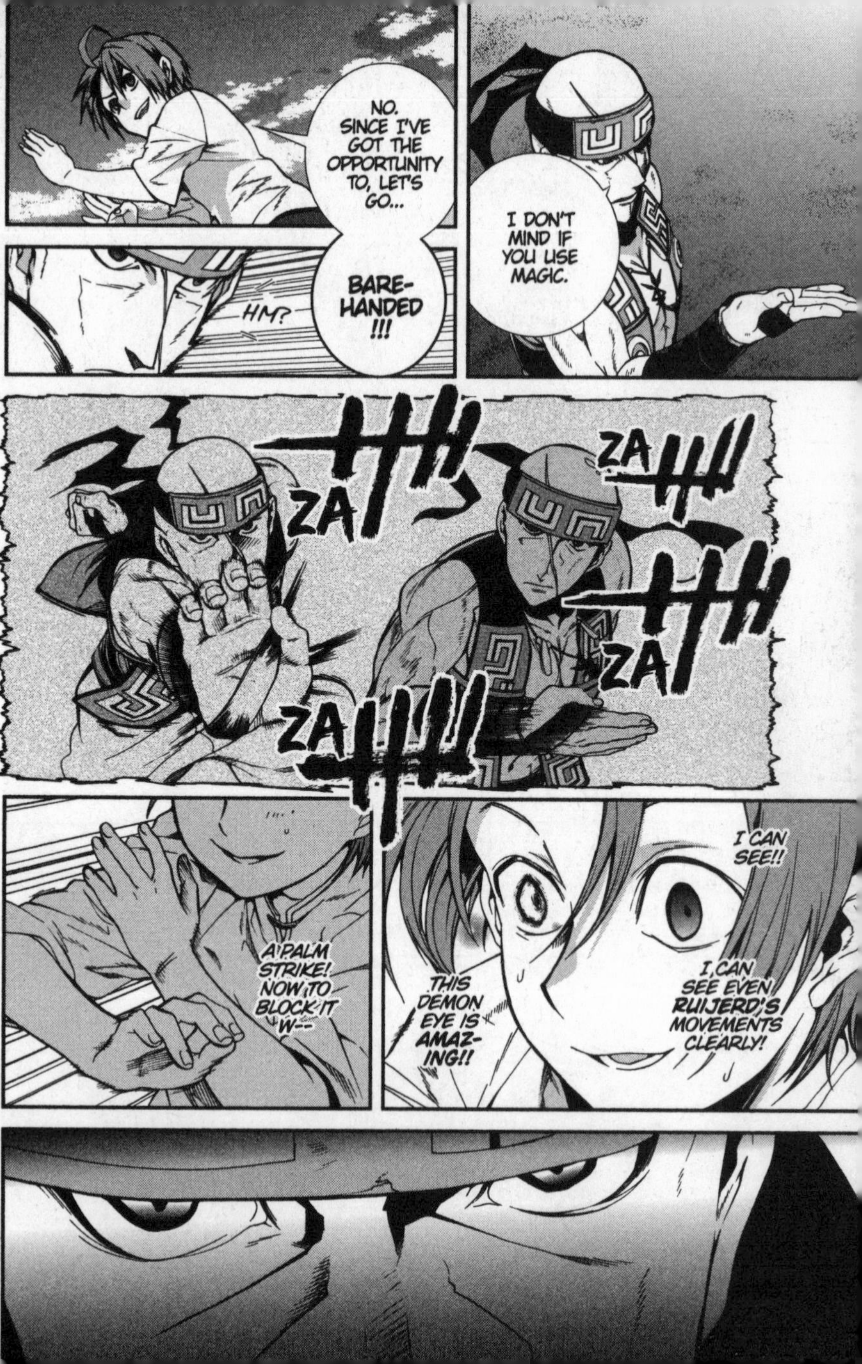
I DON'T MIND IF YOU USE MAGIC.
NO. SINCE I'VE GOT THE OPPORTUNITY TO, LET'S GO...
BARE-HANDED!!!
HM?
ZA
ZA
ZA
ZA
I CAN SEE!!
I, CAN SEE EVEN RUIJERD'S MOVEMENTS CLEARLY!
THIS DEMON EYE IS AMAZ-ING!!
A PALM STRIKE! NOW TO BLOCK IT W--

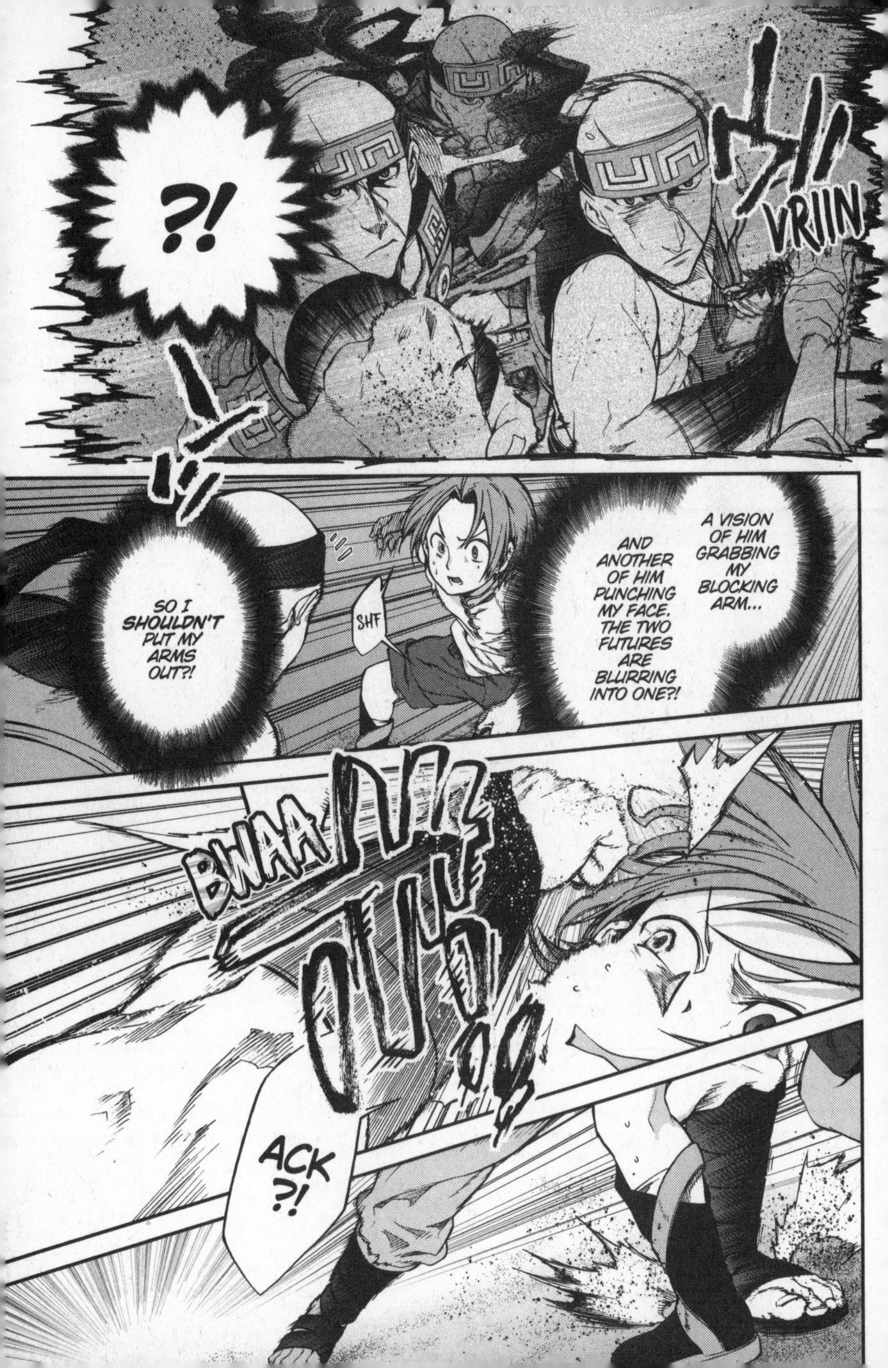
VRIIN
?!
A VISION OF HIM GRABBING MY BLOCKING ARM... AND ANOTHER OF HIM PUNCHING MY FACE. THE TWO FUTURES ARE BLURRING INTO ONE?!
SHF
SO I SHOULDN'T PUT MY ARMS OUT?!
BWAA
ACK ?!

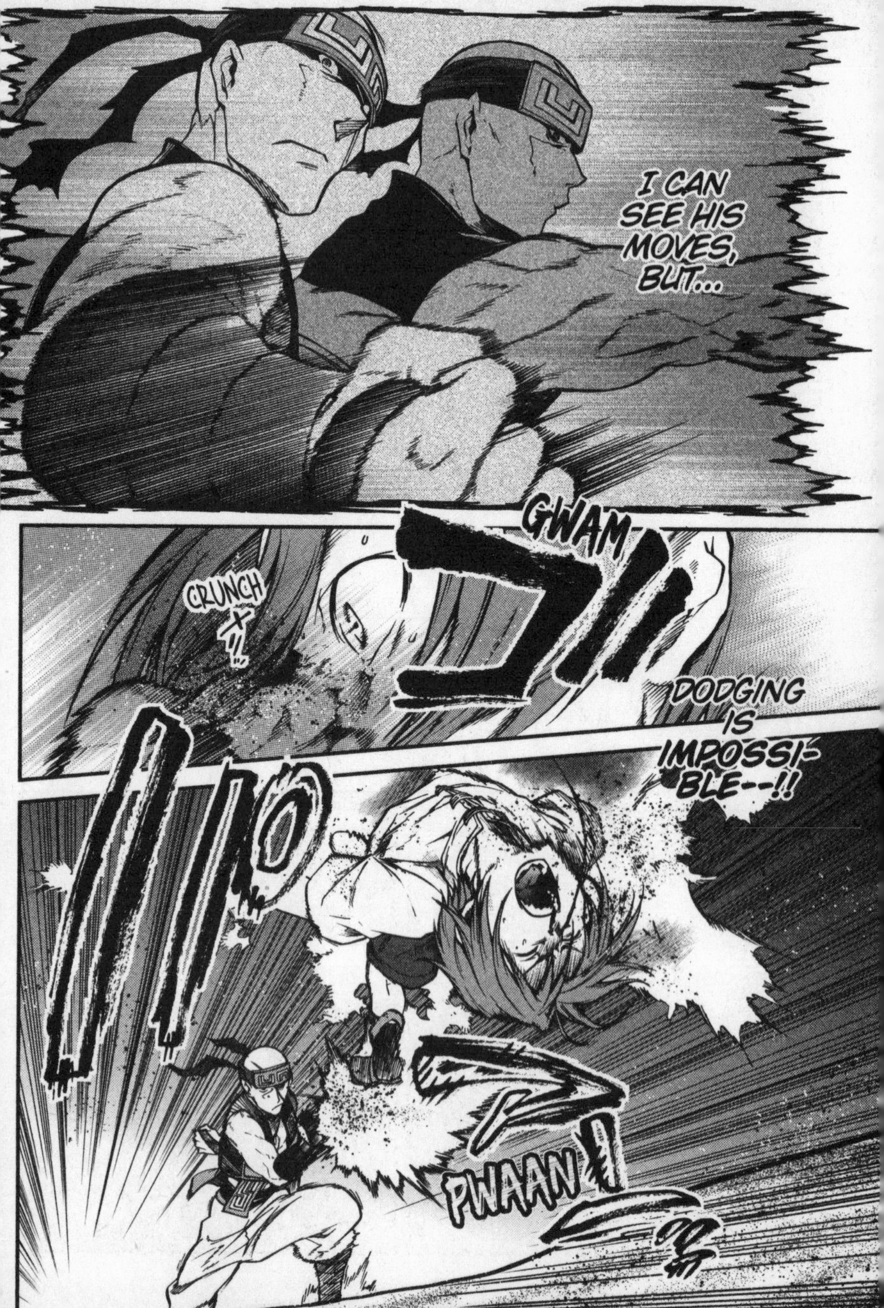
I CAN SEE HIS MOVES, BUT...
GWAM
DODGING IS IMPOSSI-BLE--!!
CRUNCH
PWAAN

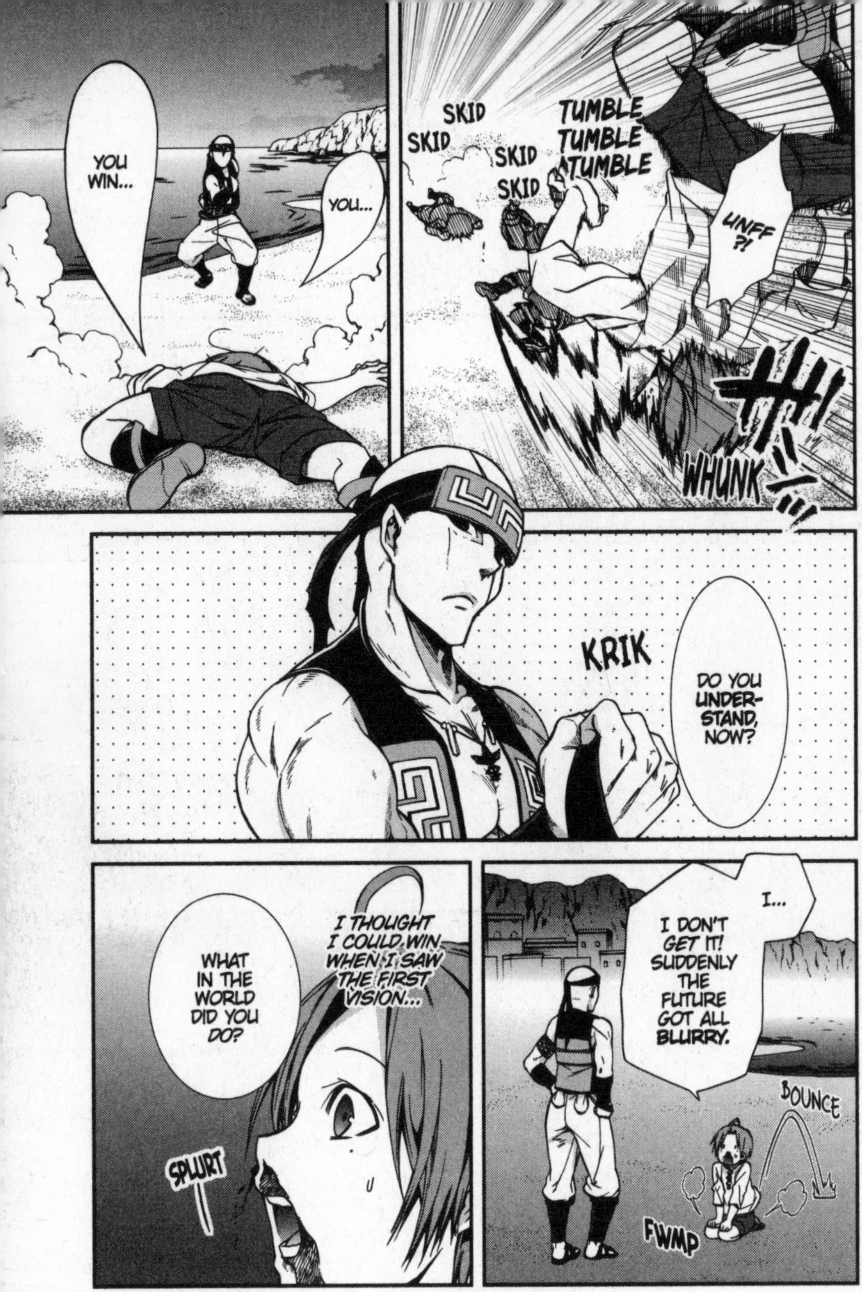
UNFF ?!
TUMBLE TUMBLE TUMBLE
SKID SKID
SKID SKID
WHUNK
YOU...
YOU WIN...
KRIK
DO YOU UNDER-STAND, NOW?
I...
I DON'T GET IT! SUDDENLY THE FUTURE GOT ALL BLURRY.
BOUNCE
FWMP
I THOUGHT I COULD WIN WHEN I SAW THE FIRST VISION...
WHAT IN THE WORLD DID YOU DO?
SPLURT

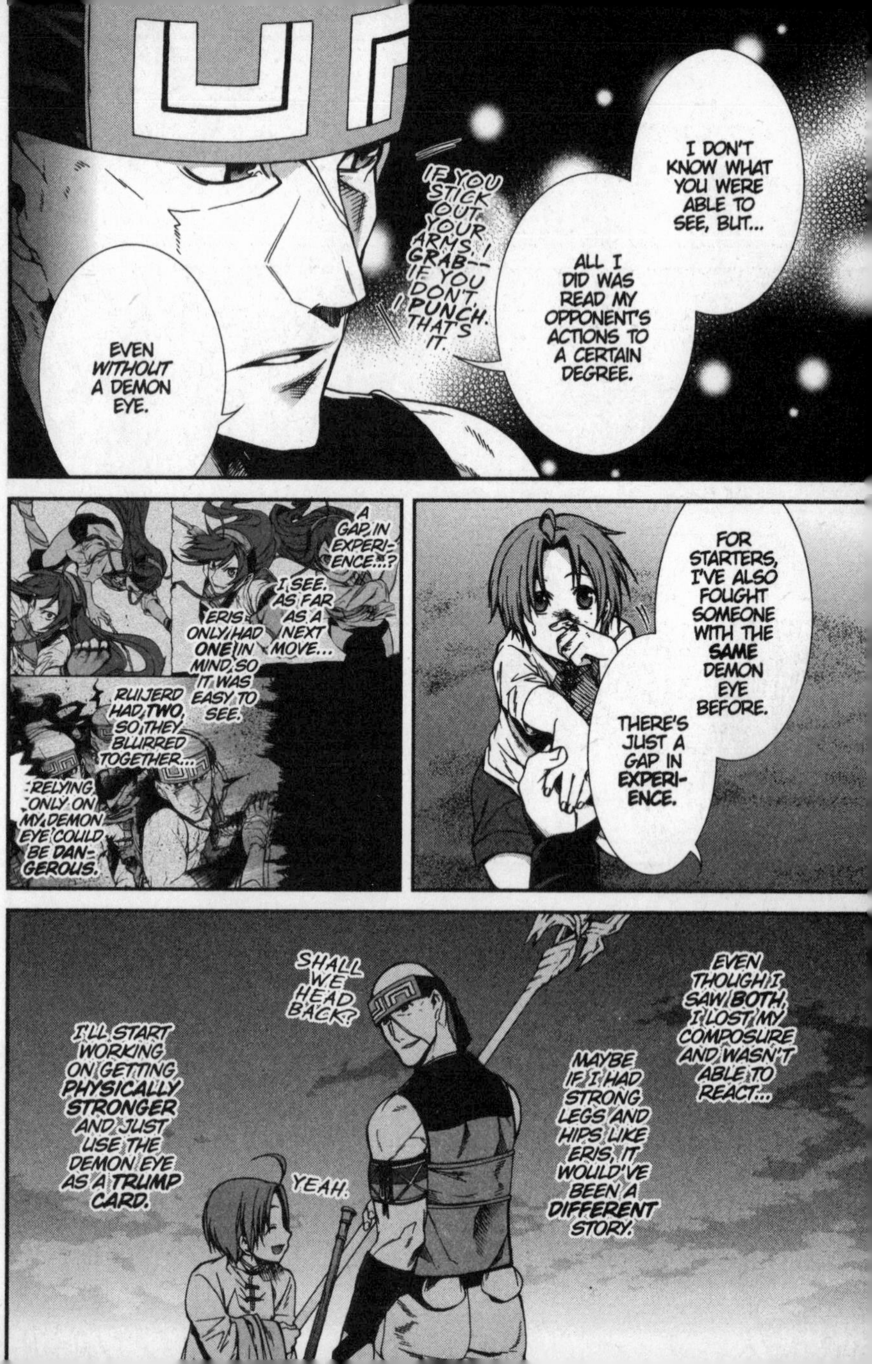
I DON'T KNOW WHAT YOU WERE ABLE TO SEE, BUT...
ALL I DID WAS READ MY OPPONENT'S ACTIONS TO A CERTAIN DEGREE.
IF YOU STICK OUT YOUR ARMS, I GRAB-- IF YOU DON'T, I PUNCH. THAT'S IT.
EVEN WITHOUT A DEMON EYE.
FOR STARTERS, I'VE ALSO FOUGHT SOMEONE WITH THE SAME DEMON EYE BEFORE.
THERE'S JUST A GAP IN EXPERIENCE.
A GAP IN EXPERIENCE...?
I SEE. AS FAR AS A NEXT MOVE...
ERIS ONLY HAD ONE IN MIND, SO IT WAS EASY TO SEE.
RUIJERD HAD TWO, SO THEY BLURRED TOGETHER...
RELYING ONLY ON MY DEMON EYE COULD BE DANGEROUS.
EVEN THOUGH I SAW BOTH, I LOST MY COMPOSURE AND WASN'T ABLE TO REACT...
MAYBE IF I HAD STRONG LEGS AND HIPS LIKE ERIS, IT WOULD'VE BEEN A DIFFERENT STORY.
SHALL WE HEAD BACK?
YEAH.
I'LL START WORKING ON GETTING PHYSICALLY STRONGER AND JUST USE THE DEMON EYE AS A TRUMP CARD.

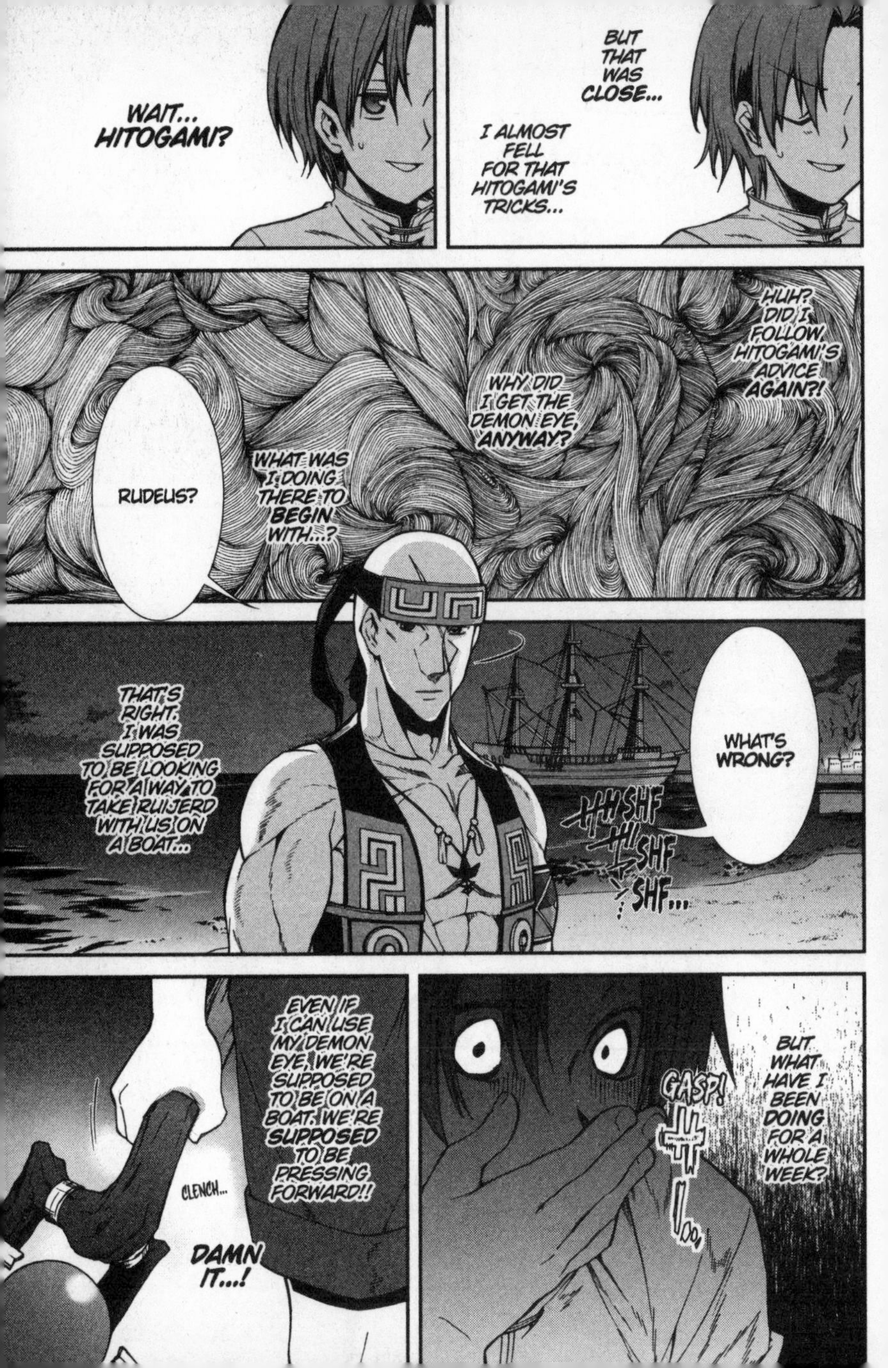
BUT THAT WAS CLOSE...
I ALMOST FELL FOR THAT HITOGAMI'S TRICKS...
WAIT... HITOGAMI?
HUH? DID I FOLLOW HITOGAMI'S ADVICE AGAIN?!
WHY DID I GET THE DEMON EYE, ANYWAY?
WHAT WAS I DOING THERE TO BEGIN WITH...?
RUDEUS?
WHAT'S WRONG?
SHF SHF SHF...
THAT'S RIGHT. I WAS SUPPOSED TO BE LOOKING FOR A WAY TO TAKE RUIJERD WITH US ON A BOAT...
BUT WHAT HAVE I BEEN DOING FOR A WHOLE WEEK?
GASP!
EVEN IF I CAN USE MY DEMON EYE, WE'RE SUPPOSED TO BE ON A BOAT. WE'RE SUPPOSED TO BE PRESSING FORWARD!!
CLENCH...
DAMN IT...!

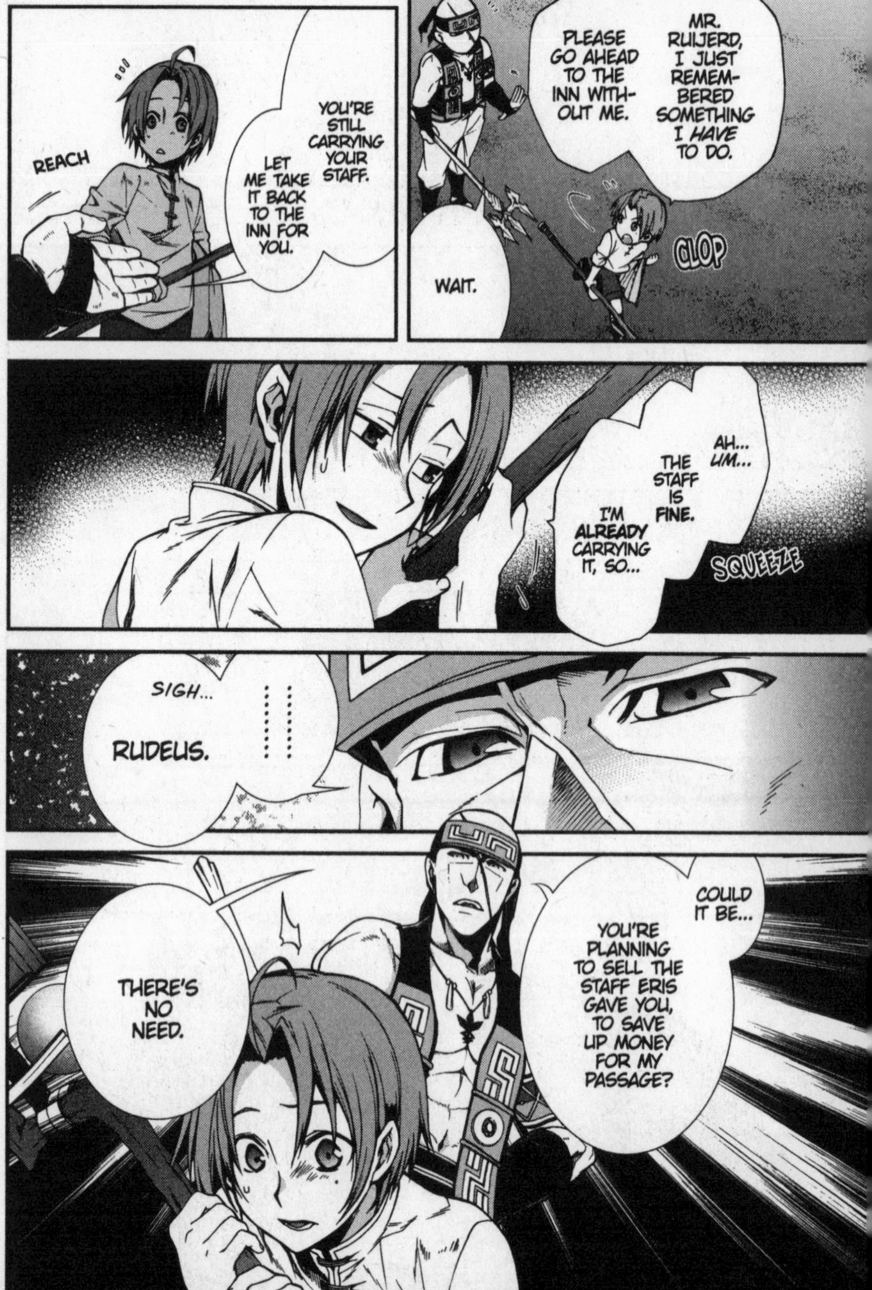
MR. RUIJERD, I JUST REMEMBERED SOMETHING I *HAVE* TO DO.
PLEASE GO AHEAD TO THE INN WITHOUT ME.
CLOP
WAIT.
YOU'RE STILL CARRYING YOUR STAFF.
LET ME TAKE IT BACK TO THE INN FOR YOU.
REACH
AH... UM...
THE STAFF IS FINE.
I'M ALREADY CARRYING IT, SO...
SQUEEZE
SIGH...
......
RUDEUS.
COULD IT BE...
YOU'RE PLANNING TO SELL THE STAFF ERIS GAVE YOU, TO SAVE UP MONEY FOR MY PASSAGE?
THERE'S NO NEED.

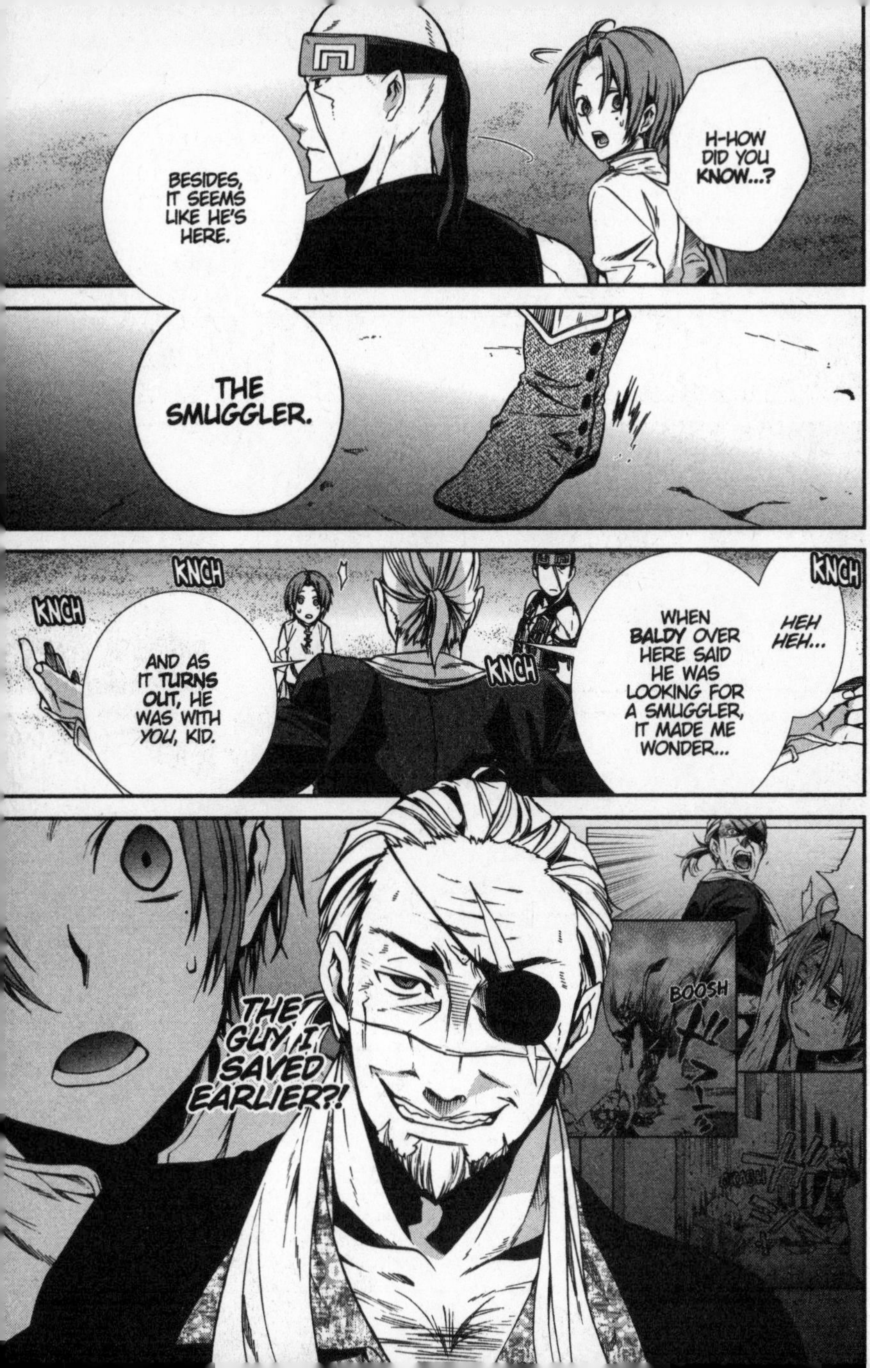
H-HOW DID YOU KNOW...?
BESIDES, IT SEEMS LIKE HE'S HERE.
THE SMUGGLER.
KNCH
HEH HEH...
WHEN BALDY OVER HERE SAID HE WAS LOOKING FOR A SMUGGLER, IT MADE ME WONDER...
KNCH
AND AS IT TURNS OUT, HE WAS WITH YOU, KID.
KNCH
KNCH
BOOSH
THE GUY I SAVED EARLIER?!

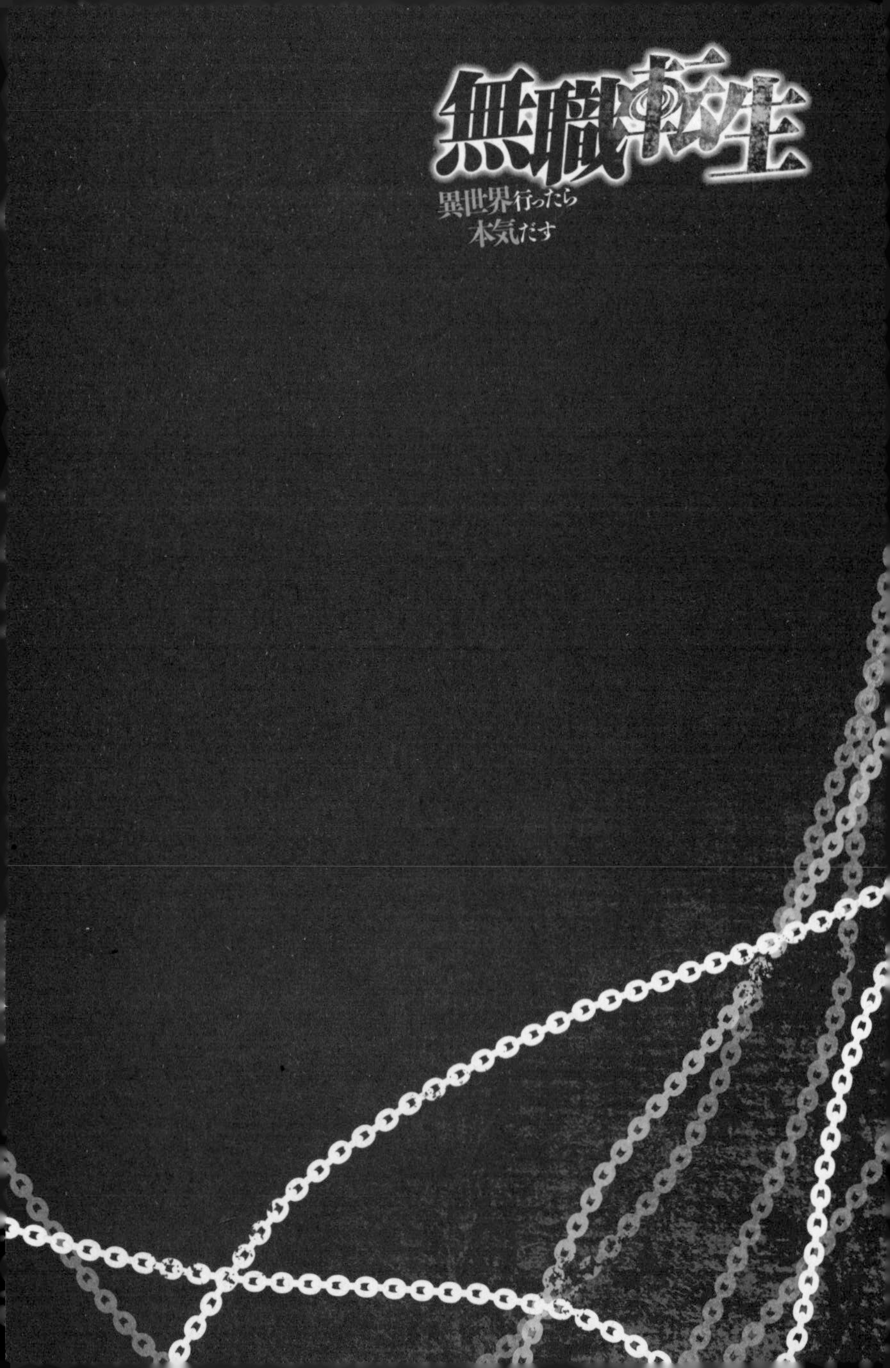
無職転生
異世界行ったら
本気だす

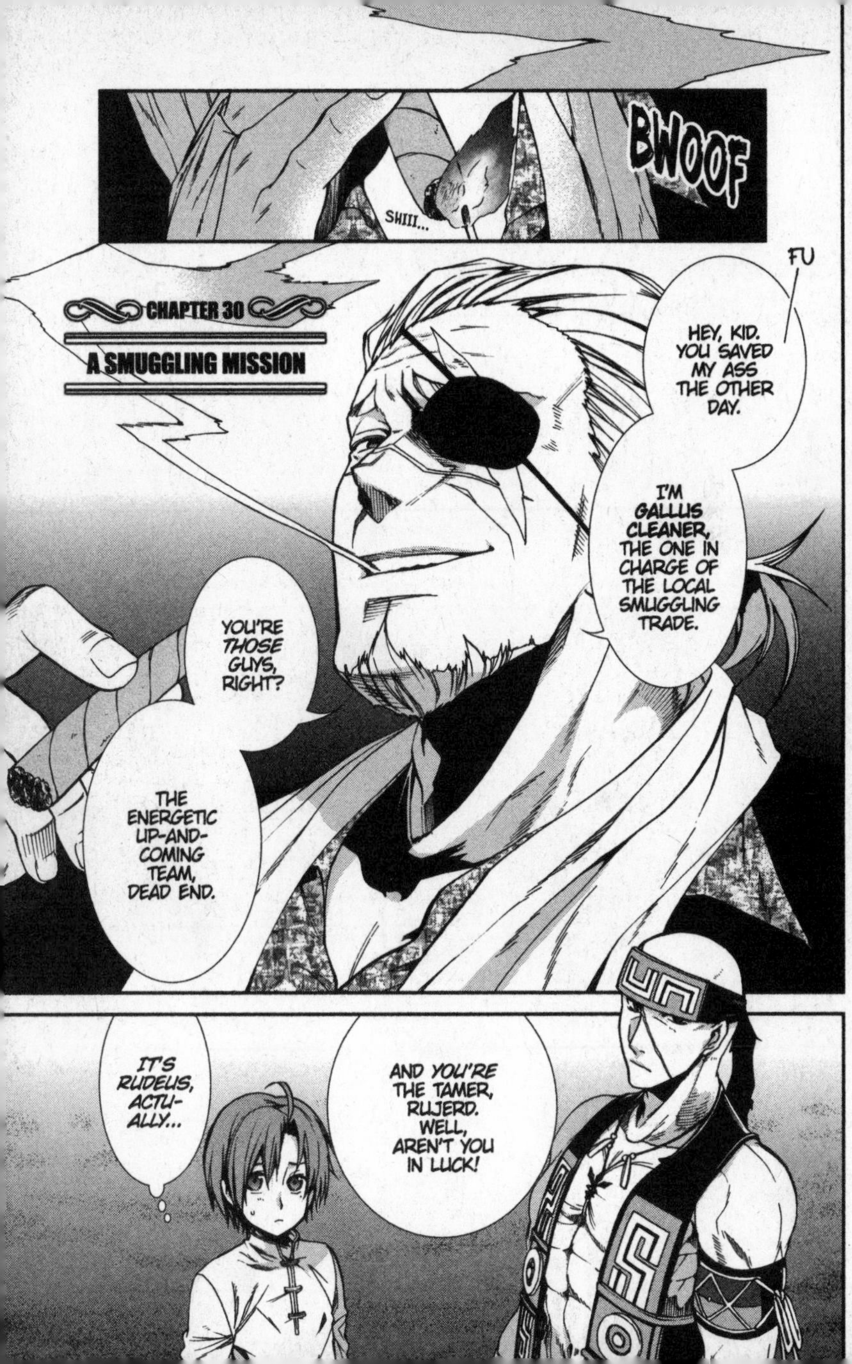
BWOOF
SHIII...
CHAPTER 30
A SMUGGLING MISSION
FU
HEY, KID. YOU SAVED MY ASS THE OTHER DAY.
I'M GALLUS CLEANER, THE ONE IN CHARGE OF THE LOCAL SMUGGLING TRADE.
YOU'RE *THOSE* GUYS, RIGHT?
THE ENERGETIC UP-AND-COMING TEAM, DEAD END.
AND *YOU'RE* THE TAMER, RUJERD. WELL, AREN'T YOU IN LUCK!
IT'S RUDEUS, ACTU-ALLY...

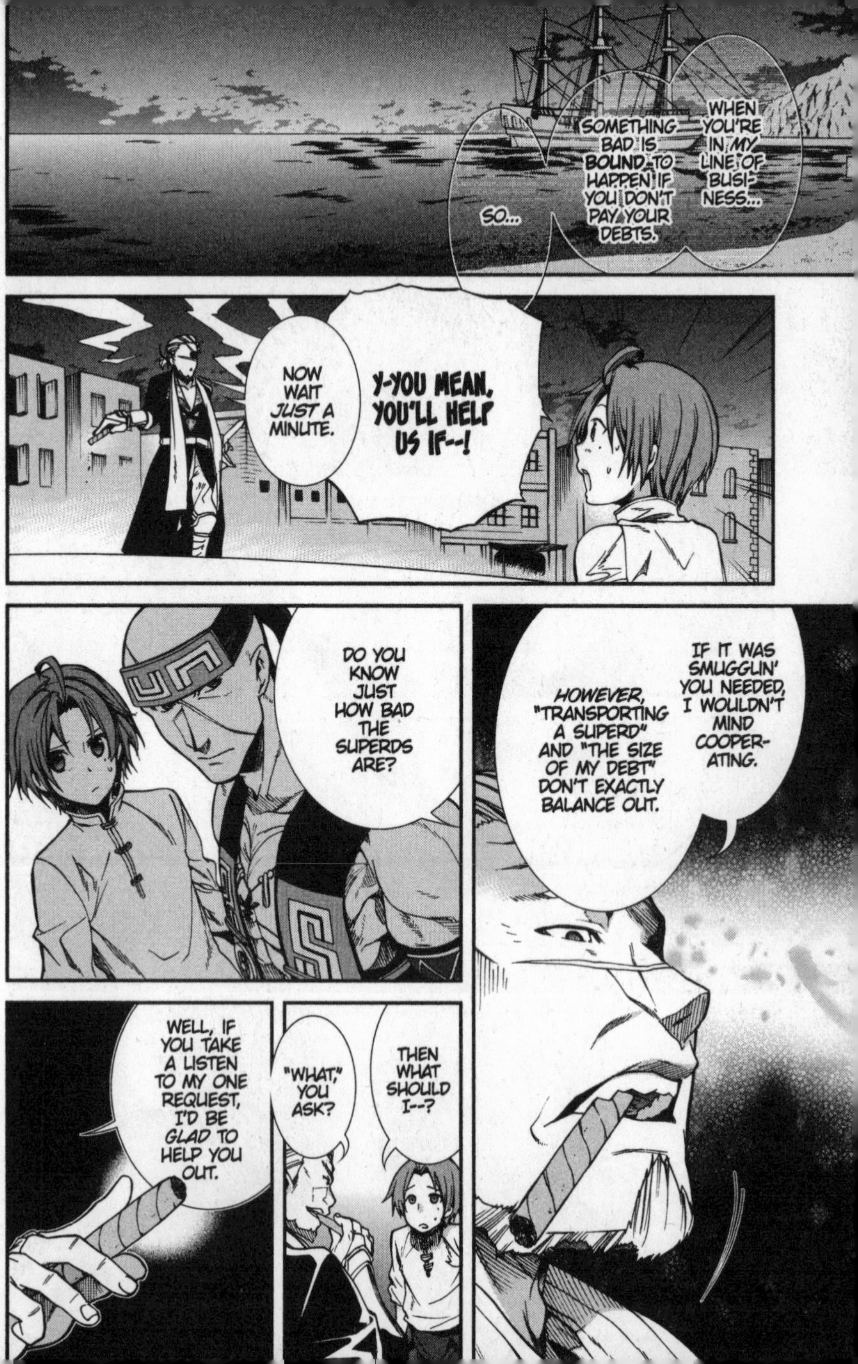
WHEN YOU'RE IN MY LINE OF BUSINESS...
SOMETHING BAD IS BOUND TO HAPPEN IF YOU DON'T PAY YOUR DEBTS.
SO...
Y-YOU MEAN, YOU'LL HELP US IF--!
NOW WAIT JUST A MINUTE.
IF IT WAS SMUGGLIN' YOU NEEDED, I WOULDN'T MIND COOPER-ATING.
HOWEVER, "TRANSPORTING A SUPERD" AND "THE SIZE OF MY DEBT" DON'T EXACTLY BALANCE OUT.
DO YOU KNOW JUST HOW BAD THE SUPERDS ARE?
THEN WHAT SHOULD I--?
"WHAT," YOU ASK?
WELL, IF YOU TAKE A LISTEN TO MY ONE REQUEST, I'D BE GLAD TO HELP YOU OUT.

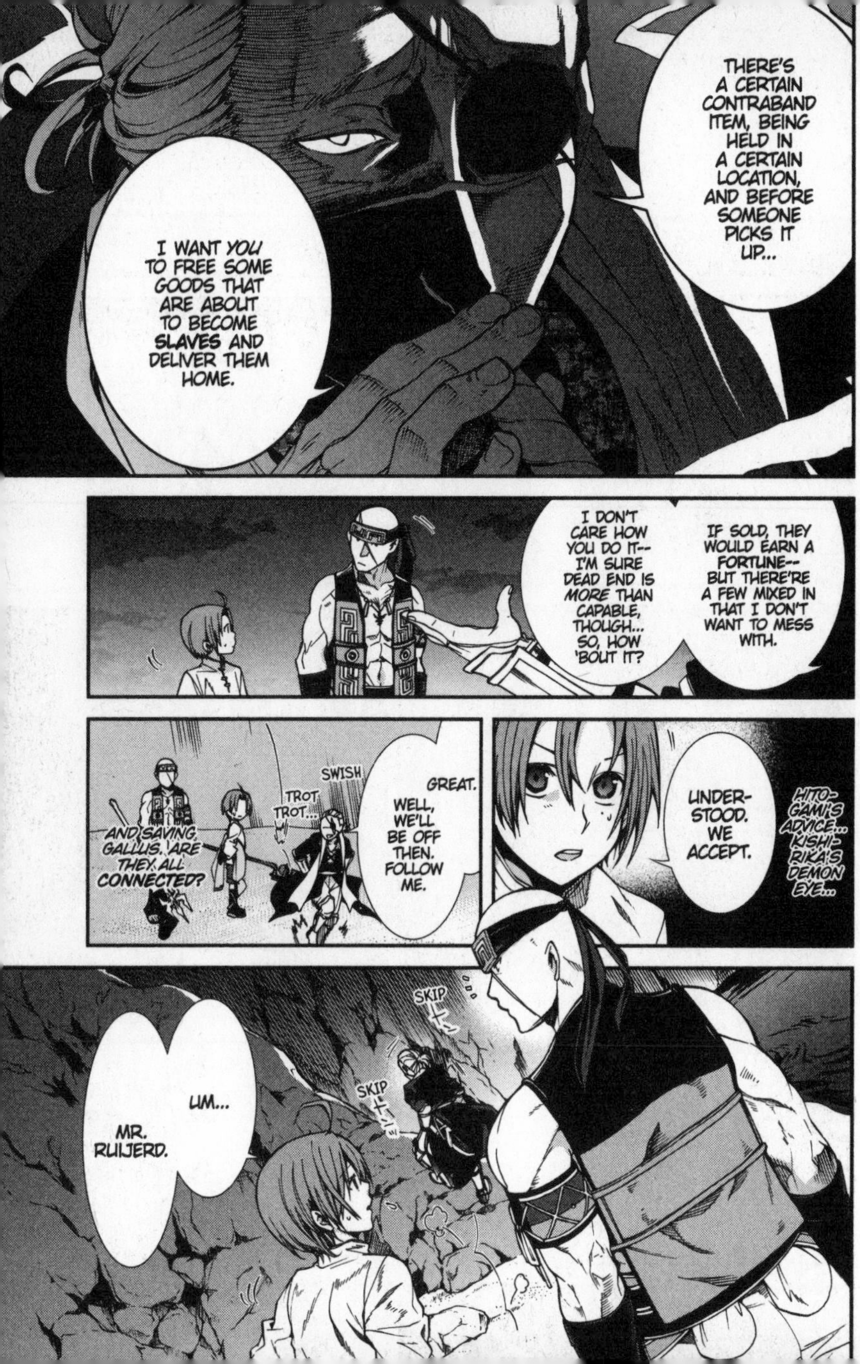
THERE'S A CERTAIN CONTRABAND ITEM, BEING HELD IN A CERTAIN LOCATION, AND BEFORE SOMEONE PICKS IT UP...
I WANT *YOU* TO FREE SOME GOODS THAT ARE ABOUT TO BECOME **SLAVES** AND DELIVER THEM HOME.
IF SOLD, THEY WOULD EARN A FORTUNE-- BUT THERE'RE A FEW MIXED IN THAT I DON'T WANT TO MESS WITH.
I DON'T CARE HOW YOU DO IT-- I'M SURE DEAD END IS *MORE* THAN CAPABLE, THOUGH... SO, HOW 'BOUT IT?
UNDER-STOOD. WE ACCEPT.
HITO-GAMI'S ADVICE... KISHIRIKA'S DEMON EYE...
GREAT. WELL, WE'LL BE OFF THEN. FOLLOW ME.
SWISH
TROT TROT...
AND SAVING GALLUS. ARE THEY ALL CONNECTED?
SKIP
SKIP
UM... MR. RUIJERD.

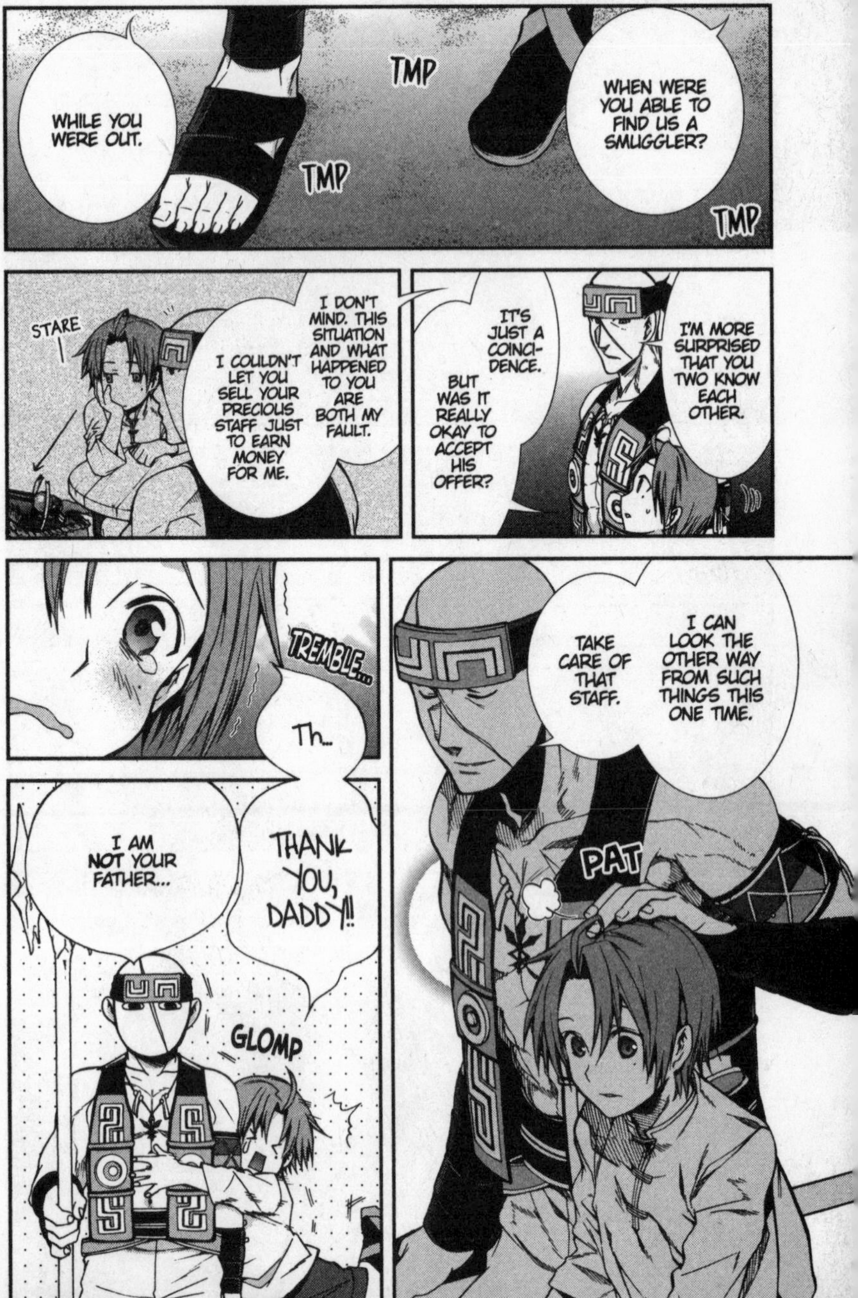
WHEN WERE YOU ABLE TO FIND US A SMUGGLER?
TMP
TMP
TMP
WHILE YOU WERE OUT.
I'M MORE SURPRISED THAT YOU TWO KNOW EACH OTHER.
IT'S JUST A COINCIDENCE.
BUT WAS IT REALLY OKAY TO ACCEPT HIS OFFER?
I DON'T MIND. THIS SITUATION AND WHAT HAPPENED TO YOU ARE BOTH MY FAULT.
I COULDN'T LET YOU SELL YOUR PRECIOUS STAFF JUST TO EARN MONEY FOR ME.
STARE
I CAN LOOK THE OTHER WAY FROM SUCH THINGS THIS ONE TIME.
TAKE CARE OF THAT STAFF.
PAT
TREMBLE...
Th...
THANK YOU, DADDY!!
I AM NOT YOUR FATHER...
GLOMP

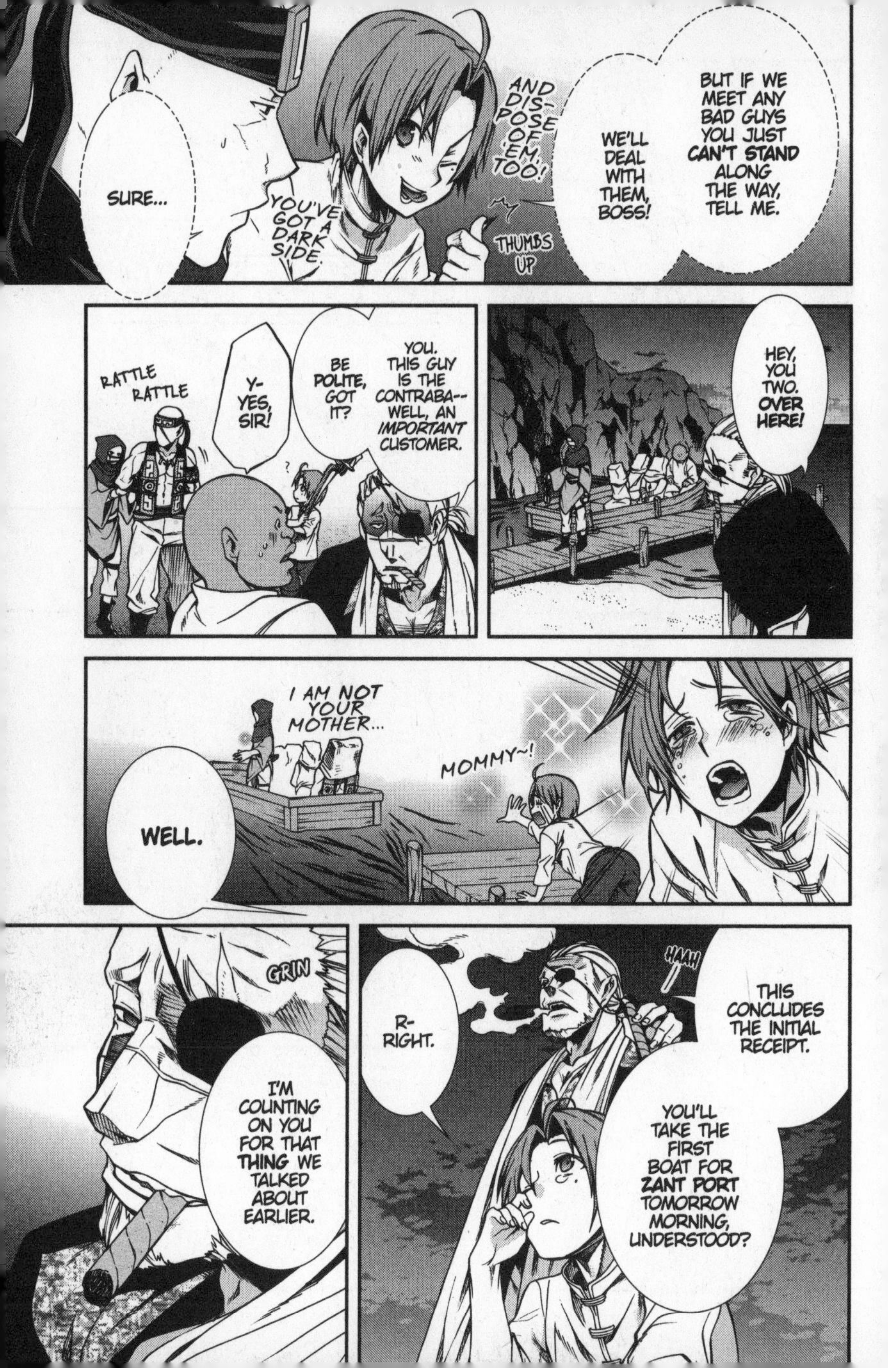
BUT IF WE MEET ANY BAD GUYS YOU JUST CAN'T STAND ALONG THE WAY, TELL ME.
WE'LL DEAL WITH THEM, BOSS!
AND DISPOSE OF 'EM, TOO!
THUMBS UP
YOU'VE GOT A DARK SIDE.
SURE...
HEY, YOU TWO. OVER HERE!
YOU. THIS GUY IS THE CONTRABA-- WELL, AN *IMPORTANT* CUSTOMER.
BE POLITE, GOT IT?
Y-YES, SIR!
RATTLE RATTLE
MOMMY~!
I AM NOT YOUR MOTHER...
WELL.
HAAH
THIS CONCLUDES THE INITIAL RECEIPT.
YOU'LL TAKE THE FIRST BOAT FOR ZANT PORT TOMORROW MORNING, UNDERSTOOD?
R-RIGHT.
GRIN
I'M COUNTING ON YOU FOR THAT THING WE TALKED ABOUT EARLIER.

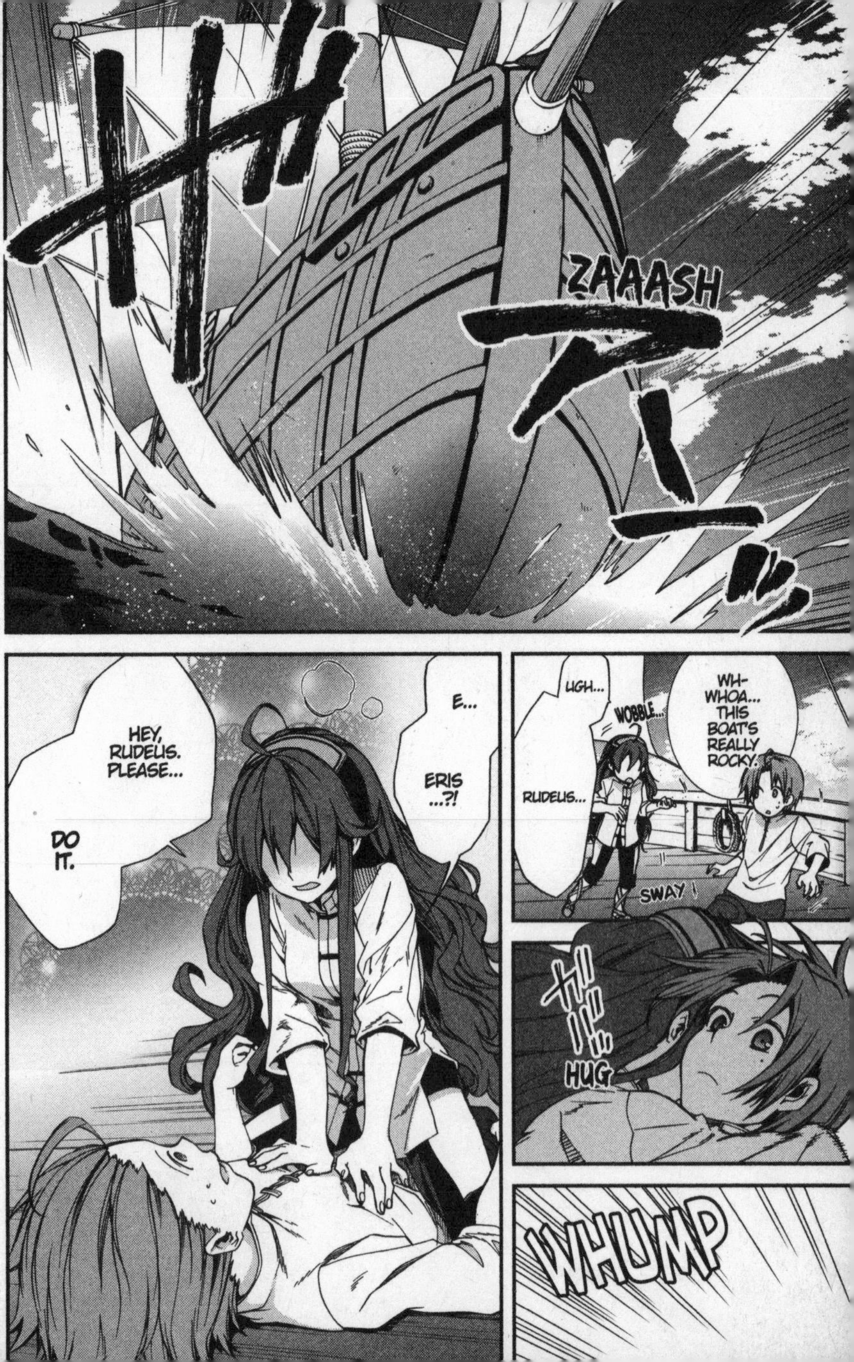
ZAAASH
WH-WHOA... THIS BOAT'S REALLY ROCKY.
UGH...
WOBBLE...
RUDEUS...
SWAY!
HUG
WHUMP
E...
ERIS...?!
HEY, RUDEUS. PLEASE...
DO IT.

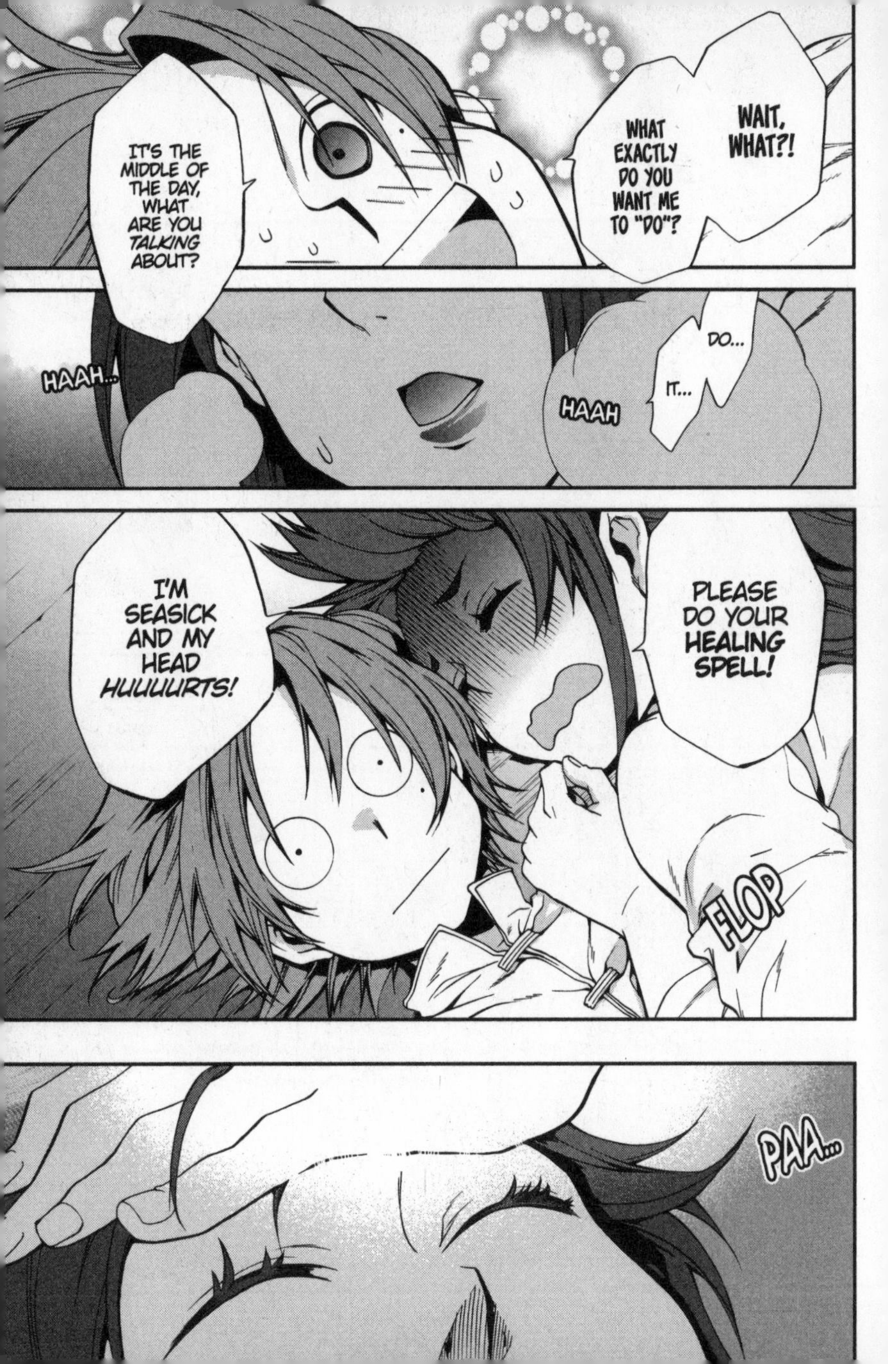
WAIT, WHAT?!
WHAT EXACTLY DO YOU WANT ME TO "DO"?
IT'S THE MIDDLE OF THE DAY, WHAT ARE YOU TALKING ABOUT?
DO...
IT...
HAAH
HAAH...
PLEASE DO YOUR HEALING SPELL!
I'M SEASICK AND MY HEAD HUUUURTS!
FLOP
PAA...

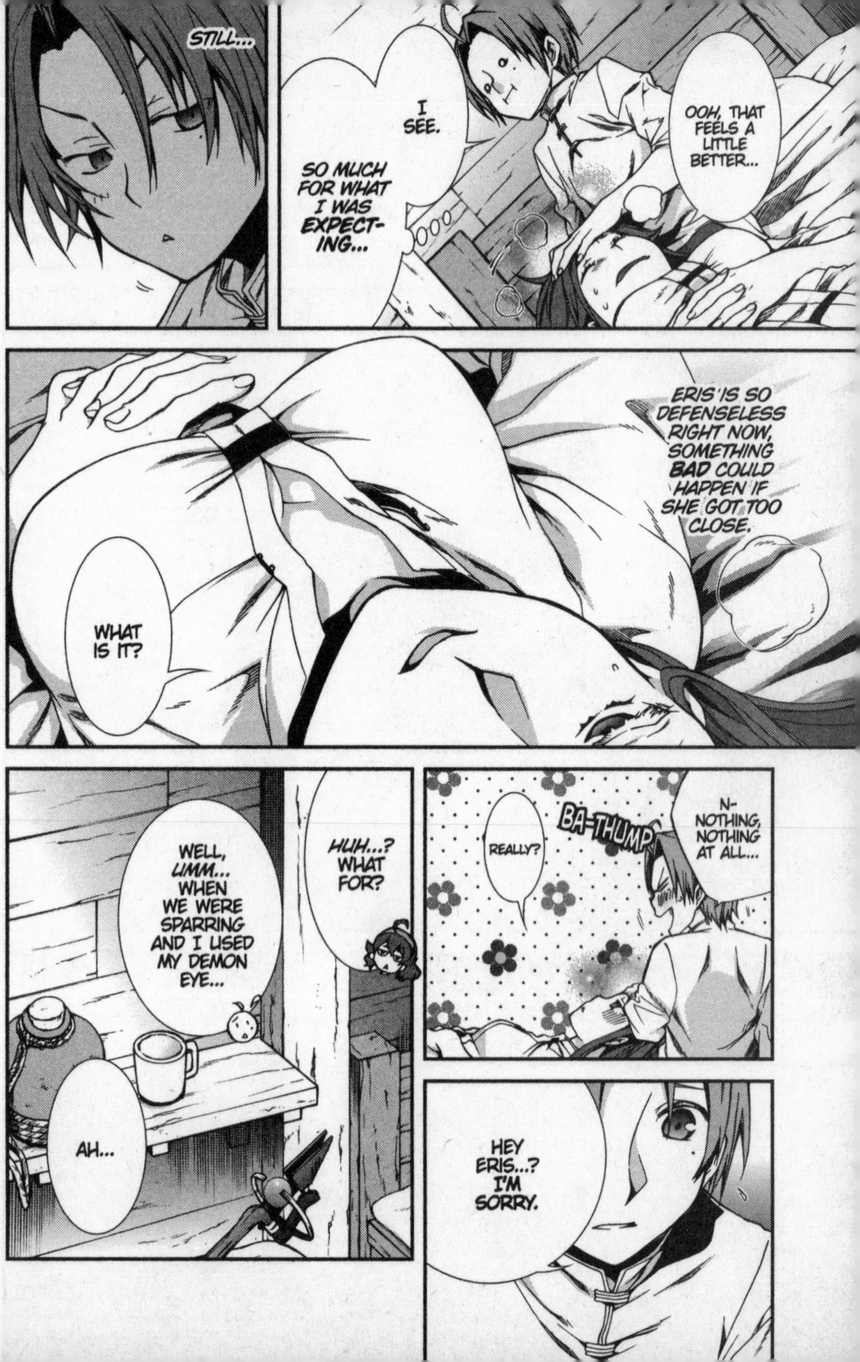
OOH, THAT FEELS A LITTLE BETTER...
I SEE.
SO MUCH FOR WHAT I WAS EXPECTING...
STILL...
ERIS IS SO DEFENSELESS RIGHT NOW, SOMETHING BAD COULD HAPPEN IF SHE GOT TOO CLOSE.
WHAT IS IT?
N-NOTHING, NOTHING AT ALL...
BA-THUMP
REALLY?
HEY ERIS...? I'M SORRY.
HUH...? WHAT FOR?
WELL, UMM... WHEN WE WERE SPARRING AND I USED MY DEMON EYE...
AH...

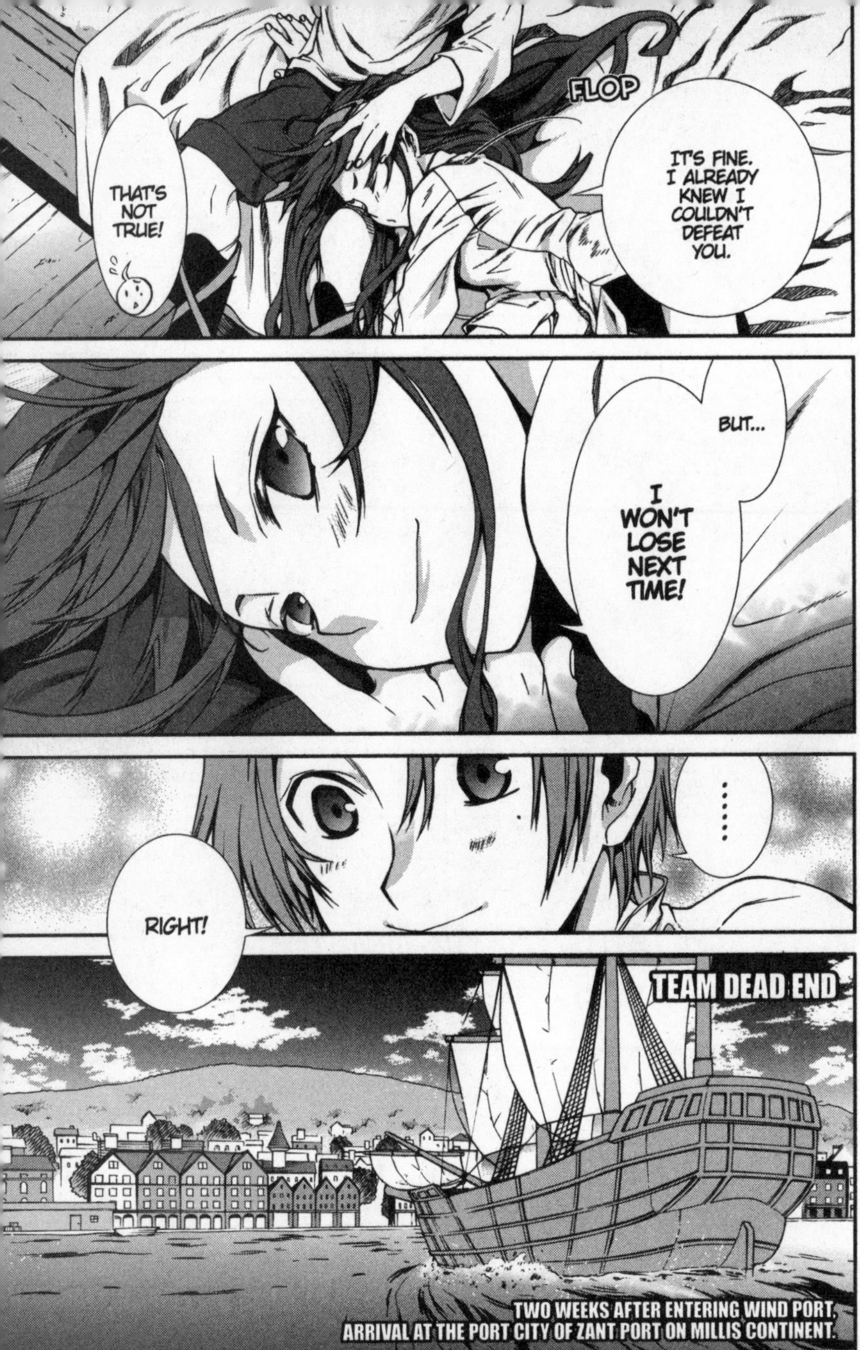
FLOP
IT'S FINE. I ALREADY KNEW I COULDN'T DEFEAT YOU.
THAT'S NOT TRUE!
BUT...
I WON'T LOSE NEXT TIME!
......
RIGHT!
TEAM DEAD END
TWO WEEKS AFTER ENTERING WIND PORT, ARRIVAL AT THE PORT CITY OF ZANT PORT ON MILLIS CONTINENT.

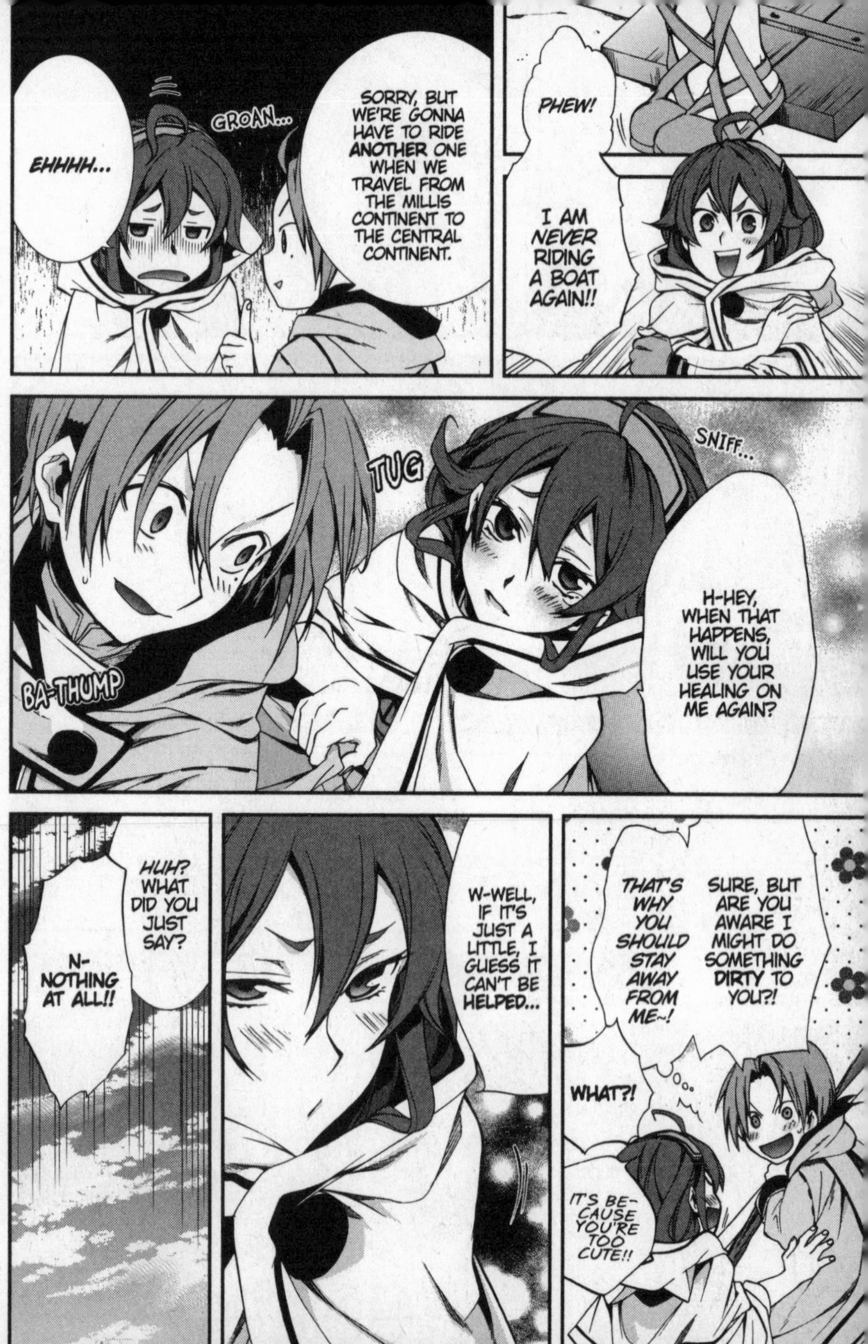
PHEW!
I AM NEVER RIDING A BOAT AGAIN!!
SORRY, BUT WE'RE GONNA HAVE TO RIDE ANOTHER ONE WHEN WE TRAVEL FROM THE MILLIS CONTINENT TO THE CENTRAL CONTINENT.
GROAN...
EHHHH...
SNIFF...
H-HEY, WHEN THAT HAPPENS, WILL YOU USE YOUR HEALING ON ME AGAIN?
TUG
BA-THUMP
SURE, BUT ARE YOU AWARE I MIGHT DO SOMETHING DIRTY TO YOU?!
THAT'S WHY YOU SHOULD STAY AWAY FROM ME~!
WHAT?!
IT'S BE-CAUSE YOU'RE TOO CUTE!!
W-WELL, IF IT'S JUST A LITTLE, I GUESS IT CAN'T BE HELPED...
HUH? WHAT DID YOU JUST SAY?
N-NOTHING AT ALL!!

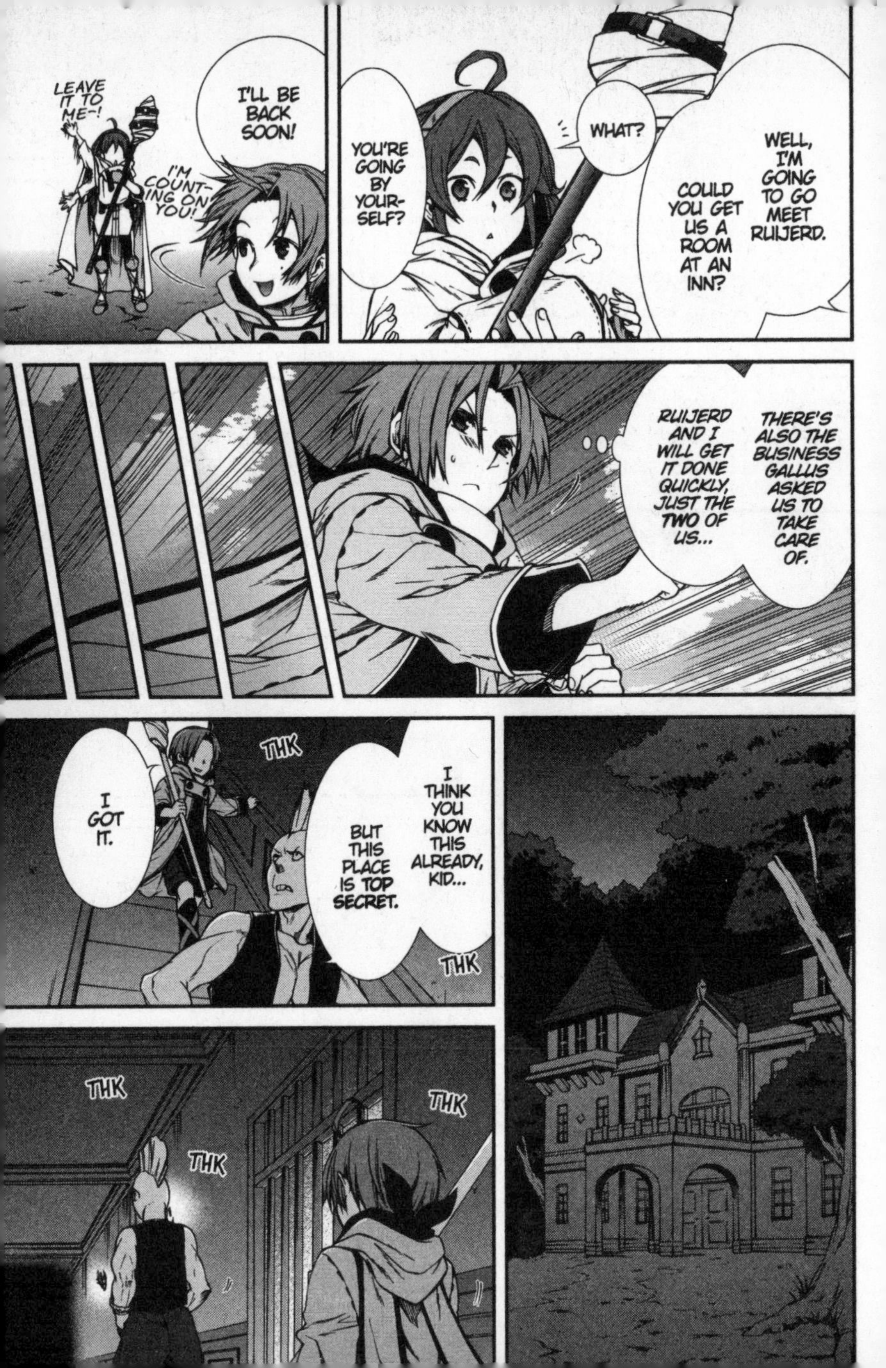
WELL, I'M GOING TO GO MEET RUIJERD.
COULD YOU GET US A ROOM AT AN INN?
WHAT?
YOU'RE GOING BY YOURSELF?
I'LL BE BACK SOON!
LEAVE IT TO ME~!
I'M COUNTING ON YOU!
THERE'S ALSO THE BUSINESS GALLUS ASKED US TO TAKE CARE OF.
RUIJERD AND I WILL GET IT DONE QUICKLY, JUST THE TWO OF US...
I THINK YOU KNOW THIS ALREADY, KID...
BUT THIS PLACE IS TOP SECRET.
THK
I GOT IT.
THK
THK
THK
THK

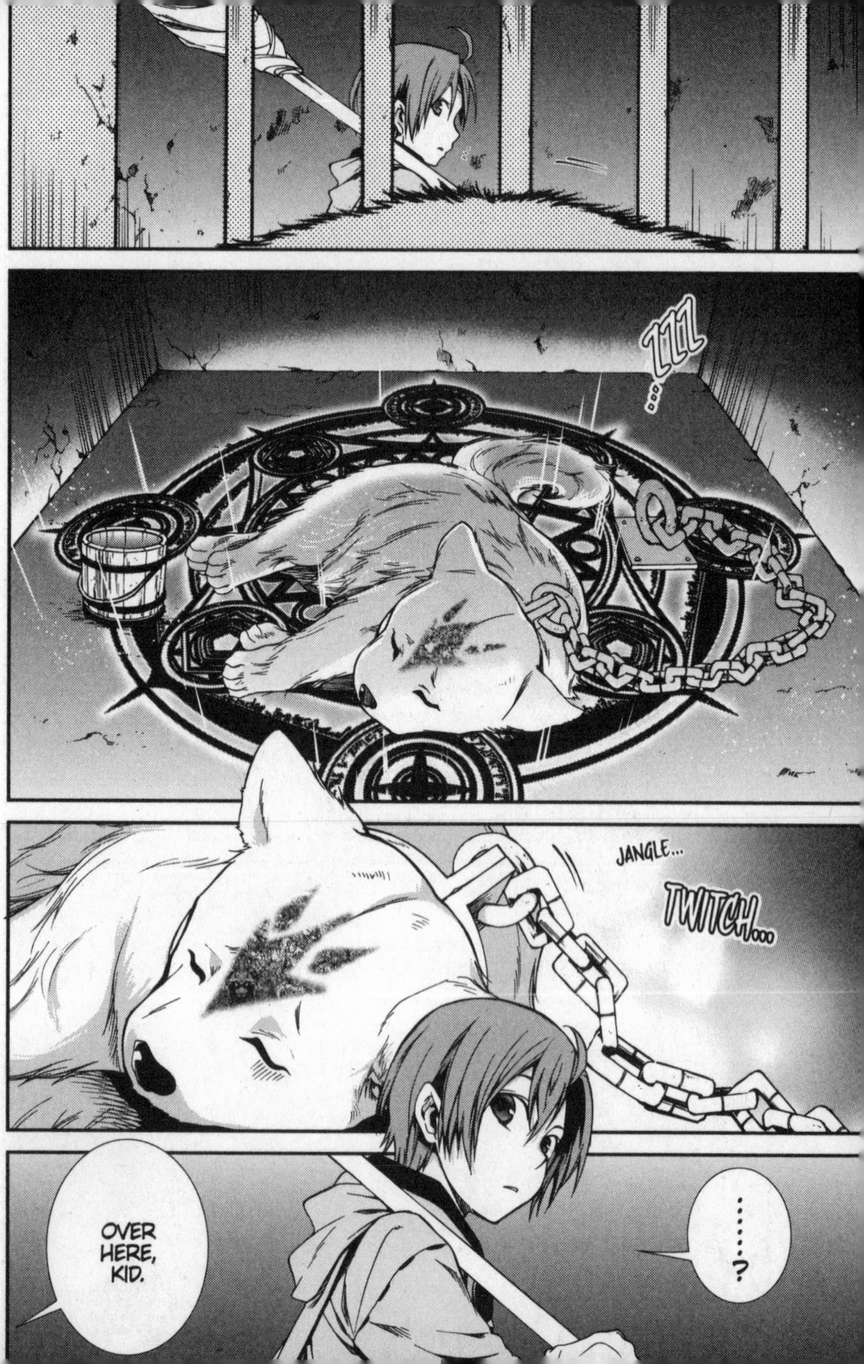
ZZZZ...
JANGLE...
TWITCH...
......?
OVER HERE, KID.

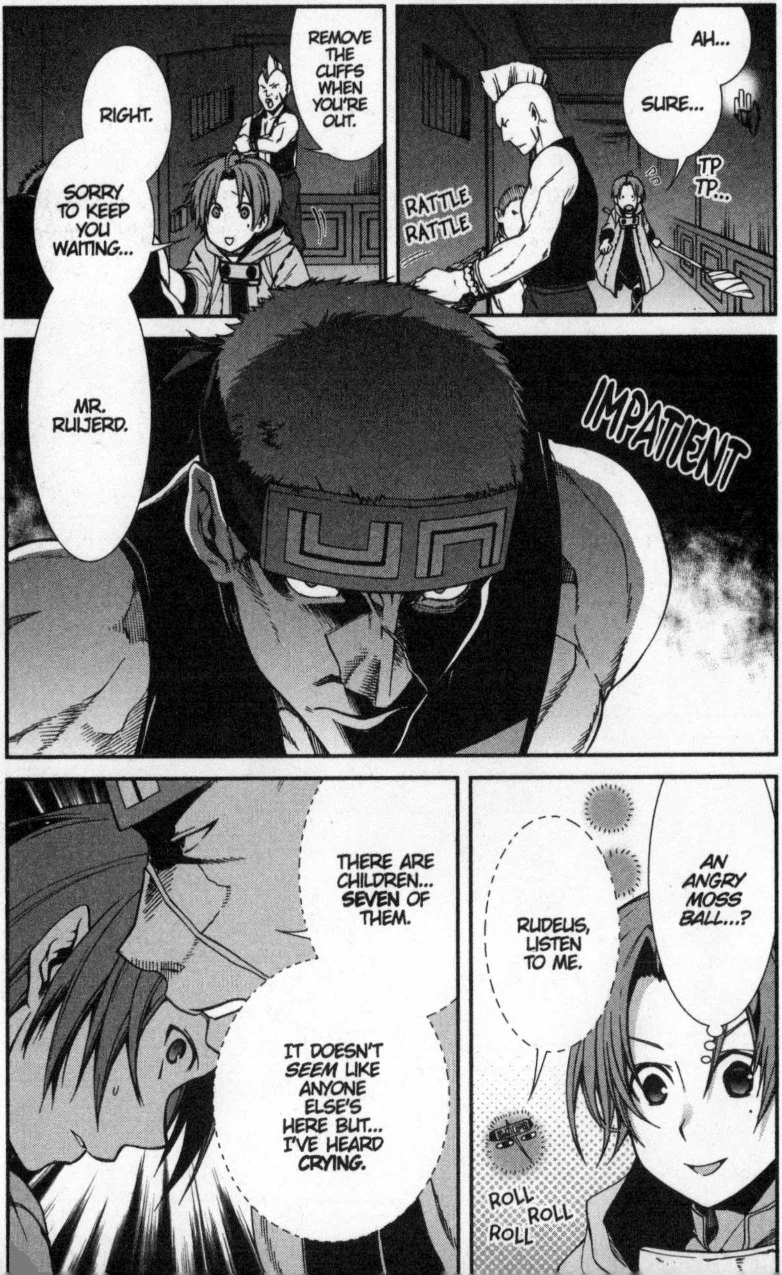
AH...
SURE...
TP TP...
RATTLE RATTLE
REMOVE THE CUFFS WHEN YOU'RE OUT.
RIGHT.
SORRY TO KEEP YOU WAITING...
MR. RUIJERD.
IMPATIENT
AN ANGRY MOSS BALL...?
RUDEUS, LISTEN TO ME.
ROLL ROLL ROLL
THERE ARE CHILDREN... SEVEN OF THEM.
IT DOESN'T SEEM LIKE ANYONE ELSE'S HERE BUT... I'VE HEARD CRYING.

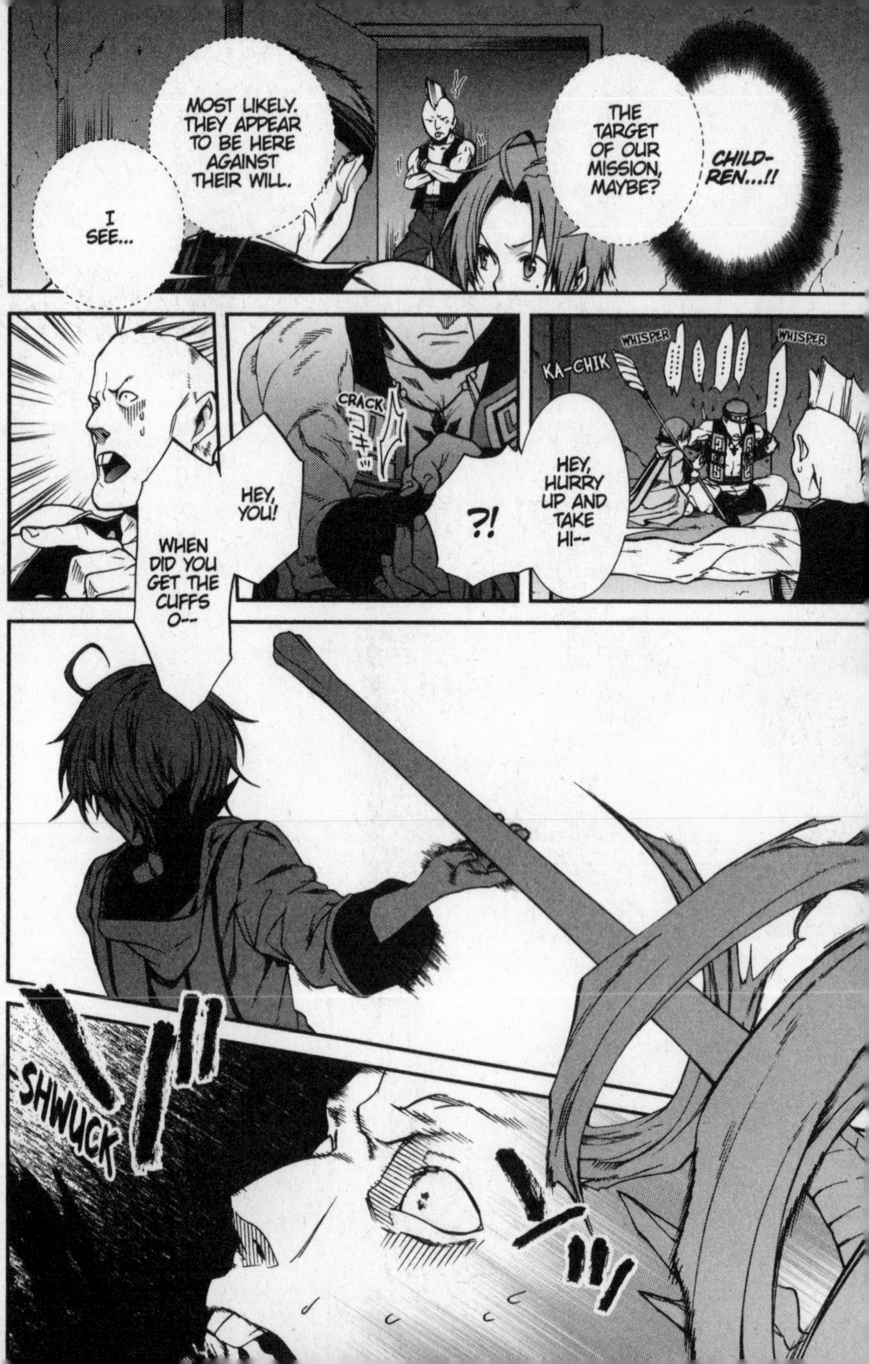
CHILD-REN...!!
THE TARGET OF OUR MISSION, MAYBE?
MOST LIKELY. THEY APPEAR TO BE HERE AGAINST THEIR WILL.
I SEE...
WHISPER
WHISPER
KA-CHIK
HEY, HURRY UP AND TAKE HI--
?!
CRACK
HEY, YOU!
WHEN DID YOU GET THE CUFFS O--
SHWUCK

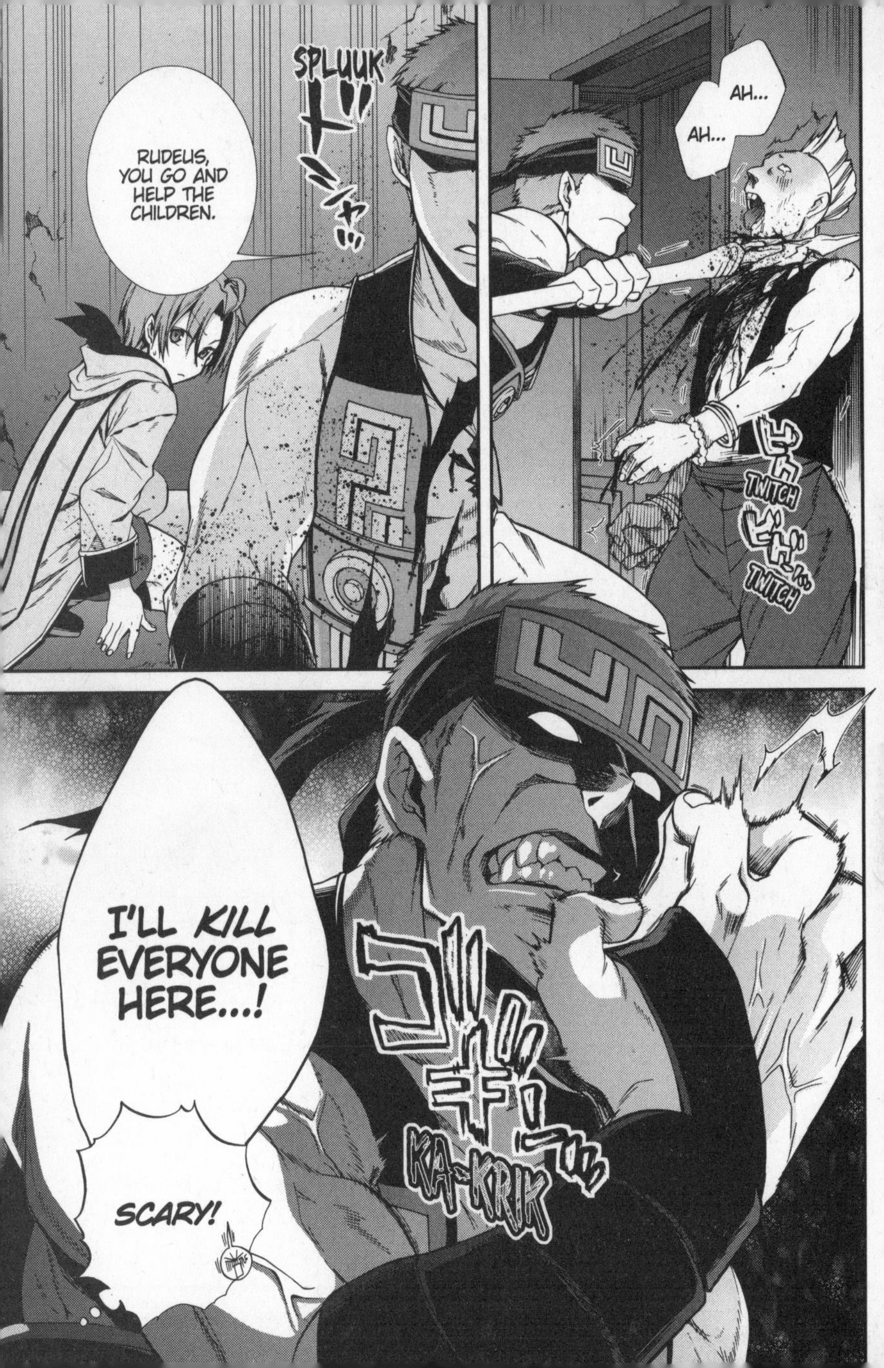
AH...
AH...
TWITCH
TWITCH
SPLUUK
RUDEUS, YOU GO AND HELP THE CHILDREN.
I'LL *KILL* EVERYONE HERE...!
KA-KRIK
SCARY!

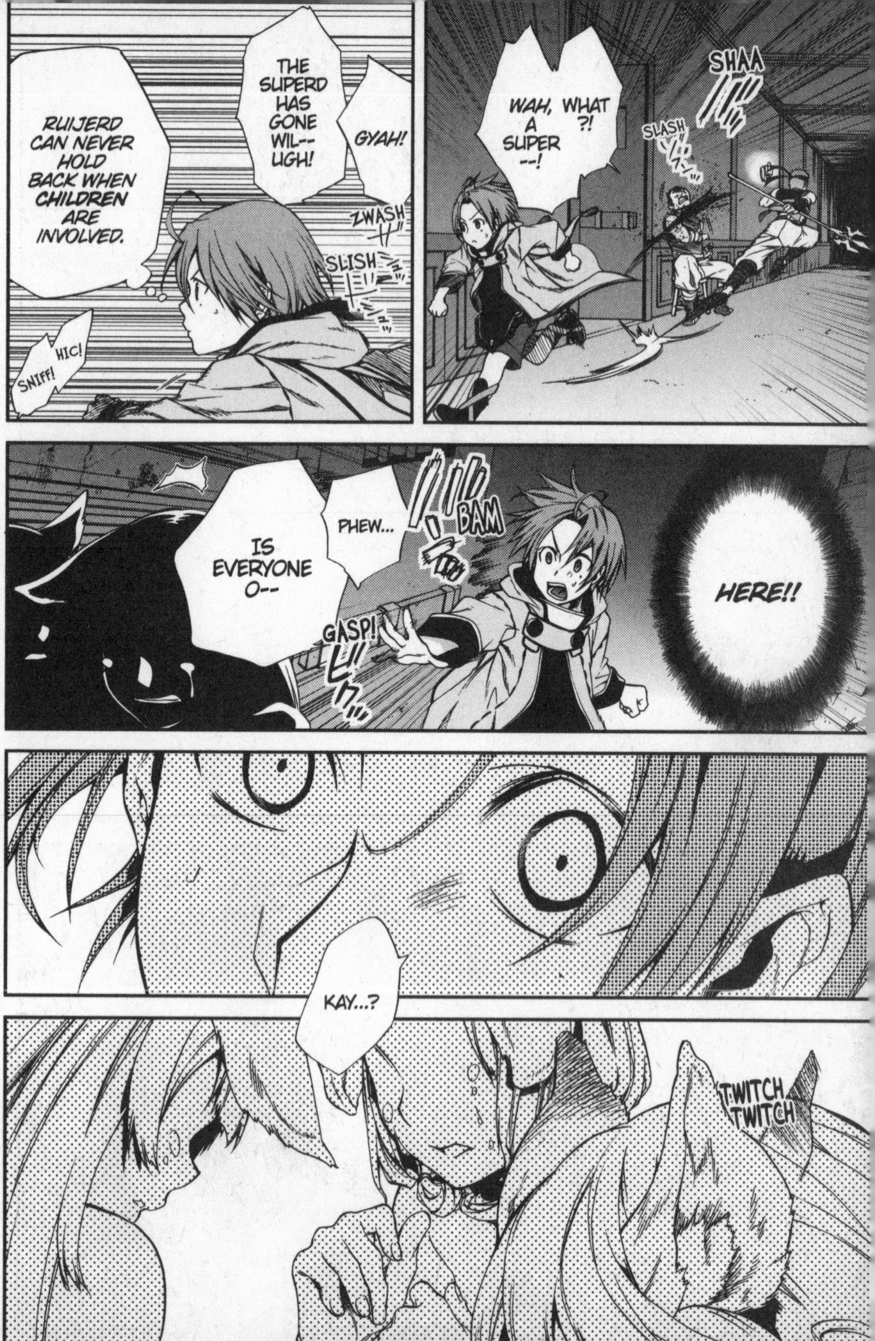
SHAA
WHAT ?!
WAH, A SUPER --!
SLASH
THE SUPERD HAS GONE WIL-- UGH!
GYAH!
RUIJERD CAN NEVER HOLD BACK WHEN CHILDREN ARE INVOLVED.
ZWASH
SLISH
HIC!
SNIFF!
HERE!!
BAM
PHEW...
IS EVERYONE O--
GASP!
KAY...?
TWITCH TWITCH

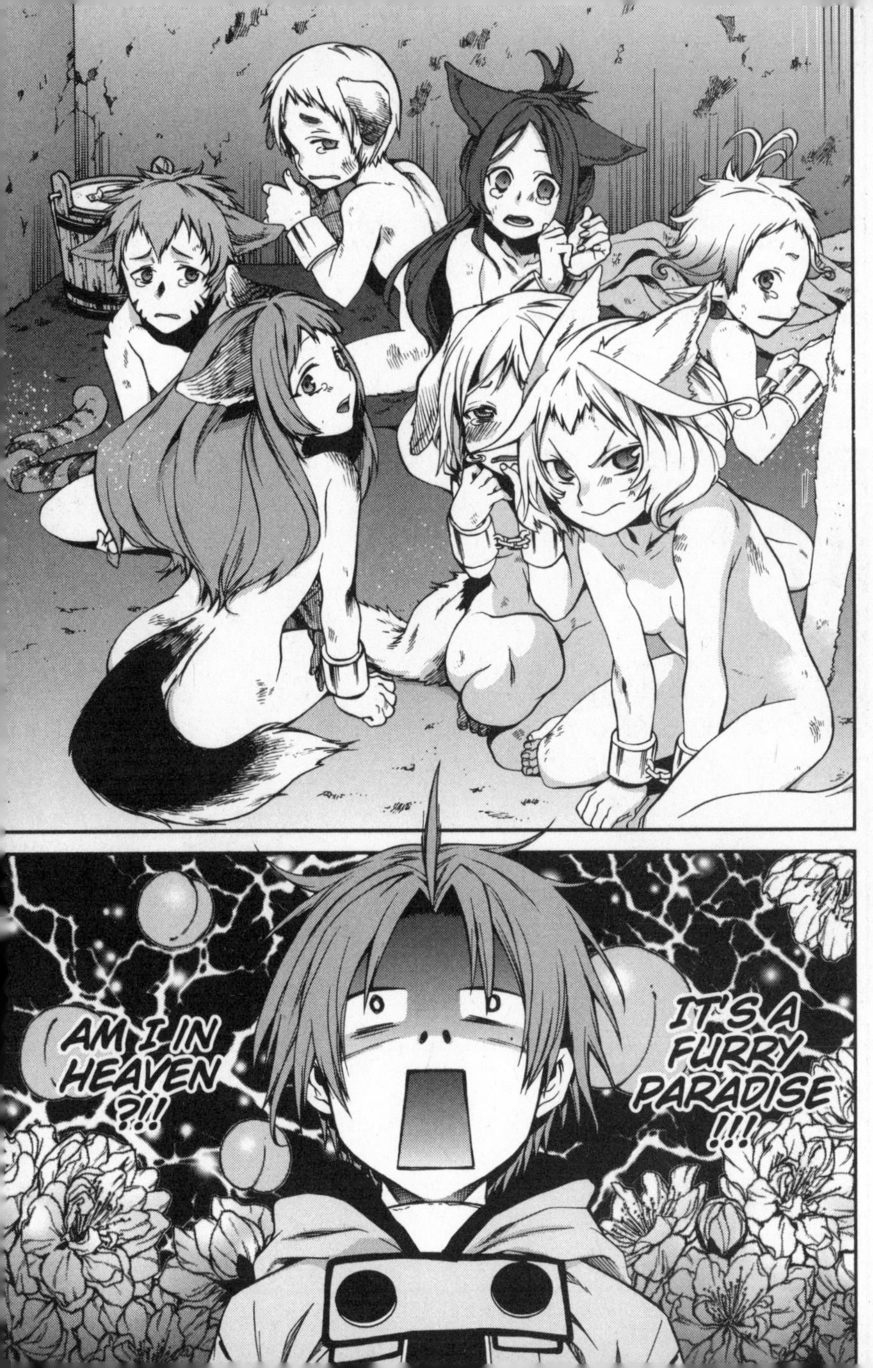
IT'S A FURRY PARADISE!!!
AM I IN HEAVEN?!!

無職転生

異世界行ったら本気だす

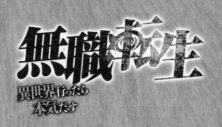

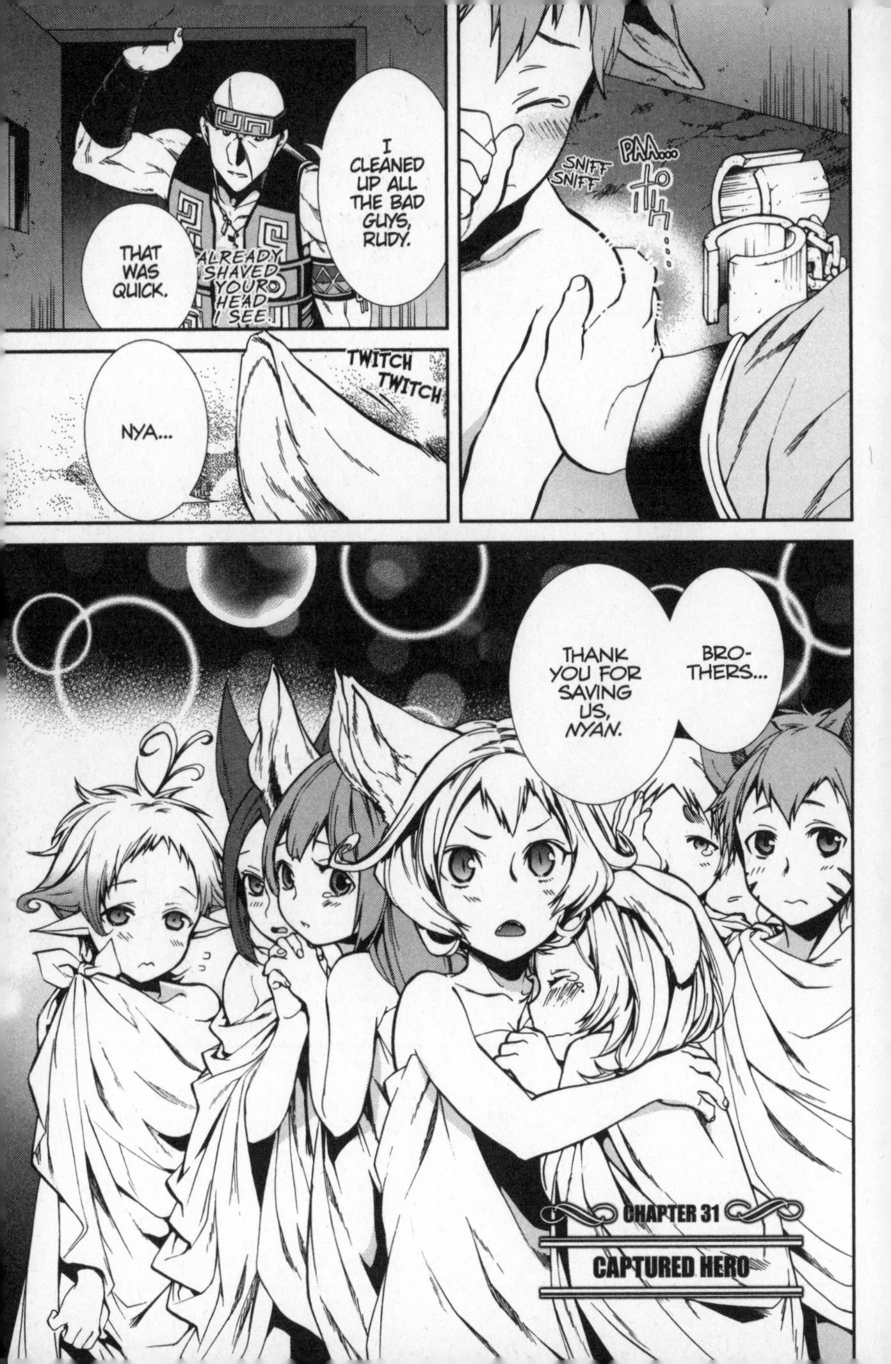
SNIFF SNIFF
PAA...
I CLEANED UP ALL THE BAD GUYS, RUDY.
ALREADY SHAVED YOUR HEAD I SEE.
THAT WAS QUICK.
TWITCH TWITCH
NYA...
BRO-THERS...
THANK YOU FOR SAVING US, NYAN.
CHAPTER 31
CAPTURED HERO

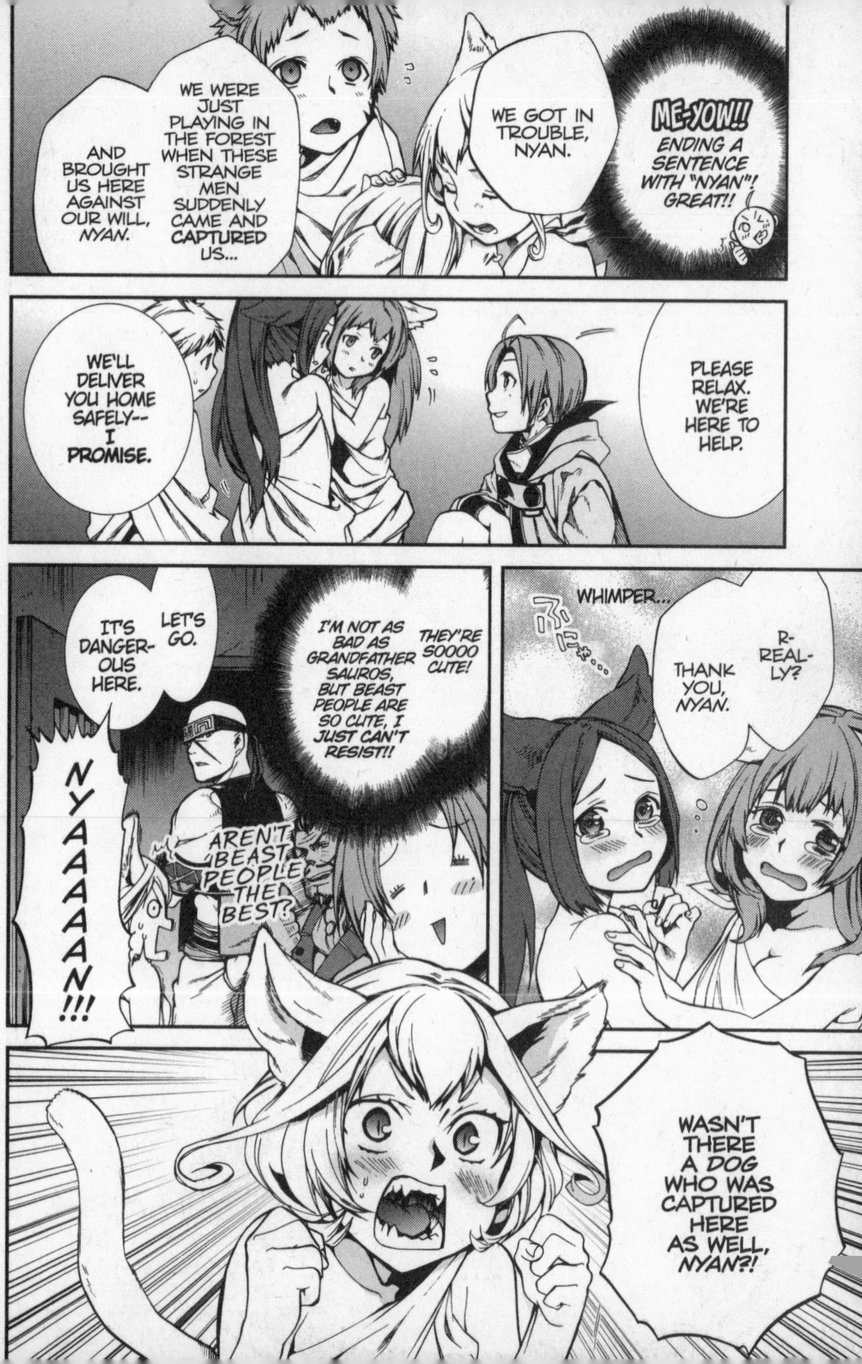
ME-YOW!! ENDING A SENTENCE WITH "NYAN"! GREAT!!
WE GOT IN TROUBLE, NYAN.
WE WERE JUST PLAYING IN THE FOREST WHEN THESE STRANGE MEN SUDDENLY CAME AND CAPTURED US...
AND BROUGHT US HERE AGAINST OUR WILL, NYAN.
PLEASE RELAX. WE'RE HERE TO HELP.
WE'LL DELIVER YOU HOME SAFELY-- I PROMISE.
WHIMPER...
ふにゃ...
R-REALLY?
THANK YOU, NYAN.
THEY'RE SOOOO CUTE!
I'M NOT AS BAD AS GRANDFATHER SAUROS, BUT BEAST PEOPLE ARE SO CUTE, I JUST CAN'T RESIST!!
LET'S GO.
IT'S DANGEROUS HERE.
AREN'T BEAST PEOPLE THE BEST?
NYAAAAAAN!!!
WASN'T THERE A DOG WHO WAS CAPTURED HERE AS WELL, NYAN?!

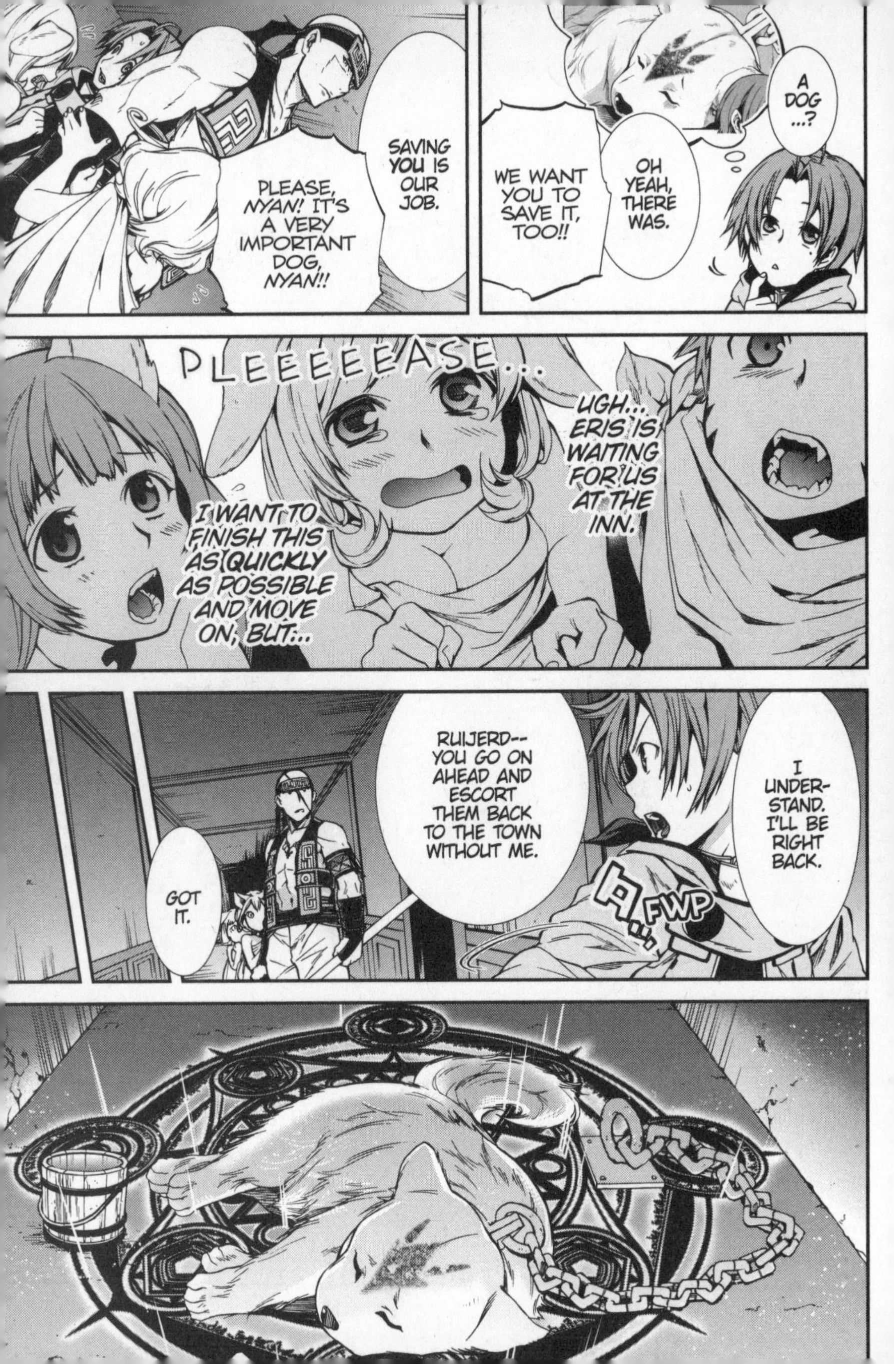
A DOG ...?
OH YEAH, THERE WAS.
WE WANT YOU TO SAVE IT, TOO!!
SAVING YOU IS OUR JOB.
PLEASE, NYAN! IT'S A VERY IMPORTANT DOG, NYAN!!
PLEEEEEEASE...
UGH... ERIS IS WAITING FOR US AT THE INN.
I WANT TO FINISH THIS AS QUICKLY AS POSSIBLE AND MOVE ON, BUT...
I UNDERSTAND. I'LL BE RIGHT BACK.
FWP
RUIJERD-- YOU GO ON AHEAD AND ESCORT THEM BACK TO THE TOWN WITHOUT ME.
GOT IT.

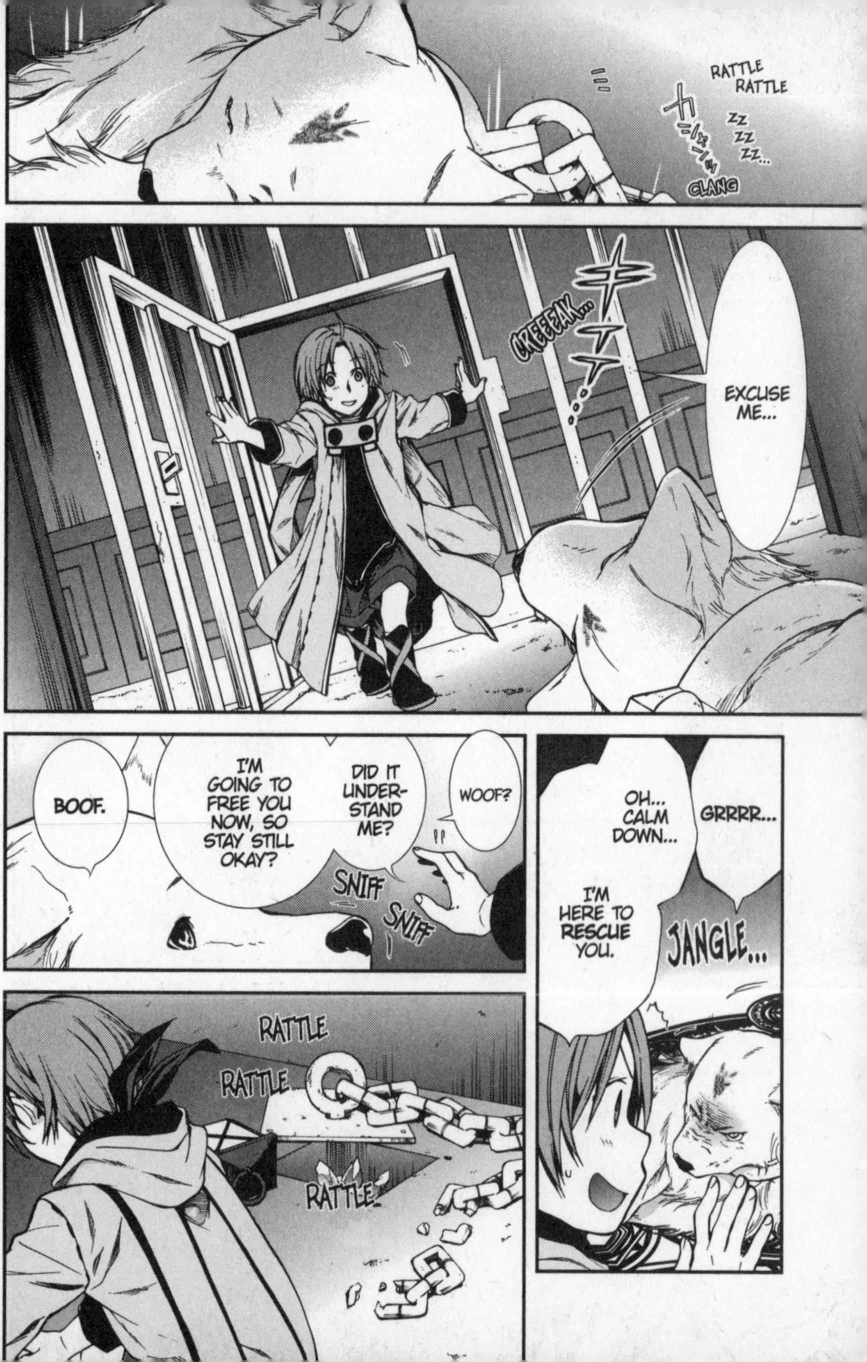
RATTLE RATTLE
ZZ ZZ ZZ...
CLANG
EXCUSE ME...
CREEEEAK...
GRRRR...
OH... CALM DOWN...
I'M HERE TO RESCUE YOU.
JANGLE...
WOOF?
DID IT UNDERSTAND ME?
I'M GOING TO FREE YOU NOW, SO STAY STILL OKAY?
SNIFF
SNIFF
BOOF.
RATTLE
RATTLE
RATTLE

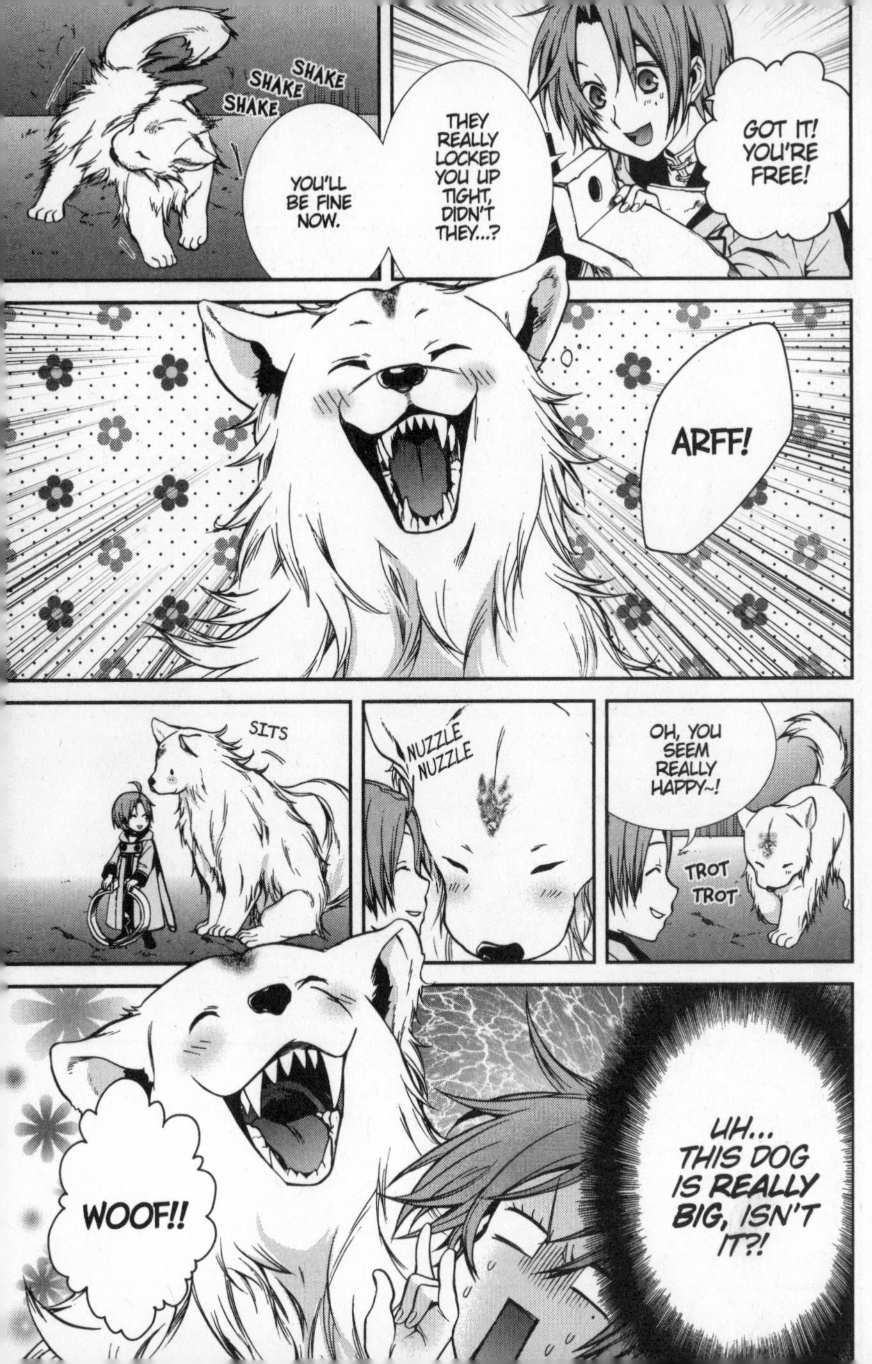
GOT IT! YOU'RE FREE!
THEY REALLY LOCKED YOU UP TIGHT, DIDN'T THEY...?
YOU'LL BE FINE NOW.
SHAKE SHAKE SHAKE
ARFF!
OH, YOU SEEM REALLY HAPPY~!
TROT TROT
NUZZLE NUZZLE
SITS
UH... THIS DOG IS REALLY BIG, ISN'T IT?!
WOOF!!

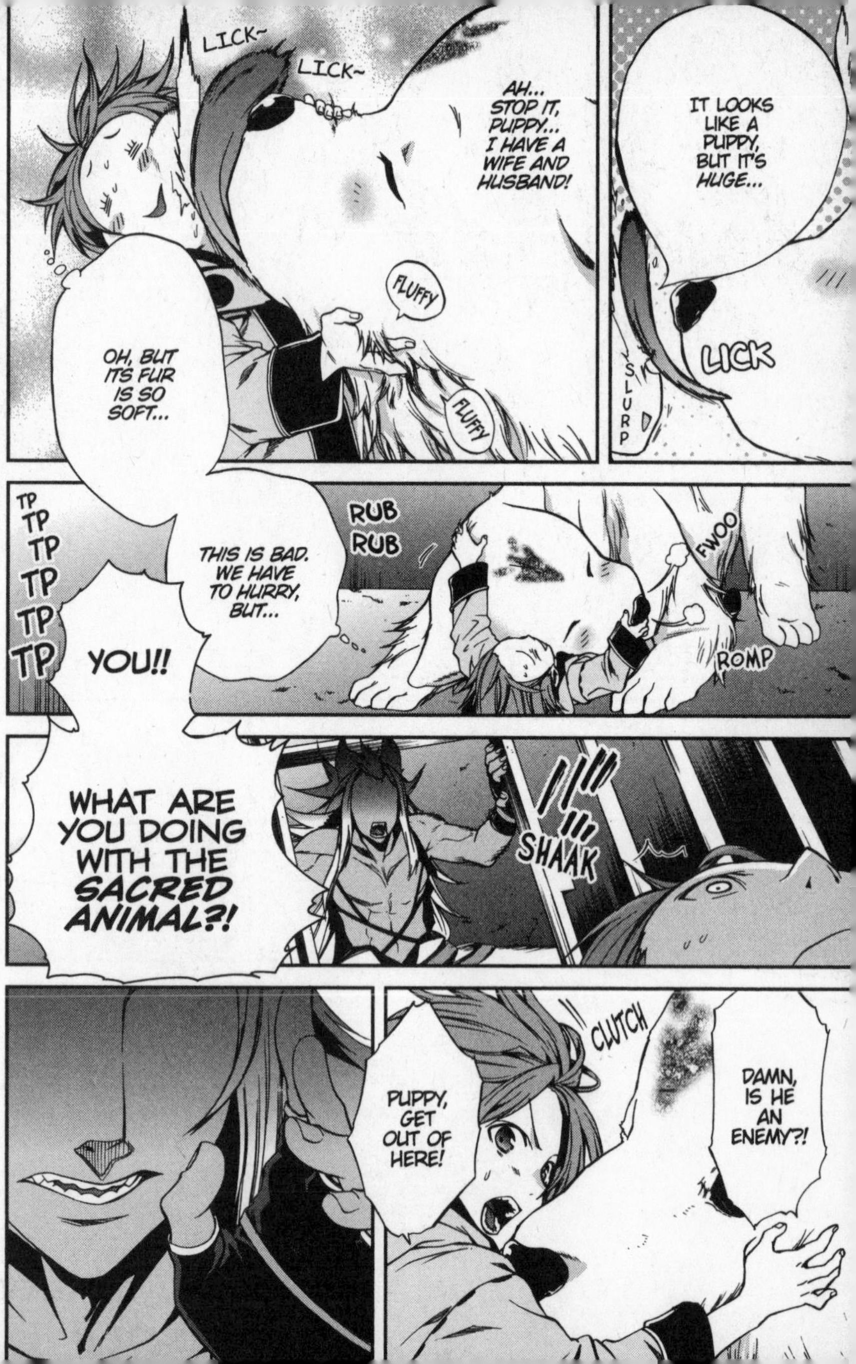

IT LOOKS LIKE A PUPPY, BUT IT'S HUGE...
LICK
SLURP
LICK~
LICK~
AH... STOP IT, PUPPY... I HAVE A WIFE AND HUSBAND!
FLUFFY
FLUFFY
OH, BUT ITS FUR IS SO SOFT...
FWOO
ROMP
RUB RUB
THIS IS BAD. WE HAVE TO HURRY, BUT...
TP TP TP TP TP TP
YOU!!
SHAAK
WHAT ARE YOU DOING WITH THE SACRED ANIMAL?!
DAMN, IS HE AN ENEMY?!
CLUTCH
PUPPY, GET OUT OF HERE!

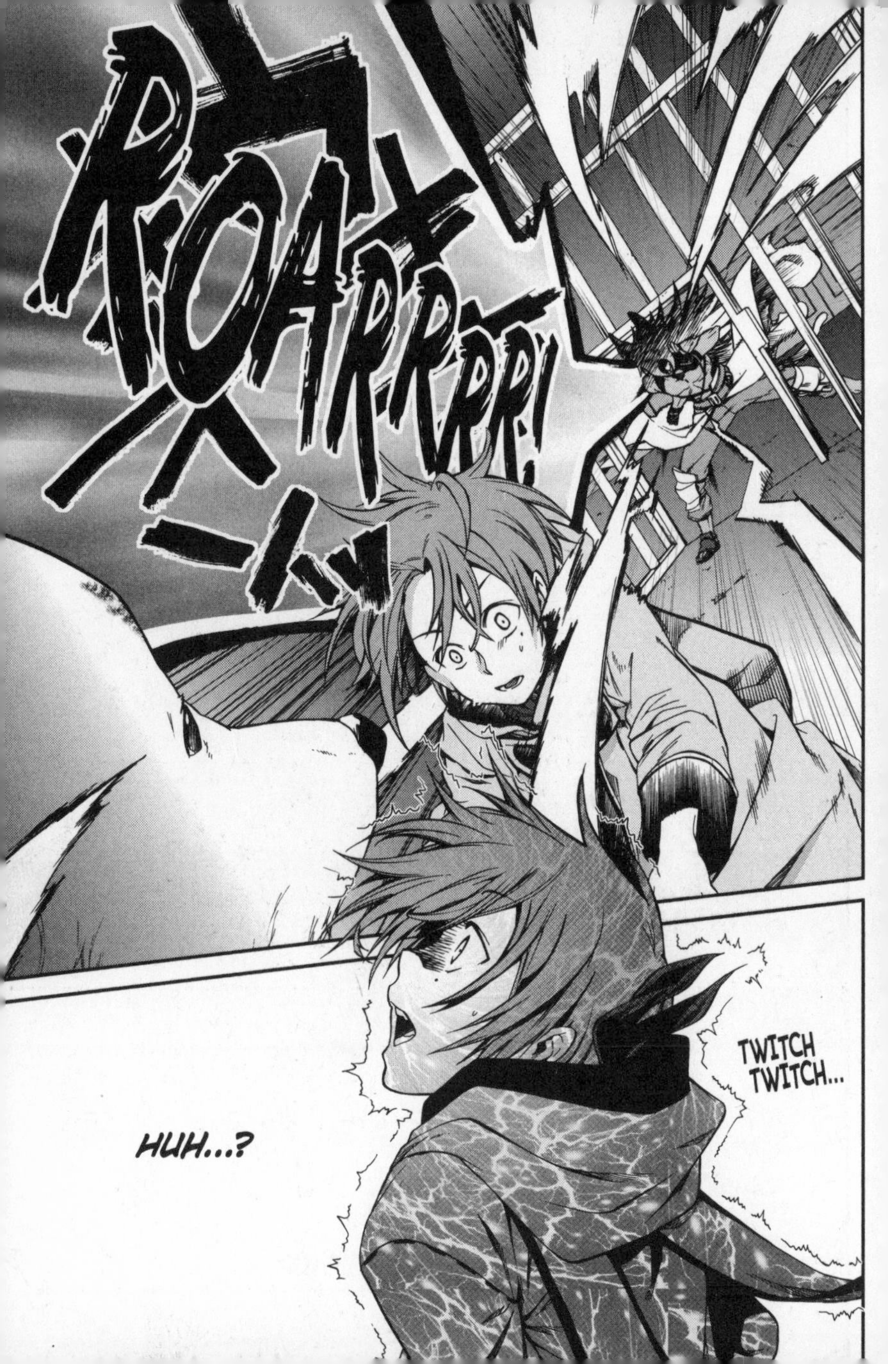
ROAARRRR!
TWITCH TWITCH...
HUH...?

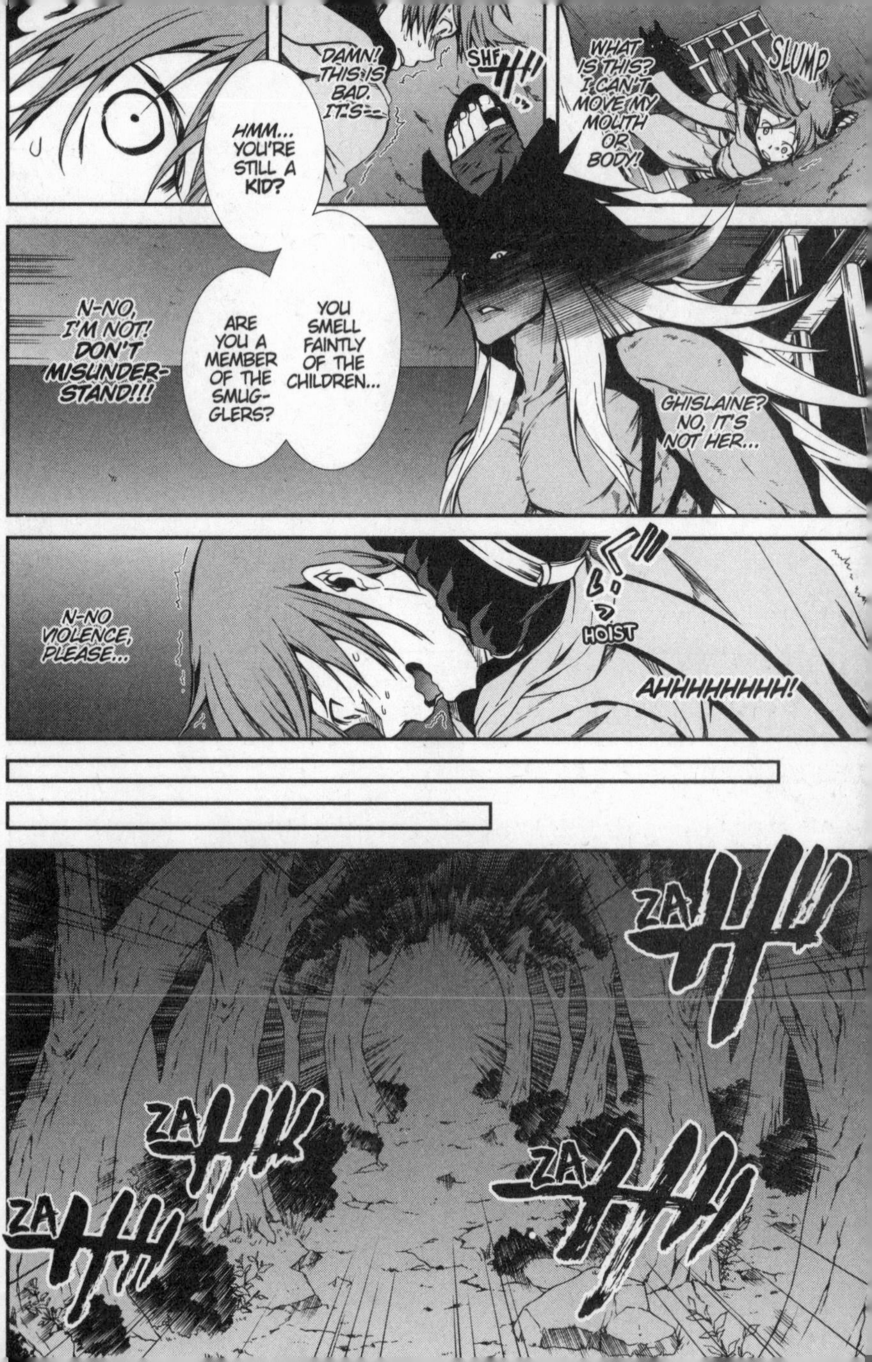
SLUMP
WHAT IS THIS? I CAN'T MOVE MY MOUTH OR BODY!
SHF
DAMN! THIS IS BAD. IT'S—
HMM... YOU'RE STILL A KID?
GHISLAINE? NO, IT'S NOT HER...
YOU SMELL FAINTLY OF THE CHILDREN...
ARE YOU A MEMBER OF THE SMUGGLERS?
N-NO, I'M NOT! DON'T MISUNDERSTAND!!!
HOIST
AHHHHHHHH!
N-NO VIOLENCE, PLEASE...
ZA
ZA
ZA
ZA

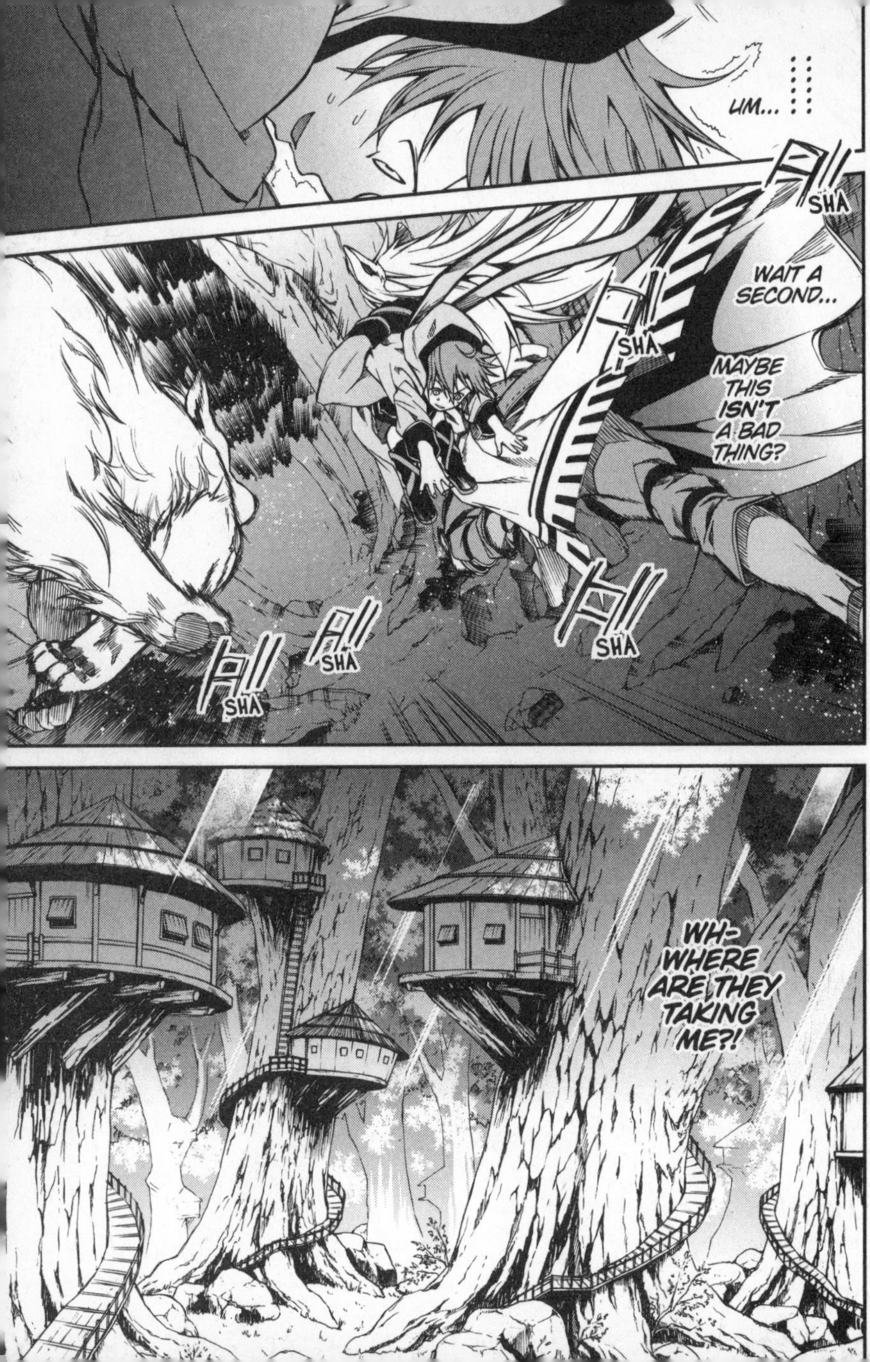
UM... ......
SHA
WAIT A SECOND...
SHA
MAYBE THIS ISN'T A BAD THING?
SHA
SHA
SHA
WH- WHERE ARE THEY TAKING ME?!

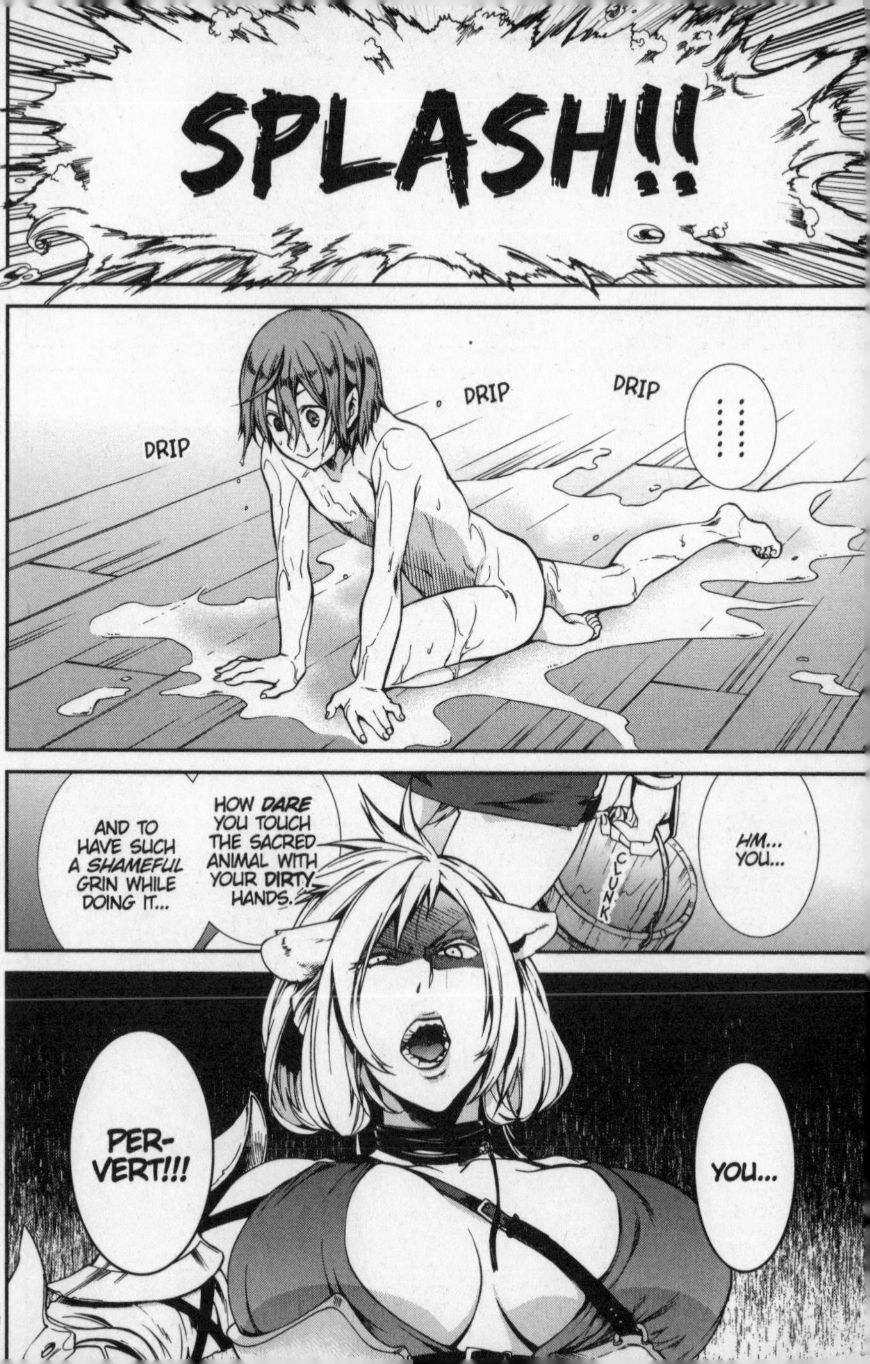
SPLASH!!
......
DRIP
DRIP
DRIP
HM... YOU...
CLUNK
HOW DARE YOU TOUCH THE SACRED ANIMAL WITH YOUR DIRTY HANDS.
AND TO HAVE SUCH A SHAMEFUL GRIN WHILE DOING IT...
YOU...
PER-VERT!!!

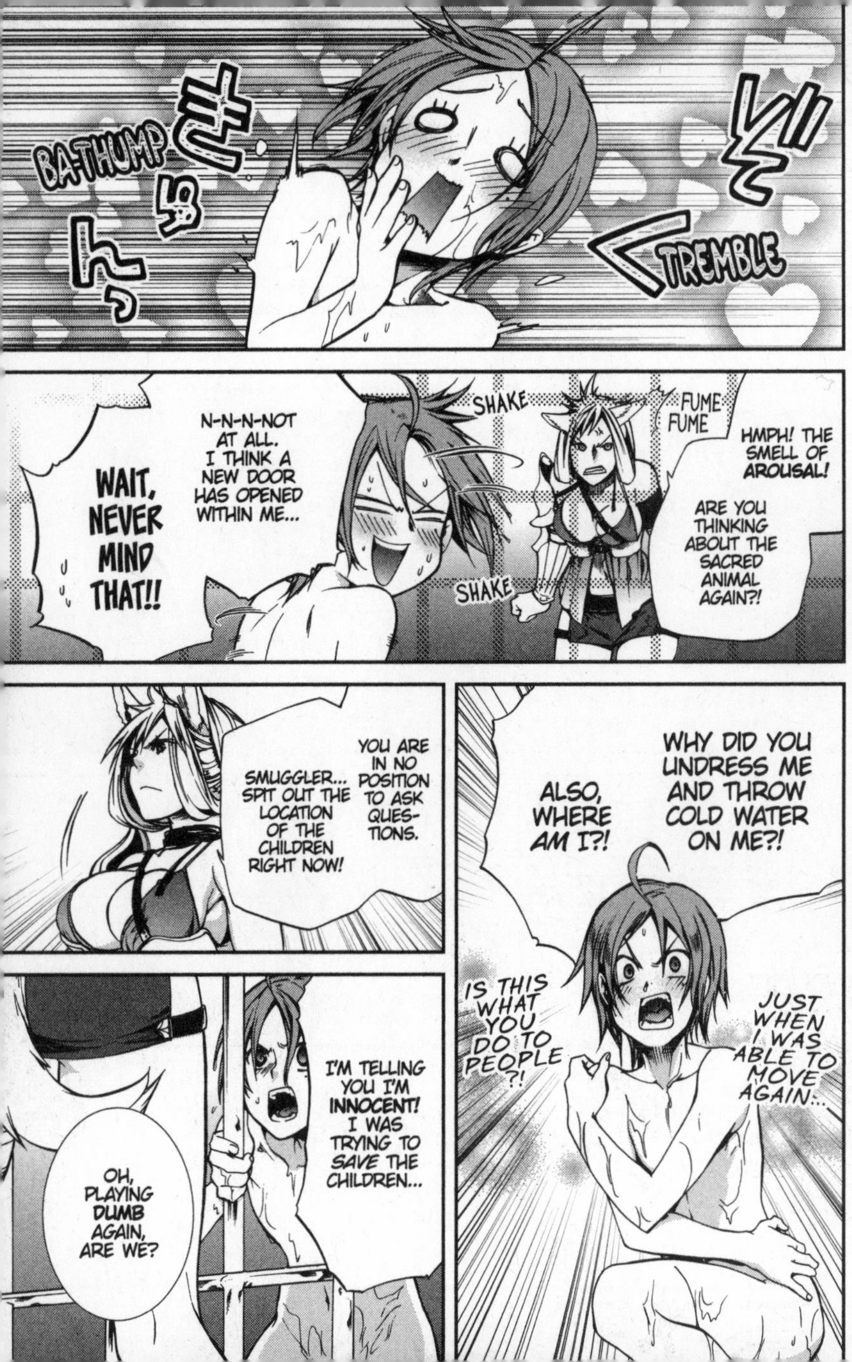
ぞく
TREMBLE
きゅん
BA-THUMP
FUME FUME
HMPH! THE SMELL OF AROUSAL!
ARE YOU THINKING ABOUT THE SACRED ANIMAL AGAIN?!
SHAKE
SHAKE
N-N-N-NOT AT ALL. I THINK A NEW DOOR HAS OPENED WITHIN ME...
WAIT, NEVER MIND THAT!!
WHY DID YOU UNDRESS ME AND THROW COLD WATER ON ME?!
ALSO, WHERE AM I?!
JUST WHEN I WAS ABLE TO MOVE AGAIN...
IS THIS WHAT YOU DO TO PEOPLE?!
YOU ARE IN NO POSITION TO ASK QUES-TIONS.
SMUGGLER... SPIT OUT THE LOCATION OF THE CHILDREN RIGHT NOW!
I'M TELLING YOU I'M INNOCENT! I WAS TRYING TO SAVE THE CHILDREN...
OH, PLAYING DUMB AGAIN, ARE WE?

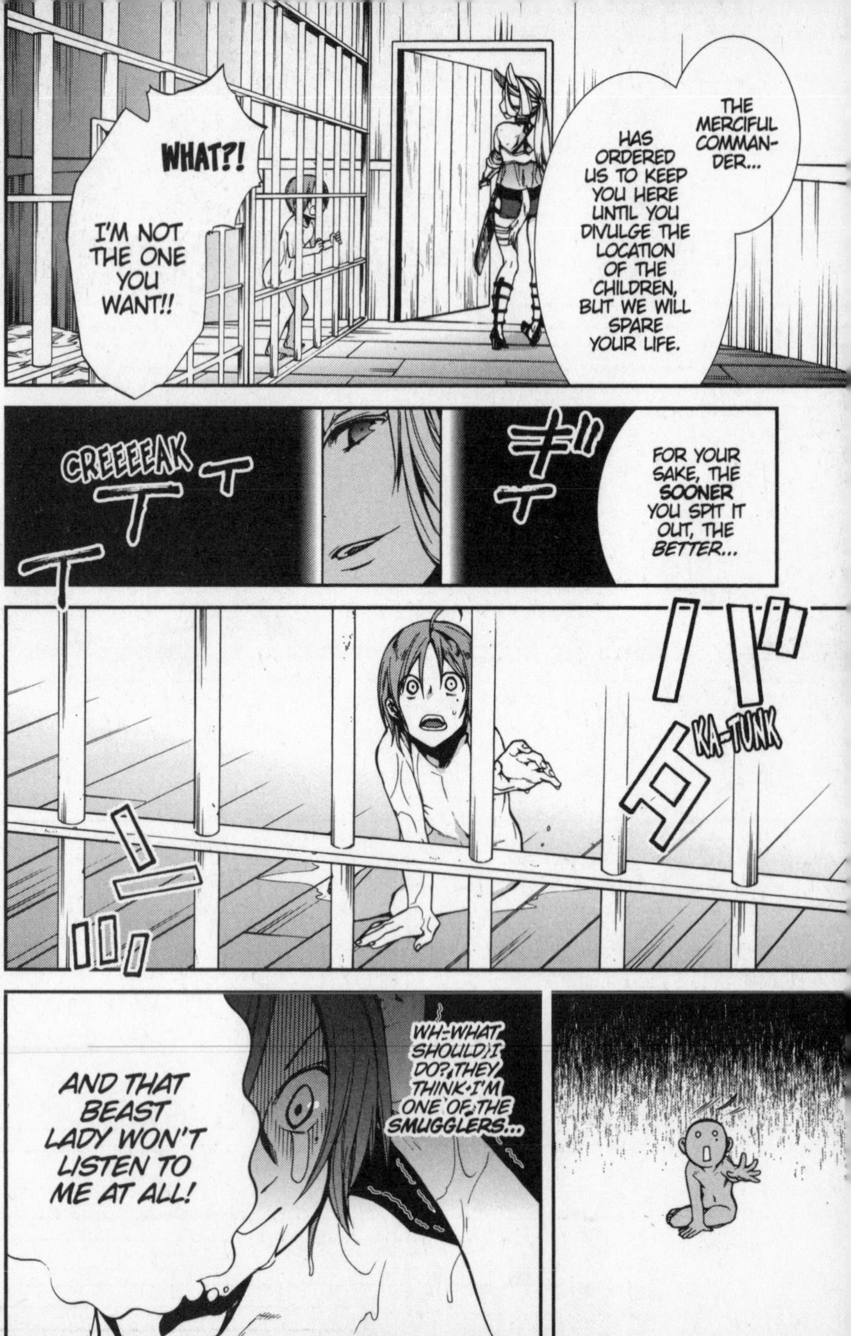
THE MERCIFUL COMMANDER...
HAS ORDERED US TO KEEP YOU HERE UNTIL YOU DIVULGE THE LOCATION OF THE CHILDREN, BUT WE WILL SPARE YOUR LIFE.
WHAT?!
I'M NOT THE ONE YOU WANT!!
FOR YOUR SAKE, THE SOONER YOU SPIT IT OUT, THE BETTER...
CREEEEAK
KA-TUNK
WH-WHAT SHOULD I DO? THEY THINK I'M ONE OF THE SMUGGLERS...
AND THAT BEAST LADY WON'T LISTEN TO ME AT ALL!

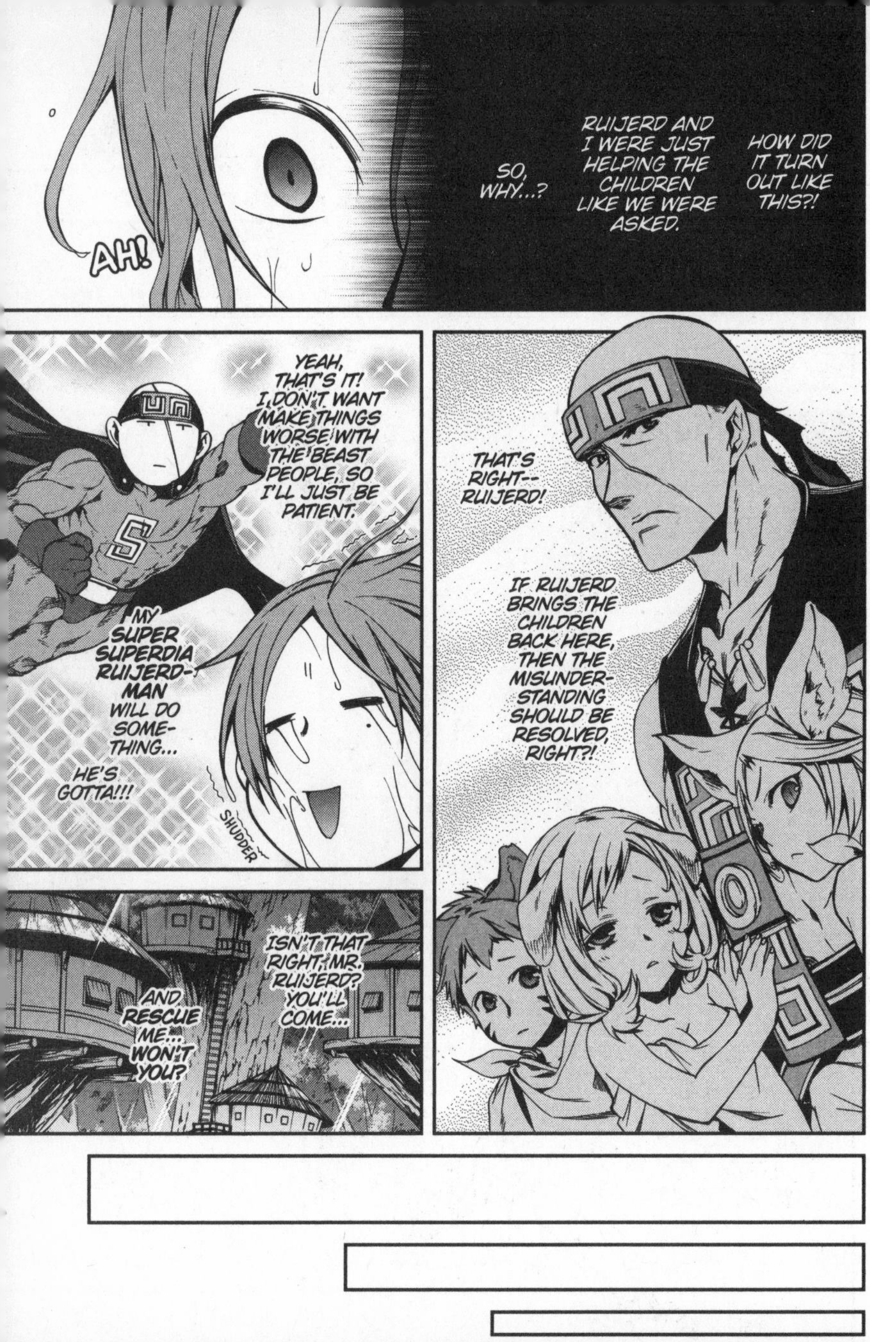
HOW DID IT TURN OUT LIKE THIS?!
RUIJERD AND I WERE JUST HELPING THE CHILDREN LIKE WE WERE ASKED.
SO, WHY...?
AH!
THAT'S RIGHT-- RUIJERD!
IF RUIJERD BRINGS THE CHILDREN BACK HERE, THEN THE MISUNDER-STANDING SHOULD BE RESOLVED, RIGHT?!
YEAH, THAT'S IT! I DON'T WANT MAKE THINGS WORSE WITH THE BEAST PEOPLE, SO I'LL JUST BE PATIENT.
MY SUPER SUPERDIA RUIJERD-MAN WILL DO SOME-THING...
HE'S GOTTA!!!
SHUDDER
ISN'T THAT RIGHT, MR. RUIJERD? YOU'LL COME...
AND RESCUE ME... WON'T YOU?

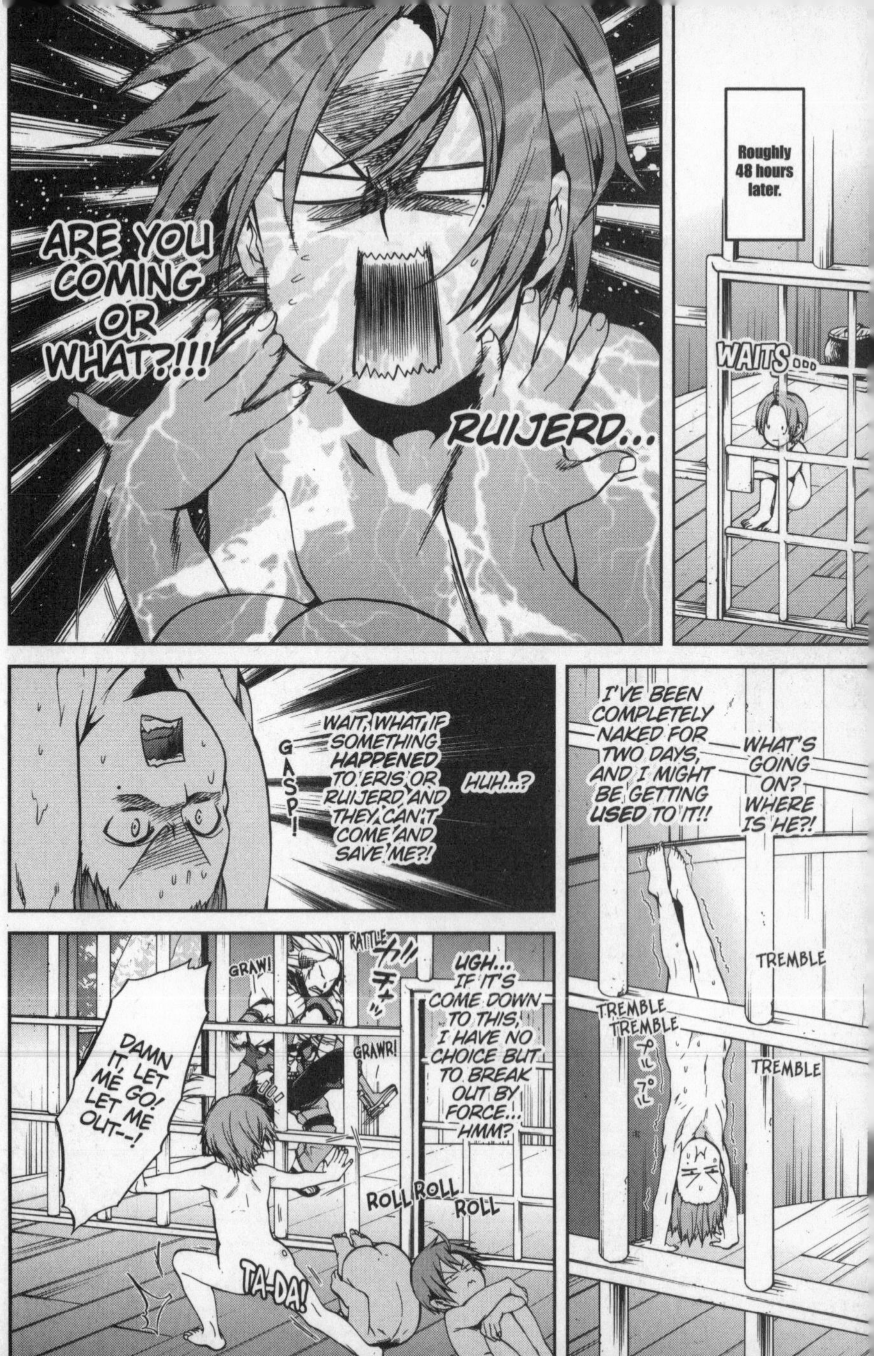

Roughly 48 hours later.
WAITS...
RUIJERD...
ARE YOU COMING OR WHAT?!!!
WHAT'S GOING ON? WHERE IS HE?!
I'VE BEEN COMPLETELY NAKED FOR TWO DAYS, AND I MIGHT BE GETTING USED TO IT!!
TREMBLE
TREMBLE TREMBLE
TREMBLE
HUH...?
WAIT, WHAT IF SOMETHING HAPPENED TO ERIS OR RUIJERD AND THEY CAN'T COME AND SAVE ME?!
GASP!
RATTLE
UGH... IF IT'S COME DOWN TO THIS, I HAVE NO CHOICE BUT TO BREAK OUT BY FORCE... HMM?
GRAW!
GRAWR!
DAMN IT, LET ME GO! LET ME OUT--!
ROLL ROLL ROLL
TA-DA!

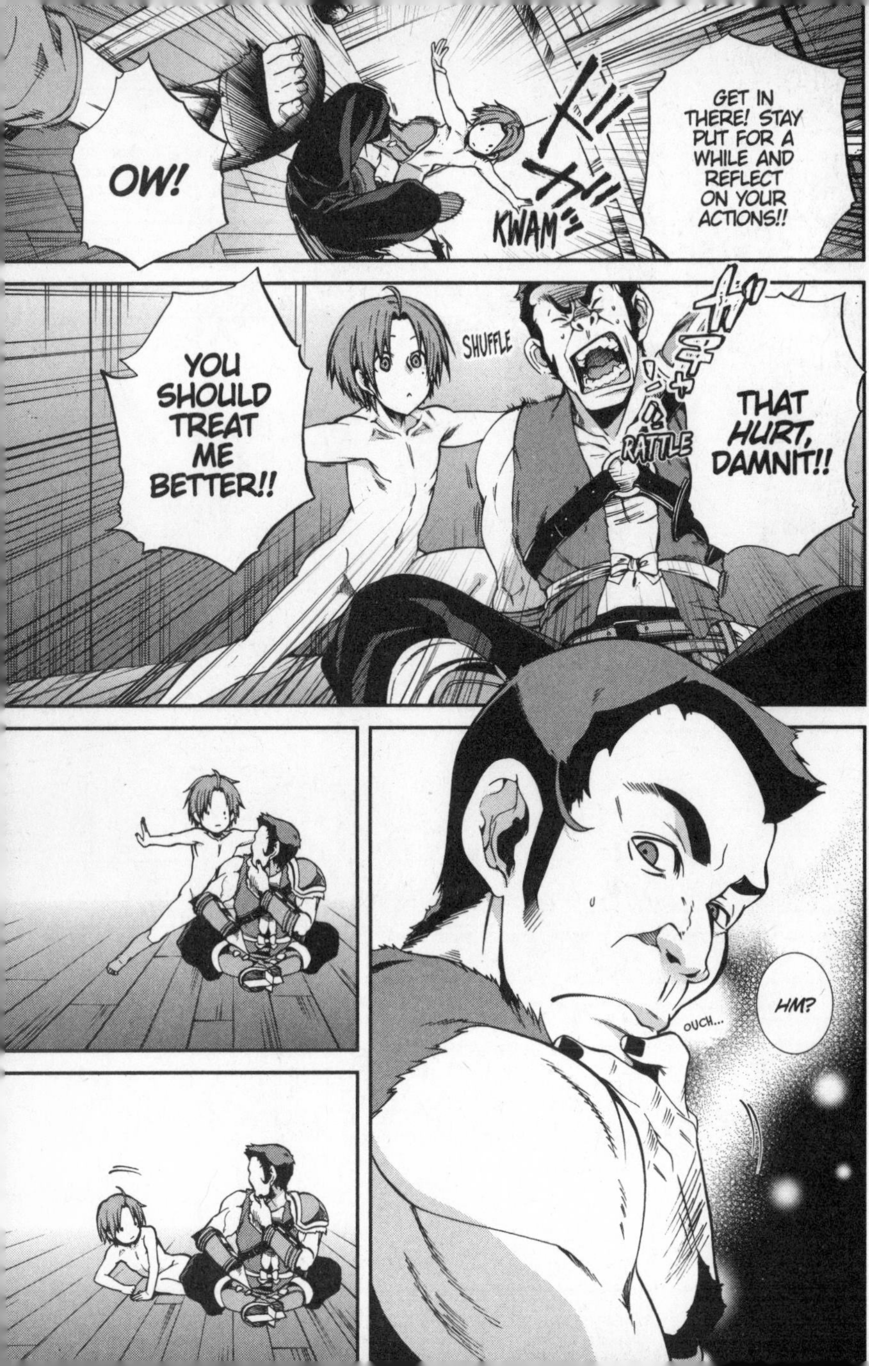
GET IN THERE! STAY PUT FOR A WHILE AND REFLECT ON YOUR ACTIONS!!
KWAM
OW!
THAT HURT, DAMNIT!!
RATTLE
SHUFFLE
YOU SHOULD TREAT ME BETTER!!
HM?
OUCH...

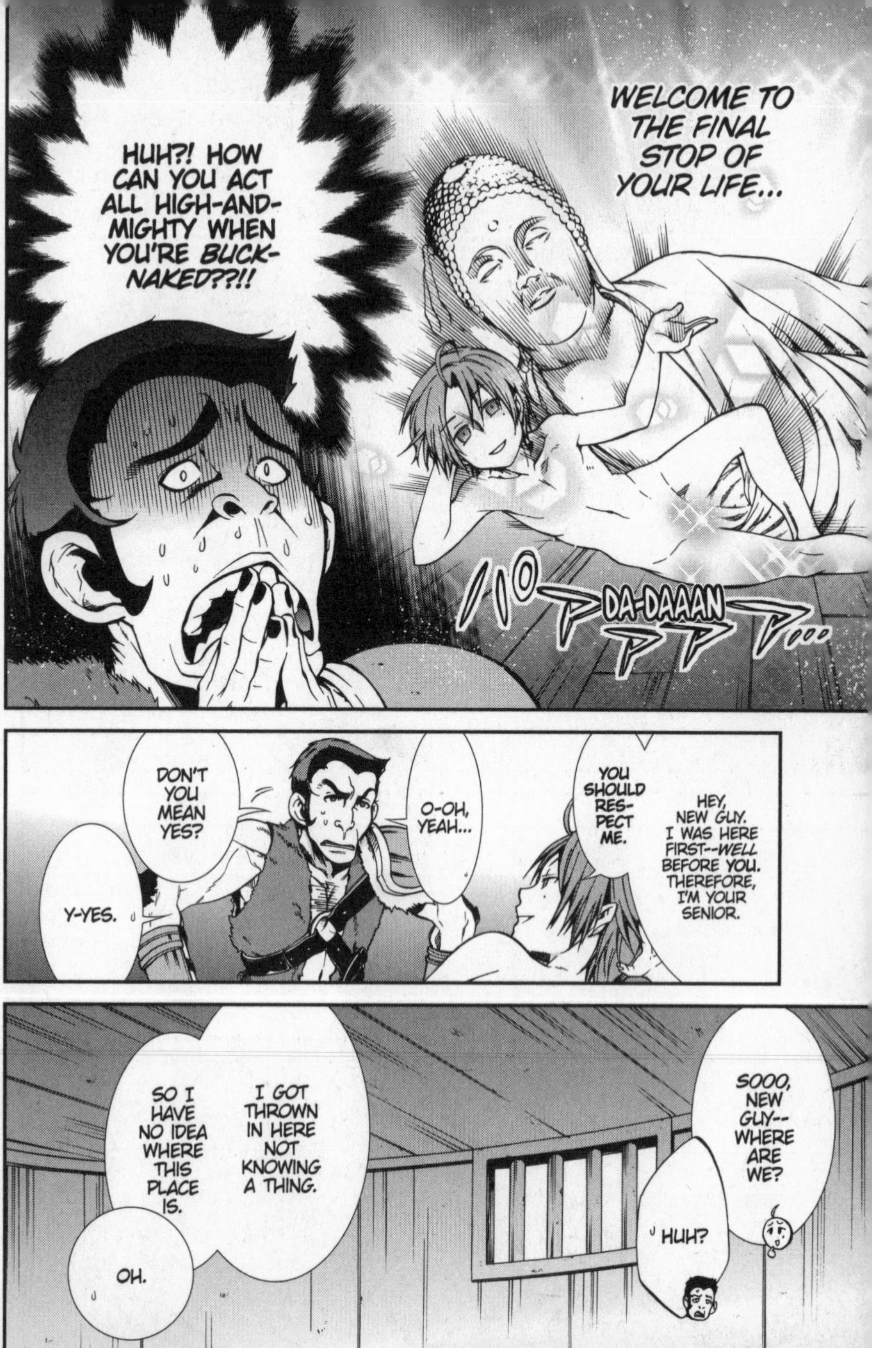
WELCOME TO THE FINAL STOP OF YOUR LIFE...
HUH?! HOW CAN YOU ACT ALL HIGH-AND-MIGHTY WHEN YOU'RE BUCK-NAKED??!!
DA-DAAAN
HEY, NEW GUY. I WAS HERE FIRST--WELL BEFORE YOU. THEREFORE, I'M YOUR SENIOR.
YOU SHOULD RES-PECT ME.
O-OH, YEAH...
DON'T YOU MEAN YES?
Y-YES.
SOOO, NEW GUY-- WHERE ARE WE?
HUH?
I GOT THROWN IN HERE NOT KNOWING A THING.
SO I HAVE NO IDEA WHERE THIS PLACE IS.
OH.

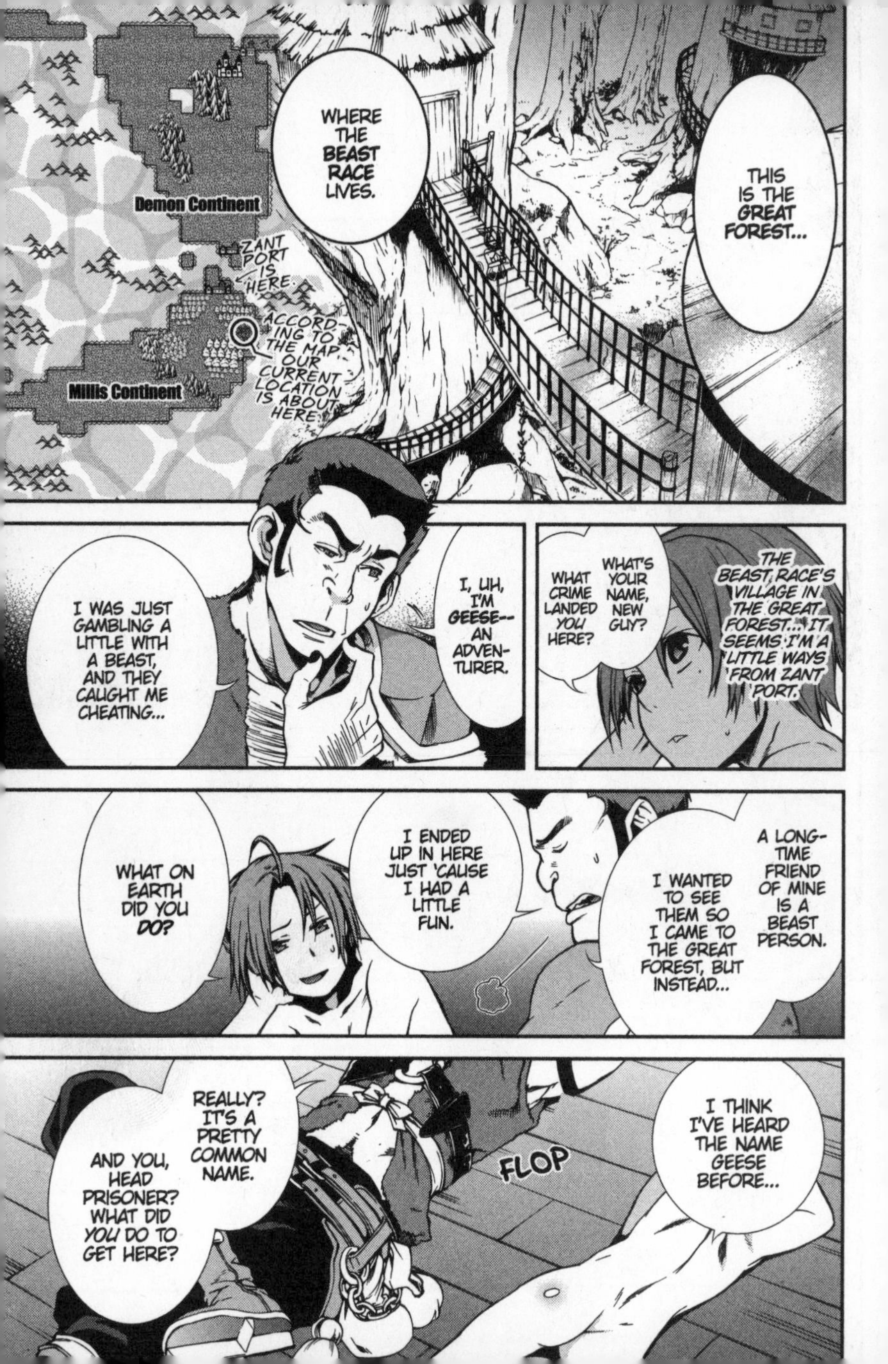
THIS IS THE GREAT FOREST...
WHERE THE BEAST RACE LIVES.
Demon Continent
ZANT PORT IS HERE.
ACCORDING TO THE MAP, OUR CURRENT LOCATION IS ABOUT HERE.
Millis Continent
THE BEAST RACE'S VILLAGE IN THE GREAT FOREST... IT SEEMS I'M A LITTLE WAYS FROM ZANT PORT.
WHAT'S YOUR NAME, NEW GUY?
WHAT CRIME LANDED YOU HERE?
I, UH, I'M GEESE-- AN ADVENTURER.
I WAS JUST GAMBLING A LITTLE WITH A BEAST, AND THEY CAUGHT ME CHEATING...
A LONG-TIME FRIEND OF MINE IS A BEAST PERSON.
I WANTED TO SEE THEM SO I CAME TO THE GREAT FOREST, BUT INSTEAD...
I ENDED UP IN HERE JUST 'CAUSE I HAD A LITTLE FUN.
WHAT ON EARTH DID YOU DO?
I THINK I'VE HEARD THE NAME GEESE BEFORE...
FLOP
REALLY? IT'S A PRETTY COMMON NAME.
AND YOU, HEAD PRISONER? WHAT DID YOU DO TO GET HERE?

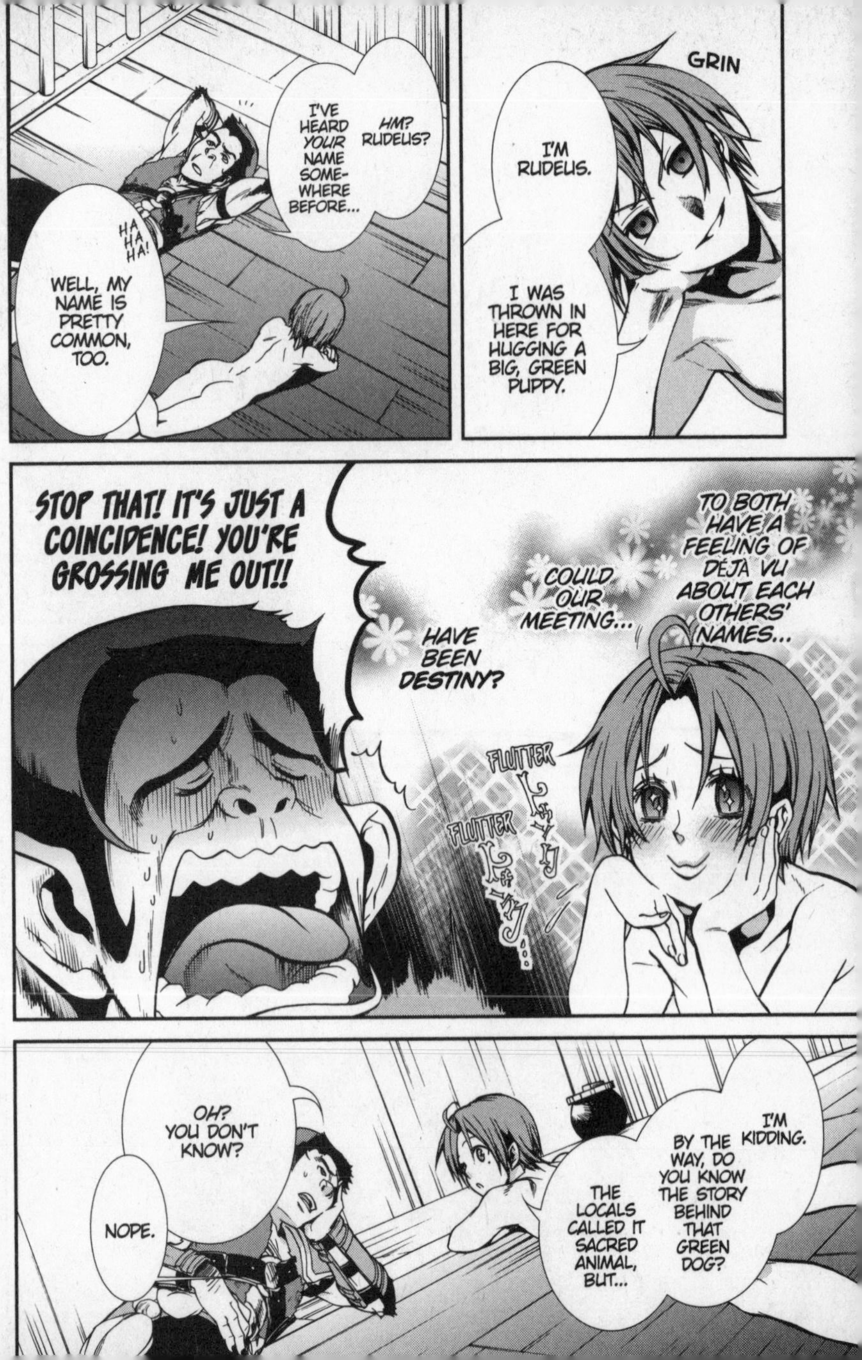
GRIN
I'M RUDEUS.
I WAS THROWN IN HERE FOR HUGGING A BIG, GREEN PUPPY.
HM? RUDEUS?
I'VE HEARD YOUR NAME SOME-WHERE BEFORE...
HA HA HA!
WELL, MY NAME IS PRETTY COMMON, TOO.
TO BOTH HAVE A FEELING OF DÉJA VU ABOUT EACH OTHERS' NAMES...
COULD OUR MEETING...
HAVE BEEN DESTINY?
FLUTTER
FLUTTER
STOP THAT! IT'S JUST A COINCIDENCE! YOU'RE GROSSING ME OUT!!
I'M KIDDING.
BY THE WAY, DO YOU KNOW THE STORY BEHIND THAT GREEN DOG?
OH? YOU DON'T KNOW?
THE LOCALS CALLED IT SACRED ANIMAL, BUT...
NOPE.

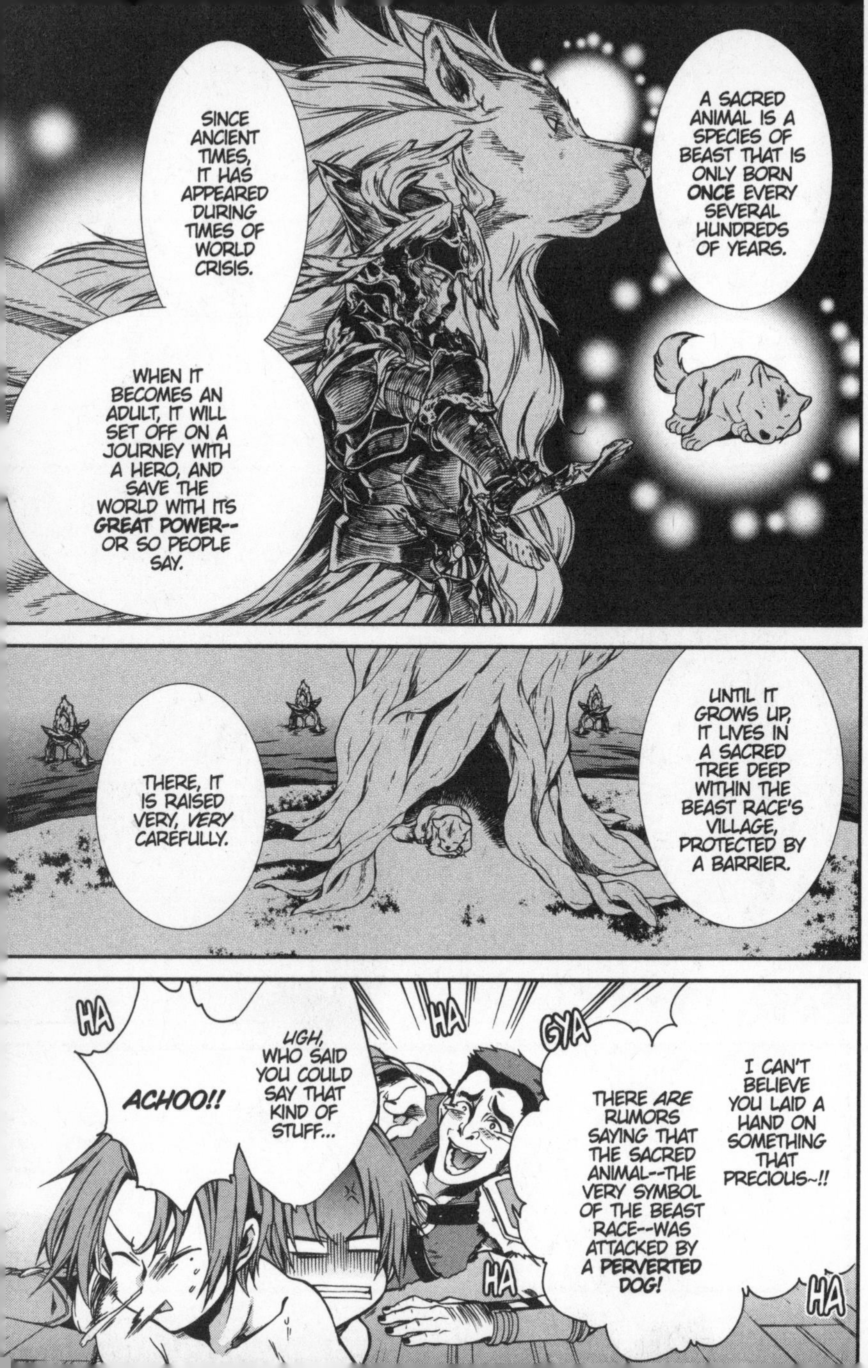
A SACRED ANIMAL IS A SPECIES OF BEAST THAT IS ONLY BORN ONCE EVERY SEVERAL HUNDREDS OF YEARS.
SINCE ANCIENT TIMES, IT HAS APPEARED DURING TIMES OF WORLD CRISIS.
WHEN IT BECOMES AN ADULT, IT WILL SET OFF ON A JOURNEY WITH A HERO, AND SAVE THE WORLD WITH ITS GREAT POWER--OR SO PEOPLE SAY.
UNTIL IT GROWS UP, IT LIVES IN A SACRED TREE DEEP WITHIN THE BEAST RACE'S VILLAGE, PROTECTED BY A BARRIER.
THERE, IT IS RAISED VERY, *VERY* CAREFULLY.
I CAN'T BELIEVE YOU LAID A HAND ON SOMETHING THAT PRECIOUS~!!
THERE *ARE* RUMORS SAYING THAT THE SACRED ANIMAL--THE VERY SYMBOL OF THE BEAST RACE--WAS ATTACKED BY A PERVERTED DOG!
HA
GYA
HA
HA
UGH, WHO SAID YOU COULD SAY THAT KIND OF STUFF...
ACHOO!!
HA

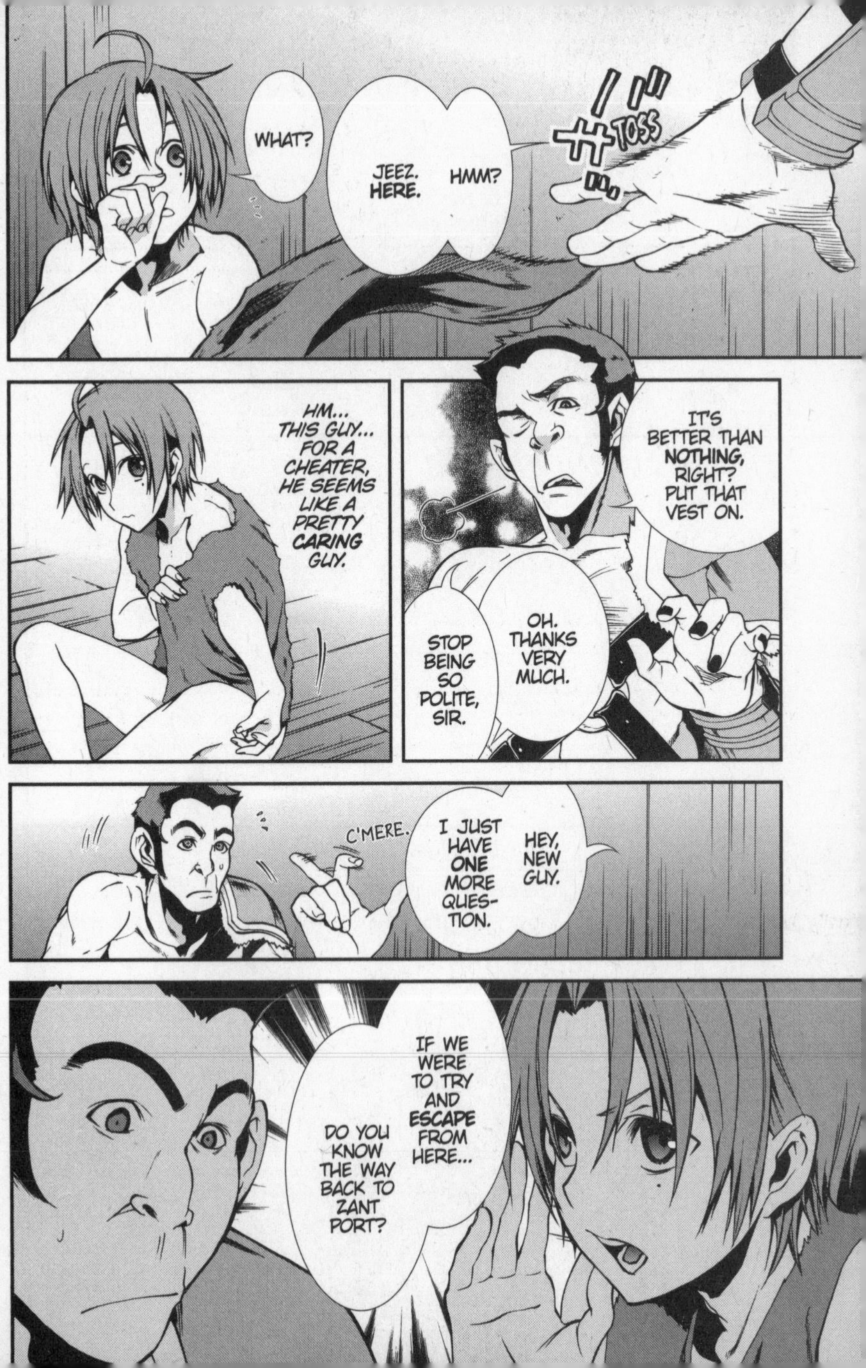
TOSS
HMM?
JEEZ. HERE.
WHAT?
IT'S BETTER THAN NOTHING, RIGHT? PUT THAT VEST ON.
OH. THANKS VERY MUCH.
STOP BEING SO POLITE, SIR.
HM... THIS GUY... FOR A CHEATER, HE SEEMS LIKE A PRETTY CARING GUY.
HEY, NEW GUY.
I JUST HAVE ONE MORE QUESTION.
C'MERE.
IF WE WERE TO TRY AND ESCAPE FROM HERE...
DO YOU KNOW THE WAY BACK TO ZANT PORT?

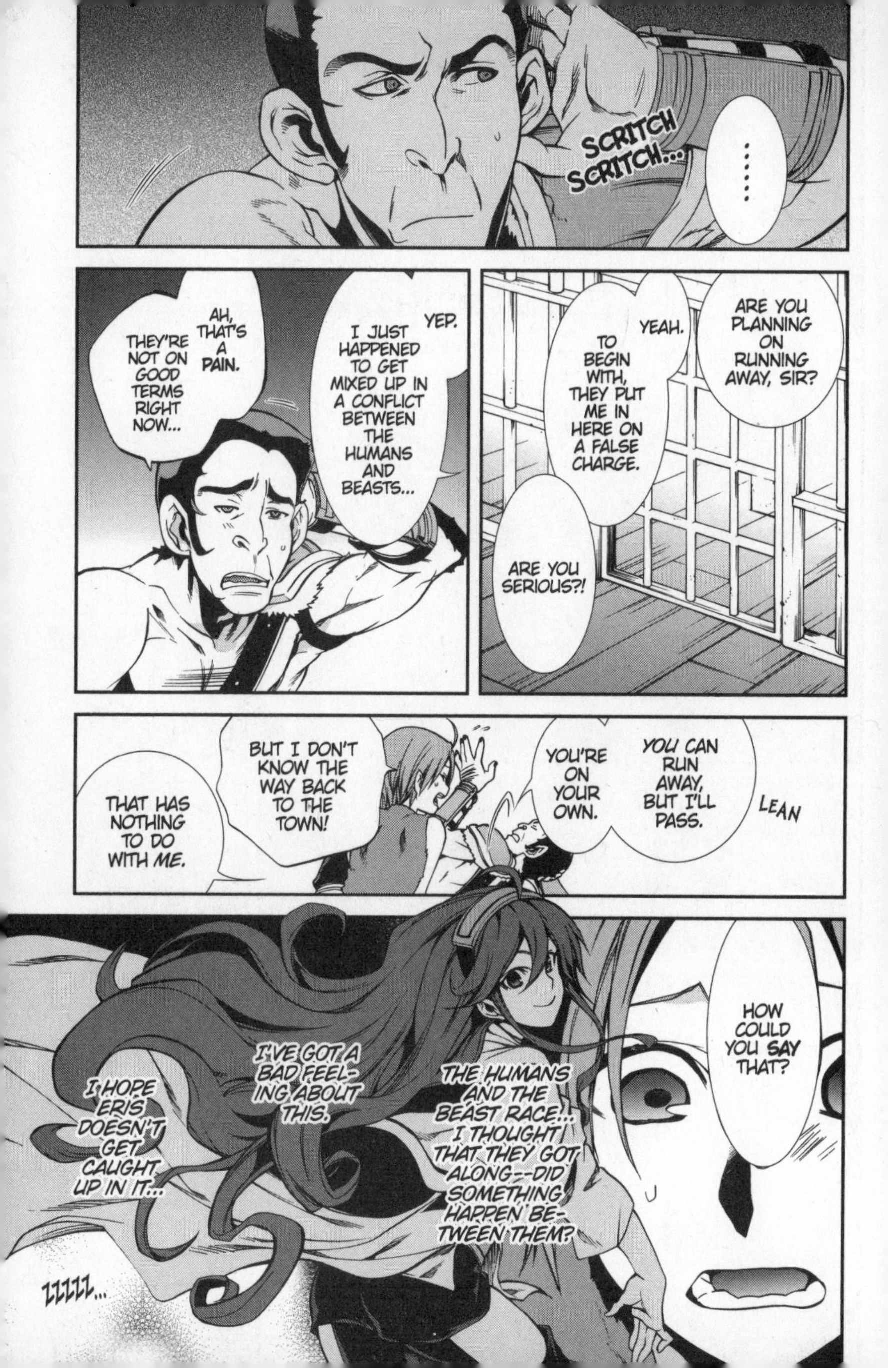
......
SCRITCH SCRITCH...
ARE YOU PLANNING ON RUNNING AWAY, SIR?
YEAH.
TO BEGIN WITH, THEY PUT ME IN HERE ON A FALSE CHARGE.
ARE YOU SERIOUS?!
YEP.
I JUST HAPPENED TO GET MIXED UP IN A CONFLICT BETWEEN THE HUMANS AND BEASTS...
AH, THAT'S A PAIN.
THEY'RE NOT ON GOOD TERMS RIGHT NOW...
LEAN
YOU CAN RUN AWAY, BUT I'LL PASS.
YOU'RE ON YOUR OWN.
BUT I DON'T KNOW THE WAY BACK TO THE TOWN!
THAT HAS NOTHING TO DO WITH ME.
HOW COULD YOU SAY THAT?
THE HUMANS AND THE BEAST RACE... I THOUGHT THAT THEY GOT ALONG--DID SOMETHING HAPPEN BETWEEN THEM?
I'VE GOT A BAD FEELING ABOUT THIS.
I HOPE ERIS DOESN'T GET CAUGHT UP IN IT...
ZZZZZ...

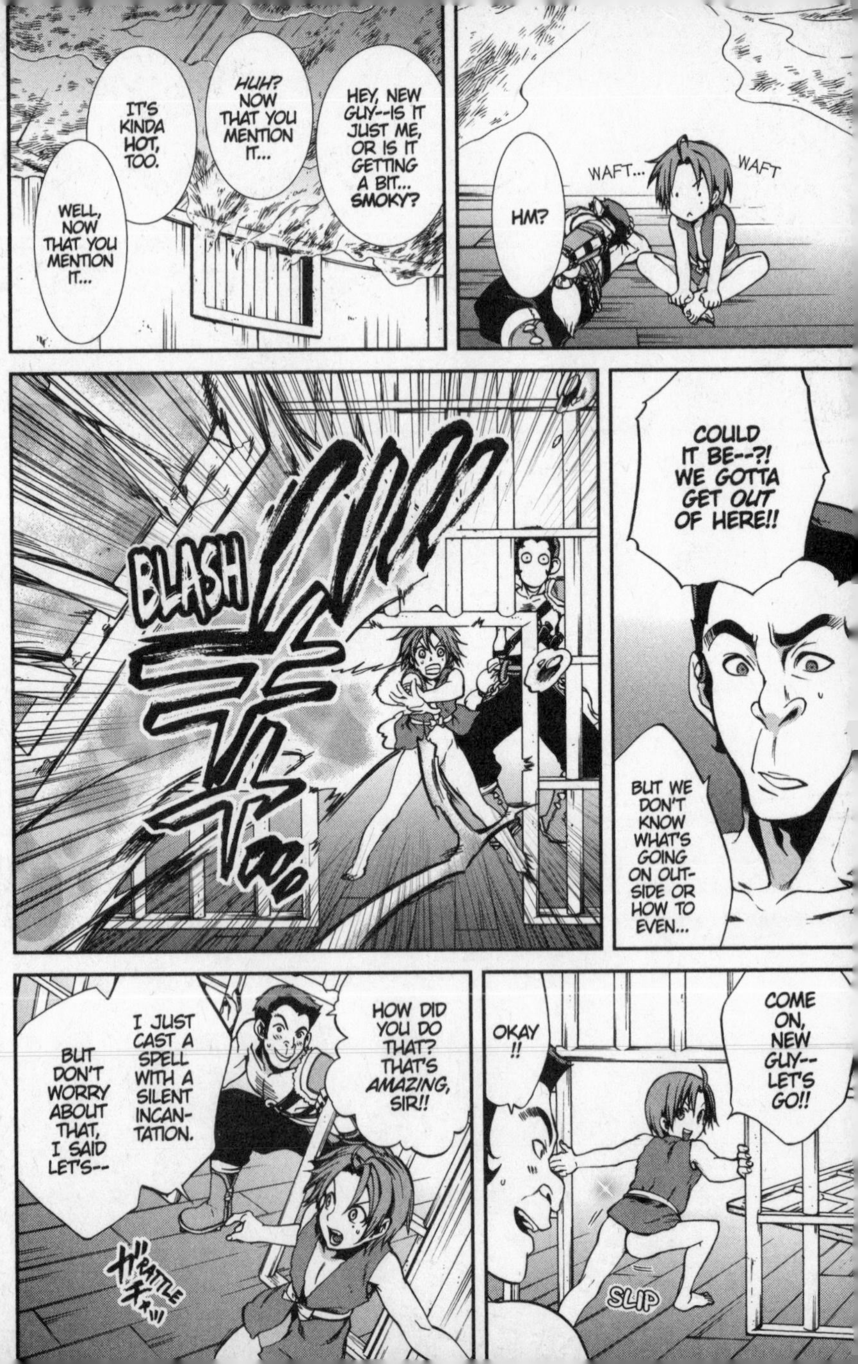
WAFT... WAFT
HM?
HEY, NEW GUY--IS IT JUST ME, OR IS IT GETTING A BIT... SMOKY?
HUH? NOW THAT YOU MENTION IT...
IT'S KINDA HOT, TOO.
WELL, NOW THAT YOU MENTION IT...
COULD IT BE--?! WE GOTTA GET OUT OF HERE!!
BUT WE DON'T KNOW WHAT'S GOING ON OUT-SIDE OR HOW TO EVEN...
BLASH
COME ON, NEW GUY--LET'S GO!!
OKAY!!
SLIP
HOW DID YOU DO THAT? THAT'S AMAZING, SIR!!
I JUST CAST A SPELL WITH A SILENT INCAN-TATION.
BUT DON'T WORRY ABOUT THAT, I SAID LET'S--
RATTLE

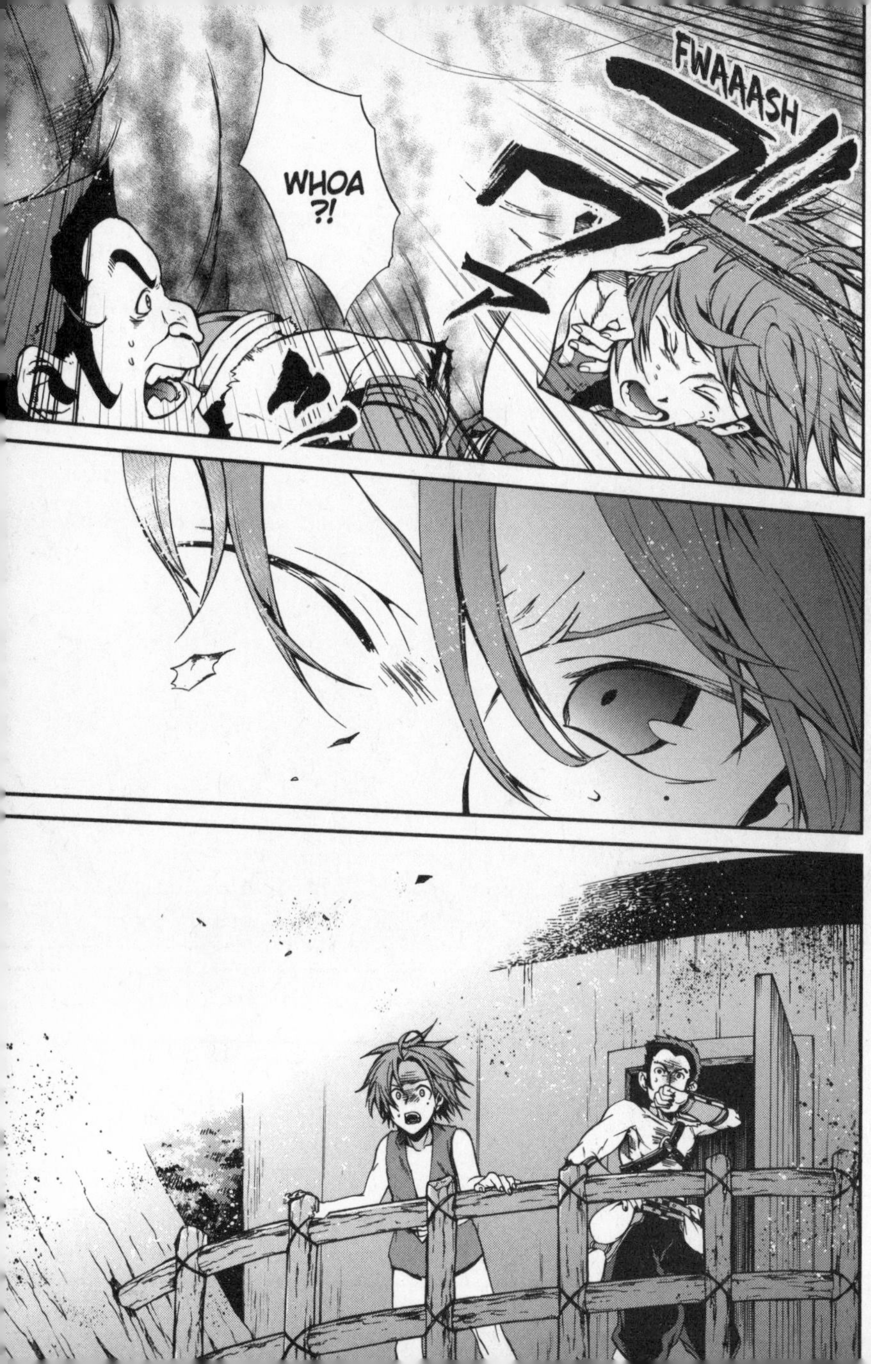
FWAAASH
WHOA ?!

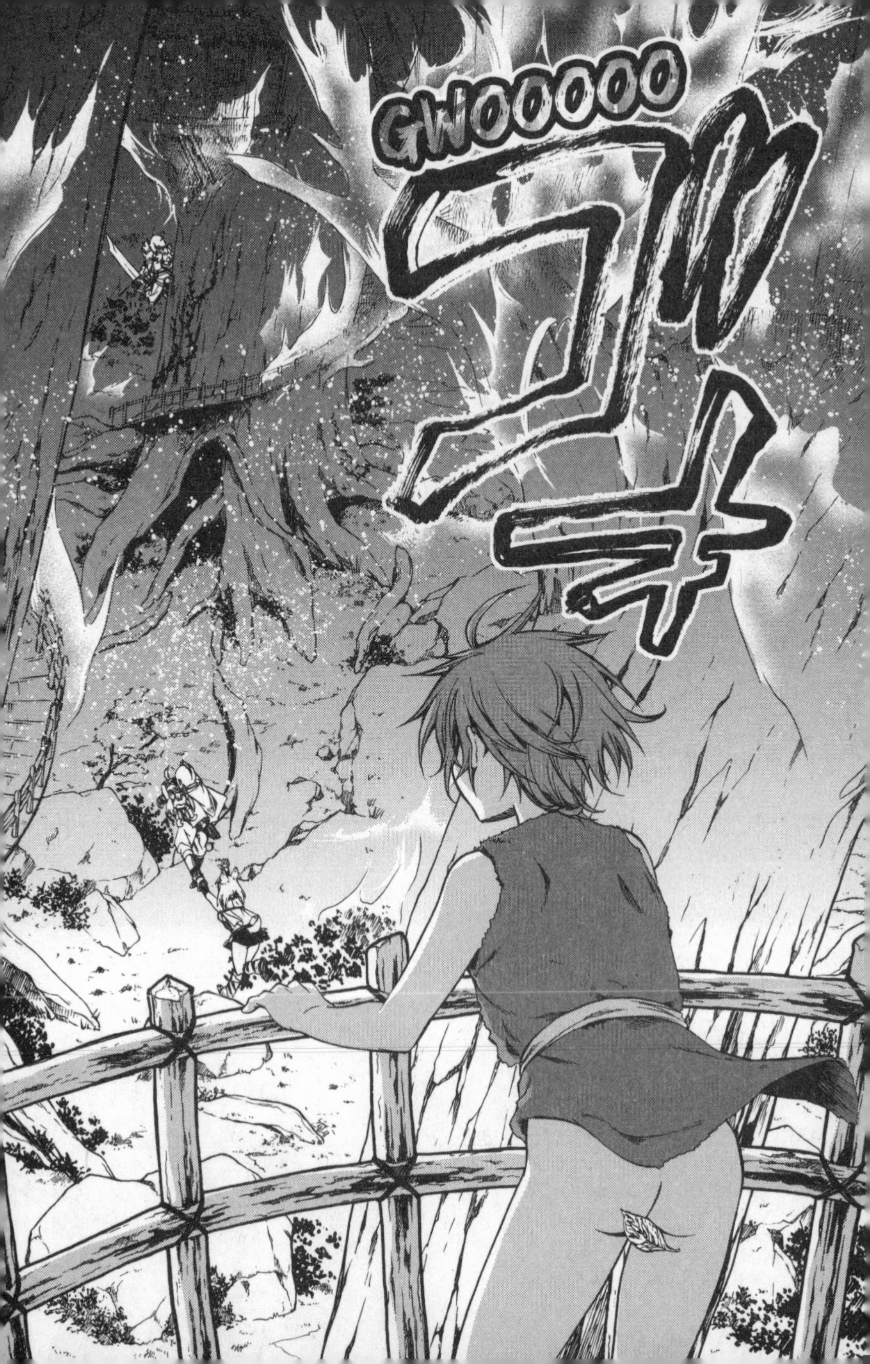
GWOOOOO

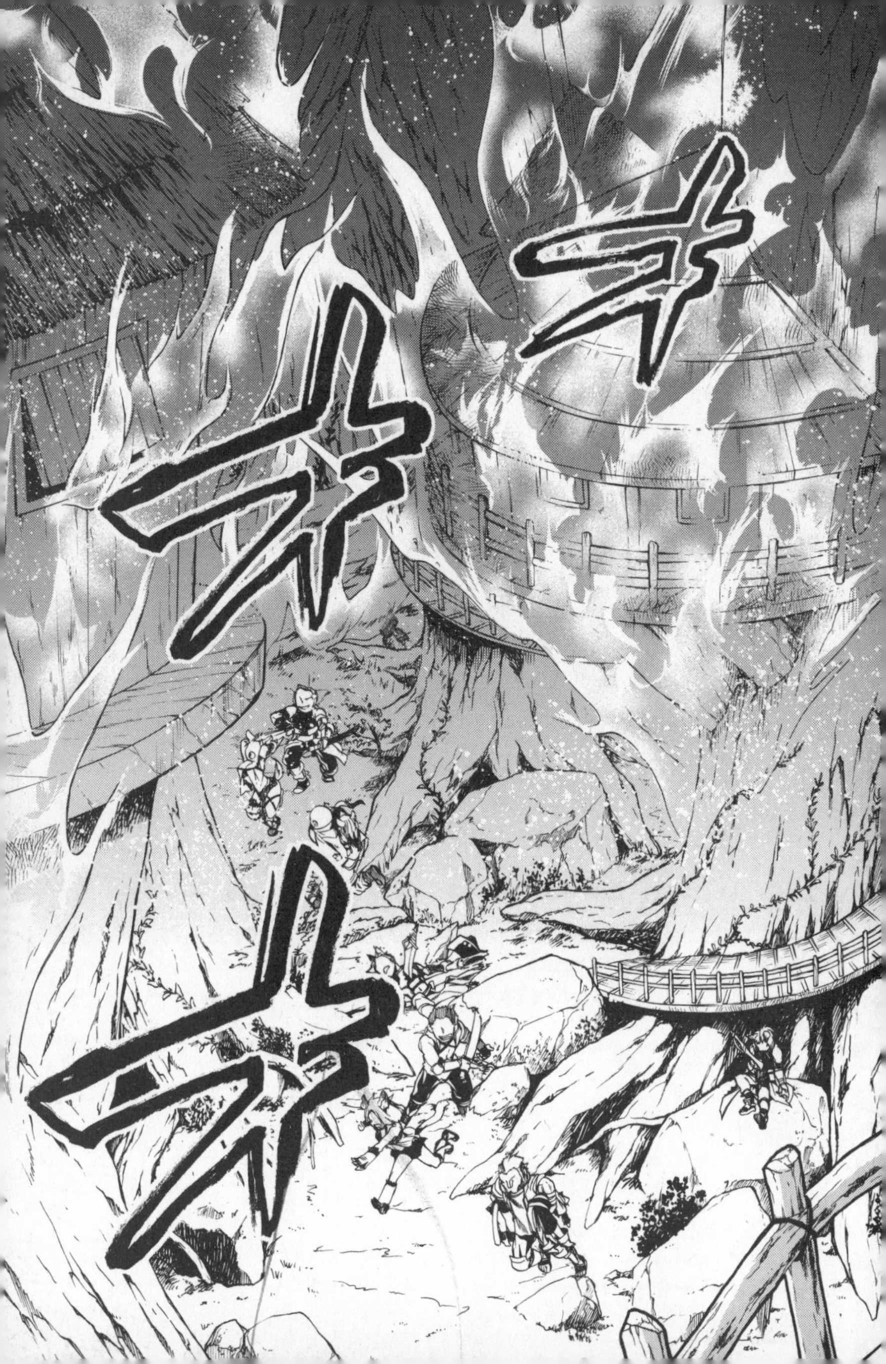

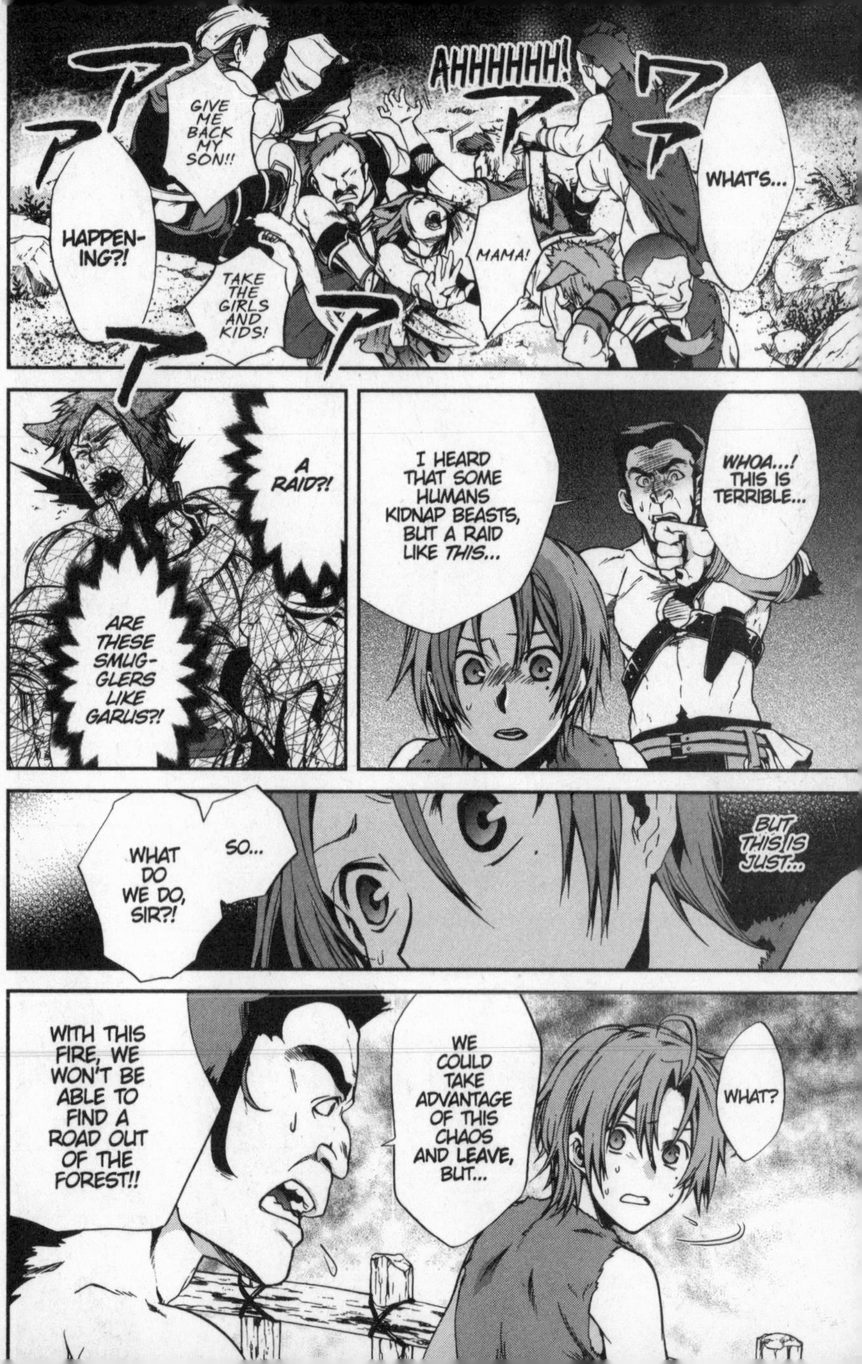
AHHHHHH!
WHAT'S...
HAPPEN-ING?!
MAMA!
GIVE ME BACK MY SON!!
TAKE THE GIRLS AND KIDS!
WHOA...! THIS IS TERRIBLE...
I HEARD THAT SOME HUMANS KIDNAP BEASTS, BUT A RAID LIKE THIS...
A RAID?!
ARE THESE SMUG-GLERS LIKE GARUS?!
BUT THIS IS JUST...
SO...
WHAT DO WE DO, SIR?!
WHAT?
WE COULD TAKE ADVANTAGE OF THIS CHAOS AND LEAVE, BUT...
WITH THIS FIRE, WE WON'T BE ABLE TO FIND A ROAD OUT OF THE FOREST!!

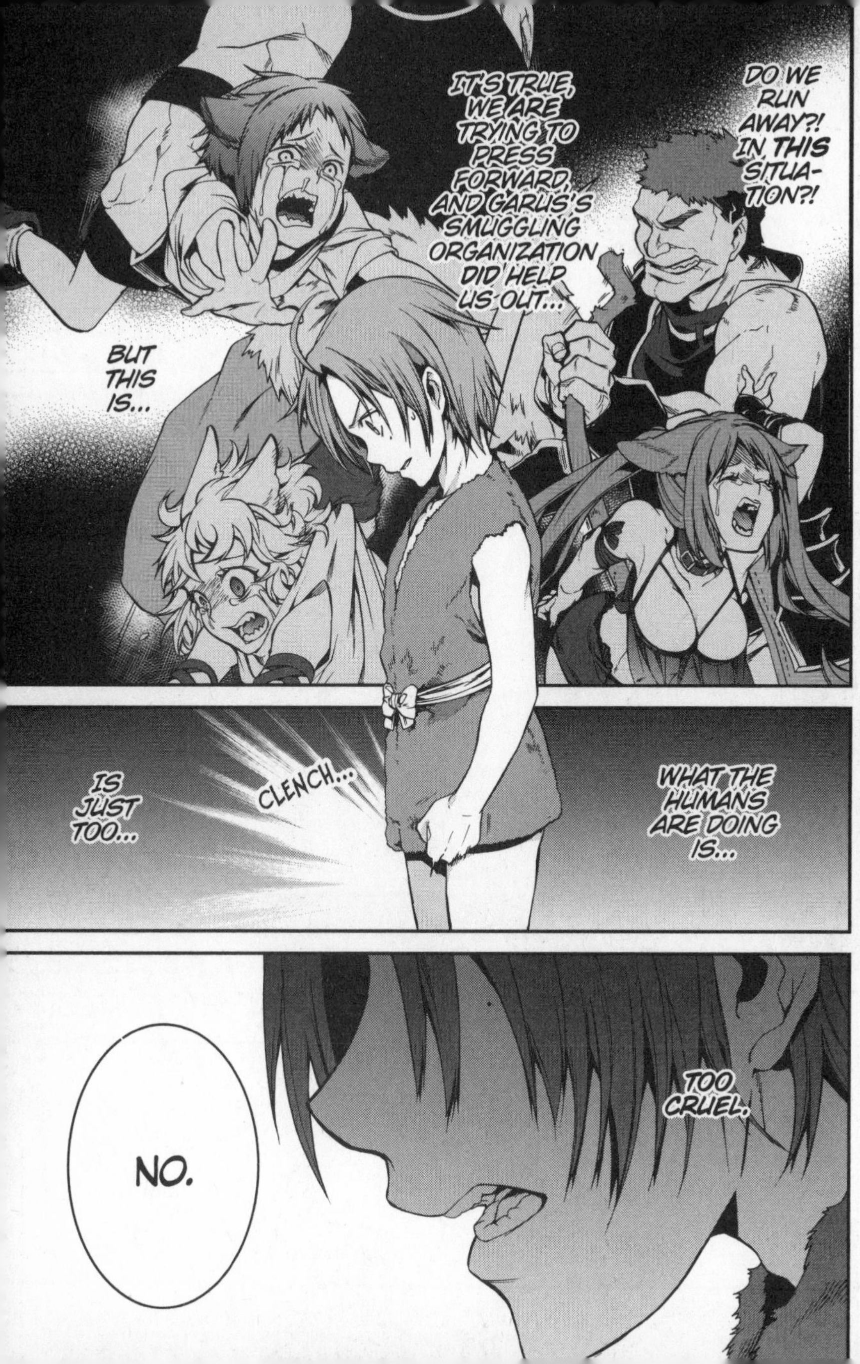
DO WE RUN AWAY?! IN THIS SITUATION?!
IT'S TRUE, WE ARE TRYING TO PRESS FORWARD, AND GARUS'S SMUGGLING ORGANIZATION DID HELP US OUT...
BUT THIS IS...
WHAT THE HUMANS ARE DOING IS...
CLENCH...
IS JUST TOO...
TOO CRUEL.
NO.

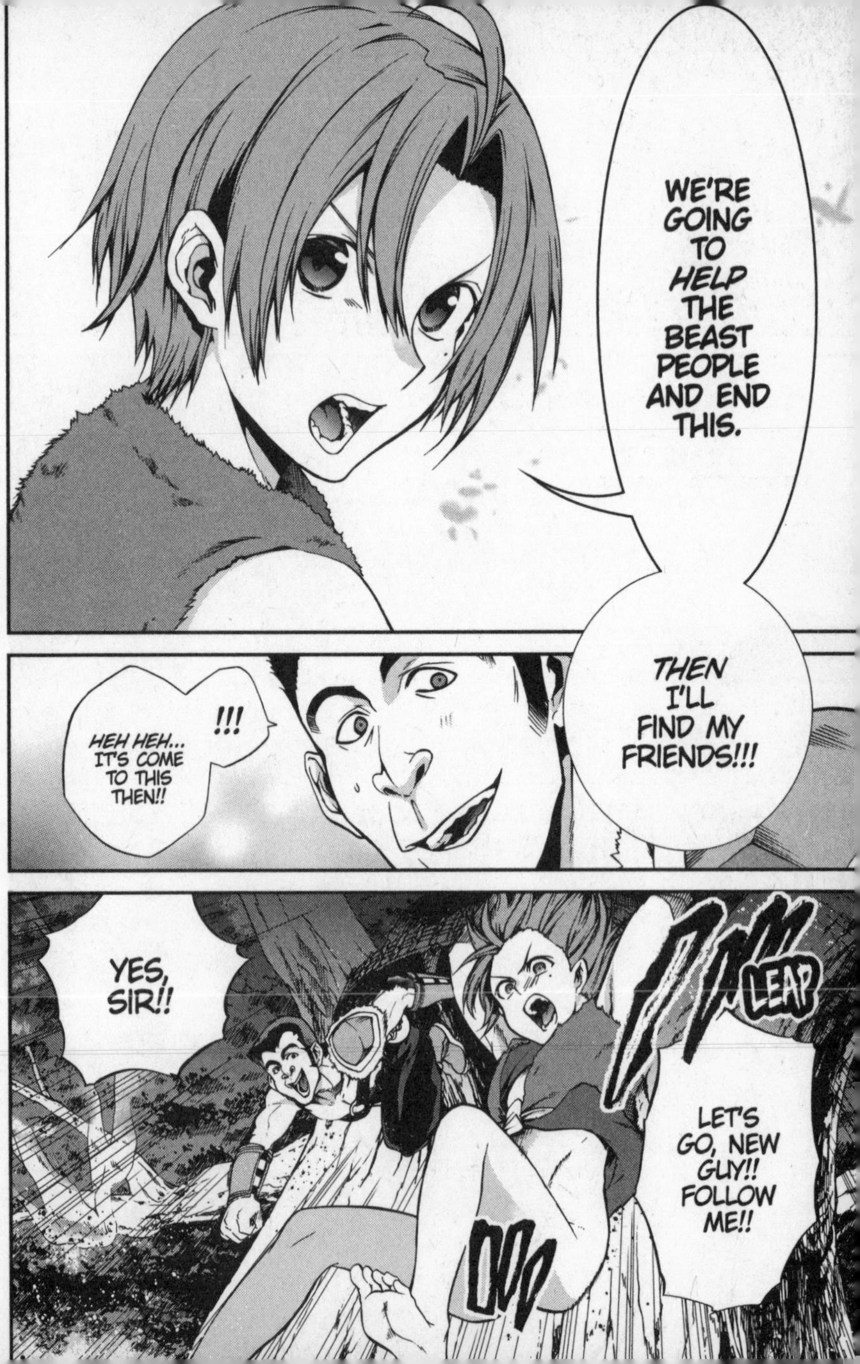
WE'RE GOING TO *HELP* THE BEAST PEOPLE AND END THIS.
THEN I'LL FIND MY FRIENDS!!!
!!!
HEH HEH... IT'S COME TO THIS THEN!!
LEAP
LET'S GO, NEW GUY!! FOLLOW ME!!
YES, SIR!!

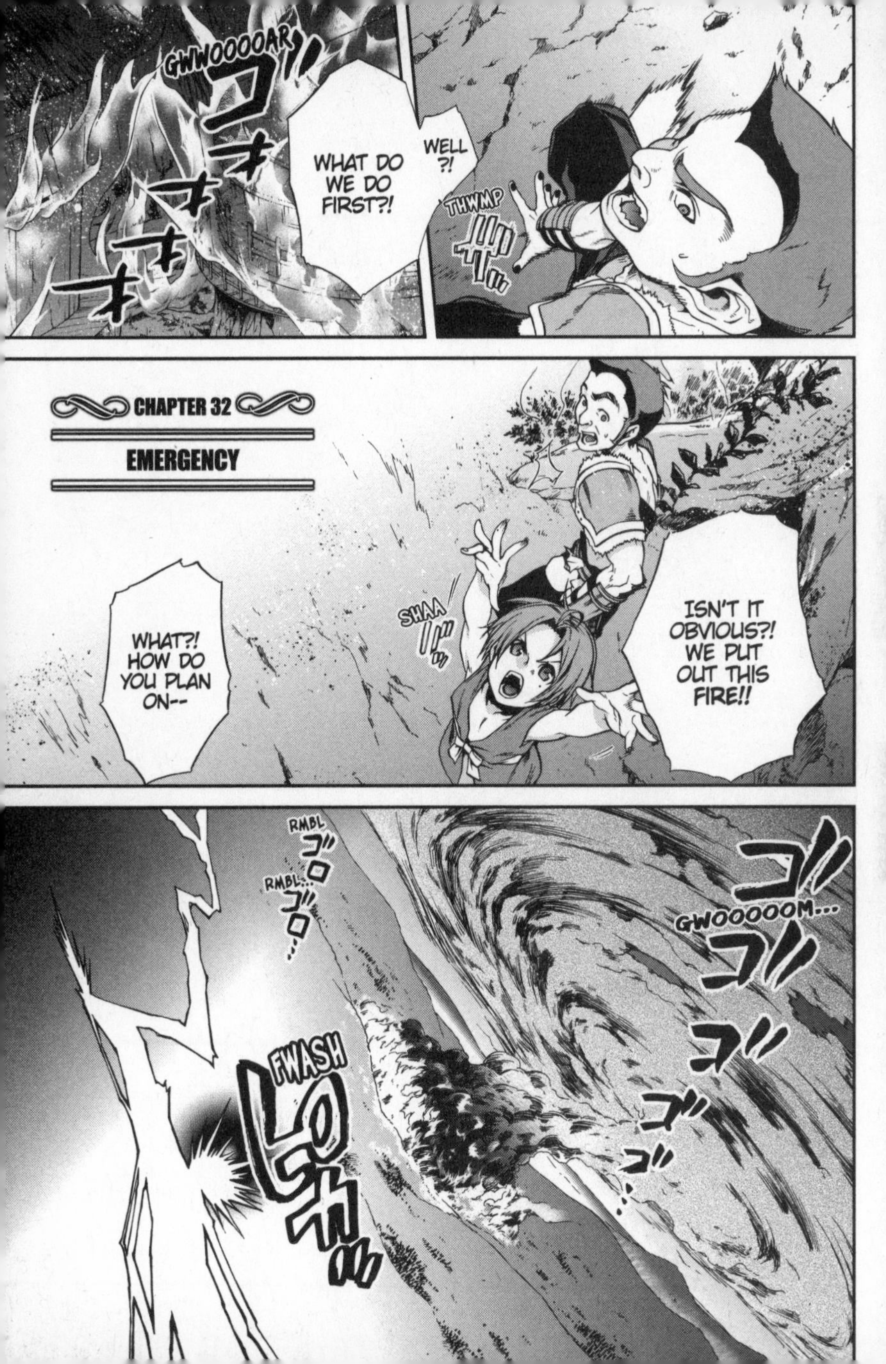
WELL?!
WHAT DO WE DO FIRST?!
THWMP
GWOOOOAR
CHAPTER 32
EMERGENCY
ISN'T IT OBVIOUS?! WE PUT OUT THIS FIRE!!
SHAA
WHAT?! HOW DO YOU PLAN ON--
GWOOOOOM...
RMBL
RMBL
FWASH

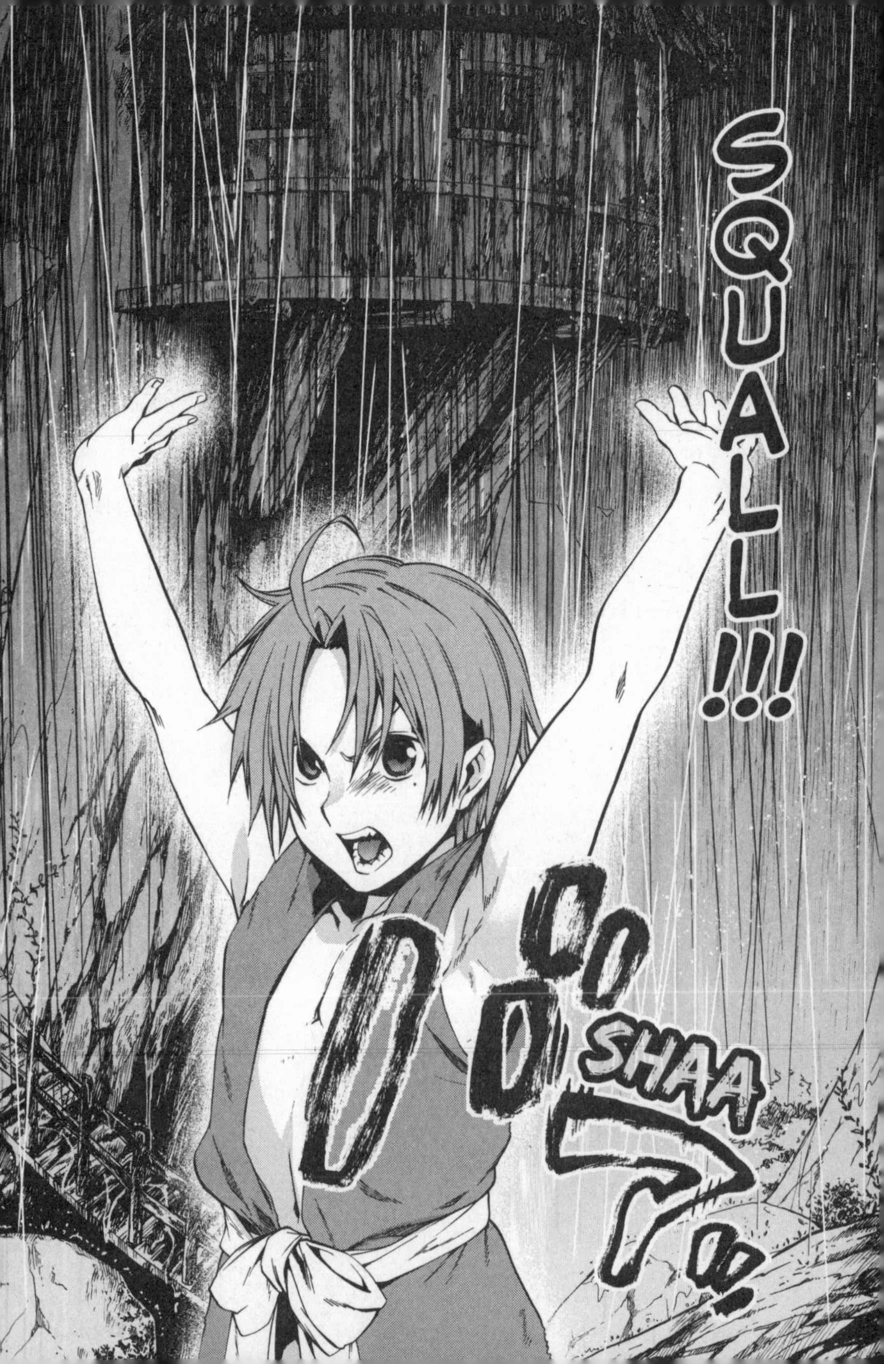
SQUALL!!!
DOOO
SHAA

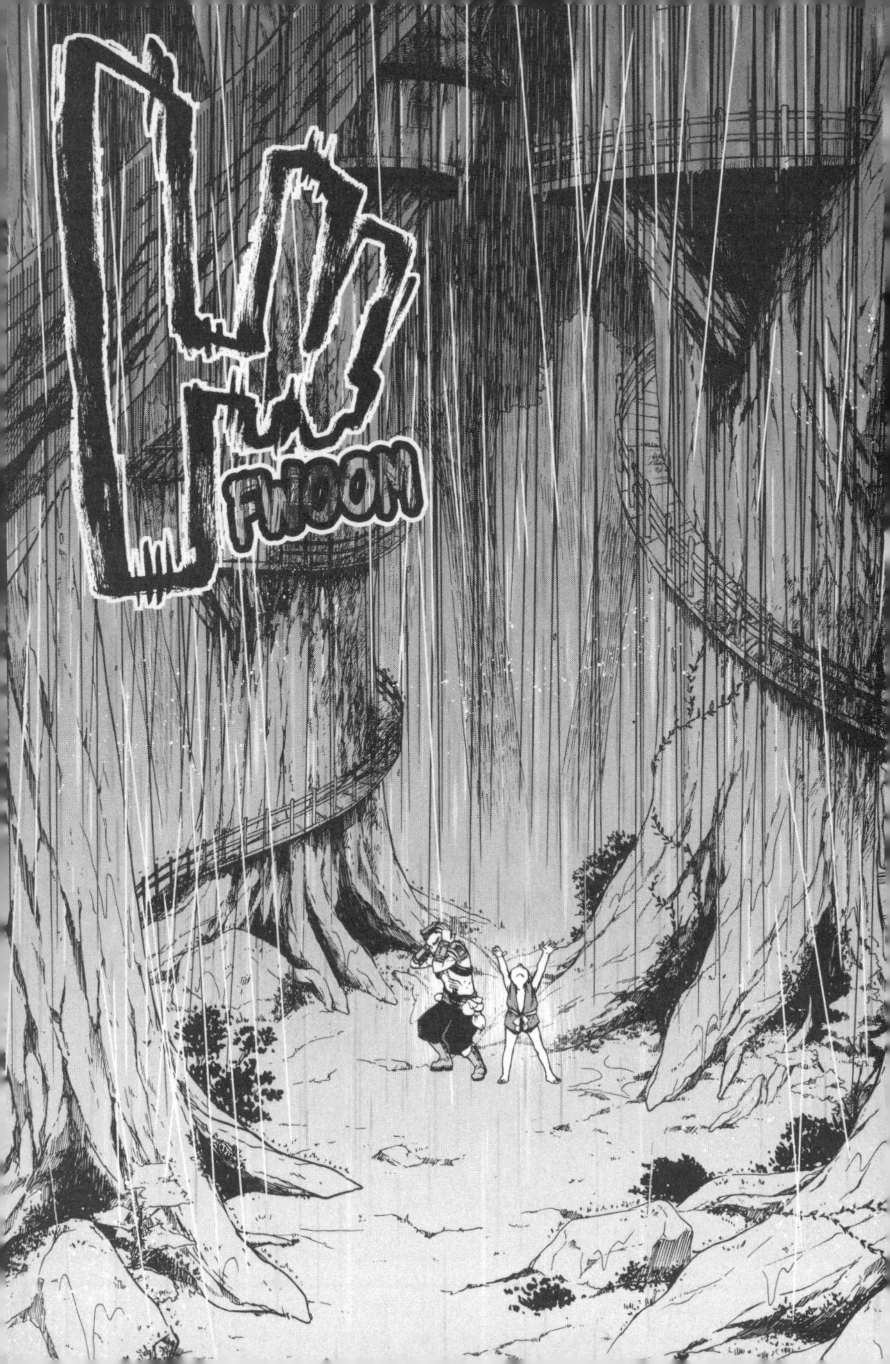
FWOOM

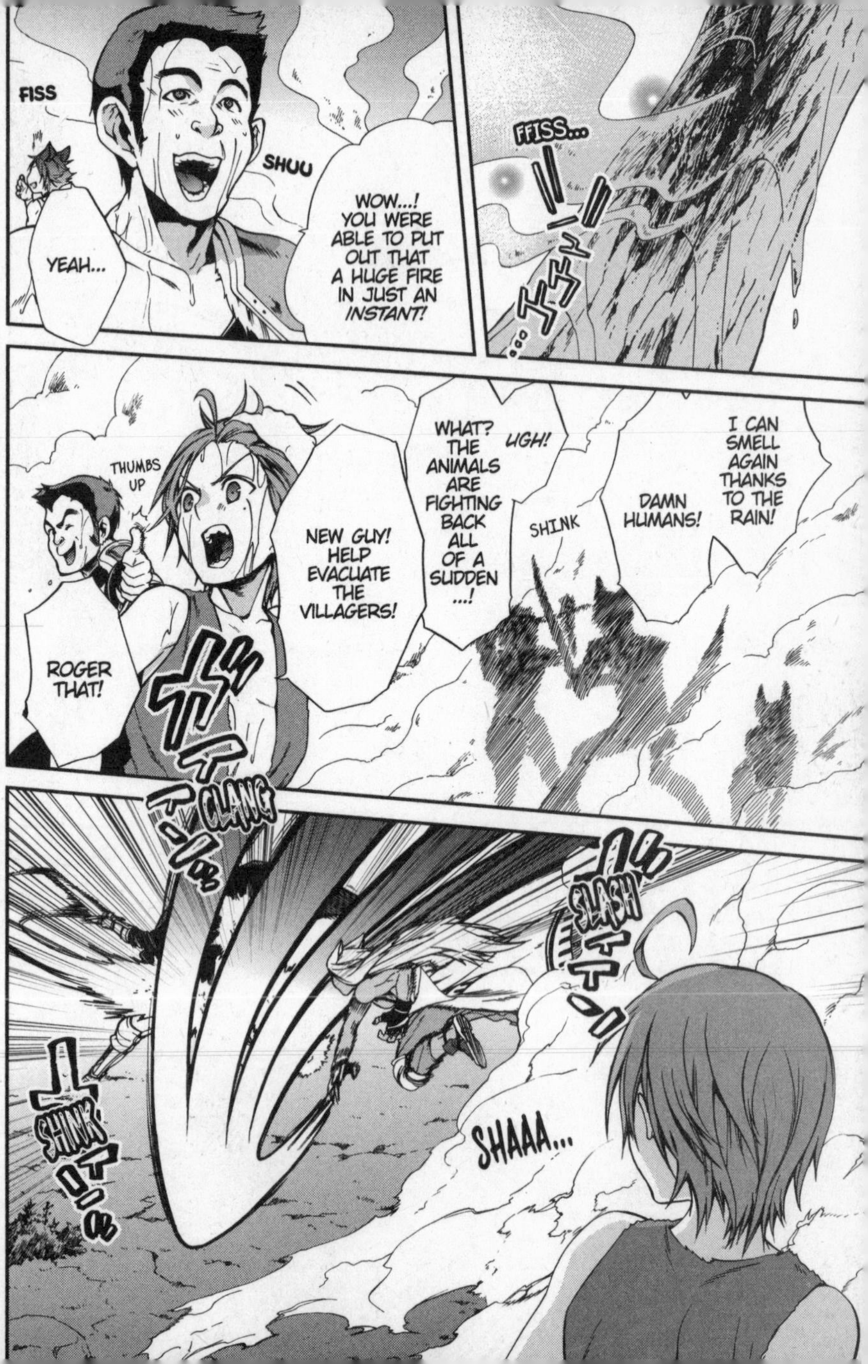
FFISS...
SHUU
WOW...! YOU WERE ABLE TO PUT OUT THAT A HUGE FIRE IN JUST AN *INSTANT!*
FISS
YEAH...
I CAN SMELL AGAIN THANKS TO THE RAIN!
DAMN HUMANS!
UGH!
WHAT? THE ANIMALS ARE FIGHTING BACK ALL OF A SUDDEN ...!
SHINK
NEW GUY! HELP EVACUATE THE VILLAGERS!
THUMBS UP
ROGER THAT!
CLANG
SLASH
SHAAA...
SHINK

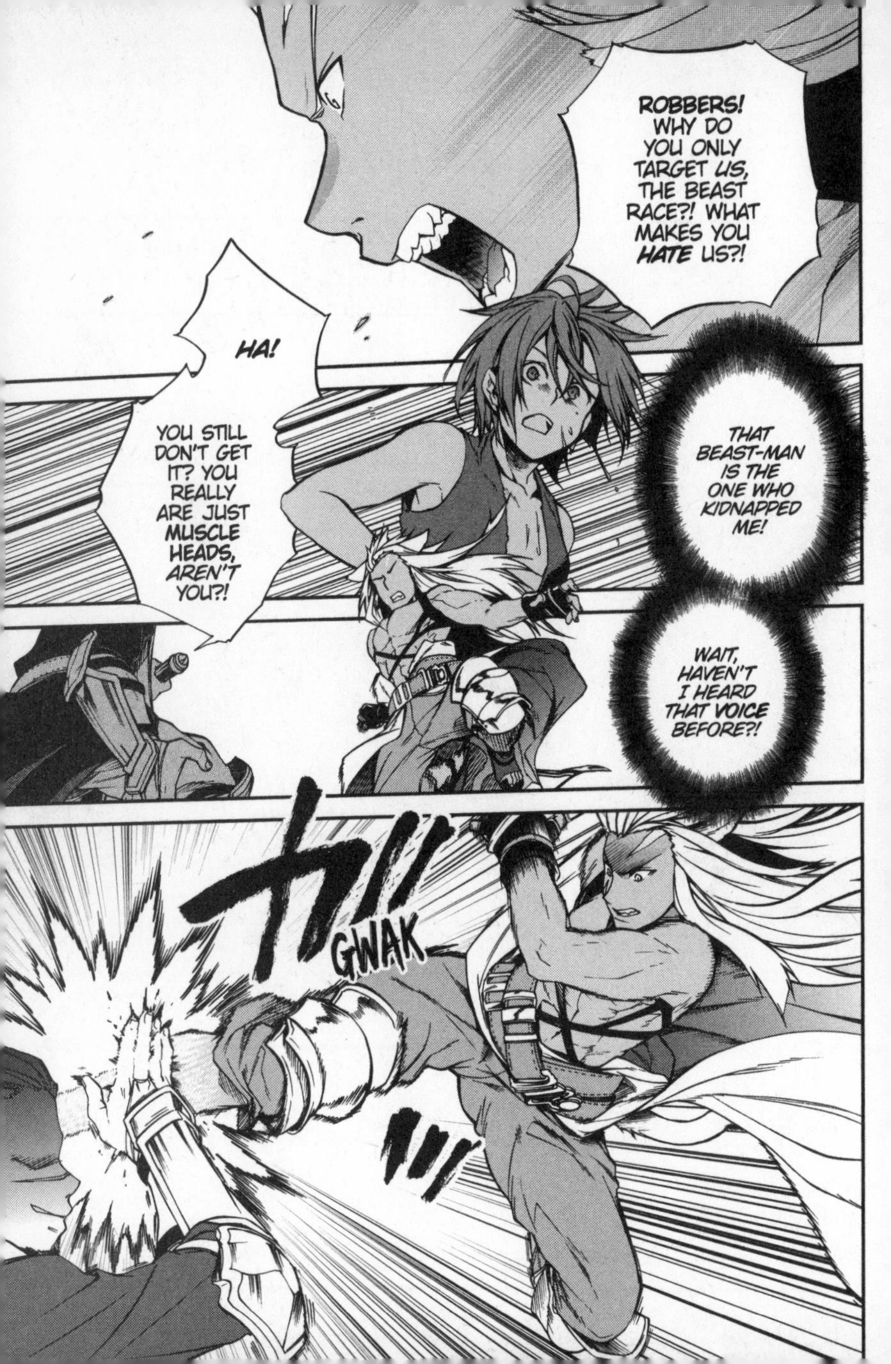
ROBBERS! WHY DO YOU ONLY TARGET US, THE BEAST RACE?! WHAT MAKES YOU HATE US?!
HA!
THAT BEAST-MAN IS THE ONE WHO KIDNAPPED ME!
YOU STILL DON'T GET IT? YOU REALLY ARE JUST MUSCLE HEADS, AREN'T YOU?!
WAIT, HAVEN'T I HEARD THAT VOICE BEFORE?!
GWAK

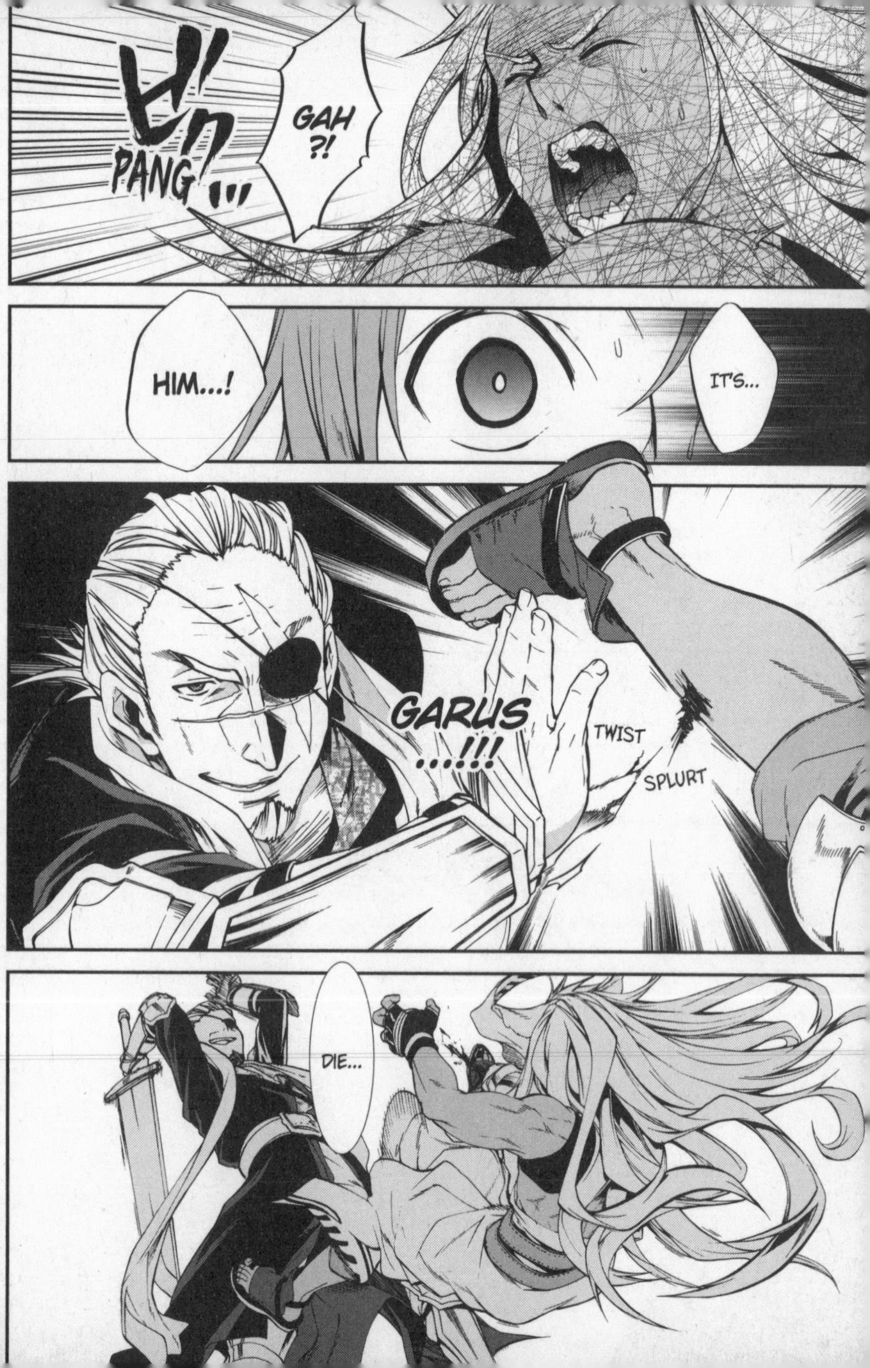

GAH ?!
PANG!!
IT'S...
HIM...!
TWIST
SPLURT
GARUS ...!!!
DIE...

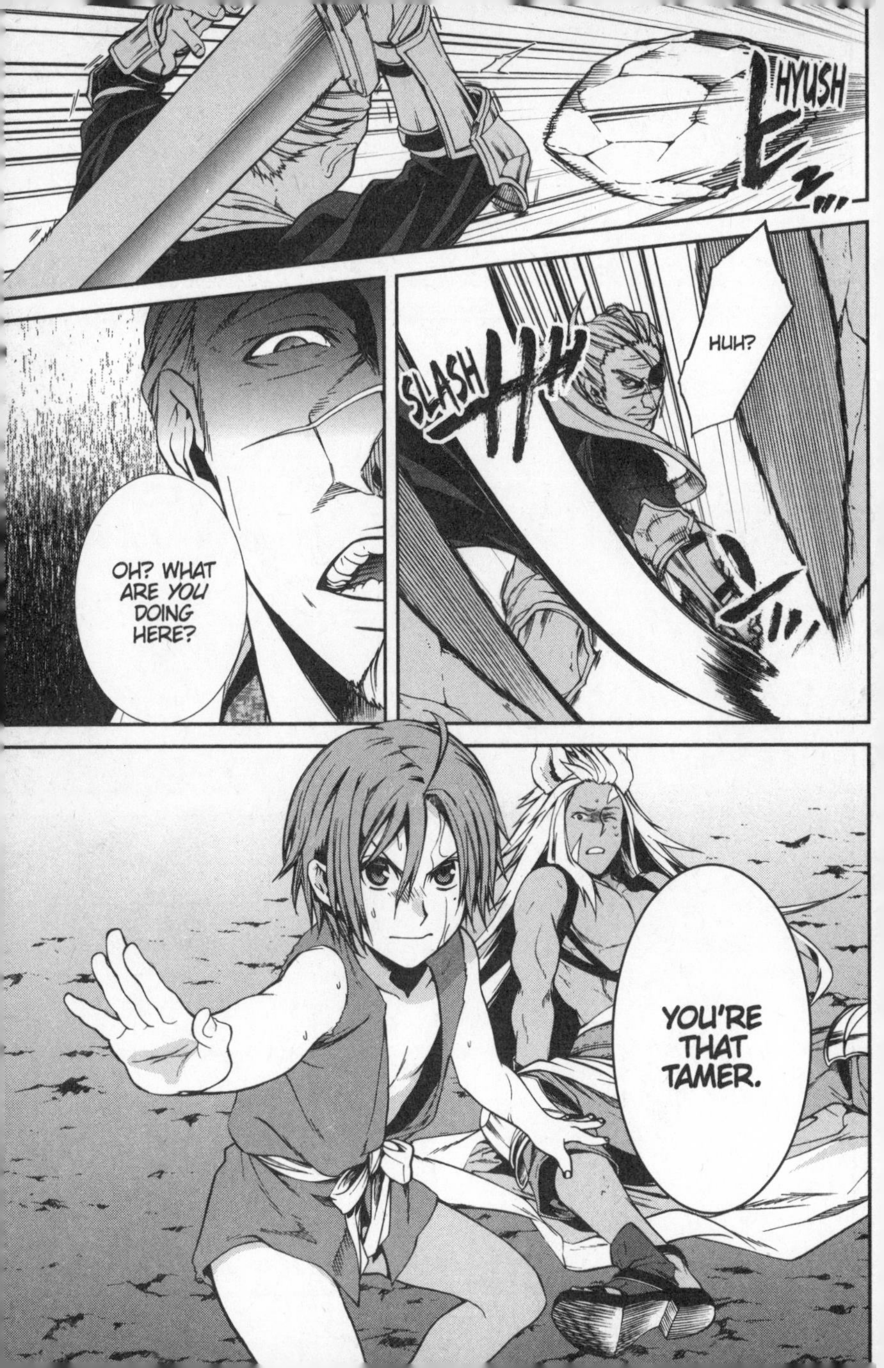
HYUSH
HUH?
SLASH
OH? WHAT ARE YOU DOING HERE?
YOU'RE THAT TAMER.

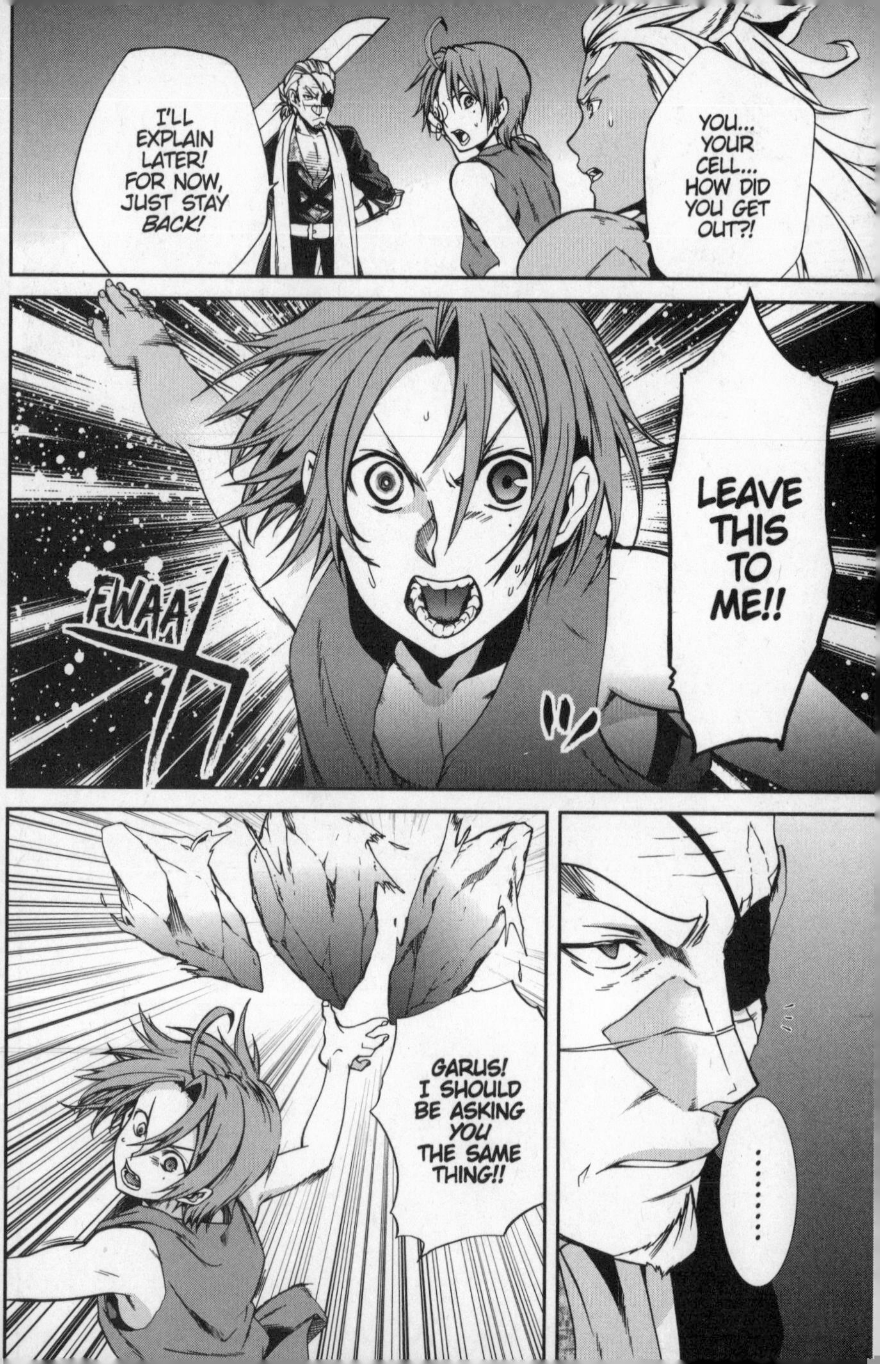
YOU... YOUR CELL... HOW DID YOU GET OUT?!
I'LL EXPLAIN LATER! FOR NOW, JUST STAY BACK!
LEAVE THIS TO ME!!
FWAA
!!
......
GARUS! I SHOULD BE ASKING YOU THE SAME THING!!

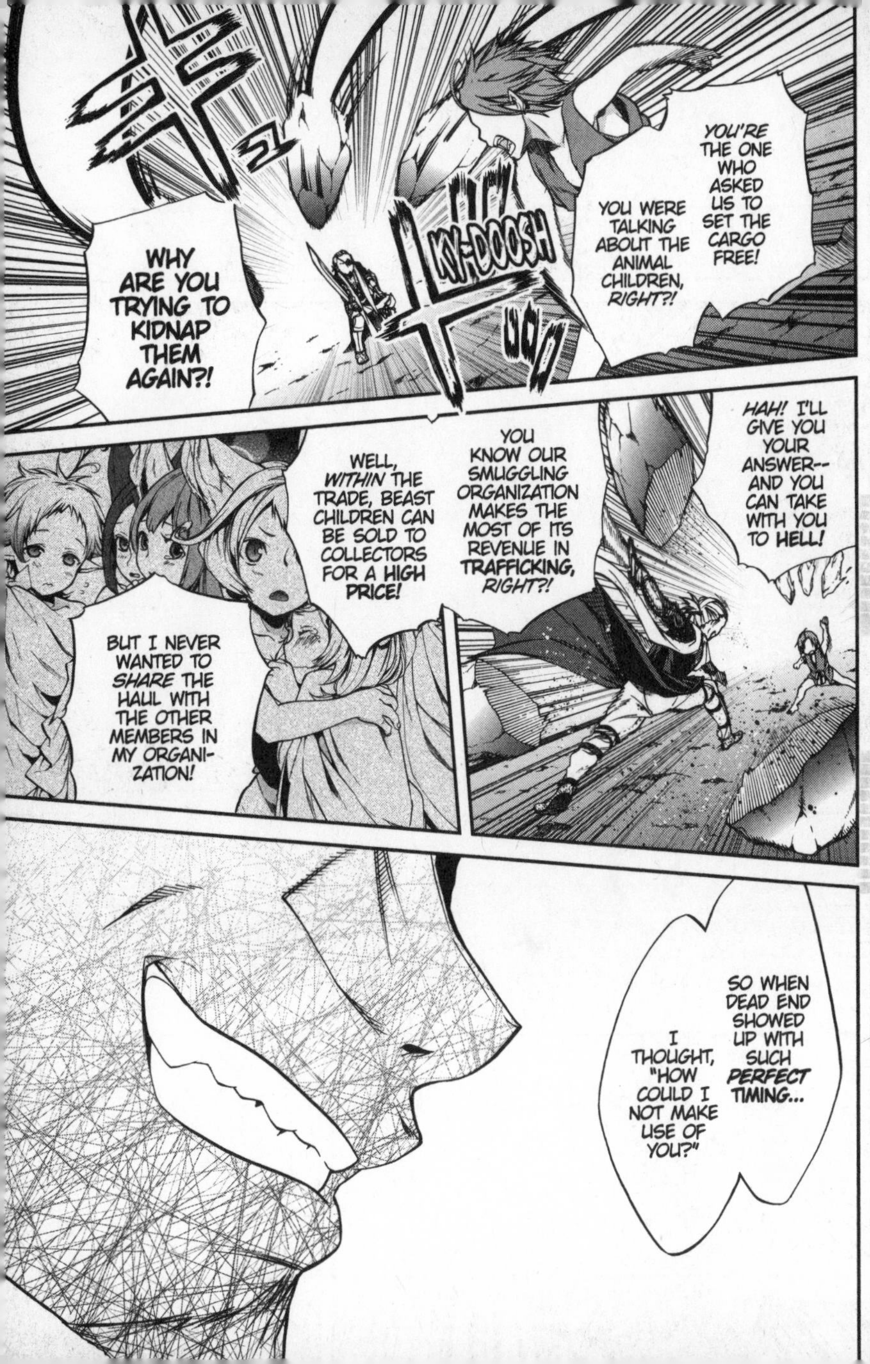

YOU'RE THE ONE WHO ASKED US TO SET THE CARGO FREE!
YOU WERE TALKING ABOUT THE ANIMAL CHILDREN, RIGHT?!
KY-DOOSH
WHY ARE YOU TRYING TO KIDNAP THEM AGAIN?!
HAH! I'LL GIVE YOU YOUR ANSWER-- AND YOU CAN TAKE WITH YOU TO HELL!
YOU KNOW OUR SMUGGLING ORGANIZATION MAKES THE MOST OF ITS REVENUE IN TRAFFICKING, RIGHT?!
WELL, WITHIN THE TRADE, BEAST CHILDREN CAN BE SOLD TO COLLECTORS FOR A HIGH PRICE!
BUT I NEVER WANTED TO SHARE THE HAUL WITH THE OTHER MEMBERS IN MY ORGANI-ZATION!
SO WHEN DEAD END SHOWED UP WITH SUCH PERFECT TIMING...
I THOUGHT, "HOW COULD I NOT MAKE USE OF YOU?"

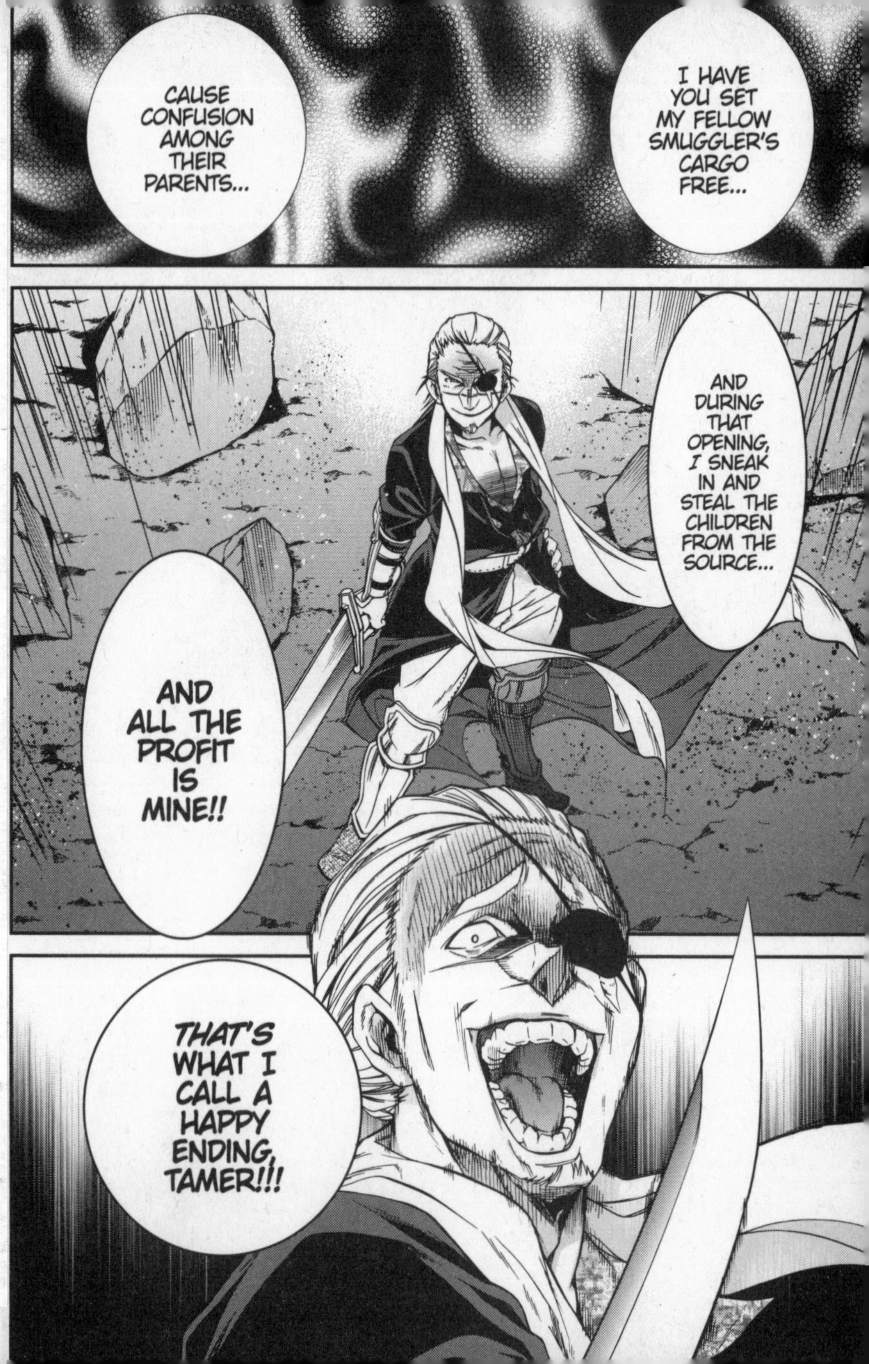
I HAVE YOU SET MY FELLOW SMUGGLER'S CARGO FREE...
CAUSE CONFUSION AMONG THEIR PARENTS...
AND DURING THAT OPENING, *I* SNEAK IN AND STEAL THE CHILDREN FROM THE SOURCE...
AND ALL THE PROFIT IS MINE!!
THAT'S WHAT I CALL A HAPPY ENDING, TAMER!!!

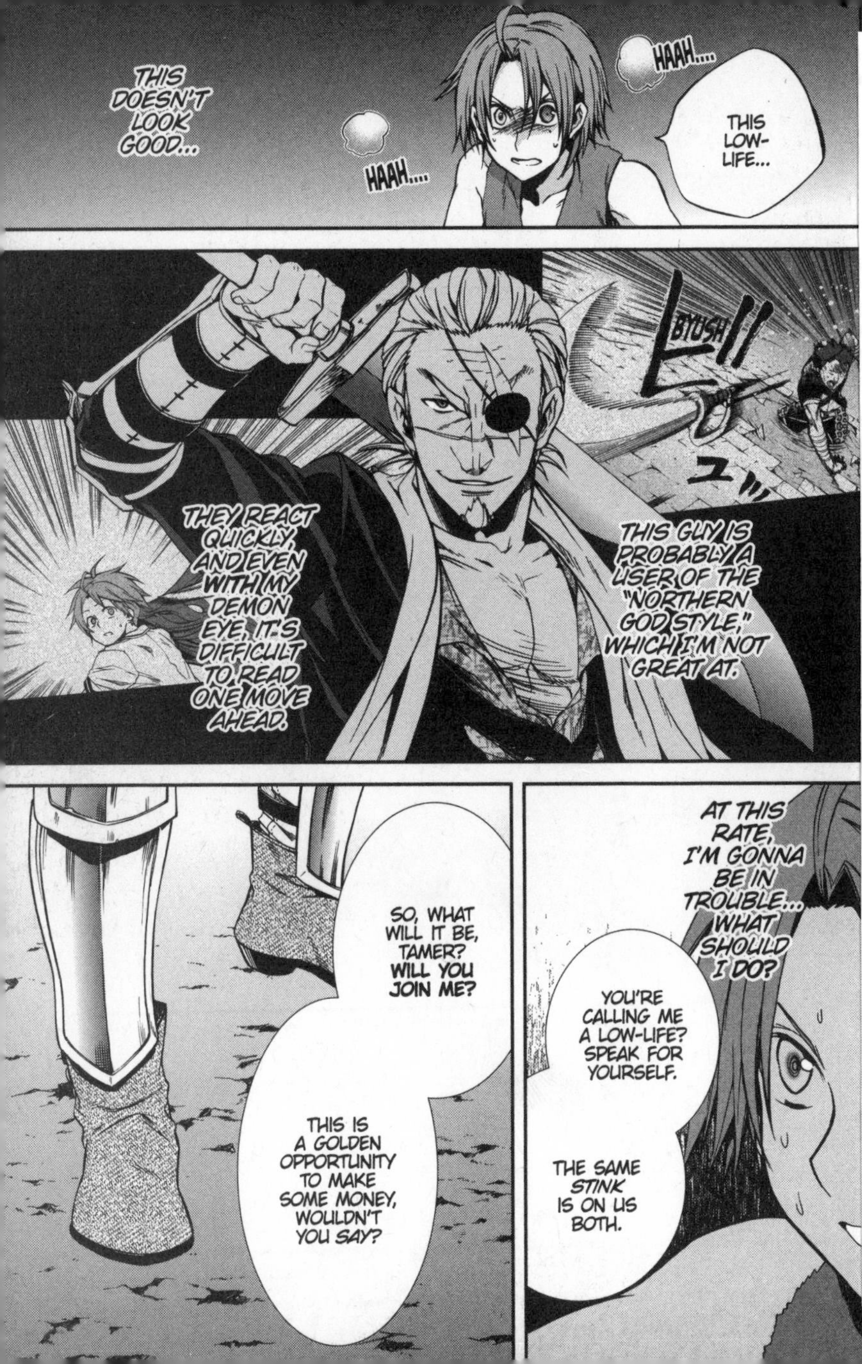
HAAH....
THIS LOW-LIFE...
THIS DOESN'T LOOK GOOD...
HAAH....
BYUSH
THIS GUY IS PROBABLY A USER OF THE "NORTHERN GOD STYLE," WHICH I'M NOT GREAT AT.
THEY REACT QUICKLY, AND EVEN WITH MY DEMON EYE, IT'S DIFFICULT TO READ ONE MOVE AHEAD.
AT THIS RATE, I'M GONNA BE IN TROUBLE... WHAT SHOULD I DO?
YOU'RE CALLING ME A LOW-LIFE? SPEAK FOR YOURSELF.
THE SAME STINK IS ON US BOTH.
SO, WHAT WILL IT BE, TAMER? WILL YOU JOIN ME?
THIS IS A GOLDEN OPPORTUNITY TO MAKE SOME MONEY, WOULDN'T YOU SAY?

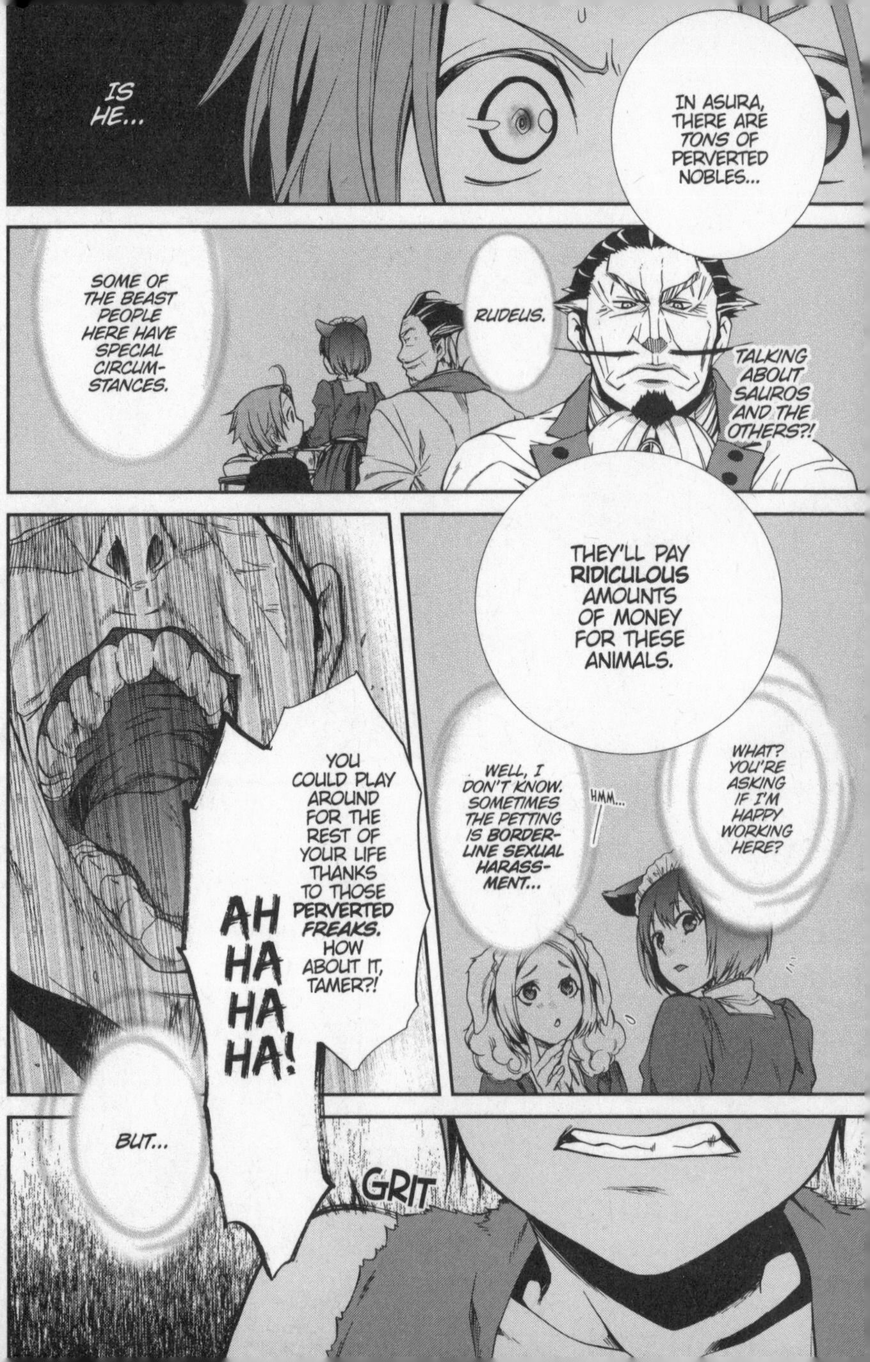
IN ASURA, THERE ARE TONS OF PERVERTED NOBLES...
IS HE...
TALKING ABOUT SAUROS AND THE OTHERS?!
RUDEUS.
SOME OF THE BEAST PEOPLE HERE HAVE SPECIAL CIRCUM-STANCES.
THEY'LL PAY RIDICULOUS AMOUNTS OF MONEY FOR THESE ANIMALS.
WHAT? YOU'RE ASKING IF I'M HAPPY WORKING HERE?
HMM...
WELL, I DON'T KNOW. SOMETIMES THE PETTING IS BORDER-LINE SEXUAL HARASS-MENT...
YOU COULD PLAY AROUND FOR THE REST OF YOUR LIFE THANKS TO THOSE PERVERTED FREAKS. HOW ABOUT IT, TAMER?!
AH HA HA HA HA!
GRIT
BUT...

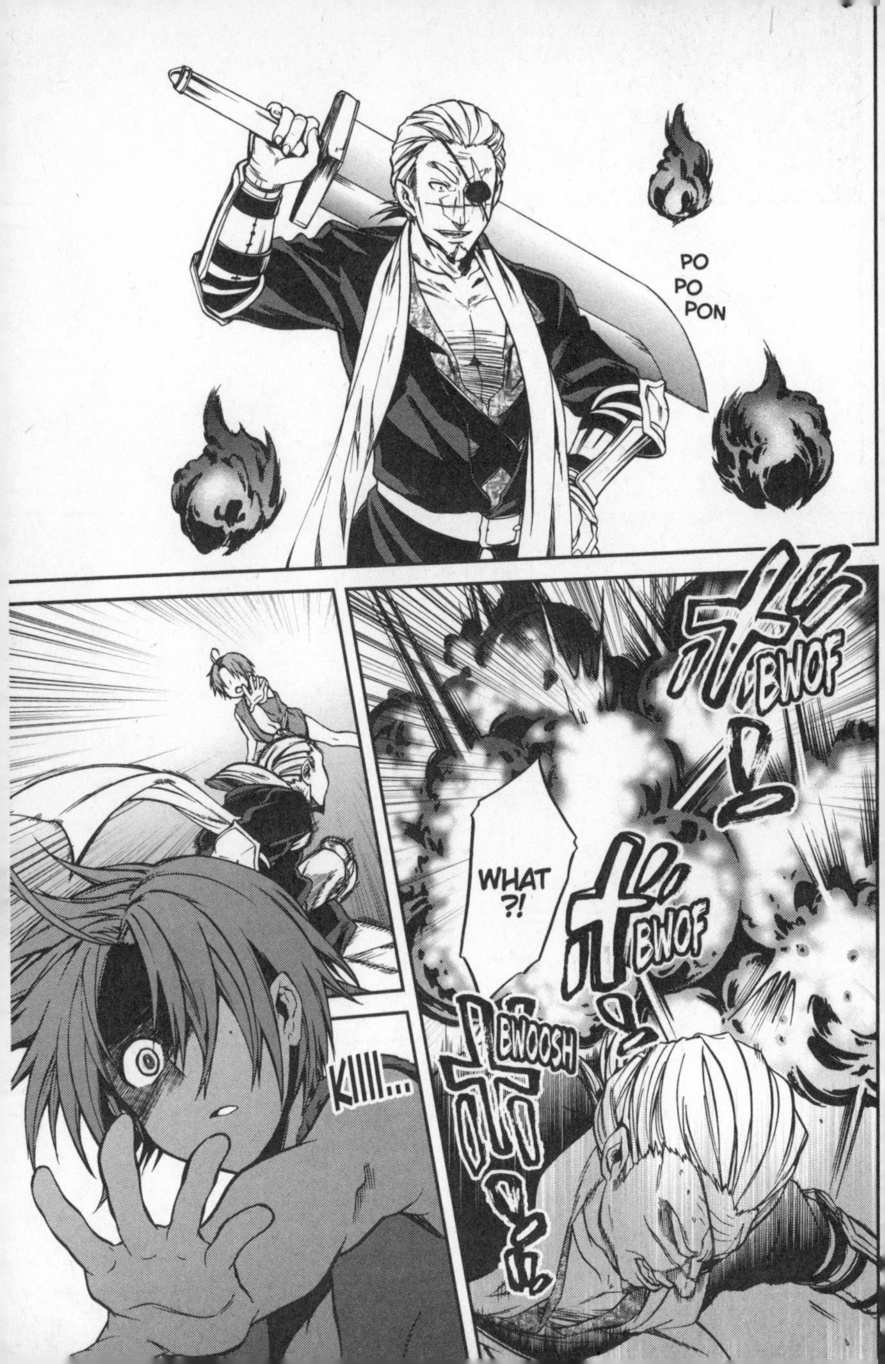
PO
PO
PON
BWOF
WHAT?!
BWOF
BWOOSH
KIIII...

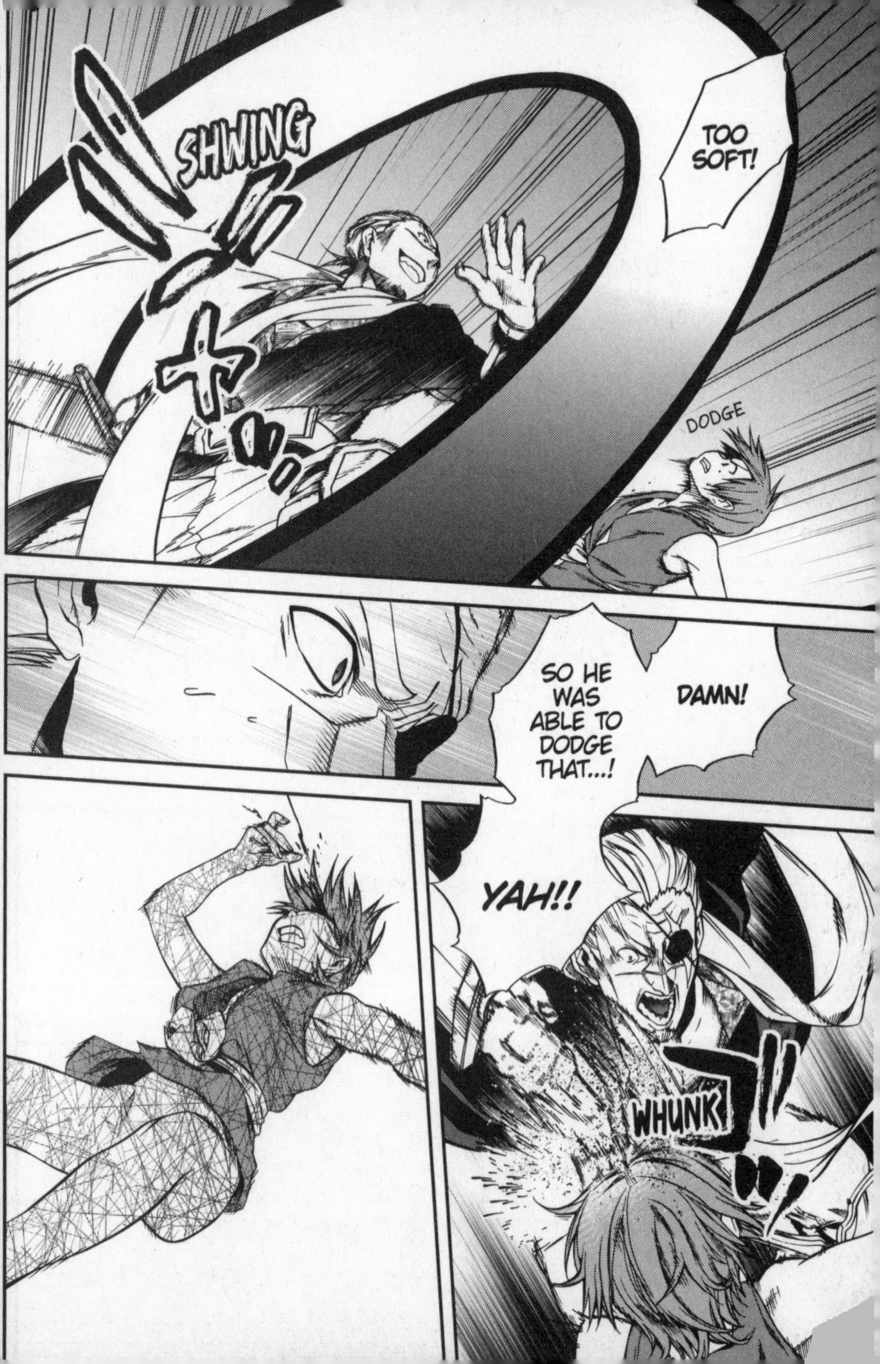
TOO SOFT!
SHWING
DODGE
DAMN!
SO HE WAS ABLE TO DODGE THAT...!
YAH!!
WHUNK

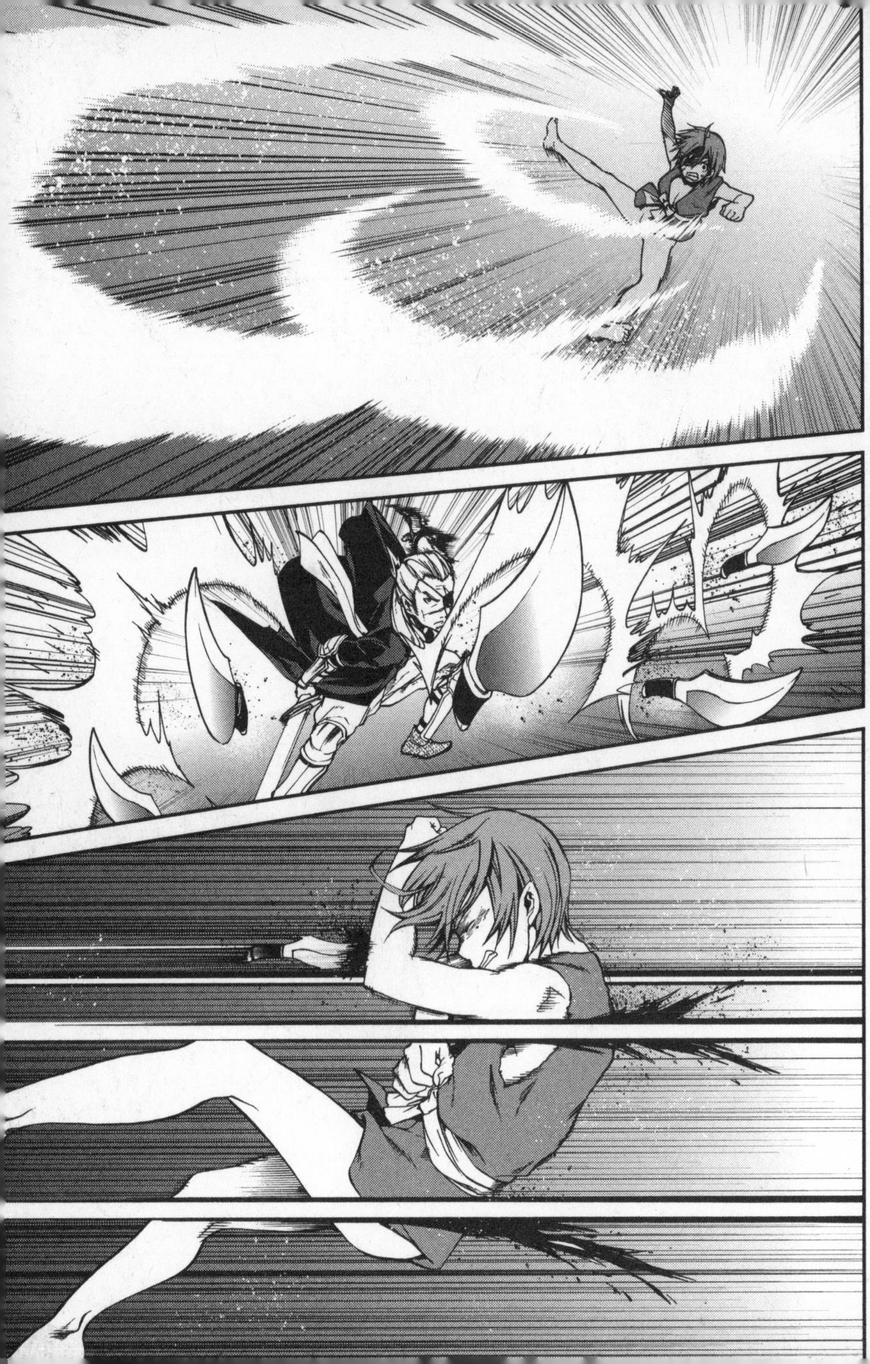

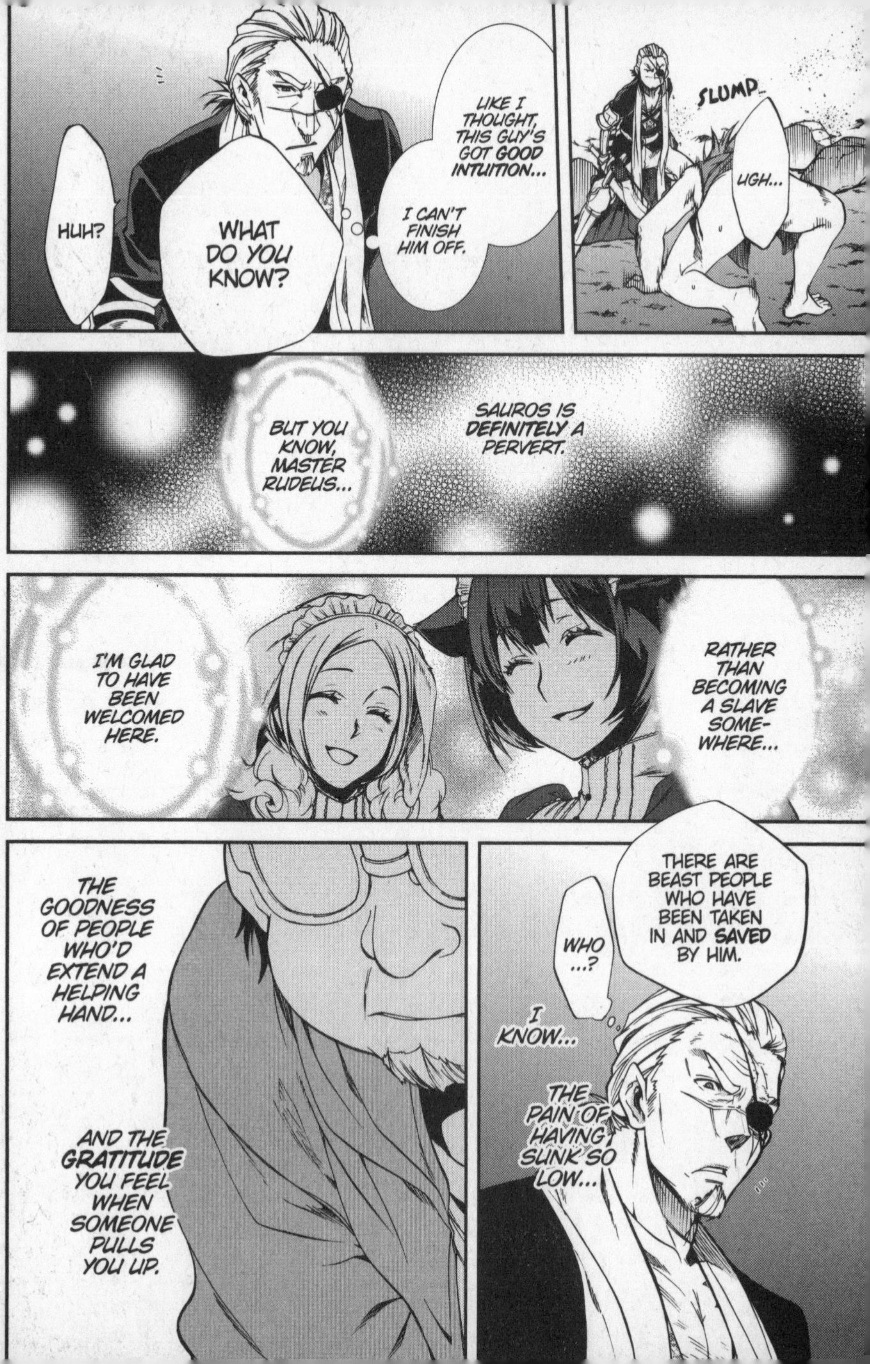
SLUMP...
UGH...
LIKE I THOUGHT, THIS GUY'S GOT GOOD INTUITION...
I CAN'T FINISH HIM OFF.
WHAT DO YOU KNOW?
HUH?
SAUROS IS DEFINITELY A PERVERT.
BUT YOU KNOW, MASTER RUDEUS...
RATHER THAN BECOMING A SLAVE SOME-WHERE...
I'M GLAD TO HAVE BEEN WELCOMED HERE.
THERE ARE BEAST PEOPLE WHO HAVE BEEN TAKEN IN AND SAVED BY HIM.
WHO ...?
I KNOW...
THE PAIN OF HAVING SUNK SO LOW...
THE GOODNESS OF PEOPLE WHO'D EXTEND A HELPING HAND...
AND THE GRATITUDE YOU FEEL WHEN SOMEONE PULLS YOU UP.

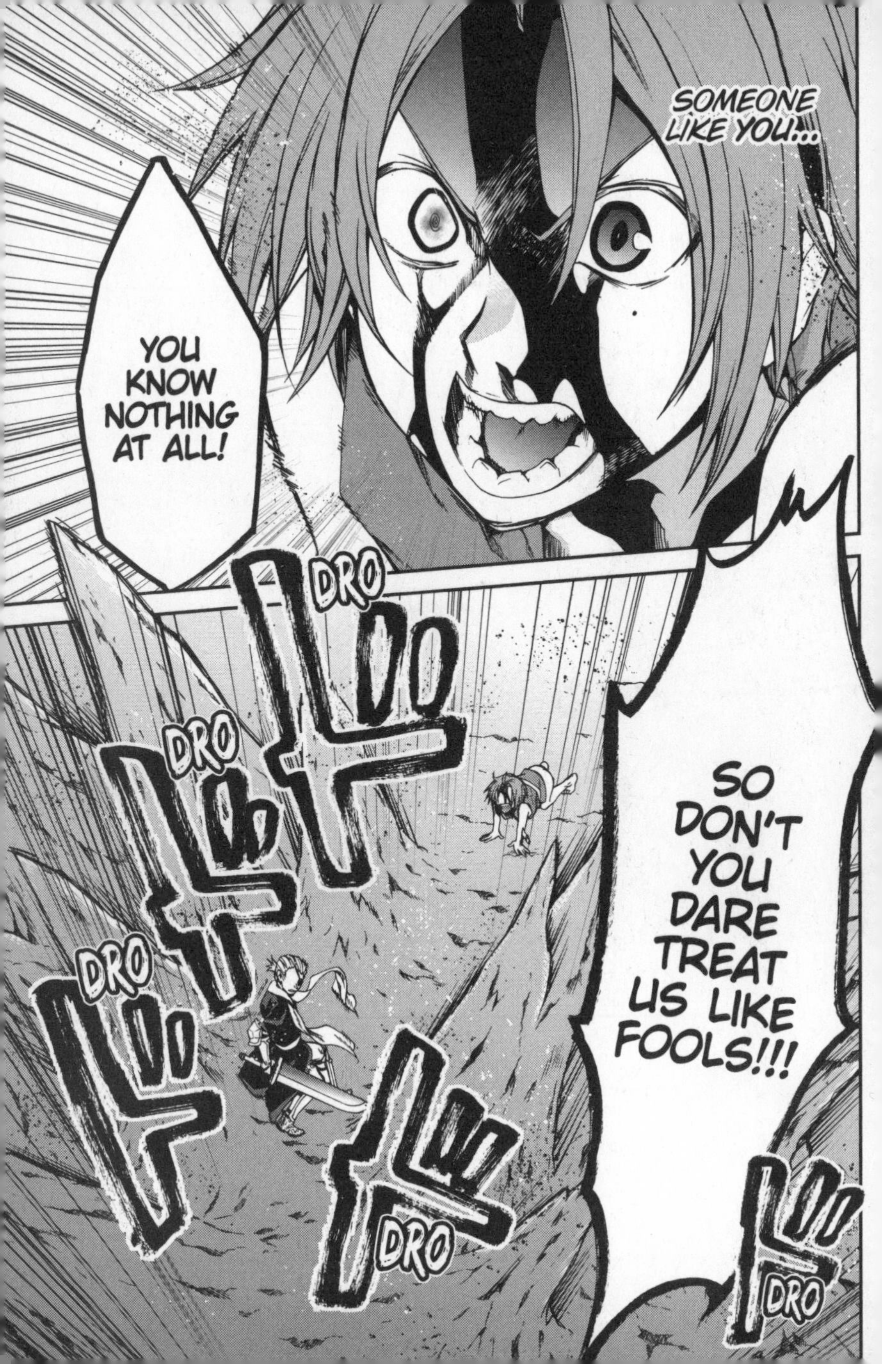
SOMEONE LIKE YOU...
YOU KNOW NOTHING AT ALL!
SO DON'T YOU DARE TREAT US LIKE FOOLS!!!
DRO
DRO
DRO
DRO
DRO

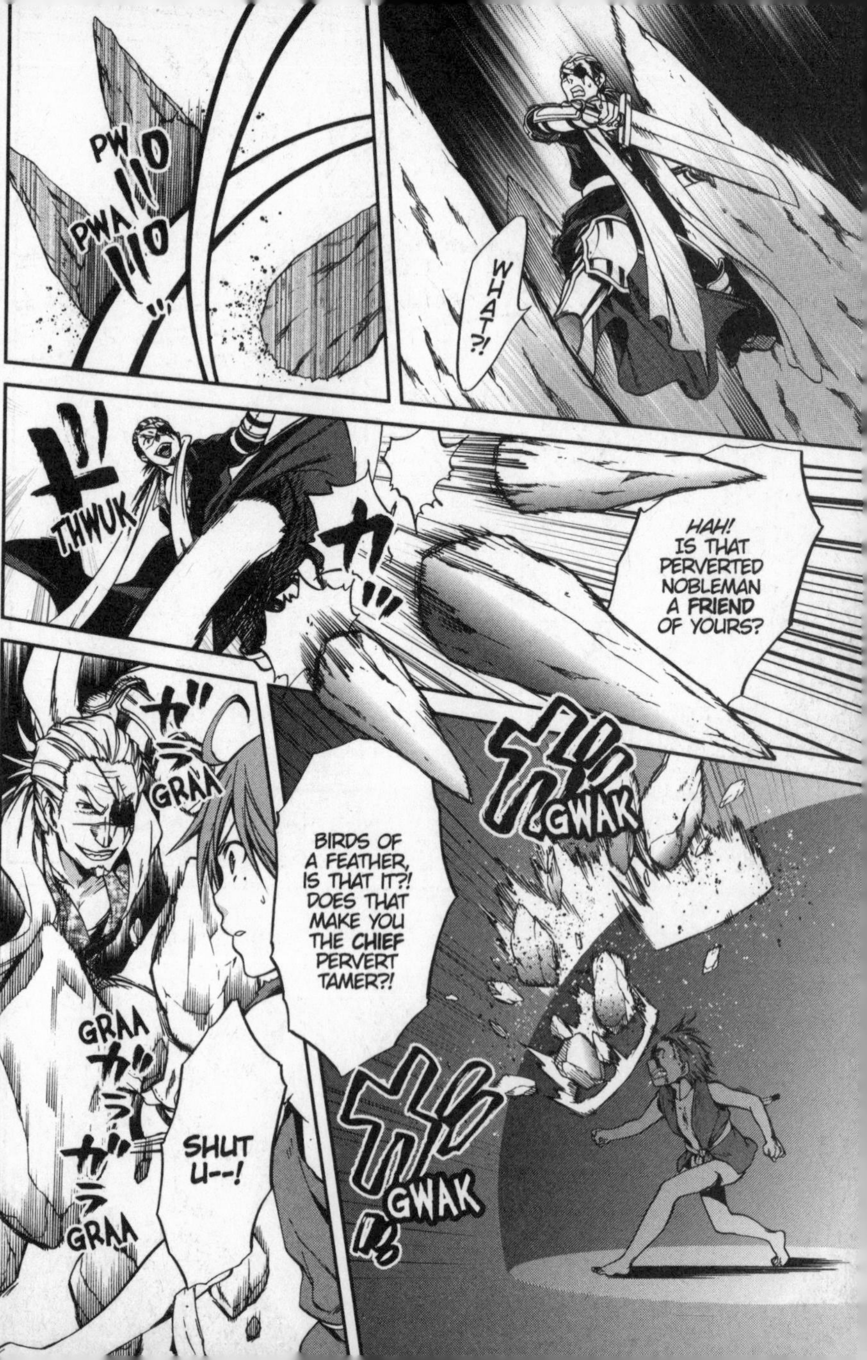
WHAT?!
PWO
PWA
HAH! IS THAT PERVERTED NOBLEMAN A FRIEND OF YOURS?
THWUK
GWAK
GWAK
BIRDS OF A FEATHER, IS THAT IT?! DOES THAT MAKE YOU THE CHIEF PERVERT TAMER?!
GRAA
SHUT U--!
GRAA
GRAA

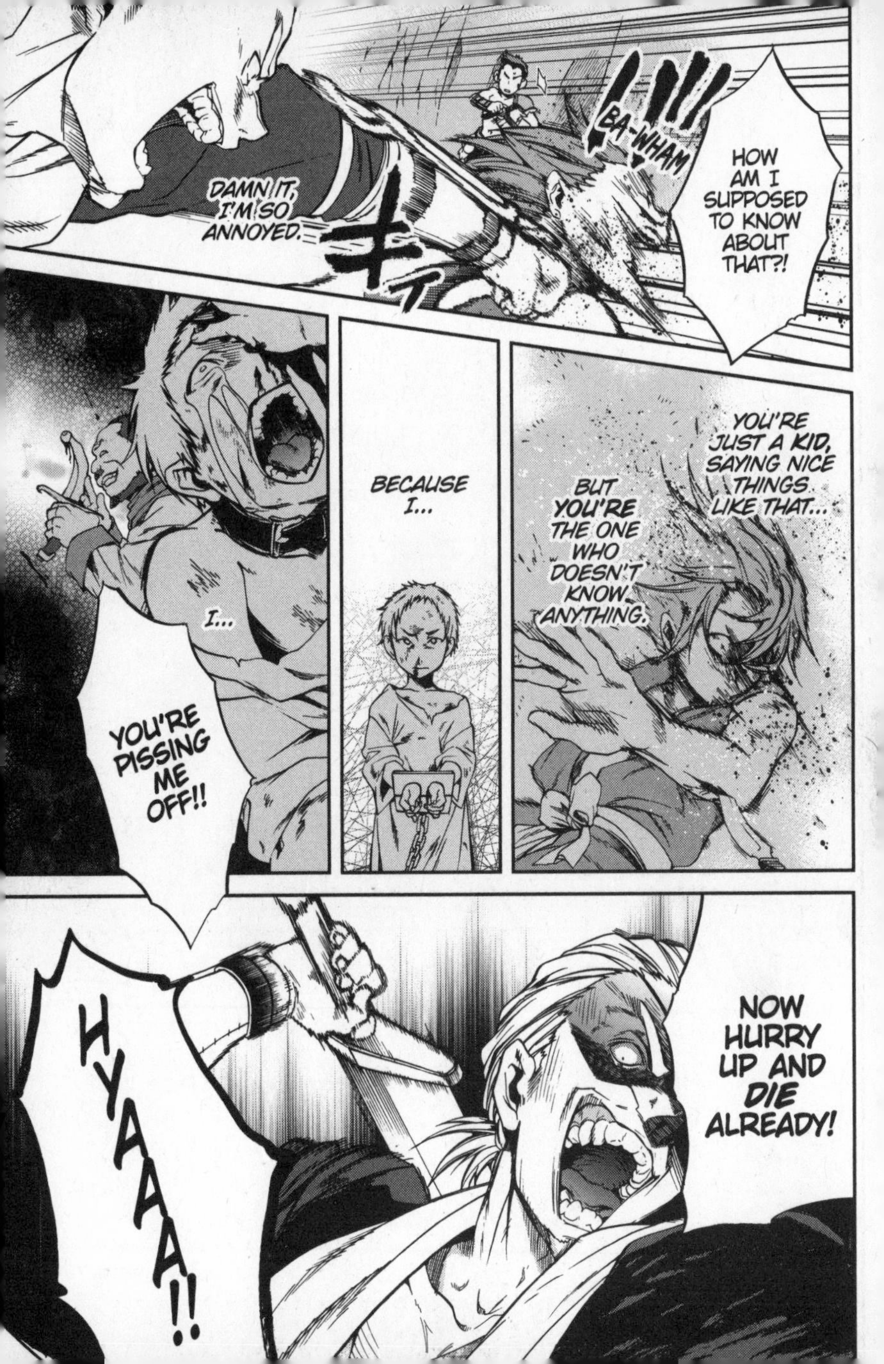
HOW AM I SUPPOSED TO KNOW ABOUT THAT?!
BA-WHAM
DAMN IT, I'M SO ANNOYED.
YOU'RE JUST A KID, SAYING NICE THINGS LIKE THAT...
BUT YOU'RE THE ONE WHO DOESN'T KNOW ANYTHING.
BECAUSE I...
I...
YOU'RE PISSING ME OFF!!
NOW HURRY UP AND DIE ALREADY!
HYAAAA!!

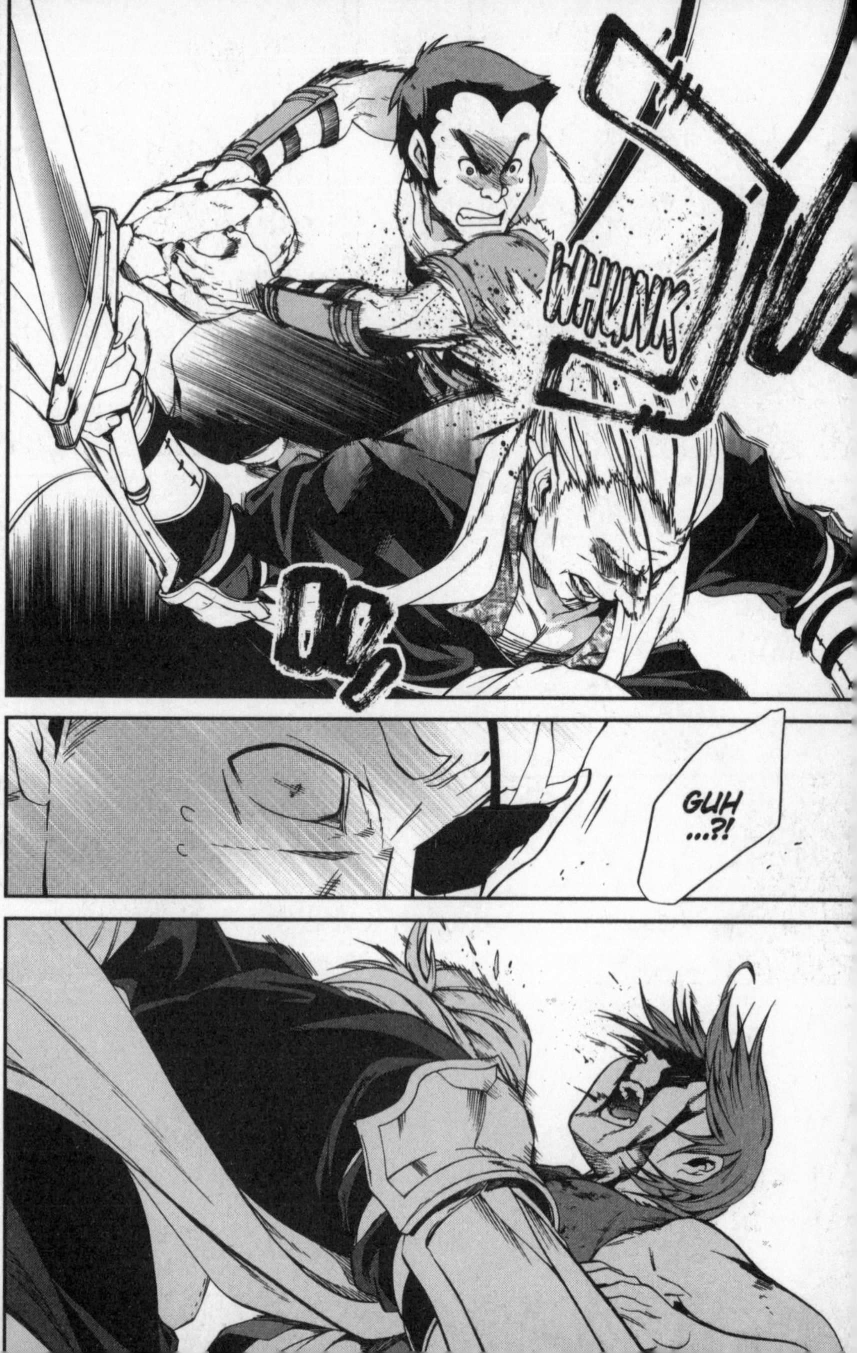
WHUNK
GUH ...?!

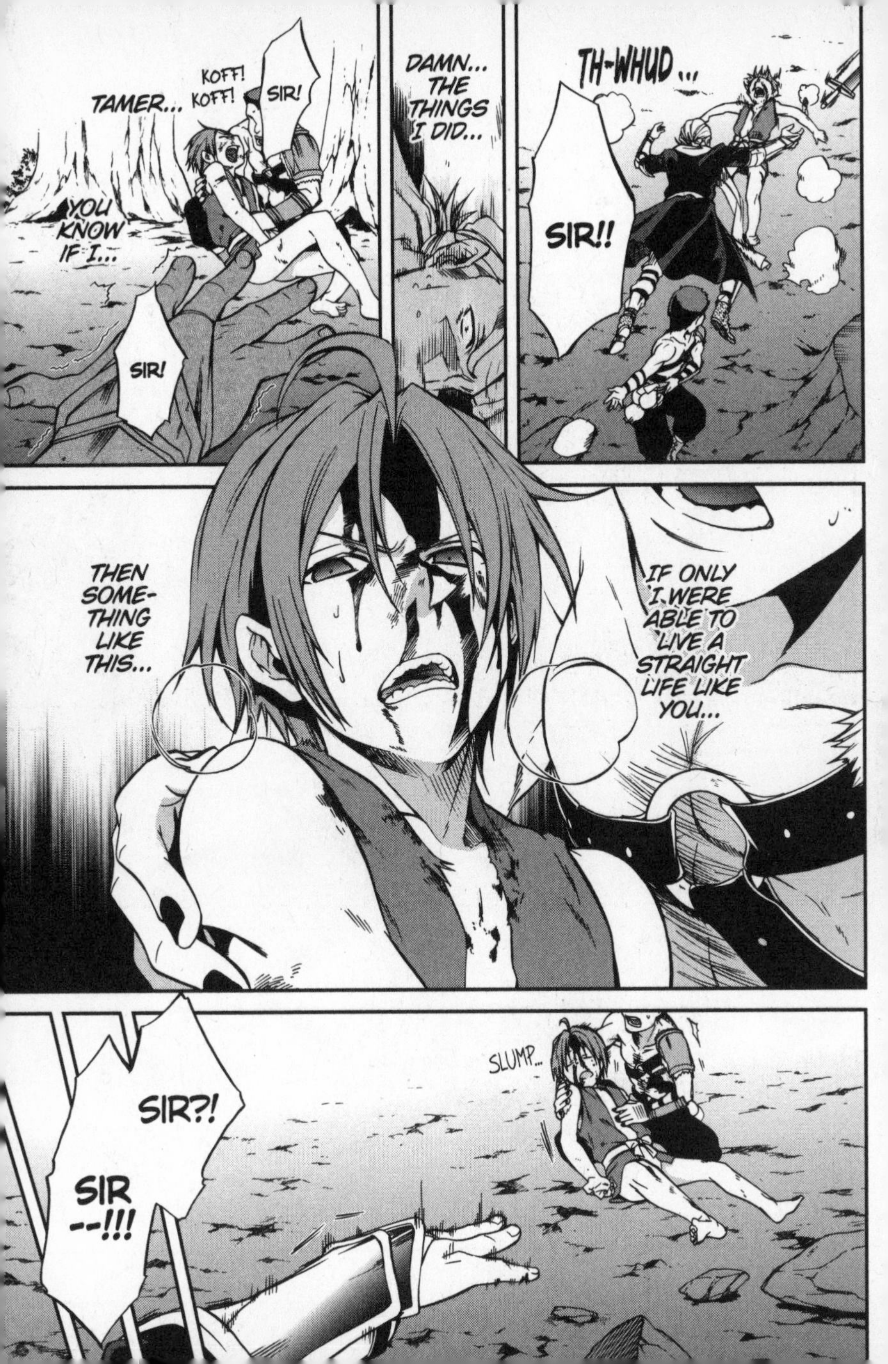
TH-WHUD...
SIR!!
DAMN... THE THINGS I DID...
SIR!
KOFF! KOFF!
TAMER...
YOU KNOW IF I...
SIR!
IF ONLY I WERE ABLE TO LIVE A STRAIGHT LIFE LIKE YOU...
THEN SOME-THING LIKE THIS...
SLUMP...
SIR?!
SIR --!!!

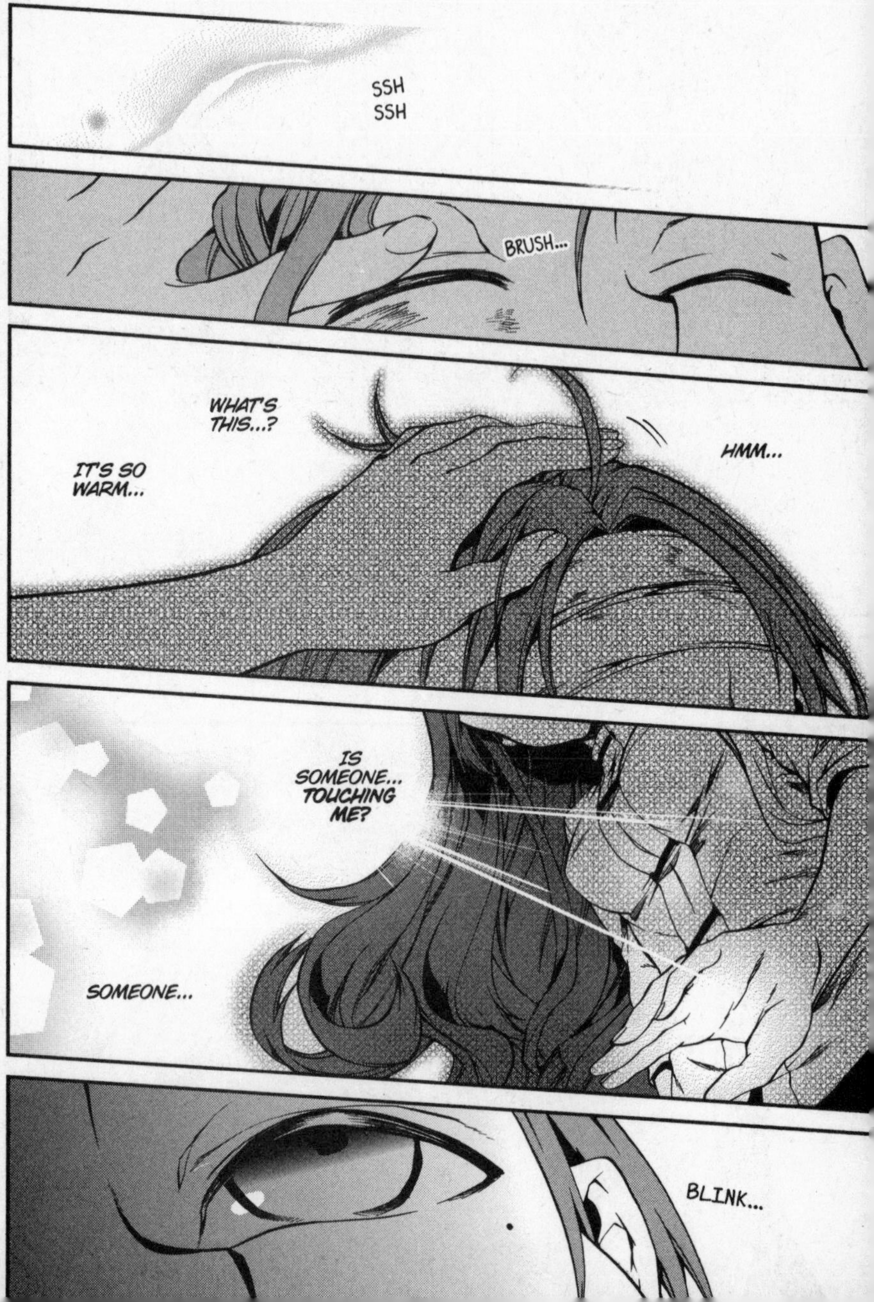
SSH
SSH
BRUSH...
HMM...
WHAT'S THIS...?
IT'S SO WARM...
IS SOMEONE... TOUCHING ME?
SOMEONE...
BLINK...

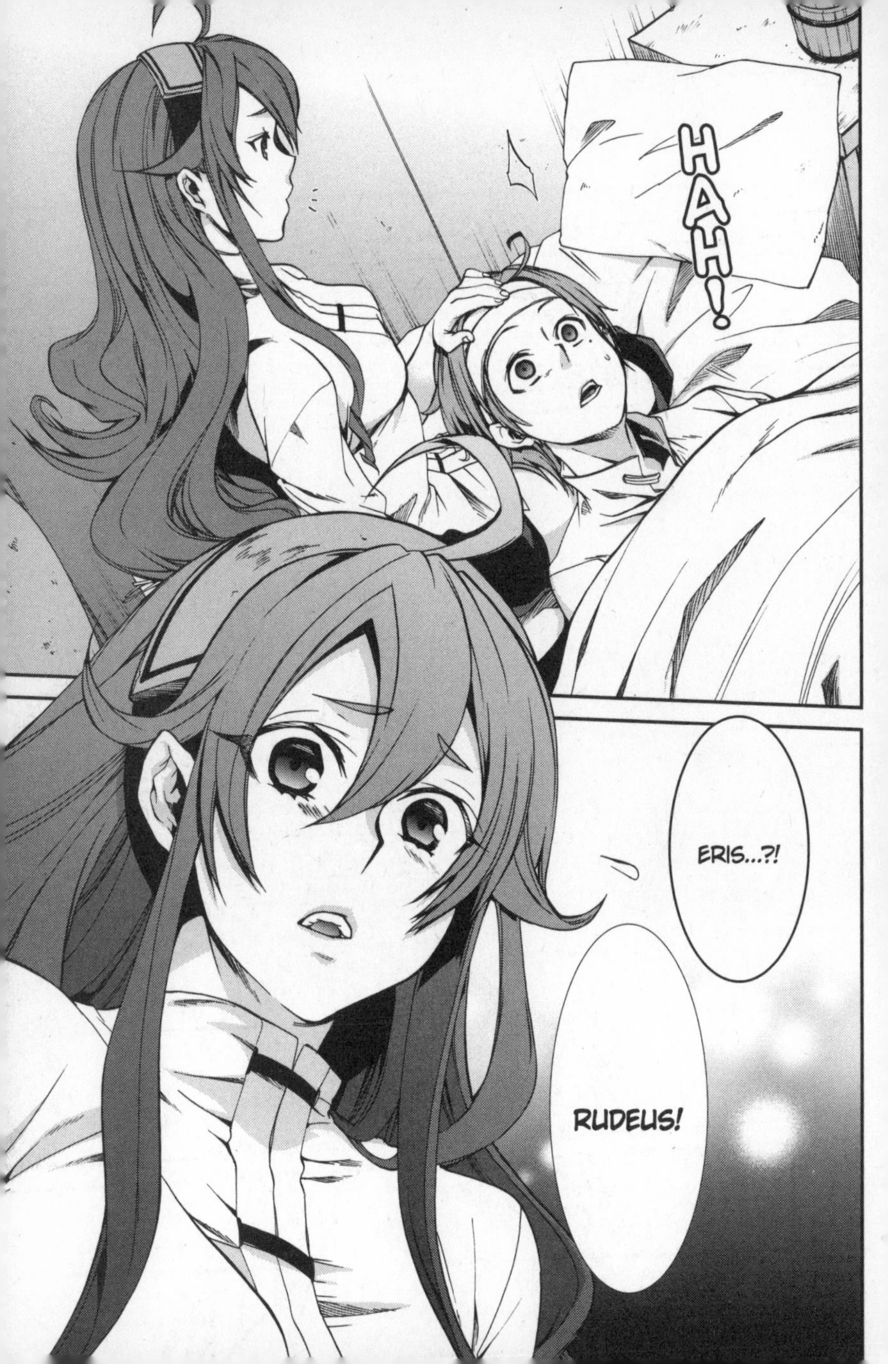
HAH!
ERIS...?!
RUDEUS!

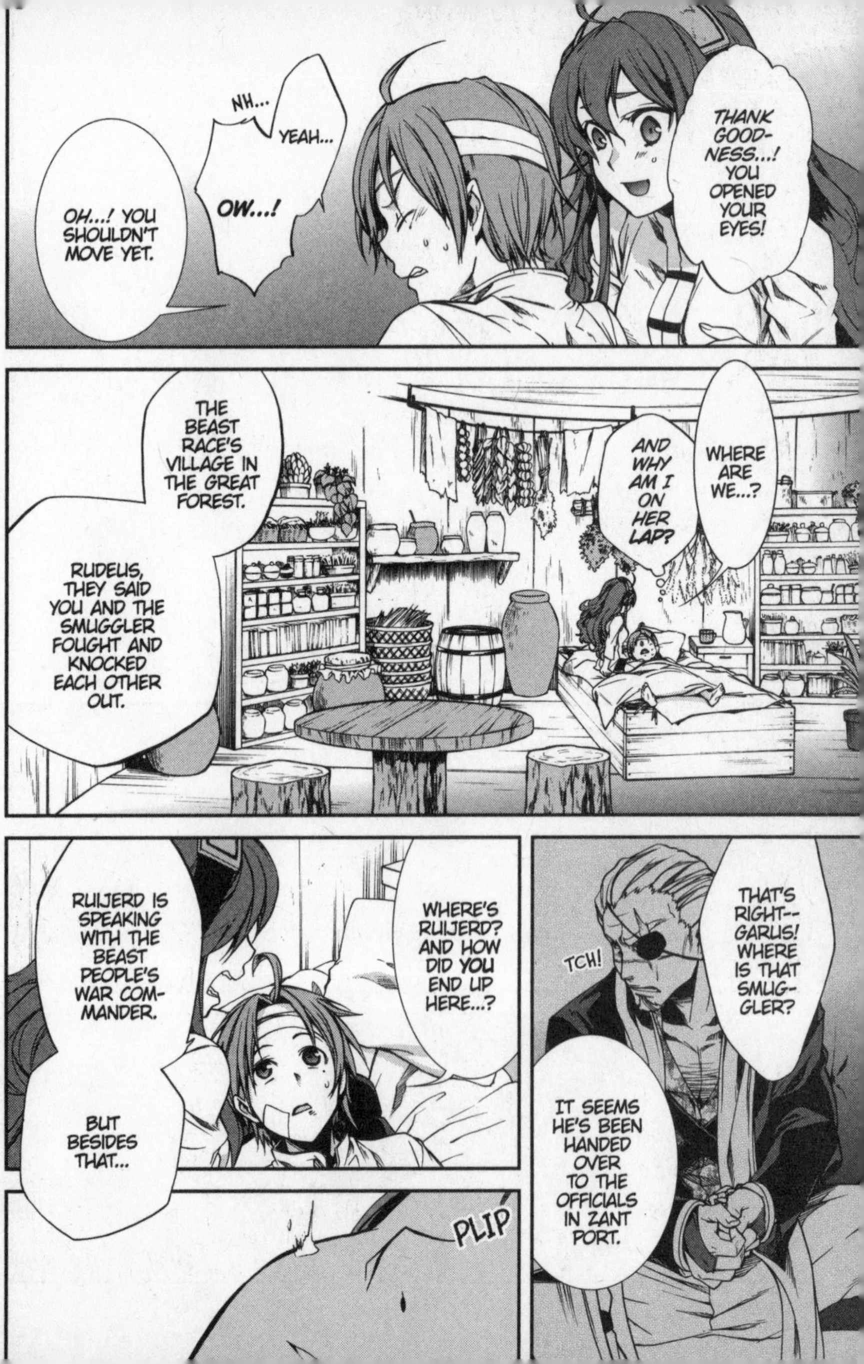
THANK GOODNESS...! YOU OPENED YOUR EYES!
NH...
YEAH...
OW...!
OH...! YOU SHOULDN'T MOVE YET.
WHERE ARE WE...?
AND WHY AM I ON HER LAP?
THE BEAST RACE'S VILLAGE IN THE GREAT FOREST.
RUDEUS, THEY SAID YOU AND THE SMUGGLER FOUGHT AND KNOCKED EACH OTHER OUT.
THAT'S RIGHT-- GARUS! WHERE IS THAT SMUGGLER?
TCH!
IT SEEMS HE'S BEEN HANDED OVER TO THE OFFICIALS IN ZANT PORT.
WHERE'S RUIJERD? AND HOW DID YOU END UP HERE...?
RUIJERD IS SPEAKING WITH THE BEAST PEOPLE'S WAR COMMANDER.
BUT BESIDES THAT...
PLIP

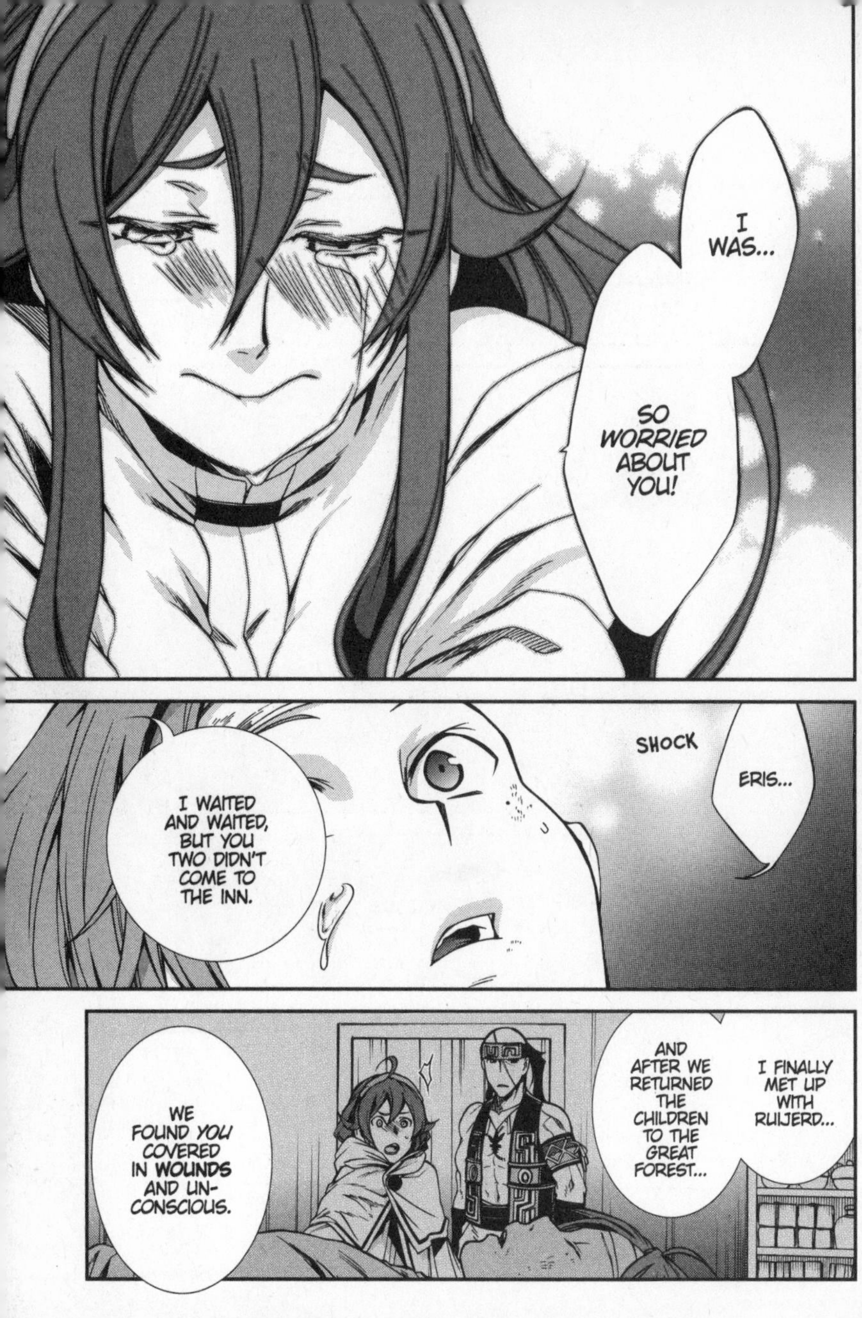
I WAS...
SO WORRIED ABOUT YOU!
ERIS...
SHOCK
I WAITED AND WAITED, BUT YOU TWO DIDN'T COME TO THE INN.
I FINALLY MET UP WITH RUIJERD...
AND AFTER WE RETURNED THE CHILDREN TO THE GREAT FOREST...
WE FOUND YOU COVERED IN WOUNDS AND UN-CONSCIOUS.

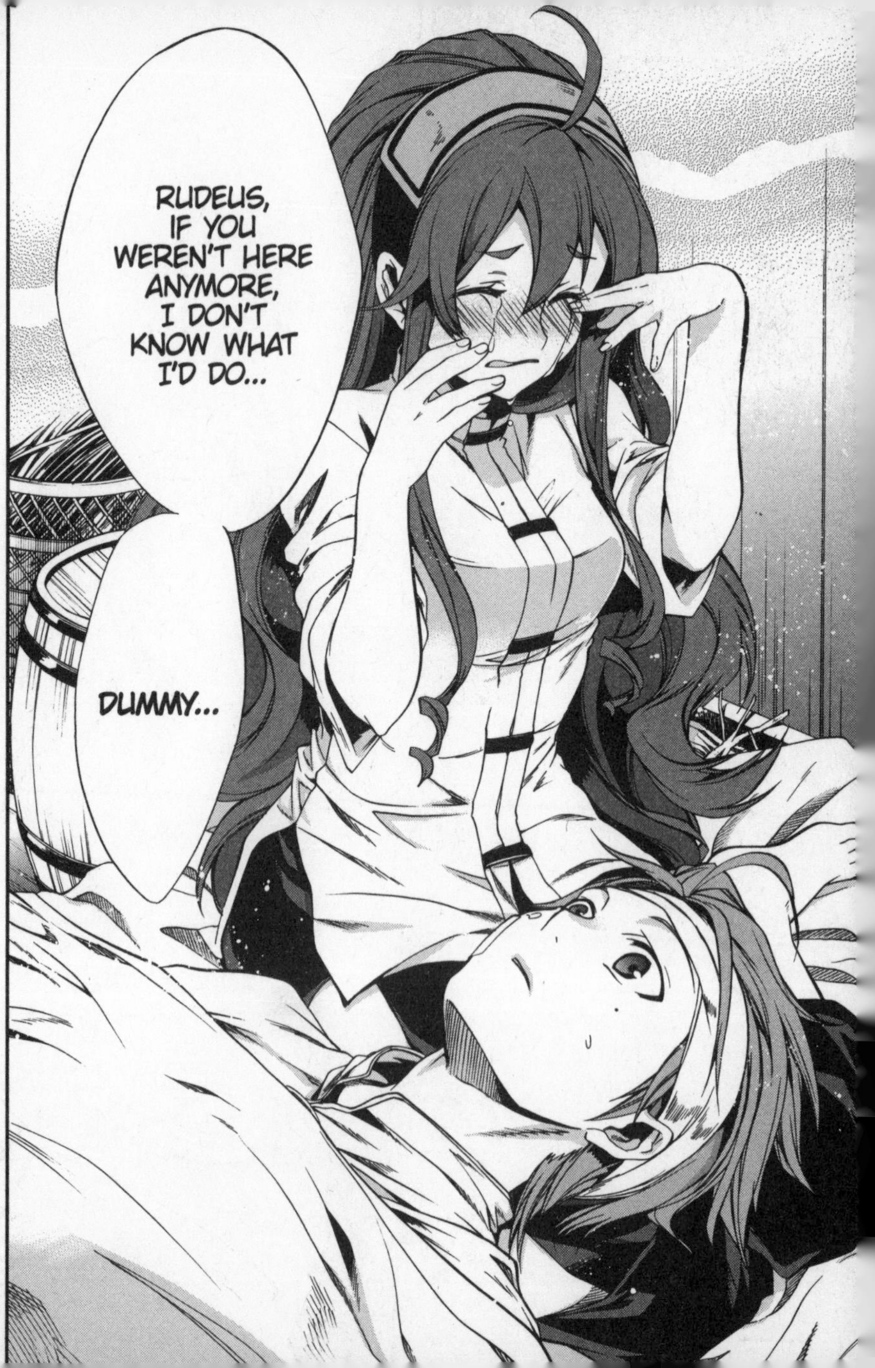
RUDEUS, IF YOU WEREN'T HERE ANYMORE, I DON'T KNOW WHAT I'D DO...
DUMMY...

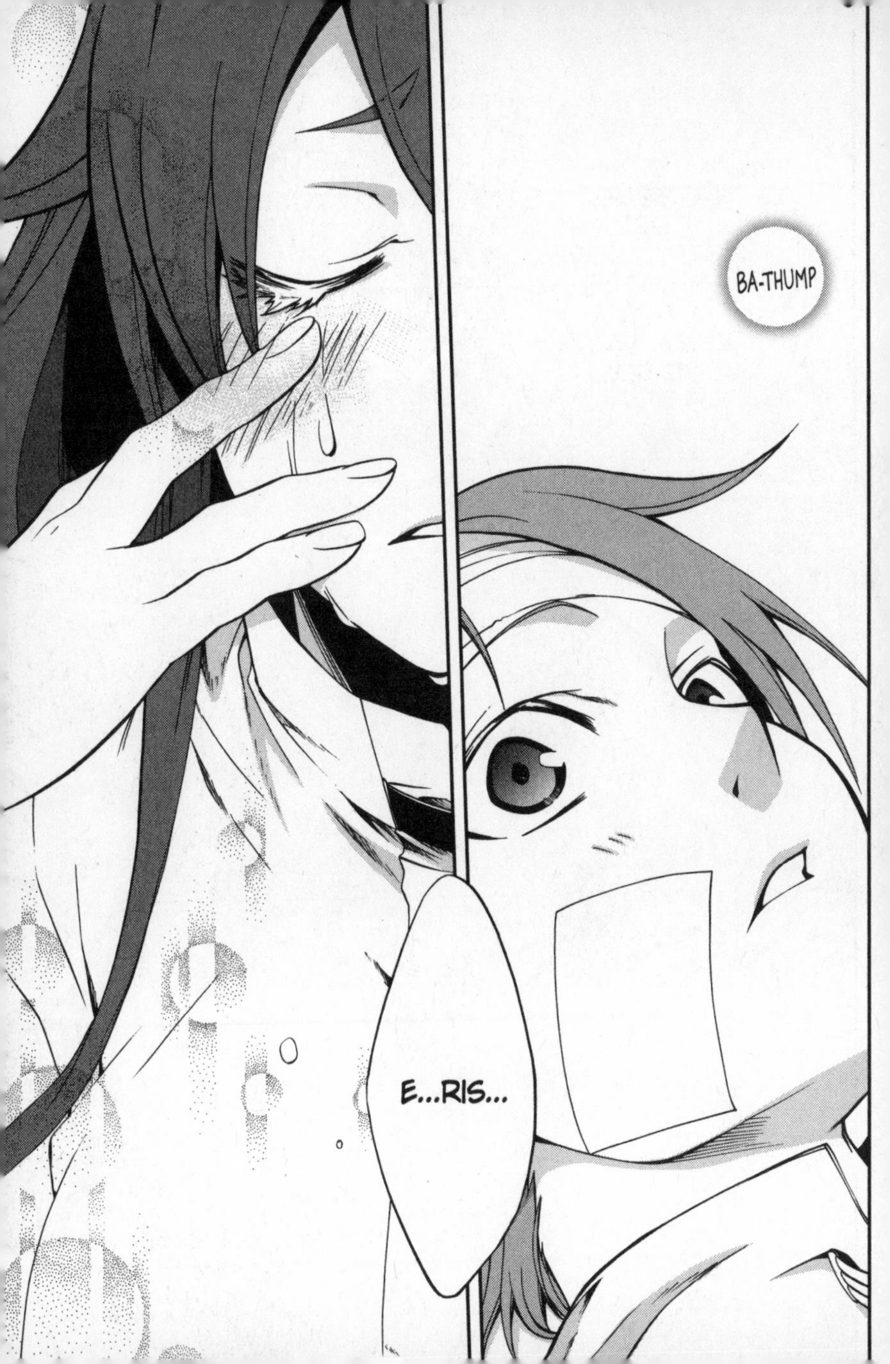
BA-THUMP
E...RIS...

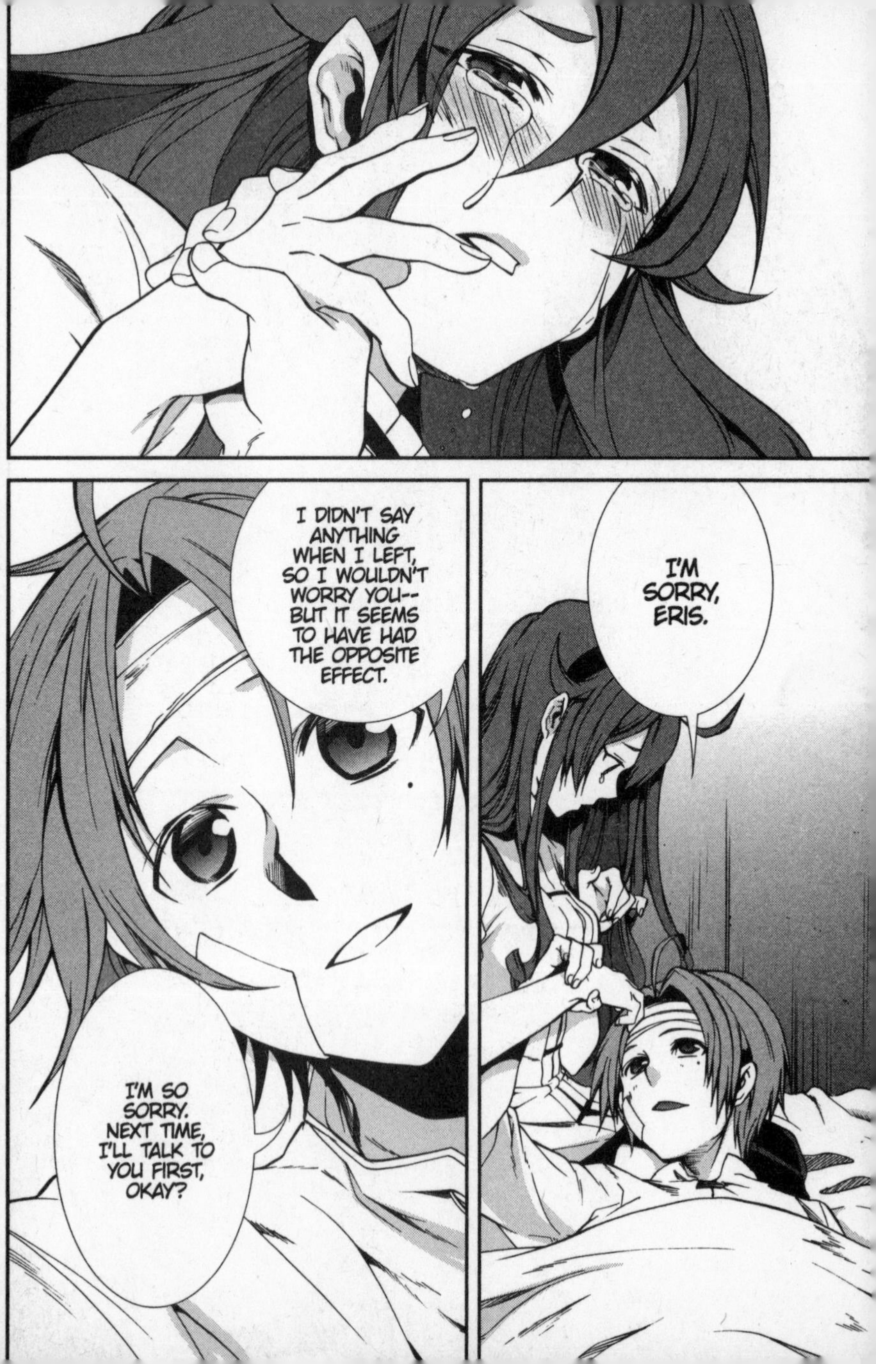
I'M SORRY, ERIS.
I DIDN'T SAY ANYTHING WHEN I LEFT, SO I WOULDN'T WORRY YOU-- BUT IT SEEMS TO HAVE HAD THE OPPOSITE EFFECT.
I'M SO SORRY. NEXT TIME, I'LL TALK TO YOU FIRST, OKAY?

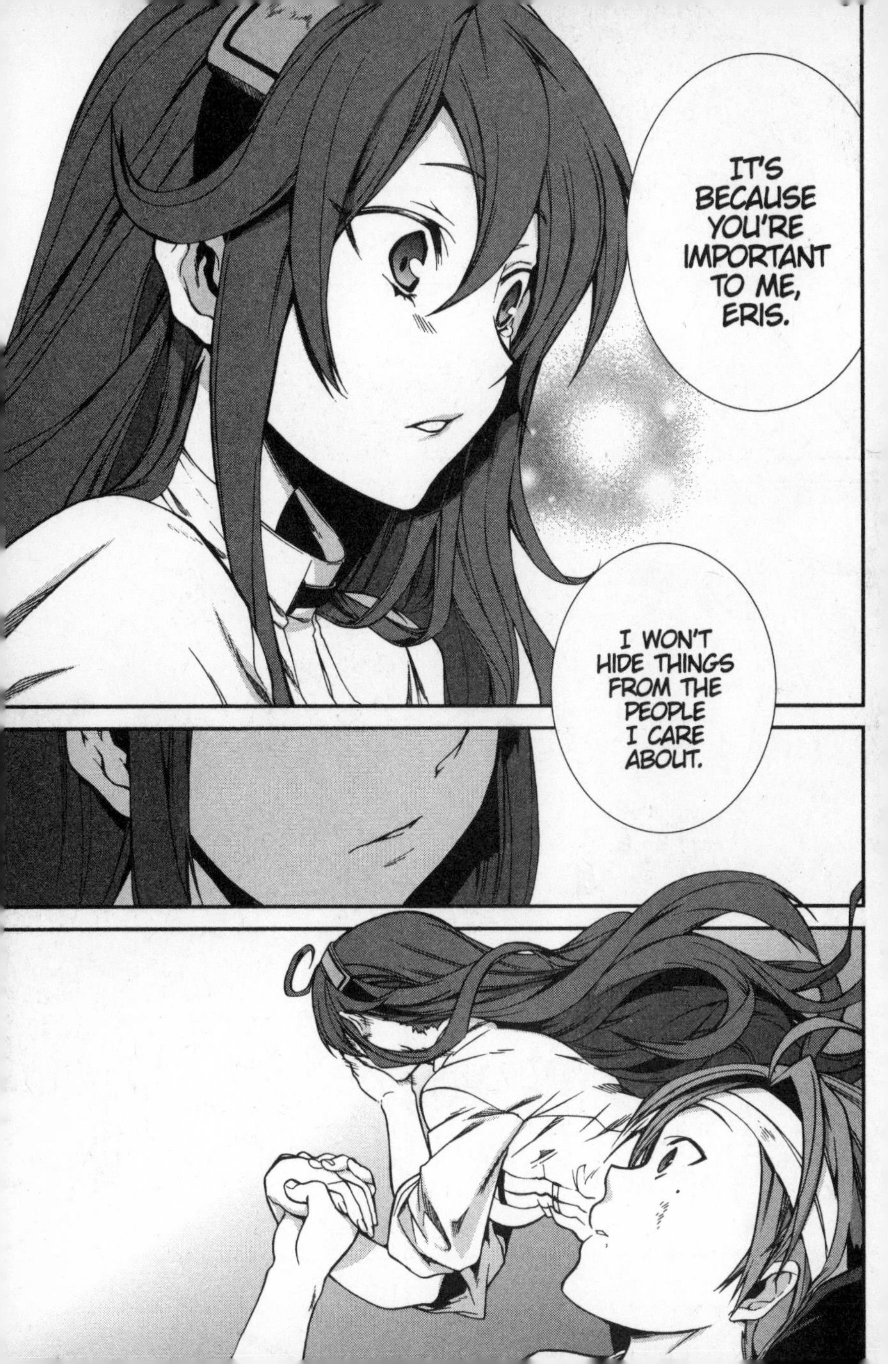
IT'S BECAUSE YOU'RE IMPORTANT TO ME, ERIS.
I WON'T HIDE THINGS FROM THE PEOPLE I CARE ABOUT.

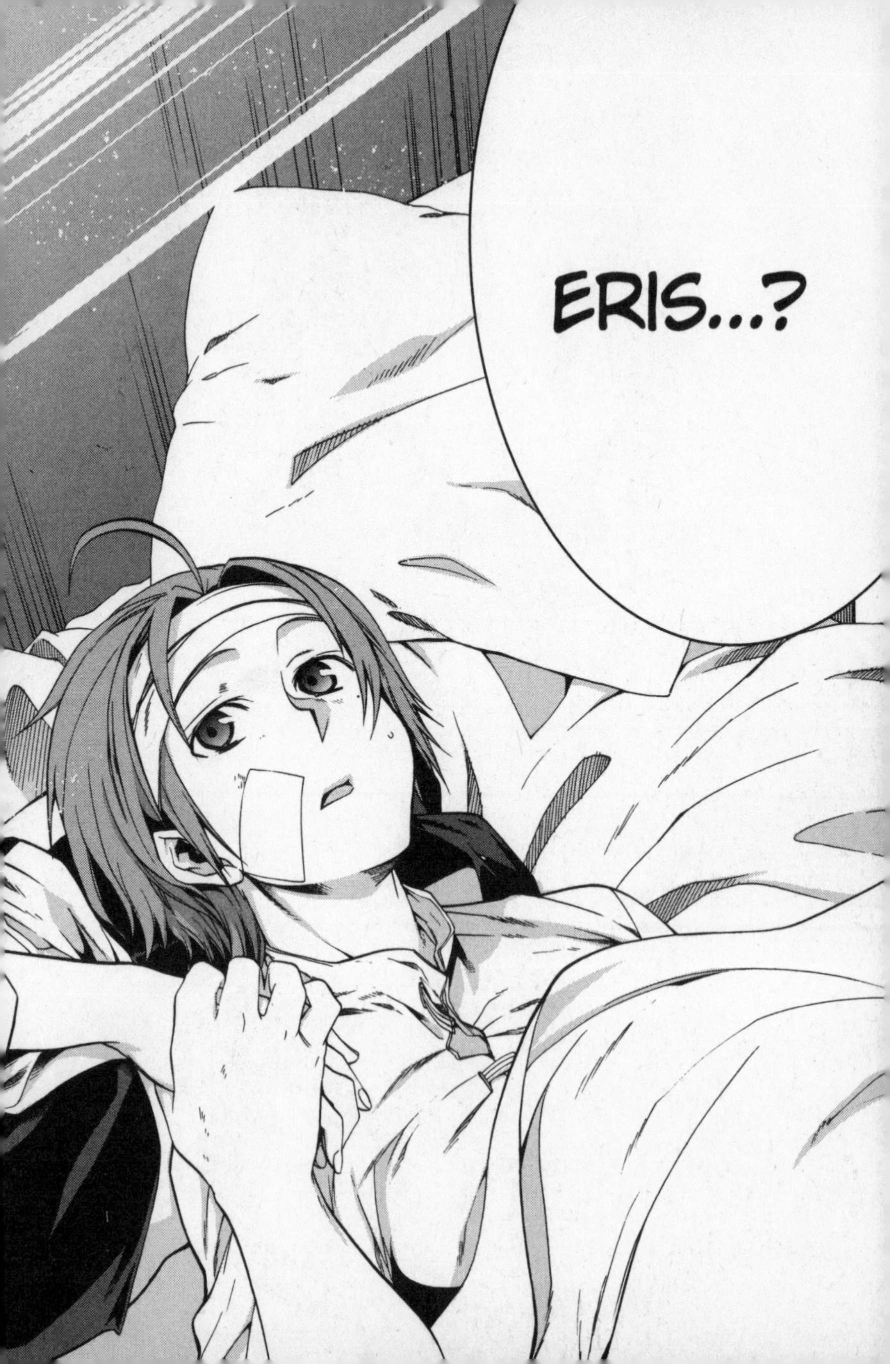
ERIS...?

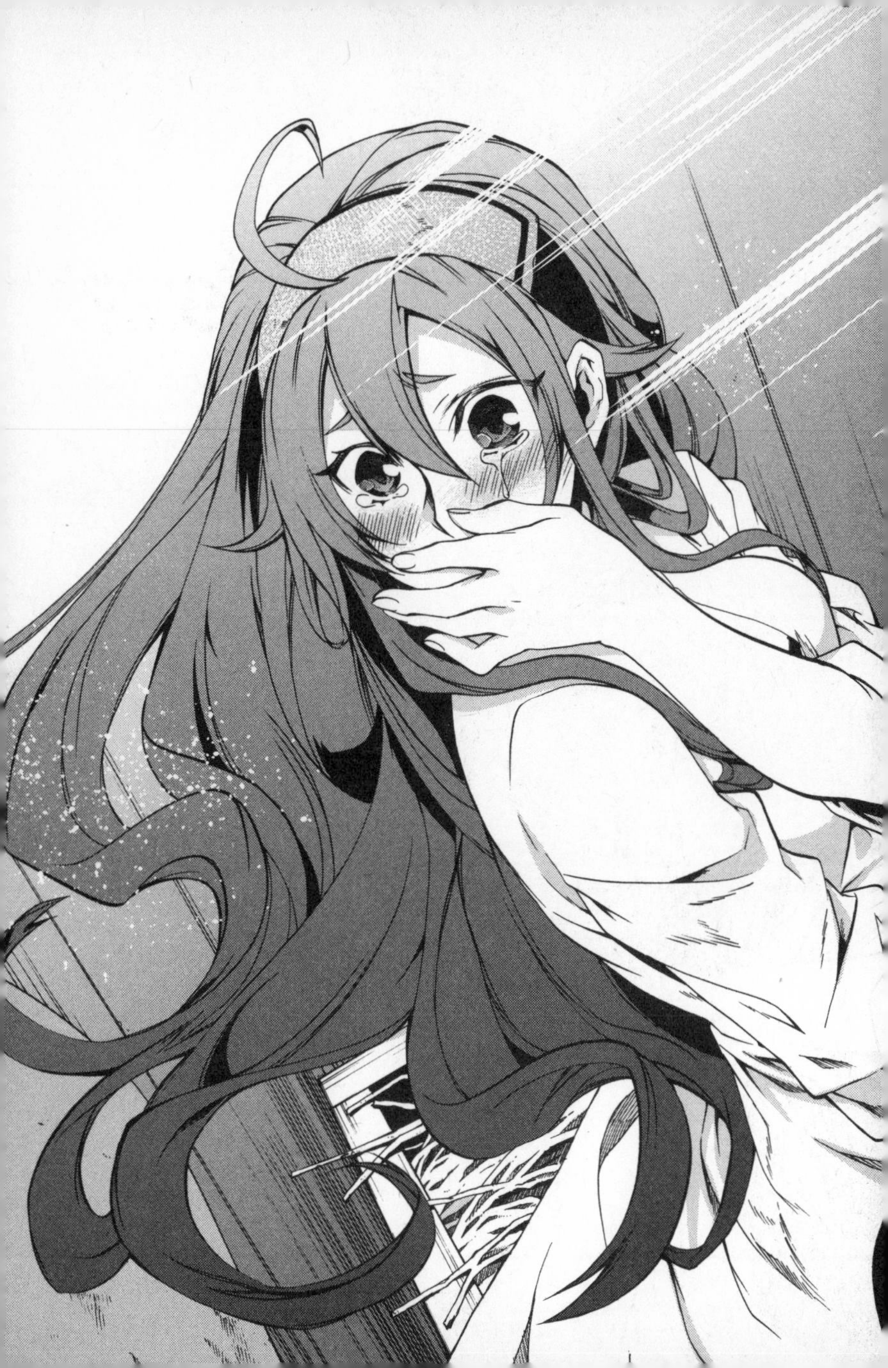

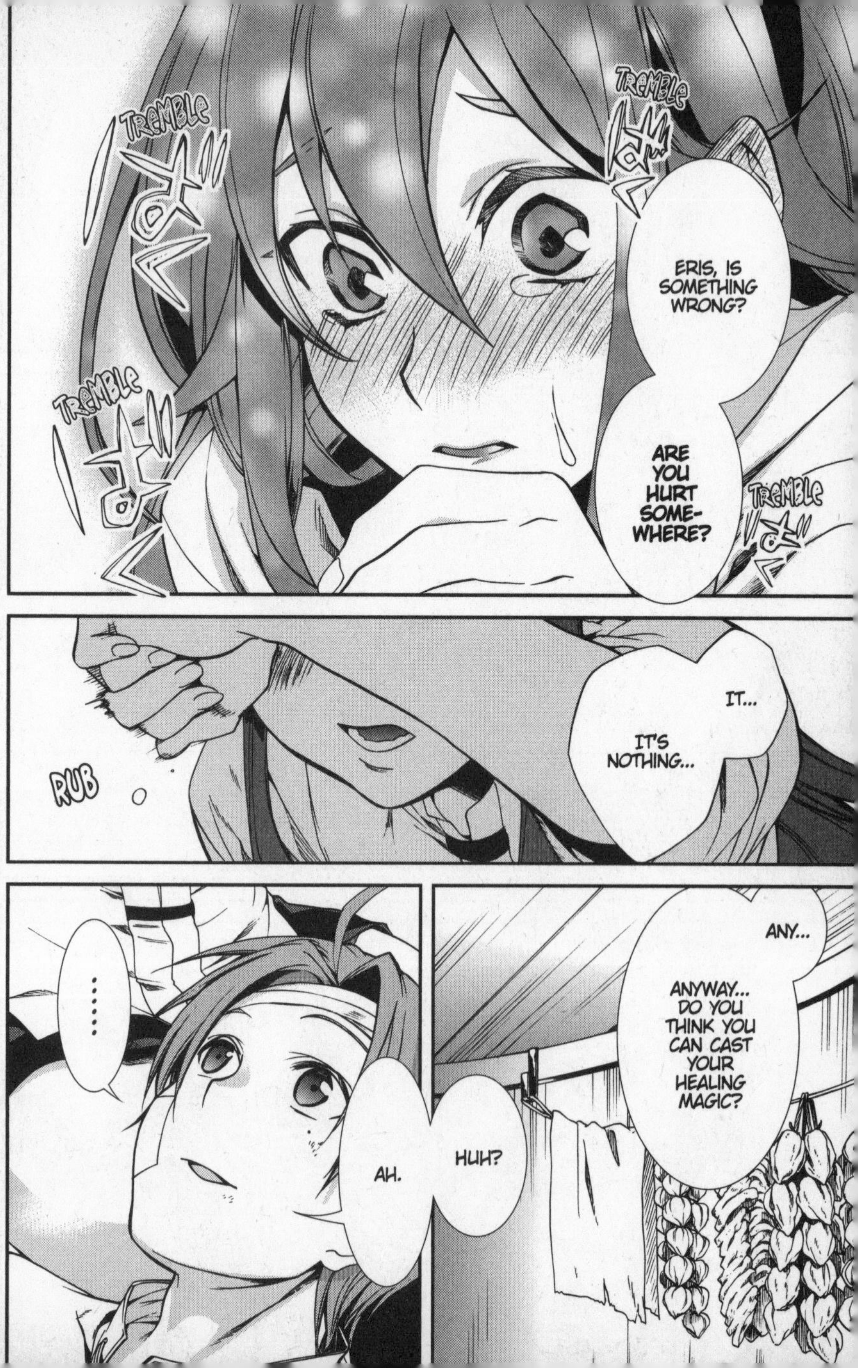
TREMBLE
ERIS, IS SOMETHING WRONG?
ARE YOU HURT SOME-WHERE?
TREMBLE
TREMBLE
TREMBLE
IT...
IT'S NOTHING...
RUB
ANY...
ANYWAY... DO YOU THINK YOU CAN CAST YOUR HEALING MAGIC?
HUH?
AH.
......

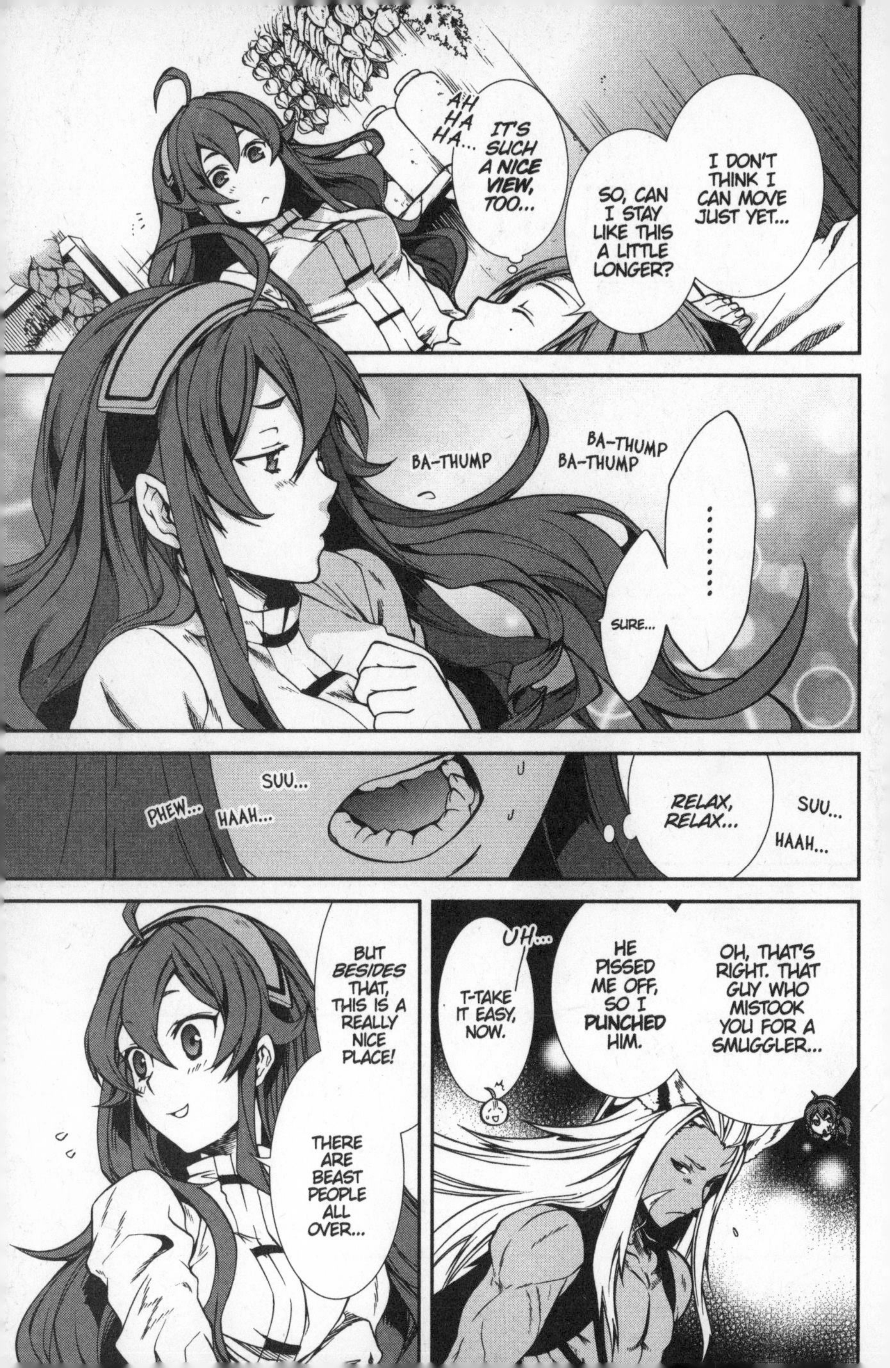
I DON'T THINK I CAN MOVE JUST YET...
SO, CAN I STAY LIKE THIS A LITTLE LONGER?
IT'S SUCH A NICE VIEW, TOO...
AH HA HA...
......
SURE...
BA-THUMP BA-THUMP
BA-THUMP
SUU...
HAAH...
RELAX, RELAX...
SUU...
PHEW...
HAAH...
OH, THAT'S RIGHT. THAT GUY WHO MISTOOK YOU FOR A SMUGGLER...
HE PISSED ME OFF, SO I PUNCHED HIM.
UH...
T-TAKE IT EASY, NOW.
BUT BESIDES THAT, THIS IS A REALLY NICE PLACE!
THERE ARE BEAST PEOPLE ALL OVER...

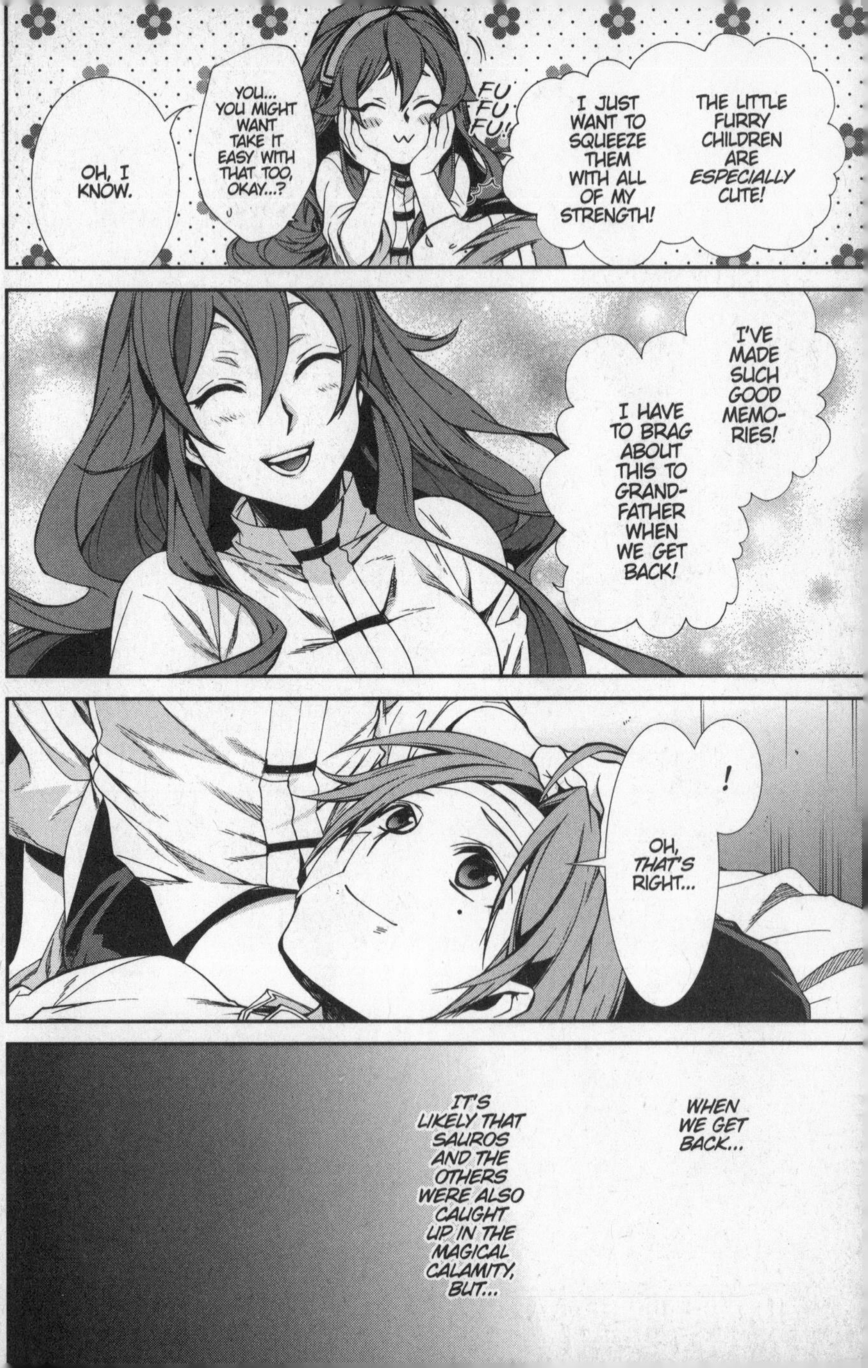
THE LITTLE FURRY CHILDREN ARE ESPECIALLY CUTE!
I JUST WANT TO SQUEEZE THEM WITH ALL OF MY STRENGTH!
FU FU FU!
YOU... YOU MIGHT WANT TAKE IT EASY WITH THAT TOO, OKAY...?
OH, I KNOW.
I'VE MADE SUCH GOOD MEMORIES!
I HAVE TO BRAG ABOUT THIS TO GRANDFATHER WHEN WE GET BACK!
!
OH, THAT'S RIGHT...
WHEN WE GET BACK...
IT'S LIKELY THAT SAUROS AND THE OTHERS WERE ALSO CAUGHT UP IN THE MAGICAL CALAMITY, BUT...

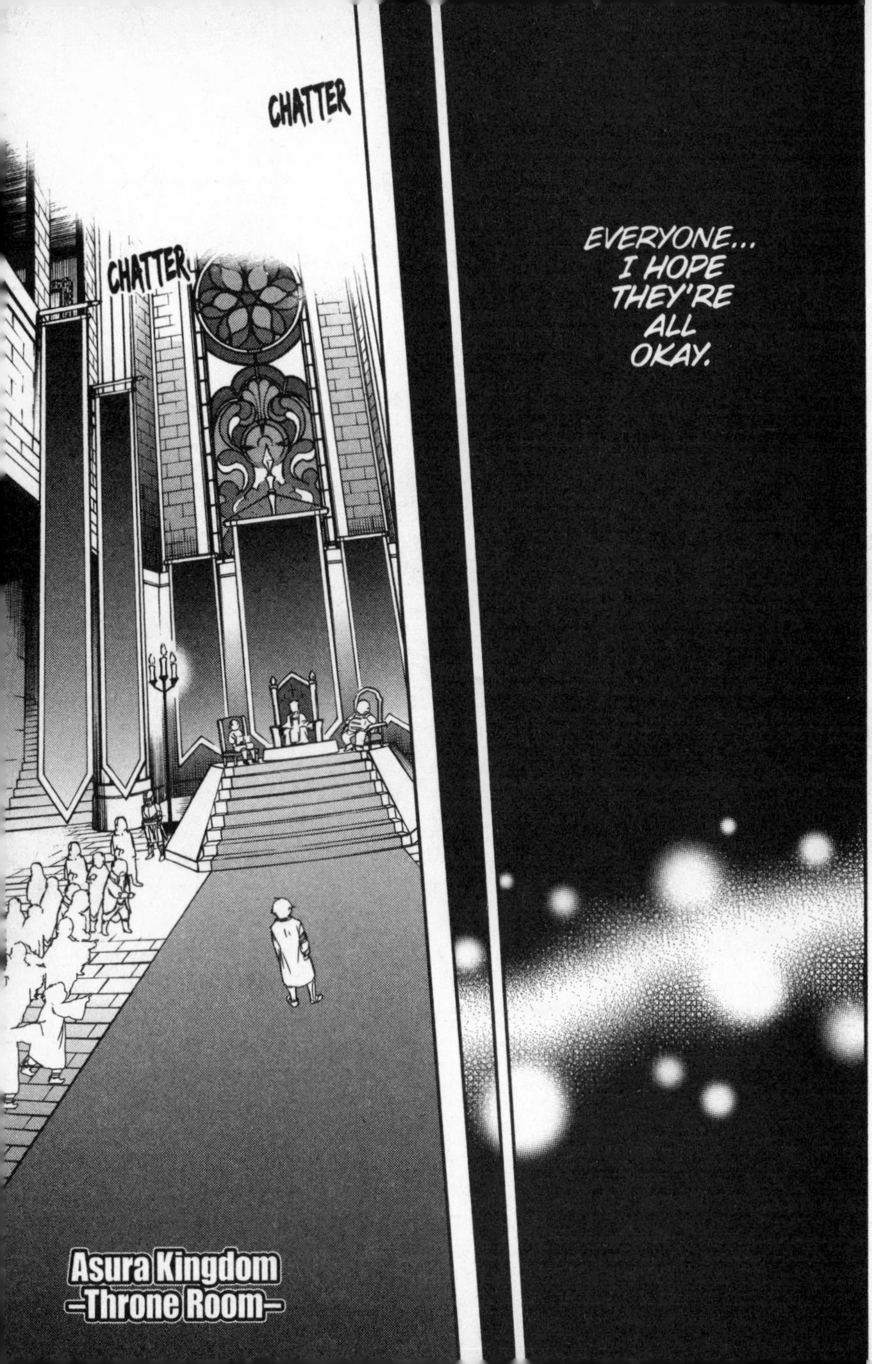
EVERYONE... I HOPE THEY'RE ALL OKAY.
CHATTER
CHATTER
Asura Kingdom -Throne Room-

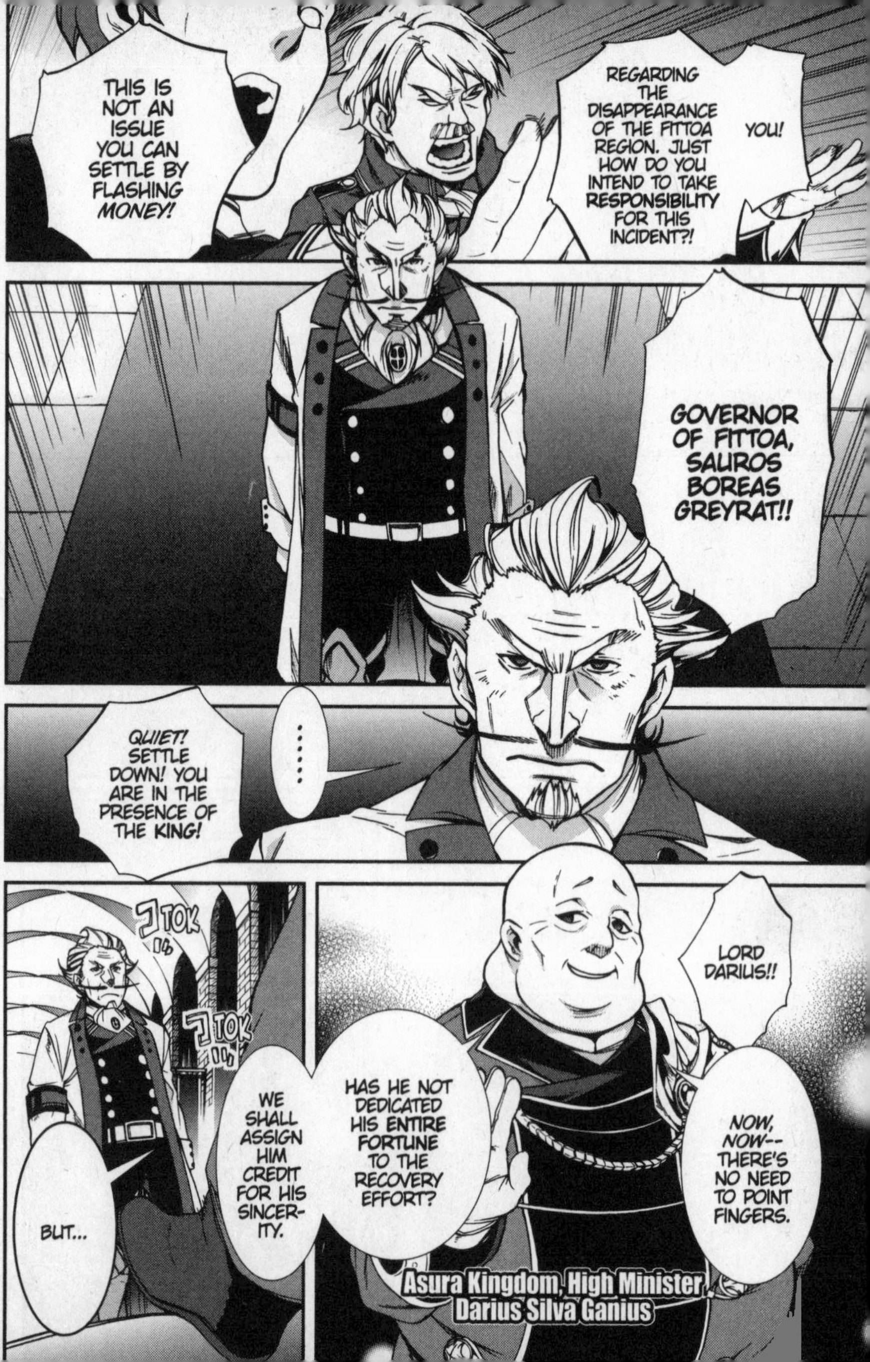
YOU!
REGARDING THE DISAPPEARANCE OF THE FITTOA REGION. JUST HOW DO YOU INTEND TO TAKE RESPONSIBILITY FOR THIS INCIDENT?!
THIS IS NOT AN ISSUE YOU CAN SETTLE BY FLASHING MONEY!
GOVERNOR OF FITTOA, SAUROS BOREAS GREYRAT!!
......
QUIET! SETTLE DOWN! YOU ARE IN THE PRESENCE OF THE KING!
LORD DARIUS!!
NOW, NOW-- THERE'S NO NEED TO POINT FINGERS.
HAS HE NOT DEDICATED HIS ENTIRE FORTUNE TO THE RECOVERY EFFORT?
WE SHALL ASSIGN HIM CREDIT FOR HIS SINCERITY.
Asura Kingdom, High Minister
Darius Silva Ganius
TOK
TOK
BUT...

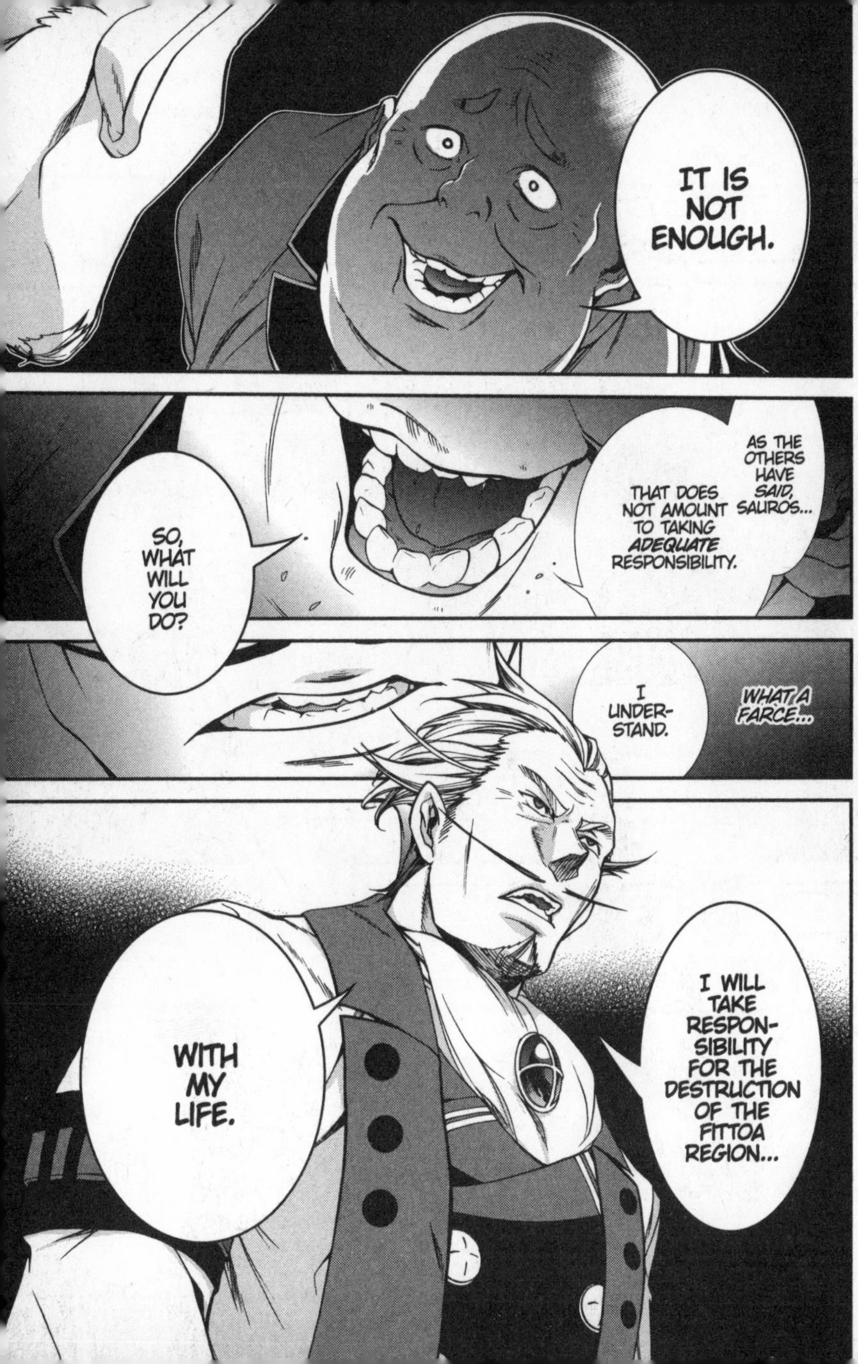
IT IS NOT ENOUGH.
AS THE OTHERS HAVE *SAID*, SAUROS...
THAT DOES NOT AMOUNT TO TAKING *ADEQUATE* RESPONSIBILITY.
SO, WHAT WILL YOU DO?
WHAT A FARCE...
I UNDERSTAND.
I WILL TAKE RESPONSIBILITY FOR THE DESTRUCTION OF THE FITTOA REGION...
WITH MY LIFE.

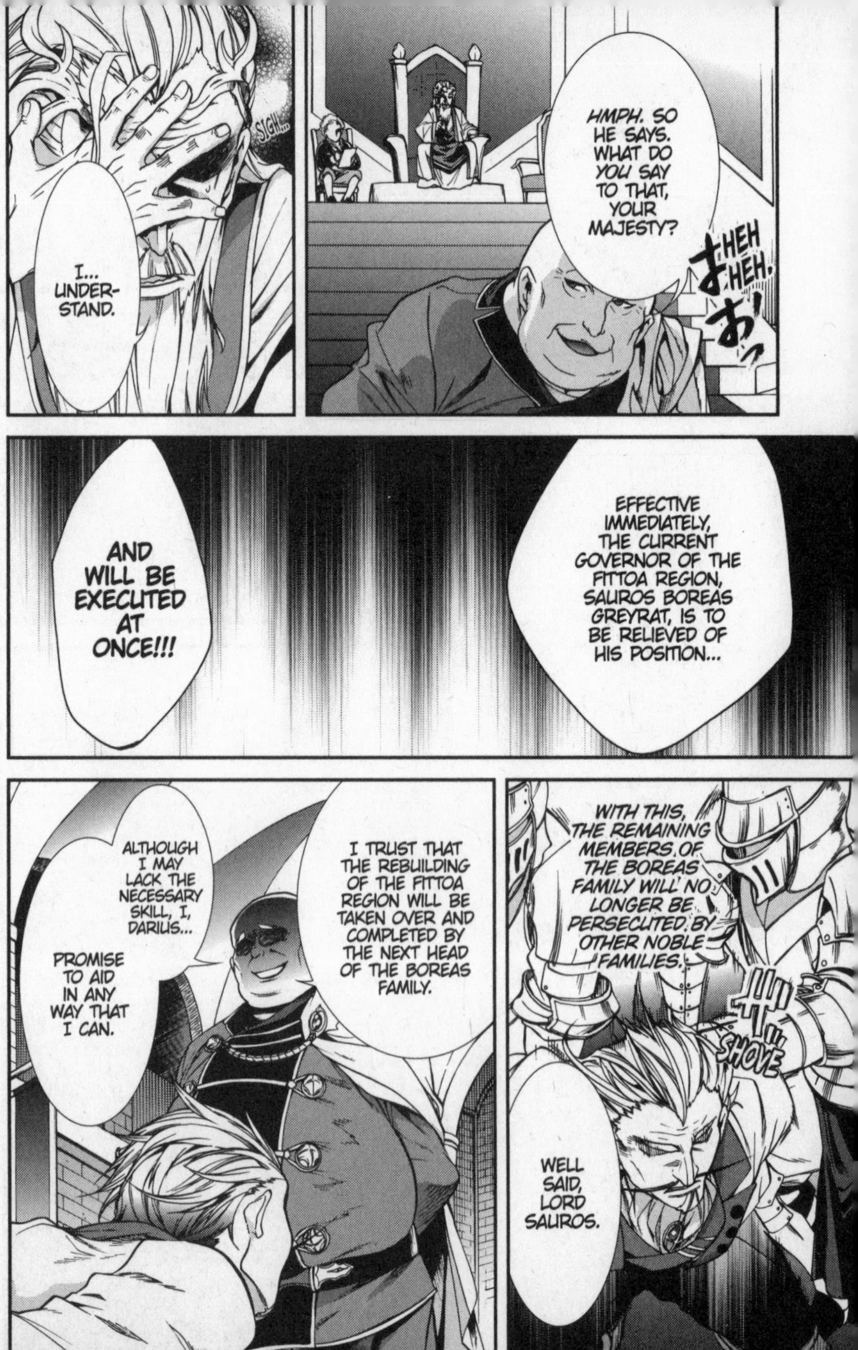
HMPH. SO HE SAYS. WHAT DO YOU SAY TO THAT, YOUR MAJESTY?
HEH HEH.
SIGH...
I... UNDER-STAND.
EFFECTIVE IMMEDIATELY, THE CURRENT GOVERNOR OF THE FITTOA REGION, SAUROS BOREAS GREYRAT, IS TO BE RELIEVED OF HIS POSITION...
AND WILL BE EXECUTED AT ONCE!!!
WITH THIS, THE REMAINING MEMBERS OF THE BOREAS FAMILY WILL NO LONGER BE PERSECUTED BY OTHER NOBLE FAMILIES.
SHOVE
WELL SAID, LORD SAUROS.
I TRUST THAT THE REBUILDING OF THE FITTOA REGION WILL BE TAKEN OVER AND COMPLETED BY THE NEXT HEAD OF THE BOREAS FAMILY.
ALTHOUGH I MAY LACK THE NECESSARY SKILL, I, DARIUS...
PROMISE TO AID IN ANY WAY THAT I CAN.

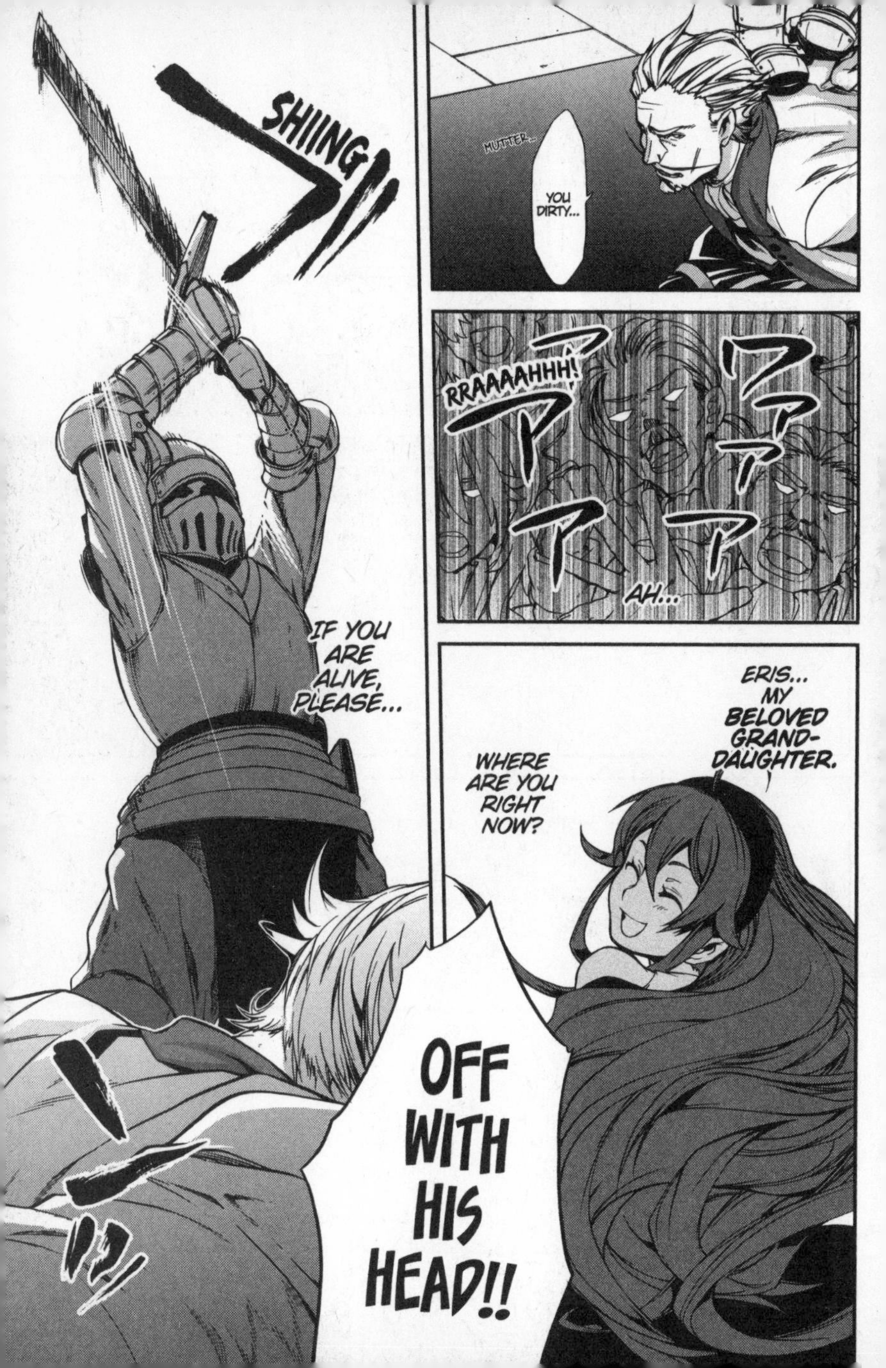

MUTTER...
YOU DIRTY...
RRAAAAHHH!
AH...
ERIS... MY BELOVED GRAND-DAUGHTER.
WHERE ARE YOU RIGHT NOW?
SHIING
IF YOU ARE ALIVE, PLEASE...
OFF WITH HIS HEAD!!

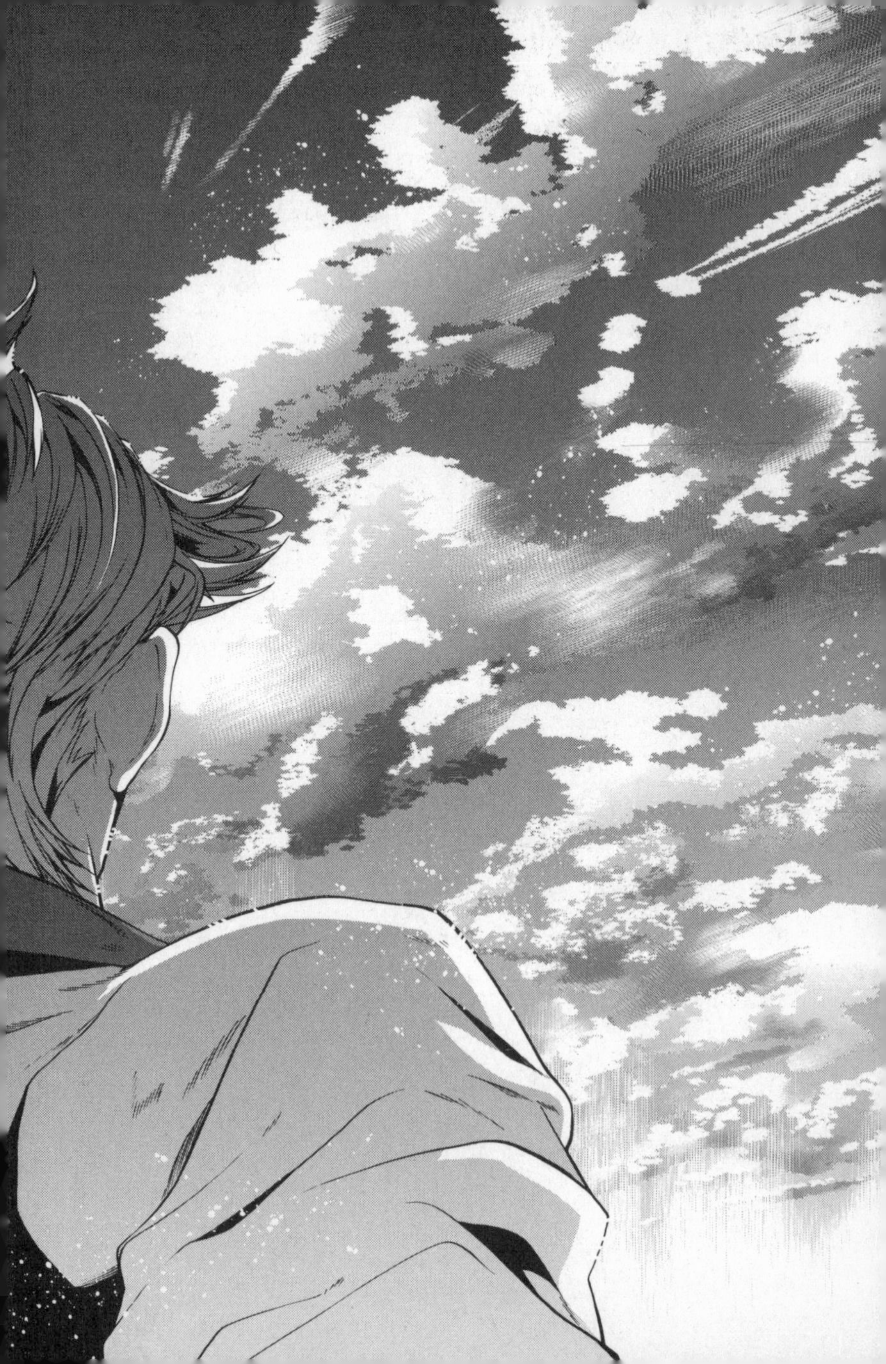

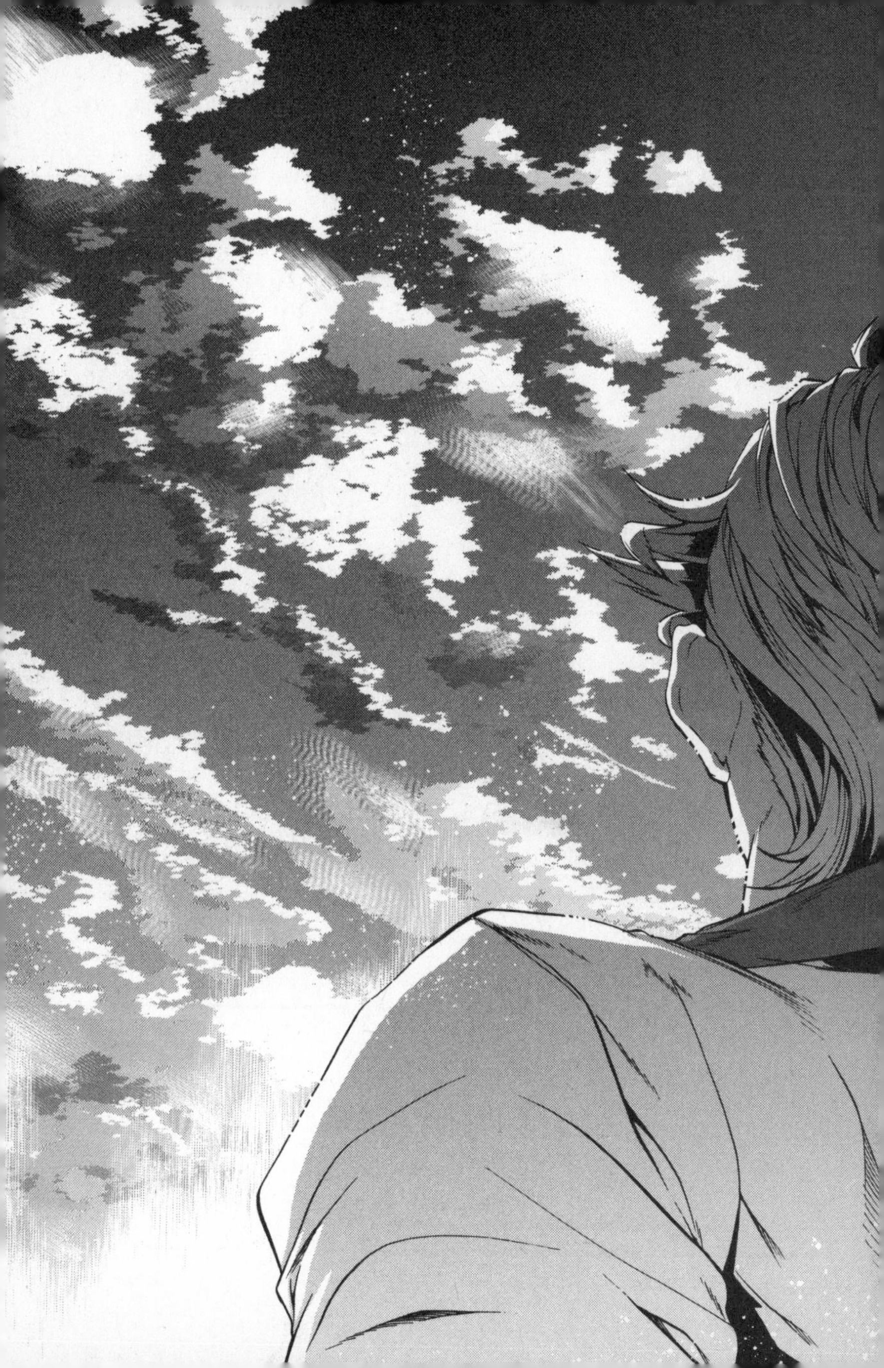

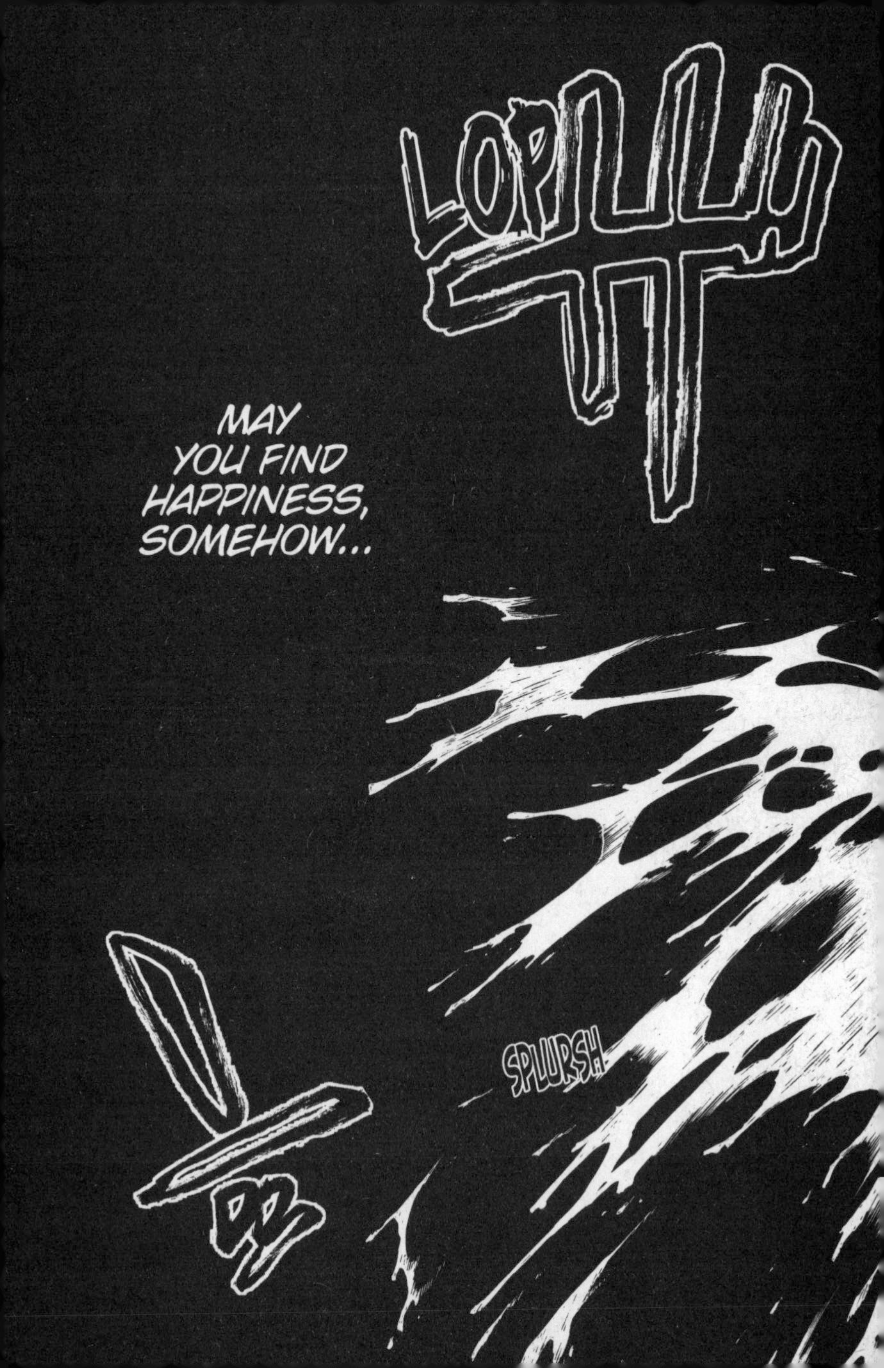
MAY YOU FIND HAPPINESS, SOMEHOW...
SPLURSH

無職転生
異世界行ったら
本気だす

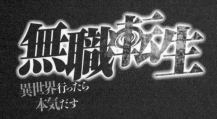

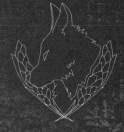

—To be continued Vol.7.

Mushoku Tensei

jobless reincarnation

SUPER ADULT LOVE STORY OF THE DEMON CONTINENT ♥

by: Rifujin Na Magonote

In a back alley of a certain town, on a certain part of the Demon Continent, a young girl was laying on the ground.

Her body was wrapped in an outfit reminiscent of bondage and sticking out from her purple hair stood two horns.She reached out with one hand toward the sky—but she didn't have enough strength and it fell to the ground.

"*Ugh*. So this is the end…" She looked like she had used up all of her strength just at that moment. "'But for one who has even been called the Demon World's Great Empress to lap at the ground, while reaching for the heavens…'" she said, then trailed off. "That line just now—it was pretty cool, wasn't it? I'll use it the next time I'm about to be done in by a hero."

Her name was the Demon World's Great Empress, Kishirika Kishirisu.

In ancient times, she was the evil empress who controlled the demon races and started a war against the people who controlled the demon king. In the present, however, without any subjects, she was just a homeless vagabond trying (and failing) to find something to eat.

"*Ugh*... I'm so hungry..."

Indeed, her empty stomach was the very reason she had collapsed. But she was the Demon World's Great Empress. As such, she could go a year without eating anything and be fine.

However, she may have been the Demon World's Great Empress, but she was also a complete dunce at the same time. In other words, her idiocy was such that she forgot she had to eat even just once a year.

When she realized that she was hungry, it was already too late. The energy required to skip around and laugh loudly had gone, and she had become a sad, pathetic beggar.

"The sky is so blue... I prefer a more purplish color—but even so, before saying my last words and dying, I must admit the blue *does* make me feel better..."

Though she had collapsed due to an empty stomach, she wasn't going to die right away—she still had enough time to appreciate the color of the sky. Such was due to the fact that being on the verge of death was an everyday occurrence for her. One could also say that she only had enough time to appreciate the color of the sky, but…

"Hmm?"

A long, narrow shadow fell across her face. Someone was staring at her.

"……?"

It was a boy with a single horn sticking out from his forehead. He was probably not yet in his teens and even then, he looked quite young. Maybe it was his sense of awareness, or lack thereof, but it was difficult to discern his age.

Wondering where the boy had appeared from, the girl looked around and saw that the back door of the house facing the back alley was open. He had probably come from there.

"What do you want?" she said. "If you intend to strip me of my possessions, then too bad—I have nothing, you hear me? Or are you a god of Death? Have you finally come to take me?"

"What's wrong?" the boy asked, not answering Kishirika's questinos. "Are you okay? Does your stomach hurt?" He looked at her with worry in his pure eyes.

She could not detect a trace of ill will in his voice, so she answered honestly. "Yes. Actually, I'm really hungry. I can't move at all."

"Really?!" The boy looked incredibly happy when he said that, then ran back to his house.

"What? Are you just making fun of me... Hey!" Kishirika shouted.

But the boy came right back, carrying a bowl with soup in it.

"Could it be, are you going to give me that?" she said. "If you intend to eat it in front of me as if it is the most delicious thing ever, then that is just too evil—"

"It's for you!"

At those words, Kishirika jumped up.

It is said that humans can find hope and muster up strength even in the most extreme of situations, but Kishirika wasn't your run-of-the-mill human. At any rate, she was the girl called the Demon World's Great Empress, and she could call upon tremendous strength whenever she liked.

GLUG GLUG GLUG SLUUURP MUNCH MUNCH GULP!

When Kishisrika took the dish from the boy,

she began drinking its contents at an incredible speed. In the bowl was a sparse soup made by dissolving something like flour into the broth. The only other ingredient it contained were several withered leaves—but to Kishirika with her empty stomach there was no better feast.

"*Ahhhhh~!* The simple flavor has spread throughout my stomach. If I had to describe to describe this feeling in one word, it would have to be 'delicious'!"

Once the energy had gathered in her stomach, Kishirika stood. Her dry hair became smooth, and her wrinkled skin had regained its tension. The miraculous absorption ability of the Demon World's Great Empress could turn all of the calories into energy in an instant.

"*Gwa ha ha ha!*" she cried. "The Demon World's Great Empress is *baaaaack!*" Kishirika voice rang out and she looked down at the boy to ask for another helping. "It must have put you out terribly to ready such a meal!" she said. "But it wasn't quite enough…" She trailed off.

The one open-mouthed beside her was a child. She took in his poor appearance and realized that the clothes he wore were tattered. The reason for his troubled demeanor was due to the fact that he had shared his only meal for the day with her. Kishirika was not smart, but even *she* was able to understand that. And although Kishirika was a conqueror, she was also someone with an empty stomach. Thus, she understood the feelings of people who were hungry.

She wasn't full yet to tell the truth, but Kishirika held back any further request for more. And since there was no more for a second helping, her next words were already decided.

"Clearly, I have received your devotion," she said. "I believe a reward is in order!" She always bestowed a gift upon anyone who fed her. She had been her rule since ancient times.

"A reward?" the boy said.

"Yes, a reward. Is there anything that you would like?"

"Something I want? Anything?"

"Anything is fine."

But though she said anything, Kishirika didn't have anything on her. If he said money—well, she didn't have any. If he wanted honor, there was little she could do, since she was a beggar like him. And if he wanted status, she'd still be at loss, as she didn't even have a house to her name.

Still, she did have *something* she was able to give that she had been born with: demon eyes. She had the power to grant someone a demon eye. Such an ability had once powerful enough to almost bring the world to its knees. It could be said that demon eyes represented the Demon world's great empress.

"Don't pretend," she said. "Stop hesitating and just say it—come on!"

"Um…"

Grinning widely, Kishirika urged the redfaced boy who was fidgeting nervously. "Well…?"

Prompted by her words, he readied himself and spoke."Please become my bride!"

"Your bride?! You want a bride at your age?! Whoa~! There sure are a lot of precocious children these days…"

The boy's face fell at the shock on Kishirika's face.

"No?" he said. He was so adorable that she almost said it was okay without thinking, but Kishirika was the type of girl who clearly stated her opinion.

"No," she said. "I'm sorry, but I already have a fiancé. I can't marry you."

"Oh…"

"Is there anything else you want?" she asked. "Come on, how about something convenient and beautiful that starts with a 'd'? Hm?"

"…Nope. I want a bride."

Possibly, if he had been at least ten years older, he may have wanted a demon eye. Using a demon eye was difficult, after all—but worth it. However, the boy didn't even know the term "demon eye" and he couldn't want something he didn't know about.

"Hmm, I'm at a loss here. I don't feel bad being wanted, but…"

She looked down at the boy with a troubled expression—but then, she suddenly thought of something.

"All right," she said. "In that case, I'll tell you the story of how I met my fiancé. If you hear that, then you should get some closure."

"A story?"

"Yes. It is, without a doubt, an exciting, heart-stopping, applause-worthy adult spectacle!"

"I want to hear it!"

"Okay, then."

And with that, Kishirika began her tale.

It happened a thousand, no two—no, three or four thousand years ago.

At the time, I was full of energy and quite popular with the demon kings.

With the gold, silver, and treasure that I had looted while invading the humans, I held parades daily, gathered handsome men from all over the territory and forced them to serve me, drew on the faces of sleeping demon kings, sent letters to human kings that caused them stress and made them go bald—in short, I did whatever I wanted.

However, at the time I reigned as the Great Empress of the Demon World, I was— unlike the mere fragment I am now—a complete crystal of beauty. Offerings from demon king and celebrity suitors from every region arrived nearly every day. Because of that, I was completely satisfied every day. I was truly invincible.

But, as I was fully enjoying my life as the great empress, there were those who stood in my way. The humans. Granted, I did invade them, so I suppose it makes sense.

Humans are weak if you eliminate them piece by piece. Every once in a while, a dangerous one rises up—but even then, it's only one every thousand years or so. I wasn't worried.

However, one every thousand years means that once every thousand years, someone like *does* come along.

I refer to such a person as a hero—and the hero always appeared without fail. Indeed, during my first war, I was defeated by a hero with some odd preferences. For example, he didn't like it when the sky wasn't blue.

Anyway. The golden knight, Aldebaran—that's what the hero was called.

Have you heard of him? That's right, the hero who single-handedly reorganized the humans' battle line and left the demon army in ruins.

At first, I didn't concern myself with people like that. Wouldn't it have been strange to regularly worry about someone who would only appear every thousand years? Even though the majority of people were calling him "The most outstanding talent of the millennia!" I figured that some other demon king would stop him.

When it came down to it, however, my subjects tried to warn me several times. "That hero is extremely dangerous," they said. "We should deal with him right away." But I thought everything would be fine, and didn't think much of it at the time.

But it *wasn't* fine. By the time I realized it, my army was in ruins, and Aldebaran had invaded my castle. That was the first time I had seen him, but I knew from just that glimpse that he was a considerable threat. With gray-speckled hair and insect-like, expressionless eyes, his entire body gave off an ominous aura. I knew that even if he had no desire to kill, he would.

And he was strong.

Because he had invaded my castle, of course, he must have been attacked by my bodyguards. They were closest to my person and of the demon races, meaning they were the best of warriors—and yet he tore those soldiers to pieces and tossed them aside as if they were cotton candy, tore them to shreds he did. And when a demon king, boasting unrivaled strength, entered the fray, he destroyed them with a single attack. Destroyed, I tell you—he *destroyed* them. You simply can't understand.

And although they may have called him the golden knight, there was no gold to be seen upon. He was so terrible that when my subjects came to warn me, spit flying everywhere, all I could do was nod. Having seen a ghost, my whole body was shaking, and I couldn't do a thing.

Do you understand? People, when it comes the time when they realize that nothing they do will help the situation, lose the ability to move. That's the real meaning of the thing called fear.

I couldn't even beg for my life—it sure didn't look like he was in the mood to listen.

All I could do was pray to the gods. I say gods, but even if I didn't even know which god I was praying to, I was praying to something that transcended existence before my very eyes.

Naturally, my prayers went unanswered. But

right as I prepared myself for death…

CRASH

Something fell from the ceiling and made a loud noise.

It was a giant man in full armor.

Oh my, is that enemy reinforcements?! is what I thought—but his stature reminded me of someone I knew quite well.

My prayers had been received!

Not by the gods, but by someone I knew!

It was the immortal demon king, Badigadi. He was the last of the demon kings.

He was wearing armor that I had never seen before and challenged the hero to a fight.

I yelled. "Stop, you're no match for him!" But he was a rare intellectual among the demon races. Despite his large frame, the words that came from his mouth were deliberate and clever. It's natural that he wouldn't have had a lot of fighting experience, but there's a saying about leaving boys alone for three days. Without my knowing, he, too, could have developed quite a bit.

Badi was not about to be outdone by a ghost, and an even match ensued.

CLASH KLING

They destroyed the castle, but still, the two kept fighting.

SLASH KLANG

They destroyed the town, but the fight wasn't over yet.

The fight continued on endlessly, and I thought all of the people would be destroyed… But there is no such thing as an eternal battle.

At the end of the long, long, struggle to the death, a victor emerged—Badi defeated the hero. But the hero was easily, and at the very end, he attempted to leave a gift.

It was a bomb. He gave up his life to kill Badi and myself.

We have to stop it! I thought, but I had no strength. I didn't have enough power to stop the hero.

Since he won the battle, Badi still had some, but at the end of such a long struggle, during which he had used his power to the fullest, he was almost completely drained…

There was nothing we could do except prepare for the end.

Removing his helmet, Badi turned his half-dead face toward me and said,"If I am reborn, may it be as your husband…"

I laughed and responded,"Naturally, if we are reborn, let's get married…"

Then, the two of us disappeared.

All the while, we were both smiling.

★ ★ ★

"Hm…No matter how many times I tell that story, it's still a good one. Especially the part when he comes to save me, even now when I think of it, it makes my heart skip a beat.

But now you get it, right? The bond between me and Badi is solid. There's no way I could become your bride…"

Kishirika looked over at the boy after finishing her story."Hm, what is it?" she asked.

Zzz… Zzz….

"Are you asleep?"

He was leaning against the wall, sleeping soundly.

It must have been time for his afternoon nap.

"Hmm, it may have been too soon for my adult love story."

Tilting her head to one side, Kishirika stood up. It wasn't his fault that he fell asleep.

"But I have to repay him for the meal! *Hmph!*"

Kishirika said cheerfully and stuck her finger into the boy's eye.

"Ouch!"

By the time the boy opened his eye because of the pain, it was already too late.

One of bis eyes had been turned into a demon eye, and Kishirika was standing by to takeoff for heaven.

"Well, this is farewell!

"What? Wait! Wait!"

"*Mwa ha ha!* Take care of that demon eye as if it were me! Marriage is out of the question, but if you become able to use it, I might be able to use you as one of my personal guards! *Gwa ha ha ha ha—koff koff! Gah!*"

Even as he struggled to find his bearings with his changed vision, he stared up at Kishirika and stretched his hand up toward her.

But his hand didn't reach her, and he was left extending his arm toward heaven…

Several years later, a single soldier became Kishirika's follower. That soldier was more loyal than any other, and was said to have been able to use his demon eye better than any other… But that's another story.

HATS OFF TO THE WORD SENSE NECESSARY TO COME UP WITH "SUPER SUPERDIA RUIJERDMAN." RUIJERD IS A SUPER RARE. A FIVE-STAR CHARACTER…!!

Teach me, Sensei!

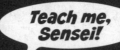

Special Talk

We press the two sensei who created the world of *Mushoku Tensei* to go deeper. This time, we reveal even more rarely heard conversations about this and that!

Q. Please tell us about a precious artifact—like the one that Rudeus treasures.

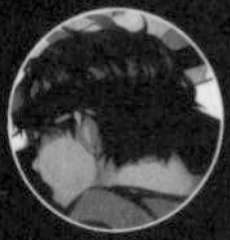

<Original work creator, Rifujin na Magonote-sensei>

I wonder how many readers are actually interested in my underwear. It would be very difficult to distribute them. I'll ask the editing section what they think. By the way, I prefer boxers.

Huh? Something else? That's not what you meant?

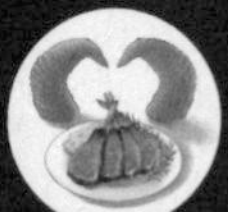

<Manga artist, Fujikawa Yuka-sensei>

....

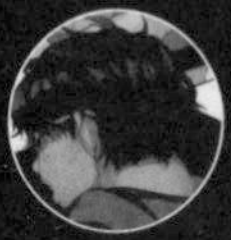

<Original work creator, Rifujin na Magonote-sensei>

Ahem. If I were to give a serious answer, I guess I'd have to say my paperback edition of *Neko no Chikyugi* is my precious artifact. Whenever I can't write or am having a rough time, I reread it and get power from it.

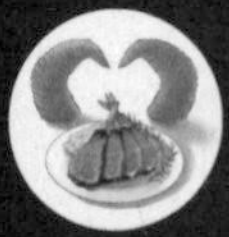

<Manga artist, Fujikawa Yuka-sensei>

For me, it would be a slome tower shaved ice cup that I bought as a souvenir while on some tour... keep it at work on my bookshelf and it's very much like a precious artifact... A more serious answer would be a memento of my old dog, Moromoro.

Q: What do you want to know about Fujikawa-sensei?

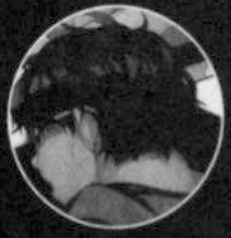

<Original work creator, Rifujin na Magonote-sensei>

I wonder what kind of precious artifact she's wearing... *Ow!* I'm sorry! It was a joke! I was joking, so please don't throw rocks at me! Fujikawa-sensei is the one who draws such wonderful manga for me every time. There's no reason I should be asking such rude things about her precious artifacts.

Ahem. Fujikawa-sensei often draws herself as a sheep, but if there is a reason, legend, or epic poem, please share it with us.

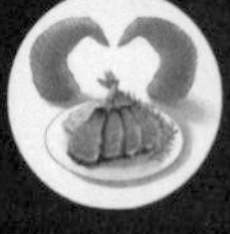

<Manga artist, Fujikawa Yuka-sensei>

I'm under the wool, so I'm not wearing any underwear! I mean, the reasons behind my self-portrait are that I like sheep, I was born in the year of the sheep, and my mental weakness is just like that of a sheep's.

Q. What have you always wanted to ask Rifujin na Magonote-sensei?

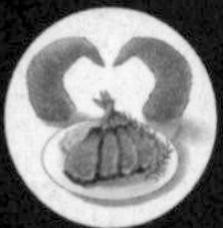

<Manga artist, Fujikawa Yuka-sensei>

It seems that Magonote-sensei is quite into muscle training, so do you have a specific muscle that you like? Incidentally, I have felt lately that both male and female abdominal muscles are quite wonderful.

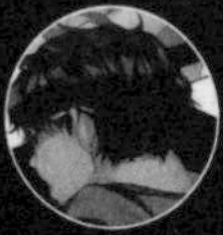

<Original work creator, Rifujin na Magonote-sensei>

Muscles! Well, the biceps, triceps, and pecs give off a "muscular vibe," so I like them, but it's the muscle training—actually it's the diet. When I tried hard to diet, my way of thinking changed slightly. I have to say that while I was on a diet, the most striking difference that appeared was around my waist.

When you lose fat from training your abdominal muscles and additional aerobic exercise, the lines of your abs appear clearly on the surface of your skin and you can achieve that upside-down V body shape.

When you see that line, it almost feels as if someone is complimenting you, telling you, "You did well."

But of course, that's just self-praise... Still, if you really think about it, isn't dieting something you start purely for your own health? To begin with, it's not something you'd be praised for, nor is it necessary to seek praise. But at some point, it begins to feel futile. That being said, trying to get praise by talking about it to others ends with no more than a "Hmm," because there's no way you could become a bulked-up macho man in just a month.

At times like those, abs—and only abs—will get others to praise you, "You must have worked hard."

That will really make you like abs.

Q. Tell us about any additional "resolutions" you plan to try your best at in 2017?!

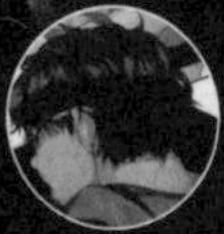

<Original work creator, Rifujin na Magonote-sensei>

This year I will lower my body fat percentage without missing any deadlines. That aside, last year I wasn't able to write many projects, so this year I want to try a little harder. But I think taking care of my mind and body is more important than working. I want to work at my own pace without being impatient.

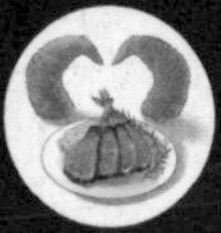

<Manga artist, Fujikawa Yuka-sensei>

My resolution this year is to complete my work as soon as possible, so I don't put any burden on the editors and printers… Sorry for always causing you problems... Also, I want to get some muscles and lose weight. If I say it here, I'll be less likely to slack off...! I'm going to do my best~!

With this it appears that the *Mushoku* team will have to hold an official muscle weigh-in. We'll do it in the fall and announce the results in volume 7!

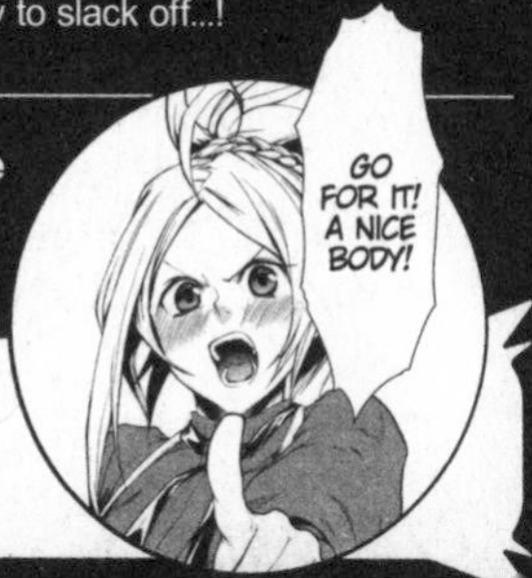
GO FOR IT! A NICE BODY!

On his way home, Rudeus crosses through the dangerous Demon continent and Great Forest! Who is the familiar face awaiting him on a new continent?!

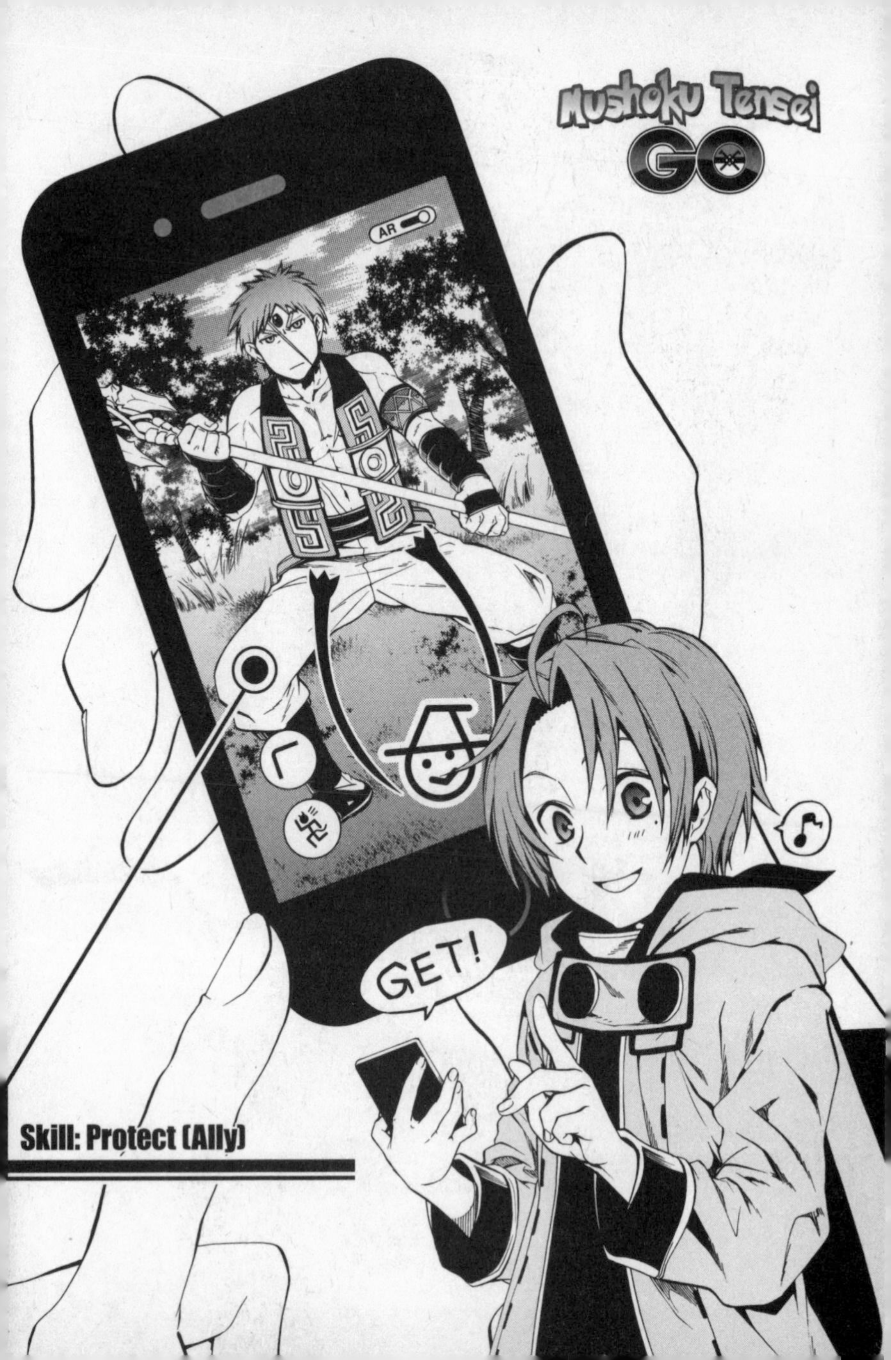

Mushoku Tensei GO
AR
GET!
Skill: Protect (Ally)